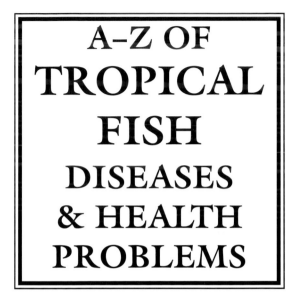

A–Z OF TROPICAL FISH DISEASES & HEALTH PROBLEMS

Signs • Diagnoses • Causes
Treatment
for Tropical Freshwater Fish

Peter Burgess, Mary Bailey & Adrian Exell

HOWELL
BOOK
HOUSE

Howell Book House

New York

HOWELL BOOK HOUSE
A Simon & Schuster / Macmillan Company
1633 Broadway
New York, NY 10019

MACMILLAN is a registered trademark of
Macmillan, Inc.

Library of Congress Cataloging-in-Publication Data
available on request

ISBN 1-58245-049-8

Printed in Hong Kong

10 9 8 7 6 5 4 3 2 1

CONTENTS

ACKNOWLEDGMENTS

The authors would like to thank the following for their assistance in the preparation of this book:
Dr Keith Banister, Dr David Ford, Dr Alastair Macartney, Gina Sandford, and Roman Sznober.

PB thanks David Bucke, Dr Tony Matthews, Stan McMahon, and Ian Wellby for their generous help in providing material and advice over the years.

MB is most grateful to Debbie and Steve Partridge for technical assistance with communications, and to all the very many aquarists who over the years have contributed to her knowledge, and hence to this book.

All photographs by the authors unless stated otherwise

4

INTRODUCTION

The keeping of ornamental fish dates back at least to imperial Rome, but it is only during the last 50 years or so that modern technology has provided the wherewithal to pursue this hobby easily and on a scientific, rather than a trial and error, basis. No longer is it necessary to heat slate-bottomed tropical aquaria with candles, or provide aeration from an inflated car inner-tube, and leakproof 'all-glass' aquaria have replaced less reliable iron-framed tanks sealed – with variable degrees of success and longevity – with putty. No longer is the hobby restricted to the enthusiast with a flair for improvisation, though the latter remains useful! Instead the equipment revolution has made fish-keeping a viable proposition for anyone with an interest in the subject, with a resulting huge increase in the number of aquarists.

At the same time there have been major advances in technique. Modern books on establishing an aquarium are – with good reason – at considerable pains to explain the importance of correct environment, and technology has provided the wherewithal to create, adjust, and monitor it. The ability to tailor the aquarium to its occupants' specific needs has greatly improved the aquarist's chances of keeping any fish alive, and, in turn, vastly increased the number of species which can readily be maintained, and often even bred, in captivity.

Fish are often regarded – especially by the uninitiated – as 'easy' pets. They do not, normally, make a noise, soil or destroy furnishings, get lost, bite visitors, or steal food from the kitchen. They do not require exercise, grooming, or litter trays. They are neatly confined to a glass box. All this is indeed true, but the would-be aquarist who thinks that fish-keeping is simply a matter of filling an aquarium with water, adding fish, and feeding them once or twice a day, is sadly mistaken. The successful aquarist needs an element of knowledge of 'water technology', ecology, and nutrition,

Specialised knowledge is needed to create the correct environment where fish can thrive.

inter alia, and the beginner must often embark on a sharp upward learning curve, luckily nowadays facilitated by the availability of literature on both aquarium techniques and the fish themselves.

The diversity of fish species now available to the hobbyist, an estimated 1,500-2,000 tropical freshwater species alone, means a concomitant diversity of size, natural origin (and hence environment), diet, habits, and other factors (including ailments and other problems), most of which should be taken into account when planning the aquarium, rather than later. Keeping fish is not like keeping a dog, cat, or horse, where just one species, albeit often numerous breeds, is involved. Tropical freshwater fish alone encompass a range of species more diverse than the entire gamut of mammals in terms of their physiology, nutrition, and ecological requirements: a *Corydoras* catfish and a Malawi cichlid are as different in their husbandry requirements as are a hamster and a horse, or an elephant and a tiger! And few of us would consider keeping those creatures in the same manner – let alone together.

Unfortunately many new hobbyists subscribe to the 'easy pets' point of view, and fail to realise the implications of this diversity, assuming they are aware of it at all. They realise their error only when an inappropriate mix of fish or an incorrect environment results in disaster, and only then – if then – resort to the literature to find out where they have gone wrong. Equally unfortunately, many aquarists, experienced as well as novice, assume that the illness or demise of a fish must be of pathogenic origin. It must be stressed from the outset – and repeatedly, whenever appropriate – that an estimated *minimum* 95 per cent of captive fish health problems are environmentally induced (including dietary) rather than pathogenic in origin. That is to say, they are, at root, the result of negligence by the aquarist. Unfortunately many aquarists find this difficult to accept, but the likelihood of any problem having an environmental basis must never be discounted, and in most cases should be considered before any other options, if the situation is to be remedied and a recurrence avoided.

The diagnosis and treatment of illness, and other problem solving, is quite different to that pertaining to most captive creatures. It is obviously not a simple matter to take an individual sick fish, let alone a tankful, to the vet. Moreover, the stress of being netted, transported, examined, and then returned to the aquarium may well exacerbate the problem and even result in the death of the fish. At the same time, few aquarists are prepared to pay for an expensive home visit for small, often cheaper-to-replace, cold-blooded creatures. And in any case, very few vets have any expertise in the diagnosis and treatment of fish ailments – a situation perpetuated by the resulting lack of demand for their services in the aquatic field, even though nowadays some ornamental fish cost considerably more than offspring of a prize-winning pedigree dog.

Instead the norm is for the aquarist to attempt to diagnose the cause of the problem, using his own experience; advice from aquatic dealers, other hobbyists, and information services provided by some aquarium magazines; and the available literature. Treatment is usually with proprietary remedies available 'off-the-shelf' from aquatic dealers, with specific chemicals, or with drugs designed for animal (usually mammal) or human use. The veterinarian is usually involved in the proceedings only if the necessary medication is not available 'over the counter', or if surgery is required.

The available literature consists of a number of highly technical works on fish pathogens and pathology, likely to confuse the amateur or induce a state of 'transferred hypochondria' regarding his fishes' health, and the problem-solving chapters, usually very limited in scope, of general aquarium manuals. The *A-Z of Tropical Fish Diseases and Health Problems* is intended to bridge the intervening gap, in terms comprehensible to the layman, by providing a guide to diagnosis and treatment not only for the hobbyist, but also for the vet unexpectedly confronted with an ailing fish.

How To Use
This Book

This book is divided into three sections, of which the first, *Health and Husbandry*, should be regarded as far and away the most important. Given that the vast majority of fish health problems are environmental, it should be obvious that prevention should be the main consideration. Accordingly, the first section provides information on the biology of fish and their relationship to the aquatic environment, on how to establish, provide, and maintain an appropriate healthy environment, and on how to acquire and maintain a compatible selection of healthy fish. As many aquarists ultimately aspire to become fish breeders, if only on a small scale, selection and care of breeding stock, and care of eggs and fry, are also covered. The section concludes with a short chapter on the types of medication available and methods of administering them.

Section II, *Signs of Diseases and Health Problems*, lists common signs of illness and possible or probable causes, to enable the aquarist to diagnose the identity of the disease or cause of the problem. Further information on specific conditions, and advice on control and treatment, can then be found in Section III, an alphabetical listing of *Treatment of Diseases and Health Problems*. Because diagnosis and choice of treatment normally lie with the aquarist, and because so many problems are environmental in origin, Section III has been expanded to include entries on drugs and chemicals and their dosages, and definitions of a small number of key environmental and biological terms.

Note on the cross-referencing system used in this book:
Terms printed in capital letters and followed by the number (2) or (3) (for example, GROWTHS [2], STRESS [3]) are cross-references to entries in Sections II and II respectively, indicating that further relevant material may be found there.

SECTION I

HEALTH AND HUSBANDRY

Chapter One

THE WELFARE
OF FISH

The majority of domestic and domesticated animals share the same environmental medium – air – as ourselves. This means that we are able readily to have regular physical, and vocal, contact with them. They tend to be obtrusive – noisy when hungry, demanding of attention and exercise, difficult to ignore. Even those which are confined, for their own safety, to cages – birds and reptiles – can be taken out and handled, and, in the case of birds, chatter or sing to us. They are very much a part of the family.

Imagine the outcry if animal welfare groups, not to mention the media, discovered that someone had bought a kitten or puppy, treated it so badly that it died within a day or so, gone back for another – and then another after that, and yet another. Imagine the outcry if it was discovered that not just one, but thousands of people, were guilty of such cruelty. Yet that is exactly what happens to fish on a regular basis. Because they are cold-blooded (and hence, it is assumed, do not suffer), confined to an aquarium full of water and thus not tactile pets, and because they are commonly relatively cheap, their lives are all too often regarded as of little or no account.

CRUELTY THROUGH IGNORANCE

The cause of this quite appalling slaughter is generally ignorance rather than deliberate neglect or cruelty. Many beginners assume that fishkeeping is simply a case of filling a tank with water and adding the fish of choice. Because they are unaware of the true complexity of the subject, they do not bother to read about what is involved. Their newly purchased fish die, so they replace them. The replacements die too, and are, in turn, replaced. The would-be aquarist blames the dealer, or the fish, but rarely himself, and often eventually gives up in disgust.

Ignorance is, however, no excuse. To continue the warm-blooded analogy, ignorance would be no defence if a cat starved to death because its owner, ignorant that it was a carnivore, fed it nothing but lettuce; or if a succession of rabbits met with a grisly end when misguidedly housed in a run with greyhounds. Yet the equivalents of these bizarre, unlikely, scenarios are commonplace in the aquarium.

Ignorance is, likewise, at the root of the assumption that fish are cold-blooded, and therefore do not suffer or feel pain. Experienced aquarists are rarely guilty of cruelty such as that mentioned above, as they have learned to regard fish in a rather different light through long-term association with them. They realise that fish are aware of the world outside their aquarium, generally learn to differentiate between people, experience fear and stress, and certainly appear to suffer when anything goes wrong. Some display an intelligence and learning ability considerably greater than that of mammals of equivalent size.

THE SCIENTIFIC EVIDENCE

Although this view has been regarded as anthropomorphic in some quarters, accumulating scientific evidence suggests that fish are capable of experiencing STRESS (3) and pain. In the UK it is now illegal to cause unnecessary pain or stress to fish for experimental purposes without government (Home Office) approval. Unfortunately, there is no reliable method for precisely measuring pain in fish, or, indeed any other animal (including man). It would, however, seem likely that fish perceive pain differently from the way humans do.

Nevertheless, there is indirect evidence for stress and pain perception in fish, based on a number of anatomical, physiological and behavioural features which show similarities to those present in the higher vertebrates, including mammals. It is known, for example, that fish assign a higher priority to pain avoidance than to hunger, and they produce adrenalin and other stress (or 'flight or fight') related hormones.

A badly stressed fish in a bare dealer's tank. Note the washed-out coloration and clamped fins. The darker fish to the right is showing normal colour for the species.

Showing fish is regarded by many as a questionable activity; the transportation involved, plus display in a small, bare tank, is undoubtedly a cause of stress.

STRESS

Of particular relevance to aquarium husbandry of fish are the negative effects of stress on disease resistance. It is known that stressful conditions, especially chronic stress, can lower the fish's immune resistance and hence render the fish more susceptible to infectious diseases. Stress can be caused by a variety of factors, for example adverse water conditions, AGGRESSION (3), inadequate shelter, inappropriate lighting, spawning, netting and transportation, to mention but a few. For this reason the chapters that follow will place considerable emphasis upon the identification of stressors and the avoidance, or at least the minimisation, of stress.

THE RESPONSIBLE APPROACH

Given that fish are evidently capable of suffering, then there is every reason to treat them with the same kindness and respect as the majority of pet owners do cats, dogs, and other 'furries'. From a humane viewpoint they are, in any case, just as entitled to live as are other creatures, and their lives should never be regarded as cheap or worthless.

Fish are more dependent on their owner than other pets. Theirs is a closed environment, and they do not have the option of running away to find a better home. They rely on their keeper not only for the food they eat, but for the provision and maintenance of their entire life-support system. That is just to keep them alive.

There are those who might argue that it is wrong to keep any creature confined permanently to a small container, but against this view is the fact that, if the environment is appropriate, the individual fish will probably enjoy a longer lifespan in captivity than it would in the wild, unconcerned about the source of its next meal or the likelihood of becoming someone else's.

However, there is little sense in prolonging life if the quality of that life is poor. How many of us would like to live a permanent, celibate existence in a small, over-crowded, smog-filled, cell. Yet this is, effectively, the life sentence to which many pet fish are condemned. The cell is, of course, too small an aquarium; the smog is water unsuited to the fish; the celibacy is when, as is often the case, just one individual of a species is kept, sometimes specifically *because* the aquarist "doesn't want to breed". These are all abuses which the aquarist can, and should, make it his responsibility to avoid.

COMMERCIAL ABUSES

There are other abuses, rooted in commercialism, which persist, once again largely because of ignorance of the cruelty they entail. Just as some breeds of dog and cat have bred-in features which cause them discomfort and sometimes serious suffering, a number of species of fish

"Red Parrots" are a grossly deformed man-made cichlid – often not red at all.

have been selectively bred to produce 'fancy' varieties. Some of these are simply harmless colour variants, but others involve serious physical DEFORMITY (2).

The worst examples are undoubtedly those involving the goldfish *(Carassius auratus)*, many of which prevent the fish from living anything approaching a normal life and may cause actual physical suffering. Breeders of other species would cull out, as worthless, non-viable, and likely to suffer, any fry exhibiting such deformities. Although in general fancy varieties of freshwater tropical fish are less extreme, the "blood red parrot", a creation of unknown provenance but thought to be a hybrid cichlid (family Cichlidae), exhibits severe body deformity akin to that of some goldfish.

Ornamental fish farmers have also produced grotesque stumpy-bodied varieties of mollies (known as "balloon mollies", due to their inflated appearance) and stumpy kissing gouramis *(Helostoma temminckii)*. Similarly, a number of long-finned varieties of various species have also been created, and in extreme cases these exhibit swimming difficulties because of the unnatural weight of their finnage.

Of more recent origin is the trend towards regarding aquaria as items of interior decor rather than homes for fish. Although an aquarium may have a decorative value, its prime function should be to provide optimum, natural, living quarters for its occupants. Its size and shape should be appropriate – tall, narrow multi-sided towers may look interesting, but they offer little scope for the horizontal movement normal to fish; and the decor should be natural and suited to the occupants, not colour-coordinated with the carpet.

Worse still are colour-coordinated fish – transparent or albino species injected with coloured, sometimes fluorescent, dyes, and often sold under various misleading names, such as 'painted fish'. This practice of dye injection, which undoubtedly causes the fish pain and stress, is associated with high mortalities following the injection process. The mass injection of fish using the same needle also increases the risk of transmitting diseases. The aquarist should not only avoid buying such fish, but also inform the dealer selling them that he is taking his trade elsewhere, and why.

THE AQUARIST'S RESPONSIBILITY

Aquarists have a responsibility not just to maintain the life of their charges, but to ensure that that life is as stress-free and natural as possible. It is to their own advantage too, as active, healthy, fish, exhibiting the behaviour nature intended, are far more likely to give pleasure to their owner than sick, frightened, harassed, or unmotivated ones.

Chapter Two
BIOLOGY AND ANATOMY

This chapter is intended to provide an insight into the anatomical and physiological diversity of fish, a basic knowledge of which is useful in order to understand disease processes and immunity.

Fish have undergone a long period of evolution compared to mammals, and this has resulted in enormous variations in anatomy and physiology. These include a wide range of adaptations to differing environmental conditions (temperature, water chemistry and quality, oxygen content, water movement, *inter alia*) and dietary items, as well as behavioural features (e.g. method of capturing prey, avoidance of becoming prey, reproductive behaviour) which, in turn, may have led to additional anatomical modifications. In fact, present-day fish are so diverse that a simple, all-embracing definition of 'fish' is impossible.

Because of this diversity, fish are the most speciose of all the vertebrate groups. Approximately 24,600 species have been described, spanning some 480 taxonomic families. Each year, many new species are discovered, such that some ichthyologists suggest the total number of extant fish species could be as high as 40,000. Many new species may be encountered in the aquarium hobby, long before they are scientifically described and classified. Around 8,500 of the described fish species inhabit freshwaters, and the number of tropical freshwater species available in the aquarium hobby is probably in the region of 1,500 to 2,000.

The existence of this enormous diversity must never be disregarded when considering aspects of fish health. Even closely related species may have quite different adaptations to their natural environment, and thus require quite different conditions in captivity. Furthermore, different species also vary in their tolerance of incorrect aquarium conditions and in their susceptibility to infectious and non-infectious diseases; in fact, some fish pathogens and parasites are specific to only one or a few fish species.

BODY SHAPE, SKELETON AND MUSCULATURE

In general terms, a fish's body comprises a head, a trunk, and a tail. Body shape varies considerably between groups of fish and even within a genus. Although some fish – for example, many cyprinids, such as the barbs – have the typical shape conjured up by the word 'fish', many species show extremes of body shape. For example, South American freshwater angelfish (*Pterophyllum* spp.) are extremely compressed laterally, whereas Borneo suckerfish (*Gastromyzon* spp.) are compressed dorso-ventrally. Some species, such as khuli loaches (*Acanthophthalmus* spp. [=*Pangio*]) are snake-like in appearance, whereas at the other extreme, pufferfish (e.g. *Tetraodon* spp.) are almost spherical. These various body profiles tend to reflect each fish's evolutionary adaptations to its environment.

Virtually all freshwater fish possess a skeleton composed of true bone, as opposed to the cartilaginous skeletons of sharks and rays. The skeleton consists of, basically, the skull, vertebrae (spine), ribs, and fin rays, and forms a framework for supporting the internal organs, musculature, nervous system, and other tissues.

The body musculature is arranged in a series of muscle blocks, known as myotomes, which allow the body to flex from side to side, producing a sideways wave-like motion which helps propel the fish through the water.

THE CIRCULATORY SYSTEM

The circulatory system is primarily involved in the transporting of oxygen and nutrients to the body tissues and the removal of the waste products of metabolism, but it also plays an important role in immunity.

Fish have a simple heart, comprising an atrium and a ventricle, which is situated ventrally behind the gill arches. The heart, which is basically a muscular pump, is linked to a single circulatory system consisting of a network of veins, arteries and capillaries. The rate of heart beat varies

Diversity of form

Synodontis multipunctatus (catfish).

ABOVE: Pelvicachromis humilis (cichlid).

BELOW: Female golden killie (Aplocheilichthys lineatus var.).

according to the fish species and the water temperature. The heart beat rate may also increase in response to STRESS (3), fright, and certain diseases.

The total blood volume of a fish is only about five per cent of its body weight. The blood is composed of various specialised cells and soluble substances which circulate within a fluid medium (the plasma). The cellular component includes the red blood cells (= erythrocytes) which are produced by the liver, kidney, and spleen. Red cells function in oxygen transportation and, in common with those of mammals, they are rich in the pigment haemoglobin. Fish red blood cells differ from those of mammals in that they contain a nucleus. The white blood cells (lymphocytes and other types) play an important role in immune defence.

Fish also possess a lymph drainage system (= lymphatic system) which is about four times the blood volume. The fluid lymph is very similar in composition to the blood plasma and constitutes the major circulatory system within the so-called white muscles (myomeres) of the fish.

ASSOCIATED HEALTH PROBLEMS
The heart may fail as a result of systemic BACTERIAL INFECTION (3) or other chronic disease. It may also fail simply due to old age. The blood of fish may occasionally be infected by bacteria (BACTEREMIA (3)) and this can manifest as HAEMORRHAGING (2) of the fins and skin. A few PROTOZOAN (3) parasites (e.g. TRYPANOSOMES (3)) may inhabit the blood; however, these are rarely of aquarium importance.

If NITRITE (3) is present in the aquarium water, this will enter the blood system where it oxidises haemoglobin into methaemoglobin. Methaemoglobin cannot bind oxygen and is therefore unable to supply the tissues with this vital gas. As a consequence the fish experiences HYPOXIA (3) and may die. In cases of severe nitrite POISONING (3) the blood may visibly turn brown owing to the presence of the brown-coloured methaemoglobin.

THE DIGESTIVE TRACT
The digestive tract comprises the mouth opening and buccal cavity, oesophagus, stomach (absent in some groups of fish) and intestine, terminating in the anus.

THE MOUTH AND TEETH

The buccopharyngeal cavity constitutes the anterior chamber of the digestive system, as well as serving to pump water for respiration.

The position and shape of the mouth opening may provide a clue to the fish's feeding behaviour. For example, species which feed mostly in midwater have mouths which are roughly forward-pointing. Underslung mouths are typical of bottom-dwelling fish which browse over the substrate, whereas upturned mouths are generally, but not always, associated with surface-dwelling fish which feed on air-breathing aquatic insect larvae or on terrestrial insects which have fallen onto the water.

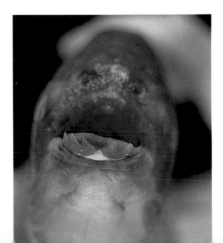

ABOVE: Arowana (Osteoglossum bicirrhosum) have lingual teeth.

RIGHT: Piranha teeth.

The mouth opening is bordered on the exterior by the lips. In some fish, such as *Plecostomus* catfish and Borneo suckerfish (*Gastromyzon* spp.), the lips are greatly enlarged and form a sucker-like apparatus enabling the fish to attach to solid surfaces over which it can then browse. Some groups of fish, such as catfish and cyprinids (barbs and their relatives) possess two or more barbels extending from the lips. These whisker-like appendages have a sensory function, enabling the fish to 'feel' and/or taste its environment *(see also Nervous System and Sensory Organs, below)*.

The teeth of teleost (bony) fish are composed of a type of dentine. Unlike the teeth of mammals they are normally subject to constant replacement, which allows not only for wear and tear but also for environmentally and/or age-induced changes in diet. The various positions, shapes, and arrangements of the teeth reflect different feeding methods and food preferences: for example, a spectacular diversity of food items and feeding methods, and associated variations in dentition, is to be found among the cichlid fish of the great lakes of East Africa.

The location of the teeth varies according to the group of fish concerned: for example, the teeth may be set in the jaw, as in characins, on the tongue (lingual teeth), for example in the osteoglossids, whose name literally means 'bony tongues', or in the throat (pharyngeal teeth or 'gill teeth'), as in carp and cichlids. Palatal or vomerine teeth (that is, situated in the roof of the mouth) are found in some fish, such as many catfish and salmonids. Most fish swallow their food whole; very few species exhibit an obvious chewing action, although the food may be processed before passing into the digestive tract proper, for example by the pharyngeal teeth in cichlids.

THE STOMACH AND INTESTINE

The stomach and intestine together form the intestinal tract. As food passes through the tract it is gradually broken down with the aid of physical, chemical and enzymatic processes. The protein, fat, and carbohydrate components of the food are finally reduced to smaller molecules, namely amino acids, fatty acids, and sugars, respectively, which can be more easily absorbed (or actively taken up) across the gut

ANATOMY OF A FISH

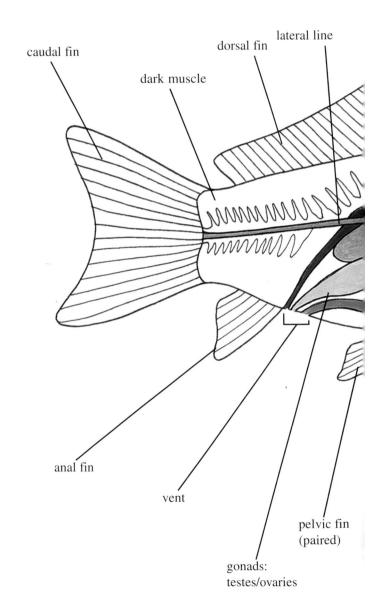

caudal fin

dark muscle

dorsal fin

lateral line

anal fin

vent

pelvic fin
(paired)

gonads:
testes/ovaries

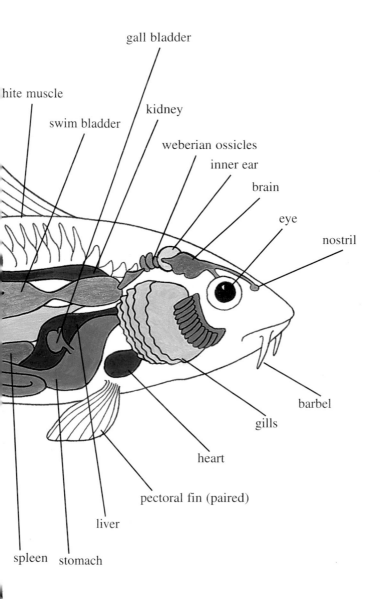

gall bladder

hite muscle

kidney

swim bladder

weberian ossicles

inner ear

brain

eye

nostril

barbel

gills

heart

pectoral fin (paired)

liver

spleen   stomach

ntestine

wall and into the blood. Once in the bloodstream these nutrients are carried around the body where they are used to provide energy and growth.

The sequence of digestive events is as follows. The ingested food passes down the short oesophagus and into the stomach, if present. Some groups of fish (e.g. cyprinids) have no true stomach and are termed agastric; the presence or absence of a stomach may be a function of diet, as when there is the need to store and partially break down large food items, such as whole fish, prior to further digestion.

The stomach contains a range of enzymes, such as pepsin and trypsin, which help break down the food. Bile fluids, which are stored in a small organ called the gall bladder, are emptied into the stomach where they aid fat digestion. In some species, such as carnivores, the stomach environment has a very low pH (pH 2.0-5.0) due to the production of hydrochloric acid (HCl) by specialised cells within the stomach wall. The acid conditions of the stomach, together with its digestive enzymes, help destroy many pathogens which may happen to be swallowed.

In some fish the stomach connects to a number of hollow finger-like processes known as pyloric caeca. These structures, which vary considerably between species in their shape and number, possibly serve to increase the surface area over which nutrients can be absorbed into the blood.

From the stomach, food passes into the intestine, which is the major site of absorption. Here the liver and pancreas aid digestion by releasing digestive juices into the anterior part of the intestine. The length and form of the intestine is a function of diet (that is, the type of food to be processed): the intestines of primarily herbivorous fish are generally much longer and more convoluted than those of carnivorous species.

The intestine terminates in the anal opening through which the faeces and copious amounts of urine are expelled. The solid faecal waste comprises undigested protein, lipids, and carbohydrates, plus cell debris and other tissue material from the fish itself.

It should be noted that the intestines of fish are also involved in immune defence and accessory respiratory activity *(see Respiratory System, below).*

ASSOCIATED HEALTH PROBLEMS

Some pathogens infect fish via the oral route. For example, larval tapeworms (CESTODES (3)) and FLUKES (3) may be transmitted by COPEPOD (3) CRUSTACEANS (3) which are a favourite prey of many fish. Once the copepod is ingested, the parasites within are released into the fish's gut where they either penetrate the gut wall and develop into the next larval stage, or remain within the gut lumen and transform into adults. Fish which are heavily burdened with gut-dwelling worms may appear swollen around the belly region due to the sheer bulk of parasites. This swelling is often the only visible evidence of a worm infection, since the majority of these gut parasites cause little damage to their fish hosts.

Certain PROTOZOAN (3) parasites (e.g. PLEIST-OPHORA (3)) and MYCOBACTERIA (3) may be acquired as a result of cannibalism, through ingesting the infected tissues of a dead fish. Incorrect diet may lead to general ill-health and digestive disorders such as constipation, which in extreme cases may prove fatal.

Fish are capable of orally ejecting foods which are too large to swallow or are toxic. Some large catfish species, such as the red-tailed catfish *(Phractocephalus hemioliopterus)* seem relatively prone to VOMITING (2). The emission of large quantities of partly digested food may overwhelm the biological filtration system and cause a serious, and sometimes lethal, water quality problem.

The teeth of fish do not normally present health problems, except in the case of pufferfish (Tetraodontidae), where the teeth are fused to form two beak-like plates which are used for crushing hard-shelled prey such as snails. The puffer's 'beak' may continue to grow throughout life and therefore need constant wear in order to prevent over-growth. Pufferfish which have been inappropriately fed on soft foods may require their teeth to be clipped – this procedure should be performed only by a veterinary surgeon.
(See also Section I: Nutrition.)

THE ENDOCRINE SYSTEM

The endocrine system helps to control and organise complex physiological processes within the fish's body, enabling the various organs and tissues to work in harmony.

This harmonization is achieved through hormones, chemical messengers which are synthesized by the endocrine system. The hormones circulate through the body via the blood and influence the activities of other organs. In fish, hormones serve to regulate important physiological processes such as osmoregulation, calcium metabolism, and reproduction.

The pituitary gland, which is linked to the forebrain, plays a key role in controlling endocrine functions. Other endocrine organs include the thymus, thyroid, pineal gland (= epiphysis, involved in circadian rhythms), interrenal gland, Corpuscles of Stannius (associated with the kidneys), urophysis, Islets of Langerhans, and the ultimobranchial glands (which secrete calcitronin). In fish the heart also has endocrine function in that it secretes peptide hormones.

Many of these endocrine organs produce hormones which are involved in the stress response of fish. For example, corticotrophin releasing factor (CRF) is produced by the hypothalamus; adrenocorticotrophic hormone (ACTH) by the pituitary gland; and cortisol and adrenalin both by the interrenal gland.

ASSOCIATED HEALTH PROBLEMS
Pituitary and thyroid TUMOURS (3) (adenomas) have been recorded in some aquarium fish (e.g. some poeciliid livebearers, *inter alia*).

STRESS (3) or DISEASE (3) can cause the fish's pigmentation to intensify or fade as a result of hormone action: a darkening of pigmentation may be due to stimulation of the melanophores by pituitary hormone, whereas pallor may be linked to adrenalin release. A partial darkening of the head, sometimes quite striking in appearance, may sometimes indicate a thyroid tumour. However, bear in mind that fish also adjust their pigmentation according to their surroundings as well as during behavioural signalling, such as visual communication and reproductive behaviour. A lack of iodine in the diet (uncommon in teleost fish, assuming a well-balanced diet is used) may lead to thyroid enlargement (goitre).

A prolonged lack of light, for example if fish are kept in a dark room for extended periods, may cause atrophy of the gonads. This is caused by lack of photic stimulation of the pineal gland, a light-sensitive area of tissue situated beneath a semi-translucent layer of skin near the forebrain, which exerts an influence on reproductive processes.

THE FINS

The number and arrangement of the fins is variable from species to species, although these appendages are normally consistent (albeit with some exceptions) within each taxonomic family. Typically there are seven fins: three unpaired (or median) fins, namely the dorsal, caudal (tail), and anal, used to maintain stability, plus two sets of paired fins, the pectorals and the pelvics, used for steering.

In most species the caudal fin works in conjunction with the myotomes to propel the fish forwards. Other fins facilitate slow, controlled movements, and general manoeuvring through the water. The fins may also play a role in courtship, mating (see Reproductive System, below), and communication. In the case of those species which venture onto land, such as climbing perch (*Anabas* spp.), *Clarias* catfish, and mudskippers (*Periophthalmus* spp.), some of the fins also aid terrestrial locomotion.

There are numerous variations on the basic fin arrangement. For example, many characins and most catfish typically possess an eighth fin known as the adipose, which lies posterior to the dorsal. The fleshy, fat-laden adipose fin is often extremely small and may be difficult to see in the case of small tetras, but is prominent in some catfish (e.g. *Synodontis* spp.).

There is also considerable variation in the size, position and fin-ray structure of the dorsal fin. In *Clarias* catfish the dorsal is ribbon-shaped and extends some two-thirds of the

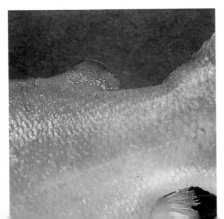

Adipose fin.

fish's length. A few groups of fish, such as the gobies (Gobiidae, *inter alia*), possess two dorsals, whereas some glass catfish (*Kryptopterus* spp.) and knife fish (gymnotids) have none. Some groups of fish have soft-rayed fins, an example being the cyprinids (carp, barbs, and their relatives). In the more advanced cichlid family (Cichlidae), the dorsal fin comprises both soft and spiny rays.

ASSOCIATED HEALTH PROBLEMS

The outer edges of the fins are often the first regions of invasion by certain microbial pathogens, and FIN EROSION (2) may reflect adverse water conditions. Fins are sometimes damaged during episodes of AGGRESSION (3). Some congenital or developmental abnormalities may produce individual fish which lack certain fins.

THE IMMUNE SYSTEM

Water is an ideal medium for single-celled organisms which are vulnerable to desiccation, such as BACTERIA (3) and PROTOZOA (3), some of which are pathogenic to fish. The whole body surface of a fish is in intimate contact with water and the organisms it harbours, and fish must therefore be able to prevent infection by pathogens. They achieve this via a complex armoury of defence systems.

The immune systems of fish are not as advanced as those of higher vertebrates, but nevertheless comprise a complex array of specialised cells, antibodies, and defence chemicals. The immune functions can be conveniently divided into innate immunity (= non-specific immunity) and adaptive immunity (= specific immunity). In some primitive groups of fish, such as the lampreys (family Petromyzontidae), the adaptive immune system is less well developed.

Innate immunity essentially provides the first line of defence against infection. This can take the form of physical barriers, notably the skin and skin mucus, which inhibit pathogen invasion, as well as an armoury of antimicrobial secretions and molecules. Examples of the latter include acid from the stomach and specialised proteins such as interferon and C-reactive protein which perform anti-viral and anti-bacterial/fungal activity respectively. Primitive phagocytic cells also play an important role in innate immunity by recognising, attacking, and engulfing a wide range of invading micro-organisms.

An adaptive immune response, on the other hand, is very specific to a particular type of pathogen. Upon exposure to the pathogen, various cells and molecular defence systems are triggered into action in order to destroy the invader. The important feature of adaptive immunity is that the immune system 'remembers' the pathogen even after it has been eliminated. If the same pathogen should happen to invade on a subsequent occasion, then the immune system is already armed for combat, enabling the pathogen to be dealt with more quickly and effectively.

The key cells involved in adaptive immunity are a group of white blood cells known as lymphocytes, which play a major role in detecting invading pathogens and in bringing other defences into play. The lymphocytes also produce antibodies – special proteins (immunoglobulins) which help neutralise or destroy pathogens and parasites. The speed of the antibody response is relatively slow in fish compared to higher vertebrates, sometimes taking several weeks, and in general it is temperature-influenced, being slower in cooler waters.

The ability of fish to develop protective immunity opens the possibility of developing vaccines. Despite a long history of fish vaccine research, only a handful of vaccines are at present commercially available for use on fish. All of these are directed against bacterial and viral pathogens, mostly of food-fish importance, with none so far developed to protect against parasitic diseases. Studies are underway to produce a vaccine against *ICHTHYOPHTHIRIUS* (3) (the parasite causing whitespot disease): such a vaccine could be highly beneficial to the health management of freshwater ornamental fish, given the frequent occurrence of this parasite in aquaria.

ASSOCIATED HEALTH PROBLEMS
Impairment of the immune system will reduce the fish's ability to ward off infections. A reduction in immune competence may arise through chronic STRESS (3), or simply through old age. In very young fish the immune systems may not be fully developed, with the result that they are more susceptible to infectious diseases. Fish which are

held under relatively sterile conditions (e.g. in water routinely dosed with antibiotics or subjected to UV IRRADIATION [3]), may exhibit a reduction in adaptive immunity due to the lack of stimulation by pathogens. Such fish are therefore more vulnerable to certain infections when introduced to normal aquarium conditions. The link between chronic stress and reduced immune ability is well documented. For example, immunosuppression causes a reduction in the number of white blood cells which play a key role in adaptive immunity. Conditions which may cause chronic stress in aquarium fish are numerous, and include overcrowding, AGGRESSION (3) by tank-mates, and adverse water conditions (e.g. incorrect temperature, pH, or OXYGEN (3) content, or toxic levels of NITRATE (3)). It should be noted that misuse of, or overdosing with, disease treatments, many of which are mildly toxic to fish, can itself be stressful, to the extent that an incorrect treatment regime can actually cause more harm than good.

THE KIDNEYS
Teleost fish possess two functional types of kidney, the anterior ('head') kidney and the posterior ('trunk') kidney. These organs, which are situated below the vertebral column, may appear quite separate in some groups of fish such as carp. The kidneys are involved in blood cell production (haemopoiesis), lymphatic function, and osmoregulation. In freshwater fish a major role of the kidneys is to excrete large quantities of urine, as part of osmoregulation. The head kidney is a lymphoid organ, involved in immunity and blood cell formation.

ASSOCIATED HEALTH PROBLEMS
The kidney may enlarge or become necrotic as a result of a systemic BACTERIAL INFECTION (3).

THE LIVER
The liver is part of the overall digestive system, and is a fairly large organ in fish, principally involved in the secretion of bile. The liver is also a storage organ, mostly for glycogen and to a lesser extent, lipids. It also plays a role in immune defence.

ASSOCIATED HEALTH PROBLEMS
The feeding of unsuitable dietary fats (= animal fats) may result in FATTY LIVER (3) degeneration, which can prove fatal.

LYMPHOID ORGANS AND TISSUES
The lymphoid organs and tissues play a crucial role in disease resistance, being the sites in which the white blood cells (lymphocytes) are synthesized and stored. In fish, lymphoid function is associated with the spleen, thymus, kidneys, and liver, and there is some evidence for gut-associated lymphoid tissue. In contrast to mammals, fish do not have bone marrow or lymph nodes.

ASSOCIATED HEALTH PROBLEMS
Certain BACTERIAL PATHOGENS (3) may invade the lymphoid organs. For example, MYCOBACTERIA (3) are often found to cause lesions in the spleen and kidney. Also, many acute VIRUS (3) infections involve the lymphoid tissues.

THE NERVOUS SYSTEM AND SENSORY ORGANS
In addition to a brain and nervous system, fish are equipped with a wide range of sense organs, several of which have no counterpart in mammals. Certain types of fish, including many catfish, are nocturnally active, and rely mostly on senses other than sight for hunting prey and avoiding predators.

The fish eye is very similar in structure to that of higher vertebrates, and most fish possess colour vision. Except in some predatory species which require acute binocular vision in order to hunt prey, sight is not so important to fish as it is to mammals. Fish which have lost one or both eyes through injury or disease may still be able to navigate through the water and feed. In fact, many cave-dwelling fish have degenerate eyes, or no eyes, one popular aquarium example being the Mexican blind cave tetra *(Astyanax mexicanus)*. These blind fish are perfectly able to swim in unfamilar surroundings (for example, when first introduced into an aquarium) without bumping into other fish or solid objects.

A small number of surface-dwelling or amphibious fish,

notably "four-eyes" (*Anableps* spp.) and mudskippers (*Periophthalmus* spp.), respectively, are capable of vision through air. In the livebearing *Anableps* each eye is divided into an upper and a lower part; the upper eye protrudes from the water during surface swimming, enabling the fish to observe its environment both above and below the water's surface – hence its common name.

Water is a good conductor of sound and fish have developed sensitive organs to be able to detect sound waves. Fish do not have external ears, but do possess inner ears whose function is balance and sound detection, just as in higher vertebrates. Although generally silent creatures, certain fish are capable of emitting sounds under water and are able to communicate with one another by this means.

A few groups of fish, such as the mormyrids, have specialised muscle cells which are capable of generating electrical pulses, and arranged over their skin are other specialised cells which can detect such electrical signals. Electrogeneration and electroreception enable these fish to communicate with one another, as well as to detect prey or avoid predators.

THE ACOUSTICO-LATERALIS SYSTEM

One special sensory feature of fish is the acoustico-lateralis system of sensory canals. This is basically a tactile organ which enables the fish to detect vibrations in the water or moving objects at close range (such as other nearby fish). It can also detect gravity as well as the direction of water movement.

In most fish the acoustico-lateralis system of canals runs beneath the skin surface, enabling the delicate sensory cells (known as hair cells or neuromasts) to be protected from accidental abrasion or other damage. The canals connect with the external environment via a series of pores. Several canals may be present over the head, and an elongate canal, known as the lateral line, runs along each side of the fish. The lateral line manifests on the body surface as an indented ridge and its pores are often clearly visible. In many species it is continuous, extending backwards from the head and terminating on the caudal peduncle; however, in cichlids and anabantoids it is usually split into two, occasionally three, sections. Groups of sensory pores are commonly found on the head of fish. In some cichlids, notably *Aulonocara, Aulonocranus,* and *Trematocara* spp., these head sensory pores are enlarged and have increased sensitivity, and are used by the fish to locate prey (small invertebrates) beneath the surface of the substrate, by detecting the minute vibrations caused by the movement of the prey.

SMELL AND TASTE

Fish are also able to 'smell' and 'taste' the water with the aid of special olfactory and palatal organs.

The olfactory system is externally visible as a pair of small pores (the nostrils or nares) which are situated on the snout. They do not play any part in respiration. In many fish each nostril has a separate inlet and outlet; however, no such division is present in the cichlids. Water entering the nostril passes over a folded epithelium which contains receptor cells, which are so sensitive that they can detect just a few molecules of 'odour' in the water. They can also distinguish between a vast range of different chemical odours. Fish use their olfactory systems to locate food as well as to detect the presence of predators. Olfactory senses are also employed for social behaviour, allowing fish to detect the presence of potential mates purely by the odours they give off in the water.

Fish also possess tastebuds, comprising sensory cells situated within the skin epithelium. The terminal end of each tastebud cell is in contact with the external environment. Unlike those of mammals, the tastebuds of fish are not confined to the tongue but are distributed over the whole body surface. In fact, the fish's tongue possesses very few, if any, tastebuds.

In many fish species the distribution of tastebuds varies considerably over various parts of the body. For example, catfish possess high concentrations of tastebuds on their barbels, but far fewer on the other body surfaces. This explains why catfish may be observed to probe the substrate or the water surface with their barbels in search of food. In fact, some catfish are known to be capable of detecting food over five metres away, purely by 'tasting' the water for food molecules using their sensitive barbels.

ASSOCIATED HEALTH PROBLEMS

The eyes of fish are often prime organs for attacks by other fish. It is not uncommon to see aquarium fish with one or even both eyes missing as a result of AGGRESSION (3). The eyes are sometimes infected by BACTERIA (3) and FUNGUS (3), as well as by a few parasites (e.g. *DIPLOSTOMUM* (3), the eye-fluke). Eye cloudiness (CLOUDY EYE (3)) and protrusion (EXOPHTHALMIA (3)) may be pathogen-induced, but are more frequently associated with adverse water conditions or generally poor aquarium hygiene. Cataracts can sometimes be the result of genetic defects (inherited) or VITAMIN DEFICIENCY (3).

The lateral line canals, being connected with the external environment by small pits (pores), may be vulnerable to infection. One occasionally encountered disease is HEXAMITIASIS (3) (hole-in-head disease [HIH]), sometimes known as head and lateral line erosion (HLLE) syndrome, which is mostly associated with cichlid fish.

The sensitive barbels of catfish and other fish are prone to abrasion and other injury from a variety of sources, including sharp gravel.

The brain and central nervous system may be damaged through water-borne toxins, notably AMMONIA (3) and certain metals.

THE REPRODUCTIVE SYSTEM

Although most fish species are egglayers which practise external fertilization, several popular aquarium fish have evolved internal fertilisation and give birth to fully formed young.

Most fish species comprise male and female individuals, though there are natural exceptions (such as the livebearer *Poecilia formosa*, which consists exclusively of females which have to be fertilised by males of a related species).

Male fish possess paired testes while females have twin ovaries, although in some species, for example many mouthbrooding cichlids which produce relatively small numbers of rather large eggs, one ovary is atrophied and inactive. The ovaries may comprise a simple assemblage of follicles, but can be quite complex organs in the case of livebearing species. The size of both male and female reproductive organs (relative to body weight) varies

34

A mouthbrooding cichlid with a mouthful of eggs.

considerably between species and according to the sexual maturity of the fish, as well as seasonal and other factors.

The chief group of livebearing aquarium fish is the poeciliids, two well-known examples being the guppy *(Poecilia reticulata)* and the swordtail *(Xiphophorus helleri)*. The male poeciliid livebearer has a specially modified anal fin known as a gonopodium. Functionally, this structure is the equivalent of the mammalian penis and can be swung forward to insert sperm into the female's genital opening. In some cultivated long-finned varieties of livebearers, such as swordtails *(Xiphophorus* sp.)*, the gonopodium is so elongated that normal mating is impossible, resulting in the fish being functionally sterile, though artificial insemination can be achieved.

Some fish have evolved specialised anatomical or physiological features to deal with the parental care of their eggs or fry. As mentioned later in this chapter (see Skin, Scales and Scutes below), some fish, such as the discus cichlids *(Symphysodon* spp.), secrete extra body mucus which is utilised as a food source by the young. In some species the buccopharyngeal cavity is used for incubating the eggs and/or fry, thus protecting them from outside predators. This so-called mouthbrooding habit is practised by certain cichlids, some catfish, and the primitive bony-tongues (Osteoglossids).

ASSOCIATED HEALTH PROBLEMS

Very few disease problems are associated with the reproductive organs of fish, though a few systemic BACTERIAL INFECTIONS (3) may attack the reproductive tissues. Deaths are more likely to arise through AGGRESSION (3) and chasing associated with reproductive behaviour than from reproductive tissue diseases.

Female fish deaths through physical exhaustion may result from producing large numbers of eggs or live young, especially if repeatedly used for breeding without adequate rest intervals. 'Overbreeding' of young females not yet fully grown may restrict their growth. The ovaries may atrophy or become otherwise dysfunctional, possibly through hormonal influences, sometimes associated with SENILITY (3). SPAWN-BINDING (3) may occur if a female is unable to lay her eggs for any reason. The influence of prolonged light deprivation on reproductive activity is discussed above under The Endocrine System: Associated Health Problems.

(See also Section I: Breeding; Fish compatibility.)

THE RESPIRATORY SYSTEM

Fish, in common with terrestrial vertebrates, must obtain OXYGEN (3) from their environment in order to live. Like terrestrial vertebrates, they also produce CARBON DIOXIDE (3) as a waste product and this must be eliminated from their bodies. The uptake of oxygen and the excretion of carbon dioxide is an important gaseous exchange process known as respiration. In terrestrial vertebrates this is achieved by means of lungs, while in most fish the primary organs of respiration are the gills.

Fish possess two sets of gills, one on each side of the body immediately posterior to the head, and these delicate organs are partially protected beneath a hard plate, the operculum or gill cover. Each gill comprises four bony arches to which are attached rows of long filaments, known as primary lamellae; each primary lamella is in turn composed of fine secondary lamellae and these are richly supplied with blood capillaries to facilitate the exchange of respiratory gases. The primary and secondary lamellae provide a large surface area over which gaseous exchange can occur. In highly

Clarias catfish crossing land.

active fish species the total gill surface area may be ten times that of the fish's body surface. Healthy gills are normally bright red in colour.

The influx of oxygen from the water into the gill capillaries, and the corresponding efflux of carbon dioxide, are processes which occur by simple diffusion. The gill membrane is very thin to allow efficient diffusion to occur. Water is some 800 times more dense than air and, as a consequence, the fish must expend a significant amount of energy in order to pump water across the gill surfaces. This pumping action is achieved by the fish opening its mouth, causing water to be sucked into the buccal cavity, followed by closure of the mouth and a muscular contraction of the buccal volume so that the water is forcibly expelled across the gills and out through the opercular openings. Although this pumping action may appear intermittent, it actually produces a constant flow of water across the gills.

The rate at which the pumping cycle occurs (the opercular rate) can easily be recorded by counting the opercular beats, and will vary according to several factors: the species, the individual fish (for example due to variations in activity, or STRESS (3)), and certain environmental conditions, notably temperature, which exerts a dual influence, by affecting the level of dissolved oxygen in the water as well as the overall metabolic rate of the fish. The opercular rate may increase dramatically when the fish is affected by disease.

When a fish is removed from the water, its gill lamellae collapse and their surface area for gaseous exchange is much reduced. Further, if the lamellar surfaces dry out then gaseous exchange cannot continue. This explains why many fish are unable to survive for extended periods out of water, despite the fact that air contains several times more oxygen than water. For this reason, fish should not be kept out of water for more than a couple of minutes, otherwise they will eventually suffocate and die. It should be mentioned, however, that the fish brain is remarkably tolerant of HYPOXIA (3) (low oxygen levels), and some fish species can survive exposure to air for many hours.

ACCESSORY METHODS OF RESPIRATION
In many fish a proportion of oxygen is also absorbed from water via the skin.

Some fish are able to obtain oxygen from the air as well as from the water, and are termed facultative air-breathers. This adaptation is common among fish which frequent stagnant waters in which dissolved oxygen levels may be critically low, and those inhabiting lakes and rivers which are prone to drying up. Certain loaches and catfish are able to absorb oxygen across their intestinal wall which is highly vascularised. Other types of fish possess auxiliary breathing organs associated with the gills, such as occur in some catfish (e.g. *Clarias* spp.), snakeheads (*Channa* and *Parachanna* spp.) and the 'labyrinth fish' (e.g. gouramis and other anabantids). Species which are equipped with auxiliary breathing organs may make occasional visits to the surface of the aquarium in order to gulp in atmospheric air. This behaviour, which can be seen in popular aquarium fish such as gouramis and *Corydoras* catfish, is sometimes misinterpreted as a sign of ill-health, or as an indicator of low oxygen levels in the aquarium water. In fact, this behaviour is perfectly normal, and may occur even when the water is saturated with oxygen.

OTHER GILL FUNCTIONS
In addition to their role in respiration, the gills also function as organs of AMMONIA (3) excretion and are the major surfaces across which salts enter and exit the fish. The influx of salts across the gills is important in

osmoregulation, because the internal body fluids of freshwater fish have higher concentrations of salts than their environment. As a result, water enters the fish by osmosis and salts are lost when this excess water is excreted. Freshwater fish must therefore compensate for this loss of vital salts by a process of active salt uptake, a function performed by special cells within the gills, known as chloride cells.

It should be noted that the gills are the major sites of uptake and excretion of immersion ANAESTHETICS (3).

ASSOCIATED HEALTH PROBLEMS

The gills, with their rich supply of blood and oxygen and their intimate contact with the external environment, are a favoured site of attack by many pathogens, including some ECTOPARASITES (3), BACTERIA (3), and FUNGI (3), which may cause serious damage to the delicate lamellae.

The gills may also be damaged by certain nitrogenous wastes (e.g. AMMONIA (3)), CHLORINE (3) and CHLORAMINE (3), incorrect pH (ACIDOSIS (3) and ALKALOSIS (3)) and heavy metals.

Because the gills play so many vital roles, any severe damage to these delicate organs is potentially life-threatening.

SKIN, SCALES, AND SCUTES

The skin forms a multi-layered barrier which separates the fish's internal tissues and body fluids from the external environment. The skin is important in maintaining the fish's internal mineral balance (= osmoregulation) as well as being the first line of defence against attack by pathogens.

The major layers of the skin are the epidermis and the dermis. The outer epidermal layer is coated with a viscous mucus which is continuously secreted by epidermal cells; this mucus coating, which is composed of glycoproteins, proteoglycans, and proteins, helps trap potential pathogens such as BACTERIA (3) and also contains components of the fish's defence system, including antibodies and antimicrobial substances such as lysozyme. The mucus coating also reduces drag in the water, thereby improving swimming efficiency. In the case of a few fish species, notably discus (*Symphysodon* spp.) and certain loricariid

Scutes.

Close-up of cichlid dorsal fin showing spinous and soft fin rays.

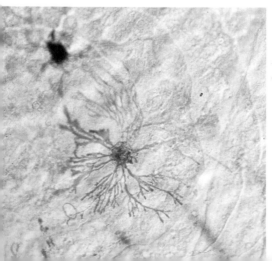

Photomicrograph of chromatophores.

catfish, the body mucus of the parent fish is a source of food for the fry. In the case of discus, there is some evidence that the parent's mucus may contain protective immuno-globulins which are taken up by the feeding fry, thereby helping to protect the youngsters from infections. In this respect the discus mucus may have a similar role to the 'first milk' (colostrum) of mammals. Beneath the epidermis lies the dermis, in which the scales are formed and anchored. The scales, which are basically calcified plates, confer additional protection to the fish. They cover the fish's body, and, less commonly, the head and/or parts of the fins. In some species the scales are so tiny that the fish appears scaleless; however, a few species, e.g. silurid catfish, are truly without scales (naked). Two basic scale forms are found among teleost fish: cycloid (smooth and roughly round in shape) scales which are common in fish with soft-rayed fins, and ctenoid (spinous and comb-like).

Certain fish, such as doradid and other 'armoured' catfish, have scutes instead of scales. Like scales, these are bony plates, but they are thicker and heavier, providing the fish with a strong defence against predators and injuries. They lie beneath the skin and thus cannot easily be dislodged, and are often equipped with spines as an additional deterrent to enemies; they also contribute significantly to the weight of the fish, thus assisting bottom-dwellers in maintaining their desired station, especially in strong currents.

Within the dermis are also found the pigment cells (chromatophores) which give the fish their body coloration. Several colour types of pigment cells exist, notably the melanophores which can influence the overall darkness of the fish's colour. These pigment cells are under hormonal control, and typically fish which appear abnormally dark are likely to be suffering from DISEASE (3) and/or STRESS (3). The fish's environment will also affect its pigmentation, with fish kept in light-coloured or over-illuminated surroundings being paler than those kept in darker surroundings. Fish which have lost their sight tend to be darker than normal. (See also Endocrine System, above.)

ASSOCIATED HEALTH PROBLEMS
The skin is in intimate contact with the aquatic environment, and not surprisingly, is vulnerable to attack by a range of

pathogens, notably VIRUSES (3), BACTERIA (3), FUNGI (3), PROTOZOA (3), and macro-PARASITES (3). Clinical signs of skin diseases include ULCERS (2), HAEMORRHAGES (2), or GROWTHS (2), these conditions resulting from pathogen damage and/or the fish's immune response. If the protective skin barrier is broken, through, for example, INJURY (3) or DISEASE (3) then the internal organs and tissues will be vulnerable to invasion by microbial pathogens. Certain ECTOPARASITES (3), such as LEECHES (3) and *ARGULUS* (3) (fish lice), puncture the skin layers in order to feed on their host's blood and tissues, and this may lead to SECONDARY INFECTION (3) (by BACTERIA [3] or FUNGUS [3]) of the resulting WOUNDS (3). Some ectoparasites partially invade the skin layers: for example, the whitespot protozoan *(Ichthyophthirius)* burrows through the epidermis but never penetrates deep into the body.

Extensive damage to the skin by invading pathogens can result in an uncontrolled osmotic movement of water and chemicals between the tissues and the external environment, causing the fish to suffer from OSMOTIC STRESS (3).

Loss of scales, for example, as a result of rough handling in the aquarium net, can give rise to infection, since the scale is ripped from the underlying dermal layer. The appearance of the scales may also be an indicator of disease.

The rate of mucus secretion may increase during skin infection or if the fish is exposed to chemical or physical irritants in the water (MUCUS HYPERPRODUCTION [2]).

THE SPLEEN
This organ is red to black in colour and contains the major secondary lymphatic tissue in fish, involved in immunity. It is also a site of blood cell formation.

ASSOCIATED HEALTH PROBLEMS
The spleen may enlarge or become necrotic as a result of a systemic BACTERIAL INFECTION (3).

THE SWIM BLADDER
The swim bladder, also known as the gas bladder or air bladder, is a gas-filled organ which enables the fish to achieve neutral buoyancy at various water depths (fish are

slightly denser than water and would tend to sink without some form of 'lift' mechanism). The organ is typically white to semi-translucent and shiny. In most fish, the swim bladder is a relatively large organ, comprising up to seven per cent of total body volume in freshwater species. It typically comprises a single chamber (but in carp is divided into two distinct chambers which are connected by a narrow duct). In the case of those fish which spend much of their adult lives on the substrate (bottom-dwellers, such as gobies), the swim bladder has become redundant, and is greatly atrophied or absent altogether. In fact, for some fish a buoyancy organ would be a positive disadvantage, for example in rheophilic species which rely on hugging the substrate to avoid being swept away, and for this reason an absence or atrophy of the swim bladder is common in such fish. The swim bladder functions by altering its gas volume, to create the desired neutral buoyancy. Structurally, the bladder wall is thin and flexible, thereby permitting the organ to expand or contract. In most adult teleost fish the swim bladder is an isolated structure with no ducts to the external environment through which gas could be exchanged; instead, gas absorption or secretion is via the blood system, mediated through a network of capillaries in the swim-bladder wall. Swim-bladder function is controlled by the endocrine and nervous systems. In some fish the swim bladder is also used for sound detection and/or sound production, and functions as a resonator and/or vibrator. This serves as a method of communication.

ASSOCIATED HEALTH PROBLEMS

Damage to the swim-bladder, for example resulting from INJURY (3) (typically the result of AGGRESSION (3)), BACTERIAL INFECTION (3), or genetic defect, may cause it to remain permanently inflated or, more usually, collapsed. Fish suffering swim-bladder dysfunction tend to float to the water surface (bladder inflated) or sink to the bottom (bladder collapsed), or to lose 'attitude control', swimming on one side or even upside-down. Such fish often struggle to regain position in mid-water. It should, however, be borne in mind that some fish naturally lack buoyancy, and that swimming upside-down or in other 'abnormal' positions is perfectly normal for some species.

Chapter Three

Signs Of A Healthy Fish

As we have already mentioned, there are many different species of tropical freshwater fish, with an immense diversity of form, behaviour, and requirements. The corollary of this diversity is that what may be a sign of ill-health in one species is often perfectly normal in another. For example, most fish swim upright and are buoyant, but there are species which normally, or sometimes, swim upside-down or on their sides, while others spend most of their time resting on the bottom because they have little or no natural BUOYANCY (2). Some fish feed almost continuously, so that loss of APPETITE (2) indicates a problem, but others, in particular piscivorous predators, may gorge themselves and then eat nothing for several days.

ESTABLISHING THE NORM
It is thus important to establish the norm for any species, both before purchasing it and in order to be able to detect any incipient problems later. There are a number of encyclopaedic manuals of fish species which will provide the necessary information about what constitutes normal; or, rather, will point out any 'abnormalities' such as those mentioned above. Sometimes a little lateral thinking may be required – most fish catalogues will tell you a fish is a piscivore, but you must use common sense in realising that when it has just consumed half its own bulk in fish, it is unlikely to be hungry again for a while!

Most fish catalogues are illustrated in colour, and these photographs can be invaluable in establishing the general appearance of a healthy individual of a particular species. If a number of individuals of a species are present, either in the

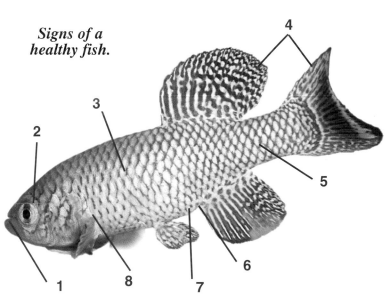

Signs of a healthy fish.

1. No ulceration or erosion around mouth.
2. Eyes clear and not bulging.
3. Scales (if present in the species) are undamaged and lie flat against the body.
4. Clean edges to fins without signs of fraying or erosion.
5. No evidence of ulcers, spots, haemorrhaging, or excessive mucus.
6. Faeces normal in terms of recent diet.
7. Belly contour is slightly convex or flat – not concave.
8. Operculum not flared (unless, like this individual, the fish is displaying). No mucus trailing from gills. Normal respiration rate.

home aquarium or the dealer's tank, then valuable comparisons can be made. It is comparatively rare for the entire group to be unwell, and if this does happen, they are generally so ill that it is obvious that something is badly amiss.

IMPORTANCE OF OBSERVATION

Some aquarium fish are large and comparatively robust, but many are small and delicate and likely to die very quickly if anything goes wrong, whether the problem be environmental degradation or disease. It is thus essential to become familiar with the normal appearance and behaviour of each individual fish, and to observe them regularly, at least once per day, to check that they are all 'present and correct'.

Probably the most convenient time to do this is during feeding. Careful observation will enable the aquarist to detect the first signs of trouble, and often, particularly with environmental problems, nip it in the bud.

APPETITE
Fish that feed on small items – invertebrates, molluscs, vegetable matter, detritus, fish eggs, and small (relative to the predator) fish – generally feed fairly continuously and can be expected always to show an interest in food unless recently fed. Only in those which feed irregularly in nature, and are fed appropriately in captivity (for example piscivores, such as that mentioned above), should lack of APPETITE (2) be disregarded. Most fish quickly learn to associate their owner's presence with feeding, especially when his or her hand goes to the hood. If a fish that normally responds to its owner in this way ceases to do so, suspect that it is unwell.

BEHAVIOUR AND DEPORTMENT
It is essential to establish – from research and observation – what constitutes normal behaviour for a particular species. Although any deviation should be a possible cause for concern, remember that some changes may be quite natural, for example at the onset of and during reproductive activity. But *never* disregard *any* change.

A fish should conform to the activity pattern of its species – unwonted LETHARGY (2) or HYPERACTIVITY (2) may denote something amiss; likewise deviation from the norm for the individual, for example when, in a species with a social hierarchy, the dominant fish loses that status. It may be sick, or it may simply be that a younger fish has become large and strong enough to assert itself and take over, in which case it may pick on the former leader.

Most species swim with their dorsal fin uppermost; a few sometimes swim upside-down or on their side, the latter usually temporarily. Whatever the position, the swimming should be controlled and regular in pattern. There is a huge difference between an upside-down catfish *(Synodontis nigriventris)* swimming upside-down at the surface, or a *Julidochromis* cichlid sidling along with its belly towards the nearest rock (and hence at a variety of angles), and a sick, unbalanced, fish desperately trying to make forward progress in an unfamiliar position.

Much the same applies to BUOYANCY (2) and normal swimming level (in the tank). Some species have atrophied swimbladders to enable them to rest on the bottom, out of the strong currents that characterise their natural habitat. Others habitually feed on the bottom, and can be expected to be found there most of the time. On the other hand, a fish which normally swims in open water, but is seen to rest on the bottom, is probably a sick fish, as is a bottom-dweller HANGING AT THE SURFACE (2).

BODY

Fish sometimes exhibit SKELETAL DEFORMITIES (3), in particular the spine. Some spinal deformities (SCOLIOSIS [3]) cause lateral asymmetry, which can be seen from above or below. Viewed from the side, in most species the dorsal (back) profile, which follows the line of the spine, runs in a regular, slightly convex, curve from the nape to the caudal peduncle. Any angularity or pronounced curvature should be regarded with suspicion.

The ventral (belly) profile in most, but not all, fish species is either slightly convex or flat between the ventral and anal

Although this fish has a split in its tail (a healed injury rather than a genetic deformity) it is obviously in robust, good health and free of stress. Its eyes are clear, its fins spread, its colour typical of its species (Archocentrus spilurus).

fins, if the fish is well- but not over-fed and in good health. Slight concavity is acceptable, and normal in wild fish which often have to work hard to find enough food. It should not be a major reason for concern when purchasing, unless the individual fish is noticeably thinner than its tankmates, or otherwise in less than 'A1' condition. Severe EMACIATION (2) is, however, generally a sign of starvation or, less often, disease, and the fish should not be purchased. Fish in dealers' tanks rarely exhibit OBESITY (2), but many aquarists do overfeed their fish on the wrong types of food, so that they gradually increase in girth. This should be avoided by providing the correct diet, as incorrect feeding generally results in the deposition of fat around vital organs (e.g. FATTY LIVER [3]), which may affect reproductive capability, health, and lifespan. It is, however, quite normal for female fish of many species to increase considerably in girth as they fill with eggs (or fry, in live-bearing species). They may also appear 'hollow-bellied' after spawning. Any massive or asymmetric SWELLING (2) of the body, in either sex, causing swimming difficulty or other abnormal behaviour, should be regarded as a cause for concern.

COLORATION

Some fish species exhibit fairly constant coloration, perhaps accentuated during reproductive activity, and significant changes in colour, usually darkening or paling, should be regarded as possible signs of illness, especially if accompanied by other signs. Many species, on the other hand, use colour as a method of communicating mood, social status, sex differences, and a whole series of behaviour-linked messages. Quite dramatic colour changes are perfectly normal in such species, although they may herald behavioural 'problems', such as territoriality during breeding, which may affect other fish present. Where a group of such a species is present, it is likely that they will establish a social hierarchy with status-linked colour patterns.

Abnormal colour for the species or individual, especially if accompanied by out-of-character HIDING (2), LETH-ARGY (2), or loss of APPETITE (2), may be a sign of illness, or of low status in a group. In the latter case the affected individual should be kept under observation as it may need to be removed if its condition deteriorates further. Provided it continues to feed and shows no significant signs of INJURY (3) from AGGRESSION (3), however, it is better to accept this perfectly natural social order. If the underdog is removed, the next fish on the social ladder will then assume that position, and the problem may be renewed.

EYES
The eyes of a healthy fish are both the same size; clear with no opaque areas or cloudiness; and alert and mobile. A fish with a glazed, rigidly staring, look to its eyes is usually a sick fish, especially when there are other behavioural abnormalities such as 'swimming on the spot' and SHIMMYING (2).

FAECES
The faeces will commonly reflect, in both colour and consistency, the recent diet, so considerable variation is to be expected. Whitish, semi-transparent, and stringy faeces may be a sign of disease. Any major deviation from the norm, unless it can be linked to a recent change of diet, should be regarded as a possible warning sign.

FINS
The fins should be intact, without splits, frayed areas, or GROWTHS (2) or nodules (which may be parasite cysts; see also Skin, below).

The regenerative powers of the fins are remarkable, and irregularities due to scarring are not a cause for concern. At the same time genetic DEFORMITIES (2) – fins split into two or more parts, or sometimes completely missing – are undesirable, particularly in breeding stock, as the deformity may be heritable. With a little practice it is easy to differentiate between splits caused by damage, where there tends to be concomitant fraying, and genetic deformities which look 'natural'. Unless it is required for showing, there is no reason why a fish with slight fin damage should not be purchased; given good conditions it will quickly heal. Some slight fin damage now and then is almost inevitable in any aquarium containing more than one fish, but if it reaches problem levels then the reasons – or the culprit(s)!

– should be identified and action taken. Avoid purchasing fish which have red streaks in their fins – other than those which form part of their natural coloration – as these may indicate a SYSTEMIC BACTERIAL (3) or VIRUS INFECTION (3) which may be difficult to cure. Much-scarred finnage, or unusually long fins with curved rays, may be a sign of age.

GILLS

Healthy gills are blood-rich and thus red in colour; pale gills are a sign of ill-health. Brownish gills, on the other hand, may be a sign of NITRITE (3) POISONING (3). In most species the gills should be effectively concealed by the operculum (gill-cover), and visible fleetingly as it opens and shuts. Swollen gills may be a sign of ill-health or overload, for example if the fish has been chased continuously. (See also Respiration, below.)

The operculum is sometimes partly or completely missing, usually unilaterally, leaving the gills partly exposed. This is sometimes a genetic deformity, and affected fish should not be used for breeding.

MOUTH

The mouth should be typical for the species, symmetric, with undamaged lips. Old, healed damage, is acceptable in some species (for example cichlids, which commonly lock mouths when fighting) provided it does not discommode the fish and/or impede feeding. The mouth should be mobile, opening and shutting as the fish breathes. A mouth which remains rigidly open (GAPING [2]) may indicate a dislocated jaw or foreign object trapped in the gullet.

If the species is one that possesses barbels, these should be intact and undamaged. It is common for bottom-dwelling fish, e.g. *Corydoras* catfish, to suffer barbel damage if kept over unsuitable (coarse or sharp) substrates.

RESPIRATION

Respiratory activity can be gauged by the rate at which a fish opens and closes its operculum, the process by which oxygen-carrying water is passed across the gills. Opercular beats should normally be slow, relaxed, and regular. Bear in mind that the opercular rate may vary between species and at different water temperatures. An increase in the opercular rate from the norm is commonly indicative of illness or STRESS (3), for example if the fish has been the victim of AGGRESSION (3) or subjected to certain adverse water conditions. Breeding activity often involves chasing and other exertions, leading to an increase in the respiratory rate. Increased respiratory rate over an extended period may lead to swollen gills and possibly permanent damage. However, swollen gills are a quite normal phenomenon in mouthbrooding cichlids, whose gills have to work harder than usual to draw water over the eggs or fry in their mouths.

SCALES, SCUTES, AND SKIN

Although the odd scale is commonly displaced by accident or during minor scuffles, more serious scale damage is a reason not to purchase, or is a cause for some concern in the home aquarium. It may be due to AGGRESSION (3) – either directly or from collision with a hard object during flight – or repeated SCRATCHING (2). Otherwise, the scales should lie flat and flush with the body.

The surface of a healthy fish is devoid of SPOTS [2] (except those forming part of its normal coloration); nodules, tufts of FUNGUS (3), and other GROWTHS (2); and other defects. The body mucus should form a virtually invisible covering; if it is clearly visible as a greyish coating, or 'peeling' off, then beware.

SENSORY PORES

The sensory pores of the head and lateral line should be small and round. Enlargement may presage disease, and there should be no matter in, or oozing from, the pores.

SIZE

When buying fish, bear in mind that a very large individual, for the species, is probably an old one, and that many fish are relatively short-lived. Undersized specimens, relative to other members of a group of their species, may be affected by STUNTING (2); equally they may be younger, or the other sex!

For further information on abnormalities of the features discussed in this chapter, see the corresponding entries (eyes, gills, etc.) in Section II.

Chapter Four

THE CORRECT ENVIRONMENT

This book is concerned primarily with aspects of fish health, and a comprehensive study of the 'mechanics' of setting up an aquarium is both impracticable and inappropriate within its scope. Indeed, there are numerous handbooks available which cover practical aspects such as what equipment to buy and how to assemble it. This chapter will instead consider these topics only insofar as they may affect fish health.

TROPICAL FRESHWATER BIOTOPES

The air we breathe is reasonably constant in its composition – pollution levels, humidity, and temperature apart – wherever we may be on our planet. The same largely applies to the seas and oceans which are interconnected to form one vast whole, in effect a single body of salt water extending around the world. The situation is, however, vastly different as regards freshwater biotopes, which are generally isolated bodies of water. For example, there is no freshwater connection between the Nile, the Amazon, and the Ganges, and conditions are different in each of these major river systems. Furthermore, the environment commonly varies considerably in or along a single freshwater system, in terms of both the physical and chemical nature of the water and other aspects of the biotope. The fact that fish originate from a single locality, habitat, or environment, whether it be a country, river basin, or lake, is no guarantee that they have the same requirements.

Generally speaking, different species of fish will have evolved, physically and behaviourally, to fit their natural

A rainforest stream with soft, acid water stained brown by organic matter.   *Photo: Paul Blowers.*

habitat, their particular ecological niche. It follows that to keep them healthy under aquarium conditions, both physically and psychologically, it is important to provide them with as accurate a replica of that habitat as is feasible. Failure to do so may stress the fish, or even kill them, rapidly in extreme cases, but more often after a period of ill-health and suffering. A very large number of aquarists fail to grasp this very basic premiss, or worse, do not even

Headland at Lion's Cove: A typical section of surf-washed rocky shoreline of Lake Malawi, habitat of mbuna, rock-dwelling cichlids, very popular with aquarists.

Senga Bay, Salima, Lake Malawi: Areas of sandy shore like this have the same water chemistry, but provide a totally different biotope, with a totally different fish fauna, to the rocky shoreline, yet aquarists commonly mistakenly mix fish from the two disparate groups.

realise that not all fish come from identical conditions.

Although some fish species are regarded as 'hardy', and thus likely to survive in whatever conditions the aquarist happens to provide, even these will benefit from the provision of an appropriate environment. Indeed a number of supposedly hardy species, the ram cichlid *(Microgeophagus ramirezi)* being a prime example, are not hardy at all, but require a specialised environment for any chance of longer term survival.

The only sensible approach is to find out about the actual requirements of *every* species before purchase; if the aquarist cannot provide what the fish needs, in any respect, he should not buy it.

THE AQUARIUM ENVIRONMENT

The aquarium environment can be considered in terms of the tank itself (size, siting, etc.) and what it contains, which is further normally subdivided into the water, the decor and the equipment. As far as each individual fish is concerned, to this list may be added the other fish, dealt with separately in Section I: Fish Compatibility.

THE AQUARIUM AND ITS EQUIPMENT

The aquarium should be of a size adequate to accommodate the fish when they are fully grown, although it is acceptable to re-house fish later when they start to outgrow their initial quarters. Stocking density is normally calculated in terms of length of fish (not including the tail) relative to tank surface area, which in turn relates to gas exchange, especially take-up of (atmospheric) OXYGEN (3) to replenish that used up by the occupants (see also below). The formula normally quoted for freshwater tropical fish is 1 inch (2.5 cm) of fish per 10 sq ins (64 sq cm) of surface area.

It should be borne in mind that the behavioural requirements of some fish (for example, as regards territoriality) *[see Section I: Fish Compatibility]* may dictate different criteria, which will normally be indicated in the literature for that species. Surface area also provides a reasonable indication of available living space. Fish tend to swim horizontally rather than vertically, and so, although a tank 24 x 12 x 12in. (60 x 30 x 30 cm) (conventionally, the last figure is the depth) may contain the same volume of water as one 12 x 12 x 2in., the surface area of the latter is half that of the former, and the fish will have a length of only 12in. to swim along, which is little effective space at all. It is important to bear this in mind, as nowadays such tall thin tanks are commonly available, but they are really quite unsuitable for the proper maintenance of fish, and little better than the now universally condemned goldfish bowl. It should always be remembered that the aquarium is primarily its residents' home, and that its decorative function, vis-as-vis the surrounding human environment, *must always* be secondary to that prime consideration. Generally speaking, the larger the aquarium the better; a large volume of water is easier to keep 'healthy', and the more swimming space the better for the fish.

THE AQUARIUM HOOD

The aquarium hood plays an essential role in fish health, by keeping dust and dirt, pets and children, out of the aquarium, and the fish in. Some species jump instinctively when frightened (to escape any potential predator), while a few, notably walking catfish (*Clarias* spp.) and snakeheads (*Channa* and *Parachanna* spp.), are able to breathe atmospheric air and migrate overland in the wild to escape from drying-up pools. They are equally likely to migrate around the house, failing a tight-fitting cover.

Check that the knob on the openable flap of the hood can be gripped firmly, even with wet fingers. Few things panic fish as readily as the lid dropping shut with a loud bang.

Cover glasses or condensation trays should be used to prevent evaporation (see below). They are also useful for ensuring that the air space above the water remains at tank temperature, important for the health of many fish that have accessory respiratory organs (e.g. anabantids) permitting them to breathe atmospheric air as well as extracting oxygen from water via their gills. Cold air may be lethal to such fish, in particular their fry. Ensure there is ample space, at least half an inch of air, between the water surface and the cover glass, otherwise gas exchange (see below) will be impaired.

SITING THE AQUARIUM
From the all-important point of view of the fish, the aquarium should be sited somewhere where it is not liable to accidental damage. Naturally nervous fish should not be housed in aquaria subject to constant disturbance (e.g. next to 'walkways' in continuous use), but at the same time siting the aquarium in a rarely visited room may cause the fish to panic whenever someone approaches. A quiet corner in a regularly used room is normally ideal.

Fish should never be subjected to the attentions of boisterous children (and adults!) and pets. Both should be kept under control near the aquarium, excluded from its vicinity, or trained to behave.

PREVENTING INTERFERENCE
Many a tankful of fish has come to grief because of unauthorised feeding, interference with external equipment, or the addition of unsuitable items to the aquarium, usually by children or visitors. If necessary, keep foods, test kits, and external equipment out of reach or under lock and key, and consider a padlock for the hood opening.

Accidental unplugging of the aquarium electrical supply, or forgetting to plug the tank back in after other use of the socket, is another common cause of losses. Parcel tape (or similar) can be used to secure the plug in the socket and the socket switch in the 'on' position, and a small warning notice – "Aquarium electrics, DO NOT UNPLUG OR SWITCH OFF" – can be added to reinforce the effect.

AQUARIUM EQUIPMENT

To avoid any risk of POISONING (3), it is important to use only items intended for aquarium use as these will be designed to work underwater and not poison the aquarium water. In addition, some plastic items intended primarily for human use can be employed, e.g. buckets, but these should be of food grade plastic. In general, coloured (including black) plastics are more likely to be toxic than clear or white. Use only silicon sealant intended for aquarium use; that sold for use on, for example, bathroom and kitchen fittings contains (toxic) fungicide.

All aquarium equipment should be kept solely for that purpose; a bucket commandeered for domestic purposes may become a bucket contaminated with detergent. If necessary, keep tempting items under lock and key. Never clean aquarium equipment with soap, detergent, bleach, or similar, because of the danger of residues which can harm fish. It is better to buy new items, if necessary.

It is wise to keep spares of essential equipment. A failed heater or airpump diaphragm can – and often does – result in a tankful of dead fish just as easily as environmental or pathogenic disease.

Equipment should be used only in accordance with the manufacturer's instructions if it is to perform correctly and safely. Moreover, it is important to understand how and why some equipment works. Many aquarists purchase expensive items unsuitable for their needs (if needed at all) because they assume, quite wrongly, that if it is available, every aquarium should have one, and that biggest and most expensive is best. In fact, unsuitable equipment may adversely affect the well-being of the fish, for example when small or slow-moving fish are subjected to violent currents from oversized filters. The same applies equally, or perhaps more so, to water treatment chemicals, fish health tonics, and other 'additives', which should be used *only* when actually required.

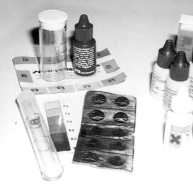

A selection of test kits.

WATER CHEMISTRY

Water is the absolute essence of life to fish; they not only live in and 'breath' it, but they constantly interchange it with their bodily fluids via osmoregulation. Keeping a fish in the wrong type of water may, in some cases, be tantamount to transfusing the wrong blood type into a human being. Most people are aware that marine fish cannot live in fresh water and vice versa, but few realise that the difference between very soft, acid water and very hard, alkaline conditions can be just as critical.

Water is generally considered in terms of its chemistry and quality, and from the point of view of the freshwater aquarium, water chemistry is normally a question of its hardness and pH, although, strictly speaking, any pollutants affecting its quality also contribute to its chemistry.

HARDNESS

The hardness of water is the measure of the amount of minerals dissolved in it (chiefly salts of calcium (Ca), magnesium (Mg), and sodium [Na]), which, in turn, normally reflects the solubility (or otherwise) of the soil or rocks over or through which it has flowed. Most people will know whether their water is hard or soft from its domestic effects – hard water requires a lot more soap to produce a lather, and 'furs' up pipework and kettles, as well as leaving limescale deposits on taps, washbasins, etc. The aquarium water may also be made harder by the presence of rocks or other decor containing soluble mineral salts.

Test kits are available for measuring the hardness of tap/aquarium water. Unfortunately these kits utilise a number of different scales of measurement (parts per million (ppm); English, French, German degrees), so when referring to the literature it is important to establish which units are quoted, and if necessary to convert the figure to correspond with the test kit used (see table 1).

TABLE 1
HARDNESS UNITS IN TERMS OF PARTS PER MILLION OF DISSOLVED CALCIUM SALTS*

1 English (Clark) degree	**14.3 ppm**
1 German degree (dh)**	**17.9 ppm**
1 American degree	**17.1 ppm**
1 French degree (fh)	**10.0 ppm**

1 ppm = 1 mg per litre

*English, French, and American degrees of hardness are expressed as ppm of calcium carbonate ($CaCO_3$), while German degrees are ppm of calcium oxide (CaO).

**Strictly speaking the abbreviation dh applies only to German degrees of hardness; it has, however, been adopted into general use in recent years.

MINERAL CONTENT
Although hardness is an important consideration, the methods of measuring it normally consider only the amount of a single calcium salt present, and not the quantities of other minerals. Many fish from 'soft' (= deficient in calcium salts) water are in actuality from mineral-depleted environments (= deficient in all mineral salts). The two are very different, and although it is not possible for the amateur to measure total mineral content, awareness of the distinction may be of importance when endeavouring to provide suitable water.

CREATING SOFTER WATER
If the aquarist's TAP WATER (3) is hard, and soft(er) water is required, a number of options are available. In each case the tap water can be replaced or 'diluted' with created/imported mineral-poor water. This may be rain water (collected), distilled water (purchased, for example,

from a pharmacist), water purified via a reverse osmosis (RO) unit (available from aquarium suppliers – equipment, sometimes water), or water treated with an ion-exchange softening resin (use only those intended for aquarium, not domestic, use). It is important to select an ion-exchange product that de-ionises the water treated, rather than one which simply exchanges calcium ions for those of another metal, for example sodium (Na), such that it is still rich in minerals even though it tests as soft. Table 2 indicates the advantages and disadvantages of each source. The latest development in softening aquarium water is liquid addition chemicals, which irreversibly bind up the salts that cause hardness, effectively softening the water. These products also contain a pH buffer to maintain the pH at 6.7. These chemicals have the obvious advantage of convenience, but only long-term use will reveal whether or not there are any disadvantages. At the time of writing we have been unable to ascertain the nature of any residues from the process, and whether the resulting water is soft or mineral-poor.

TABLE 2
SOURCES OF SOFT WATER

SOURCE	ADVANTAGES	DISADVANTAGES
Rain water	No cost.	May be very acid and polluted (see RAIN WATER [3]). Unpredictable supply.
Distilled water	Pure.	Expensive. Needs to be transported.
RO water	Pure.	Wasteful of water, hence possibly expensive. Expensive equipment.
Ion-exchange water	Pure, provided the correct resin is used.	Some resins simply exchange calcium ions for those of other metals.

Both distilled and RO water are almost pure H_2O, and contain virtually nothing else, including the free oxygen needed by fish in order to breathe. Water purified by these methods must therefore be well-aerated before use. It must also have a small amount of minerals added in order to satisfy the metabolic requirements of the fish; this can be achieved either by adding a little tap water or by using special remineralisation salts available from aquatic dealers.

pH

pH is the measure of the acidity or alkalinity of a liquid. The pH scale is used internationally, and extends from 0 (extremely acid) to 14 (extremely alkaline), with 7 defined as neutral. The majority of freshwater fish are found in waters with a pH between 6 and 8, but some species require an acidity down to 4.5 or an alkalinity up to 9.5. The scale is logarithmic, that is each unit of pH is 10 times different to that either side, so the 'normal' range between 6 and 8 in fact encompasses a considerable variation in water chemistry. Colorimetric test kits and electronic meters are available for measuring the pH of aquarium water.

pH is commonly related to the mineral content of water; in general the minerals that make water hard also make it alkaline. Mineral-depleted water is acidified by dissolved carbon dioxide and organic material; although these acidifiers are commonly found in hard water too, they are counteracted (buffered) by the alkalising mineral salts present.

Sudden changes in pH can cause SHOCK (3) (see also below), usually with fatal results. In general a sudden change from alkaline to acid, or vice versa, is more dire than a dramatic change within the acid or alkaline range, but any rapid pH shift can have serious results. (See also Section III: Acidosis, Alkalosis.) In the longer term, incorrect pH can have a serious effect on the fish's health, vigour, and resistance to pathogens, and may also result in REPRODUCTIVE FAILURE (3).

REGULATING pH

Mineral content is the secret of regulating pH; it is pointless to try to acidify hard water as its mineral content will simply buffer the pH back to neutral/alkaline. Equally, the pH of mineral-depleted water can be increased only by the addition of mineral salts.

Although proprietary chemical pH adjusters are available from aquatic outlets, some types should be used with extreme circumspection, and preferably not at all. Unless the instructions are followed to the letter the result may be a tank full of poisoned water and dead fish, and it is not uncommon for a tank to 'go wrong' even where the adjuster has been used as directed. Modern balanced buffer salts produced by reputable manufacturers are, however, regarded as safe and foolproof.

The natural approach is nevertheless preferable. Soft water can be acidified organically by the use of peat (as a filter medium (see below) or as peat extract), while the use of calciferous material, as part of the decor (substrate, rocks) or, again, as a filter medium, will increase pH. The acidifying effect of peat varies with the type used and its source, as well as the buffering capacity of the water (the pH of mineral-depleted water is notoriously unstable) and must be carefully monitored using a pH test kit.

Only small adjustments to pH (maximum 0.2-0.3 units per day, e.g. from 7.0 to 7.2 or 7.3) should be made to water which contains fish. The use of natural buffers such as peat (in filters) and calciferous decor will normally remain within these bounds. Sudden changes in pH are a major causative factor of CHEMICAL SHOCK (3) in fish.

CHEMICAL SHOCK
Sudden changes in water chemistry can cause serious illness, and usually death, from CHEMICAL SHOCK (3). Such problems sometimes occur where a partial water change (see below) is made without properly adjusting the new water, but are more common where fish are moved from tank to tank. Newly-purchased fish, for example, may have been kept in quite different conditions (not necessarily the correct conditions) and it is important to provide the same conditions initially, in a special tank if need be. Water chemistry should always be adjusted slowly, over a period of days or even weeks (depending on the degree of change), from that in which the fish have been living to that in which they are to live in future. This adjustment can usefully take place during the QUARANTINE (3) period. The normal

method is to perform small daily partial water changes (see below) using water of the intended chemistry for refilling.

It follows that the aquarist has a responsibility to find out the water conditions in which fish have been kept, *before* purchase. It is unfortunate that few aquarium dealers display water chemistry information for the customer's benefit; however, it is not unreasonable to ask for the necessary information, or even to request that tests are made specially. If those conditions differ significantly (and different fish have differing degrees of tolerance) to those of the destination aquarium, and the aquarist lacks the facilities to provide the correct conditions temporarily in a separate tank, then the fish should not be purchased.

Even so it may be wise to test the water in the bags to confirm water chemistry; should this prove to be different to that anticipated, then it may be possible to save the fish by decanting it and the water in the bag into an opaque bucket which is floated in an aquarium to keep it warm, with gentle aeration. Water from the destination aquarium is then siphoned into the bucket, via a clamped airline, a drop at a time, over a period of 24-48 hours, so that the fish can adjust slowly to the new water chemistry. This is, of necessity, likely to cause major STRESS (3), and should be regarded as a last resort. Alternatively, floating the new fish in a buoyed plastic container with a small hole (ca. 0.5 cm diameter) bored in the side will allow the gradual equilibration of water chemistry (partly by osmosis) between the container and aquarium.

These measures should, however, be reserved for emergencies; proper acclimatization in a special tank should be regarded as the norm.

WATER QUALITY

In aquarium literature, 'water quality' generally refers to the amount of pollutants it contains. Strictly speaking, however, any measurement of water quality should include undesirable aspects of water chemistry *vis-a-vis* the fish kept, but in practice the term is normally taken as relating to "toxins and organic pollutants". Pollutants may be present in tap water, derived from the surrounding environment or the aquarium decor/equipment, or produced by the flora and fauna of the aquarium.

TABLE 3

COMMON TAP WATER POLLUTANTS
COPPER (3)
Source 1: Domestic plumbing.
Solution: Run tap before use to clear water standing in pipes. Never use water from the hot water cylinder. Use a copper-removing conditioner.
Source 2: Natural contamination.
Solution: Use alternative source*.
Copper removing conditioner.

NITRATE (3)/ Phosphate
Source: Inadequate removal of agricultural fertilisers or sewage by-products.
Solution: Use alternative source.*
Use nitrate/phosphate-removal device.**

CHLORINE (3)
Source: Added by water company as purifier.
Solution: Drive off gas by running tap hard into bucket.***
Let water stand overnight, preferably with aeration, to let chlorine disperse. ***
Chlorine-remover.

CHLORAMINE (3)
Source: Added by water company as purifier.
Solution: Chloramine-remover.
Use alternative source.*

PESTICIDES
Source: Agricultural residues or used by water company to destroy invertebrates in mains.
Solution: Use alternative source.*
* This may be water from another supply, distilled, rain, or RO water.
** A number of methods are available from aquatic retailers, including RO and nitrate removal resins.
***If there is still a smell of chlorine from the water after using either of these methods, allow further time and/or use additional aeration to dissipate the chlorine, or use a dechlorinator.

TAP WATER

Tap water is normally required to be of a particular standard, but that standard is based on what is deemed harmless to humans, not fish, and levels of some pollutants nominally harmless to the former may be quickly lethal to the latter. Table 3 shows the commonest pollutants of tap water and how they may be removed.

Test kits are available for nitrate and copper. Chlorination is commonplace, but easily dealt with. The aquarist *must* ask his water company if chloramine is used, and use a chloramine remover if so. He should also ask the water company to notify him if and when they plan to use pesticides in the mains, and avoid using (untreated) water during the active life of the chemical, as advised by the company.

There are many other, less usual, sources of tap water contamination; if cases of POISONING (3) can be traced to no other source, then it is advisable to have a sample analysed by an appropriate laboratory. The water company or veterinarian may be able to advise on, or perhaps provide, this professional help.

POLLUTION

Pollution by decor, equipment and external sources may result in sudden acute POISONING (3) and is best avoided. In the event that it does occur, removal to an unpolluted aquarium may be the only chance of saving the fish. Less severe cases may sometimes be remedied by elimination of the source of toxicity followed by successive partial water changes (see below). In general, external toxins such as insecticides (e.g. fly spray), paint fumes, furniture polish, require immediate transfer to alternative accommodation; while poisoning from sources within the aquarium (slight pesticide residues on decor items, rocks with veins of toxic minerals, use of unsuitable equipment) can be remedied by elimination of the source and partial water changes (see below). Some toxins can be removed by filtering the aquarium water through activated carbon. *(See also: The Aquarium and its Equipment, above; Aquarium Decor, below.)*

THE NITROGEN CYCLE IN THE AQUARIUM

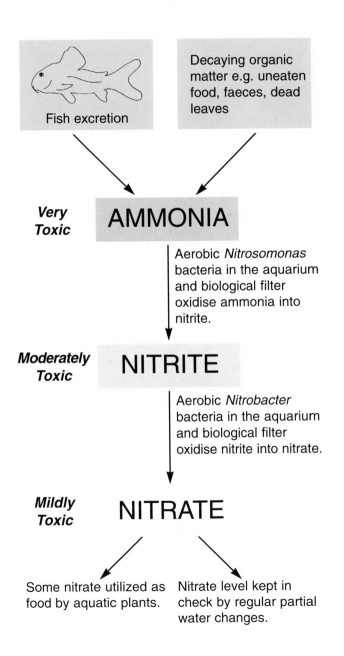

Fish excretion

Decaying organic matter e.g. uneaten food, faeces, dead leaves

Very Toxic

AMMONIA

Aerobic *Nitrosomonas* bacteria in the aquarium and biological filter oxidise ammonia into nitrite.

Moderately Toxic

NITRITE

Aerobic *Nitrobacter* bacteria in the aquarium and biological filter oxidise nitrite into nitrate.

Mildly Toxic

NITRATE

Some nitrate utilized as food by aquatic plants.

Nitrate level kept in check by regular partial water changes.

ORGANIC WASTES

All living things produce organic wastes, either as excreta of various kinds, or through decay after death. These are recycled via various natural processes, the most important being the nitrogen cycle (Page 66).

During the nitrogen cycle organic wastes are processed by certain types of bacteria. An understanding of the nitrogen cycle and its implications in the aquarium is essential to the successful maintenance of a healthy aquarium and healthy fish. Test kits are available for measuring levels of AMMONIA (3), NITRITE (3), and NITRATE (3).

If the cycle is functioning correctly then any ammonia and nitrite (both highly toxic to fish) produced will be converted to relatively harmless nitrate before they can build up to harmful levels. The aquarist must, however, ensure he has the necessary bacterial population before he starts to keep fish; and he must tend it carefully thereafter, keeping it intact and healthy and avoiding any sudden overload with which it may be unable to cope: overfeeding; failing to remove dead fish; adding significant numbers of new fish without compensatory action (usually a temporary reduction in rations followed by gradual increase back to normal, to allow the filter to adjust).

In nature any given volume of water will generally contain fewer fish and more vegetation than are commonplace in the same volume in the domestic aquarium, so although it is possible to achieve a balanced aquarium in which fish wastes are all processed and utilised by plants, it is far from easy. The aquarist must therefore use other measures to avoid pollution, the chief of these being filtration and water changes.

FILTRATION AND WATER CHANGES

BIOLOGICAL FILTRATION

Biological filtration is used to optimise the nitrogen cycle by collecting wastes together in a relatively localised area (the filter) together with a suitable habitat for the necessary nitrifying bacteria (the filter medium, which also serves to trap solids), and a good supply of oxygen-rich water to encourage the growth of these aerobic nitrifiers.

There are a number of different types of filter, ranging from small to large and slow to fast turnover. The aquarist

Progressive dirtying of filter foam cartridges from new (left) through recently rinsed to very dirty.

should not make the common mistake of assuming the largest, most powerful and expensive filter is the best for every purpose. Generally speaking, powerful turnover is required only for very large aquaria or those which are 'overloaded' (too many fish or fish with messy feeding habits, both problems which are often better ameliorated by reducing the population or changing the diet, respectively). Filter volume (= the amount of filter medium it can contain, or, in the case of undergravel filters, the depth of the filter bed) is equally important, and both flow and volume should be appropriate to the aquarium and its occupants. Pumping large amounts of water rapidly achieves little positive effect if there are few wastes to be processed, as the size of the bacterial population will be a function of the loading normally imposed on it (hence the need to avoid sudden overloads); but on the negative side it may cause considerable discomfort to the fish, hinder plant growth, and suck in fry.

(See also: Oxygen Content and Water Circulation, below.)

CARE OF BIOLOGICAL FILTERS

It generally takes approximately 15-28 days for a tropical tank and its biological filter to mature, in terms of developing an adequate population of nitrifying bacteria. The process can be accelerated by using a 'starter culture' of bacteria, which can be purchased, or taken from another aquarium in the form of a handful or two of substrate, or some used filter medium (provided there is no risk of affecting water chemistry or introducing disease).

During this maturation period first ammonia and then nitrite will peak at dangerous levels, and no fish should be present. The beneficial nitrifying bacteria within the aquarium will need to be 'fed': proprietary maturation treatments are available, but simply adding a small pinch of flake food each day will also have the desired effect. The sometimes-advocated practice of using one or two 'hardy' fish to mature an aquarium (with their wastes) is cruel, and may even cause their death; monitor the ammonia and nitrite levels daily during the maturation period and add fish *only* when both have peaked and returned to minimal, safe, readings. Failure to mature a tank before adding fish will result in the problem known as NEW TANK SYNDROME (3), commonly resulting in heavy losses.

Nowadays proprietary 'starter cultures' of filter bacteria can be purchased, which will accelerate the maturation process. However, the old-fashioned natural method is safer, and will also allow water chemistry to stabilise; alert the aquarist to any undesirable (or possibly desirable!) side-effects of decor (e.g. increasing hardness and pH, staining the water), likewise to any problems with the equipment; allow any initial CLOUDY WATER (2) to dissipate; and, above all teach the aquarist the all-important quality of patience, essential to successful fishkeeping.

Even when a filter has been properly matured it should not be expected to cope with its final intended loading immediately. Either add fish in small numbers over an extended period, or if this is impracticable (e.g. one large fish, or territorial fish likely to attack later additions) then add all the fish at once but feed them very lightly initially, gradually increasing rations to optimum. A further option is to pre-mature a filter in an established aquarium and transfer it to the new one, provided there is no risk of thus introducing disease. Although this may appear to rob the established aquarium of part of its filtration, in practice there appears to be no deleterious effect, possibly because an established bacterial population will quickly multiply back to optimal.

Biological filters should be left undisturbed as much as possible. They should never be switched off for more than a couple of hours at a time (as little as one hour for 'enclosed' external filters (i.e. motorised canisters), because there can be no oxygen absorption from the atmosphere), otherwise the aerobic bacteria may be starved of oxygen and begin to die. Any cleaning of the filter medium (including the highly inadvisable practice of regularly 'hoovering' the substrate where undergravel filtration is employed) will result in the loss of large numbers of bacteria.

Only part of the filter medium should ever be replaced at any one time, and cleaning should consist of gentle rinsing in a bucket of aquarium water. The chlorine in tap water is a BACTERICIDE (3). Very hot water will also kill beneficial filter bacteria. After (major) filter maintenance it is a wise precaution to reduce feeding for several days while the bacterial population recovers, increasing rations gradually, as with a new filter.

Some types of medication are bactericidal and thus harmful to biological filtration; these are indicated in the A–Z section. Very low pH can also reduce filter efficiency: below 6.5 is sometimes stated to be sub-optimal, nevertheless in practice biological filtration has been found to remain adequate at considerably lower pH levels.

OTHER TYPES OF FILTRATION

Filtration may also be mechanical, and/or chemical. Virtually all filters are mechanical, in that they contain media which trap solids. A purely mechanical filter is one which is cleaned out regularly before it can acquire a population of nitrifying bacteria and thus become biological.

Chemical filtration may be mechanical, and commonly biological, but uses media which chemically alter the water. Chemical filtration includes the use of media which alter pH (e.g. peat, calciferous material such as limestone chippings), or remove certain pollutants (e.g. zeolite, which removes ammonia). Some chemical media, notably carbon/charcoal, may remove certain medications. Such media should therefore be removed during treatment, but may be useful for removing unwanted slow-breakdown chemicals after the prescribed treatment period.

WATER CHANGES

Unfortunately, biological filtration does not remove nitrate, the end product of the nitrogen cycle, and unless there are few fish and many plants the latter are unlikely to have any significant effect on its build-up. Excess nitrate can cause gradual deterioration in health, reduced growth, increased susceptibility to pathogens, and problems with ALGAE (3); it may also cause death in newly-introduced fish which are unaccustomed to high levels and experience NITRATE SHOCK (3). Nitrate shock should not be avoided by gradual adjustment (as with CHEMICAL SHOCK [3]), but by ensuring that the problem never arises by keeping nitrate levels low. This is effected by exchanging part of the aquarium water for new water with minimal nitrate levels. If the tap water is itself high in nitrates, then it must be treated (as described earlier) before use.

The frequency and volume of partial water changes must be established by trial and error, that is by testing nitrate levels regularly to ensure that the regime is proving adequate. Twenty to 25 per cent weekly is a good starting point; avoid changing more than one third of the aquarium water at any one time, unless it has been properly aged and conditioned, and even then large changes are best avoided. Freshly-drawn water is commonly gas-saturated and, in excess, may cause GAS BUBBLE DISEASE (3).

The new water should be of approximately the same chemistry and temperature as that of the aquarium to avoid any chance of shock. It should be free of CHLORINE (3) and CHLORAMINE (3), as well as any other contaminants, and aerated if necessary, as described earlier. Ideally it should be siphoned slowly into the aquarium from a bucket or similar, to minimise disturbance of fish and decor.

COMPENSATING FOR EVAPORATION

If the aquarium water level drops through evaporation, it will need to be topped up, using properly matched water as during water changes. Because only pure water, and not the minerals it contains, evaporates, topping-up (unless with mineral-free water) will cause an increase in mineral content which may be undesirable. The need for topping-up can be avoided by preventing evaporation through, for example, the use of cover glasses or a tight-fitting aquarium hood.

TEMPERATURE

In general fish are adapted for life within a particular temperature range, which may vary considerably in extent from species to species. Although some accept a degree of latitude which enables many tropical species with nominally different requirements to be housed together, a degree of care must be exercised. Abnormally (for the species concerned) low temperature may result in LETHARGY (2), poor APPETITE (2) and ultimately greater susceptibility to disease; fish should never be kept at too low a temperature in order to reduce the electricity bill. If the aquarist cannot afford to keep fish properly, he should not keep fish at all. At the other end of the scale, an abnormally high temperature will increase oxygen requirement (see below) and hence cause RESPIRATORY STRESS (3), sometimes with permanent gill damage.

A deliberate increase in TEMPERATURE (3) is sometimes used to increase the fish's metabolic rate in order to promote healing/recovery, and/or to speed up the life cycle of certain PARASITES (3), the quicker to eliminate them. However, it should be remembered that the warmer the water, the less oxygen it contains (see below), such that increased aeration may be required.

Sudden changes of temperature, in particular where these involve chilling, can occasion TEMPERATURE SHOCK (3). Such fluctuations are normally the result of introducing new fish to the aquarium without equalising temperatures *(see Section I: Purchasing, Transporting, and Introducing Stock)*, or refilling the aquarium with water at the wrong temperature (during topping up, water changes). The situation is best avoided, but if a mistake does occur, the temperature should be returned to normal (for the fish concerned) as soon as possible.

Where slow chilling has taken place, however, for example through heater failure, there will be no shock, and the aquarium should be returned to normal temperature over a period of an hour or more, to avoid shock. Simply allowing the replacement heater to warm the aquarium is adequate.

In cases of overheating (e.g. thermostat failure), increase aeration to compensate for any oxygen deficiency (see below), and allow the aquarium to cool naturally. As a general rule, however, if the temperature is above 90 degrees F (ca. 32 degrees C) and any fish are still alive, then perform a partial (10 to 20 per cent) water change, refilling with cold water which is slowly siphoned into the aquarium, as well as increasing aeration.

OXYGEN CONTENT AND WATER CIRCULATION
OXYGEN CONTENT AND GAS EXCHANGE

Fish breathe free OXYGEN (3) absorbed by water from the atmosphere, although some species, generally from polluted and/or oxygen-depleted waters, have the ability to utilise atmospheric oxygen. Oxygen requirement is generally a function of the oxygen content of the natural habitat; fish from well-oxygenated biotopes, such as fast-flowing streams and rivers, will require more oxygen.

If the oxygen content of the aquarium is inadequate, this may manifest as RESPIRATORY DISTRESS (2) – increased respiratory rate and GASPING (2) at the surface. Surface gasping occurs not because the fish affected can thus take in atmospheric air, but because the surface water has a higher oxygen content (see also HYPOXIA [3]).

Oxygen content may be depleted or inadequate because the aerobic requirements of its occupants outpace absorption rate, and/or because the water contains excessive CARBON DIOXIDE (3) (CO_2) (produced by various life processes) which hinders oxygen uptake. A high organic loading in the aquarium, with its associated bacterial population, will also consume oxygen from the water.

Water can absorb oxygen from the air only where the two elements meet, which is at the water's surface. The oxygen content of the aquarium can be increased by agitating the surface of the water, thereby increasing the effective surface area available for gas exchange – discharge of carbon dioxide and absorption of oxygen. Circulating the water is also helpful, in that it brings water rich in carbon dioxide to the surface and carries newly-oxygenated water to the lower layers of the aquarium. This can be achieved by means of the filtration system, and/or by aeration with a diffuser ('airstone') connected to an airpump. Contrary to common belief, the bubbles of air produced by a diffuser do not themselves add any significant amount of oxygen to the water through which they pass; it is the water circulation and surface movement they cause that is beneficial. The oxygen content of water is also affected by its temperature: the warmer the water, the lower its oxygen content – but at the same time the faster the metabolic rate of the fish, and hence the greater their oxygen requirement.

It should be remembered that while plants produce oxygen as a by-product of photosynthesis under light, at night they produce carbon dioxide and consume oxygen. Although many fish are inactive at night and their oxygen requirements thus lower, heavily planted aquaria may suffer nocturnal oxygen depletion.

WATER MOVEMENT

Although water circulation may be beneficial in terms of gas exchange, it is important to bear in mind that fish which have evolved for life in still or slow-moving waters may find it difficult to cope with strong currents and turbulence, which may lead to STRESS (3) and ultimately physical ill-health. In general, fish adapted to highly-oxygenated water – fast-flowing rivers or large lakes with waves – will require high oxygen levels in captivity and be untroubled by the water movement this may necessitate. Conversely, fish from calmer waters will generally have a lower oxygen requirement so that, provided they are not overcrowded, vigorous water circulation is unnecessary. It must be accepted that fish from the two extremes are not normally compatible in the aquarium, as it is impossible to accommodate the needs of both.

Fry and juveniles may also experience difficulties in aquaria with turbulent conditions – even those of rheophilic or lacustrine species: in nature such juveniles are commonly found in different (calmer) habitats to those of their parents (who may breed outside their normal habitat), or in sheltered micro-habitats within the overall biotope.

Vigorous water circulation may also impede plant growth, particularly in association with undergravel filtration.

LIGHTING

Lighting in the aquarium serves two main purposes: to enable the aquarist to see his charges, and to encourage plant growth. In addition, of course, it is a feature of the natural environment of the fish, and one which regulates some aspects of their behaviour, including swimming activity and reproductive function. Some fish require light in order to locate and attack their prey.

The natural photoperiod in the tropics is 12 to 14 hours and this is the appropriate length of time for which the aquarium should be illuminated daily. In this way both diurnal and nocturnal species will have an active period approximating to what is natural.

Light intensity is a vexed question. Very many species kept in aquaria originate in forest streams where light intensity is low; those from more open biotopes generally have the benefit of shade from aquatic vegetation or the option of retiring to deeper water; few are obliged to remain in brilliant light if their inclination is otherwise. On the other hand, the aquatic plants beloved of many aquarists do generally require fairly strong light to produce healthy growth.

As ever, the aquarist should learn to research his subject and compromise (his preferences, but never the fishes' health) if necessary. If plants are the chief interest, then the fish should be light-tolerant species. Shade-loving fish can be combined with floating plants, or those with long stems and floating leaves. Whatever the lighting chosen, it is important that fish are not subjected to sudden changes from light to darkness or vice versa, for example by switching the tank light off and the room light immediately thereafter, or the tank light on in a room which was in darkness until a few seconds previously. Sudden illumination is likely to induce panic, and hence STRESS (3) or even INJURY (3), in the short term, and in the longer term can lead to NERVOUSNESS (2) and a tendency to hide. Sudden darkness is less obviously stressful, but it should be remembered that in the aquarium, as in the wild, diurnal species often seek out shelter at nightfall, in areas where they hope to be safe from nocturnal predation. Such predation may be a genuine hazard in some cases, for example where parental fish such as cichlids are guarding fry in a community aquarium; these fish commonly take their young to a place of safety (e.g. the breeding cave or a clump of plants) at nightfall, and quickly learn that total 'night' is signalled by the turning off of the tank light. 15 to 30 minutes is an appropriate period for both 'dawn' and 'dusk'.

ALGAE
ALGAE (3) are inevitable where water and light are combined, and, unless the aquarist wishes to keep the aquarium in total darkness, he must accept some algal growth. In fact a coating of green on rocks and other 'hard' decor items is not unattractive, and far more natural than stark cleanliness. Algae utilise some of the NITRATES (3) generated by the nitrogen cycle, and can act as a useful indicator of rising nitrate levels in consequence. They harbour micro-organisms and are thus a useful feeding ground for fish fry. They do, however, often have an adverse effect on aquatic vegetation in the aquarium. A common error in such cases is to shorten the photoperiod or reduce light intensity to hinder algal growth, but while this may affect the type of algae that thrive, there are plenty that will burgeon in dim light. But plants are unlikely to thrive under such conditions, so the problem is only exacerbated.

Healthy, growing, plants continually produce new leaves, and it takes some time, under normal circumstances, for algae significantly to affect these. It is perfectly normal (in nature) for old, slowly dying, plant leaves to carry an algal coating. It is unhealthy plants, showing little or no growth, that are normally overwhelmed by algae, and the answer is not to try and eliminate the latter, but to improve the cultivation of the former.

DECOR
The decor may not be an immediately obvious factor when considering fish health, but in practice it (or its absence) can have a considerable positive or negative effect.

The purpose of the aquarium decor should be primarily to simulate the natural habitat of its occupants. Its decorative function *vis-a-vis* the aquarist's home should be regarded as incidental, though with careful planning both parties can be accommodated. However, it is not acceptable under any circumstances to subject fish to unnatural, gaudily-coloured decor simply because the blue/mauve/yellow concerned matches the carpet/curtains/chairs.

Equally, dazzling white or light-coloured decor may cause considerable STRESS (3) – most freshwater tropical aquarium fish originate from dimly to moderately lit biotopes 'decorated' in shades of beige-brown and yellow-green, where the environment below them is dark (or poorly lit) and lighter above.

THE NEED FOR DECOR

Most of the tropical freshwater fish kept in aquaria live quite near to the bottom of the food chain; even the largest fish may fall prey to birds, crocodiles, otters, and other larger creatures. Few have the confidence to cruise alone in open water away from the protection of the shoreline or the shoal – and even shoaling fish also sometimes take cover, if their habitat provides it.

Imagine, then, how stressful it must be for a captive fish to be kept in a bare, undecorated aquarium, with nowhere to hide should the occasion arise – from the fish's point of view, not the owner's. The fish does not know that its environment is safe, and its natural instincts will instead warn it that any environment is potentially hostile.

Yet many aquarists and dealers use bare tanks, for a number of reasons:

● "Bare tanks are hygienic." It is true that it is easy to siphon off solid wastes from a bare aquarium; however, remember that fish do not excrete just solids, so siphoning off visible excreta is only part of the story. The nitrogen cycle takes place in aquaria even without filtration to optimise it;

It is essential to provide the right type of decor in the aquarium.

The effect of background. In the photo above where there is no background, the fish is trying to merge with surroundings. The dwarf waterlily is totally inappropriate to the hard alkaline water and rocky habitat required by the fish.

In the photo below the same fish, in good colour, is seen against a background of rocks.

bacteria colonise all the surfaces of the decor, including the substrate. The colonisable surface area in a bare aquarium is much reduced. A more efficient filtration system may assist the bacterial shortfall, but all too often bare aquaria have only a small filter, or no filtration, because they are supposedly 'clean'. Bare tanks require constant monitoring and frequent small water changes, and are probably no more hygienic than decorated aquaria. They can be utilised for treating sick fish *(see Section I: Treating Fish Diseases)* and as temporary quarters, but are unkind as long-term accommodation.

● "If cover is provided, the fish hide." If, however, the fish are properly maintained in a stress-free environment, then after a very short time they will gain in confidence and swim around in the open, hiding only if some external stimulus frightens them temporarily. Fish which require the security of cover, but are denied it, will commonly skulk in the rear corners of the aquarium, sometimes facing the rear glass as fewest external stimuli come from that direction. They will be highly stressed, and likely to suffer from poor APPETITE (2) and increased susceptibility to disease.

● "The fish move the substrate around." Fish dig for a number of reasons, all instinctive, none intended deliberately to make their environment unattractive to their owner. Some, such as khuhli loaches (*Acanthophthalmus* spp.), burrow in the substrate for safety. The fact that this makes them impossible to catch excuses absence of substrate only in dealers' tanks. Some sift the bottom for food. Some, in particular cichlids, dig as part of their reproductive behaviour, commonly to create 'nursery pits' for their fry. Preventing such highly instinctive behaviour may in turn lead to REPRODUCTIVE FAILURE (3).

● "Convenience" (in particular in commercial aquaria). This is undoubtedly true; however, convenience for the owner in no way excuses the cruelty involved. Particularly deplorable is the practice of maintaining tiers of aquaria with no substrate so that the fish are subjected to light from below as well as above, with no shelter from either. Fish kept in such an environment, even if only temporarily, are likely to be suffering severe STRESS (3) and should not be purchased. It should always be remembered that the aquarium is its occupants' home; if the aquarist is not prepared to allow certain fish to enact their natural behaviour, then he should keep other, less antisocial, species.

ASPECTS OF DECOR
The decor is generally divided into three parts: substrate, background, and main decor, each important to the aquarium occupants.

The substrate, as well as serving the purposes mentioned above, avoids stressful reflection of the overhead lighting and mirror effects from the bare glass bottom. It is also used to secure other parts of the decor – plants and rocks.

The background is an analogue of the bank of the river, pond, or lake, the solid and secure backdrop against which many small fish live out their lives in the wild, the area to which they can flee for cover, away from the hazardous open water further out. An aquarium with no background offers no sense of direction to its occupants; a tank used as a room divider, or free-standing, is an insecure and unnatural environment indeed. In addition, the background is a natural backdrop against which to arrange the main decor.

The main decor is the chief source of actual cover for the aquarium occupants. It may also provide shade and spawning substrates.

THE IMPORTANCE OF SPECIFIC DECOR
It is not possible exactly to simulate every aspect of a biotope in all cases – muddy bottoms, for example, are not practicable. However, it is important to consider the natural requirements of the fish to be kept, as unnatural cover may not be recognised as cover at all: a cave-dweller from a rocky habitat will not be at home in a densely-planted aquarium, and a fish from a densely-vegetated biotope will feel exposed, insecure, and stressed in a tank full of rocks. Nevertheless, provided the fish concerned are compatible in other aspects (see Section I: Fish Compatibility), and the aquarium is large enough, there is no reason why decor of various types cannot be mixed. The presence of rocks or plants is unlikely to cause stress to fish unaccustomed to them in nature, provided their own shelter requirements are satisfied.

DANGERS FROM DECOR

Inappropriate decor items are a common source of POISONING (3) in the aquarium (see also Water Quality, above). Decor originating in natural bodies of water or tanks of fish (shop or other aquarists') may harbour DISEASE (3), PESTS (3) such as SNAILS (3) (sometimes themselves vectors of disease) and *HYDRA* (3) and/or PARASITES (3), and is best avoided. It is important to consider the provenance and nature of every single decor item, and to reject any that is any way suspect.

Some items of decor contain interesting holes and/or cracks through or into which fish may swim. Unfortunately it is not unknown for some fish, especially when frightened, to try to swim through or into spaces which are too small (this includes gaps between equipment and decor, or between decor items), and become stuck, sometimes with fatal consequences. Discus (*Symphysodon* spp.) are particularly noted for this behaviour; luckily most fish are more sensible.

All decor should be thoroughly cleaned and prepared, where necessary, before use.

The following sections detail some common types of decor, possible dangers, and methods of preparation. It should be added that in cases of illness in newly set-up aquaria, or where a new decor item has recently been added, decor toxicity should always be suspected.

ROCKS

Rocks can be purchased from many aquarium dealers, but this in no way guarantees their suitablility for the purpose in hand, or for aquarium use at all. Some rocks, in particular calciferous types (including the popular tufa), will increase hardness and pH. Rock is heavy and expensive to transport, and increasingly aquatic outlets obtain supplies from nearby garden centres, together with highly suspect geological identifications. Moreover, even rocks normally quoted as suitable for aquaria are sometimes safe only if the sample has been chosen by someone with a basic knowledge of geology. For example, granite may contain tin ore, usually accompanied by arsenic deposits, and slate sometimes has thin layers of undesirable minerals sandwiched between its laminae. Thus, whether the aquarist buys rocks, or collects his own, a little knowledge of geology is useful. Always avoid the following:

- soft or crumbly rocks (except tufa)
- plain white, cream, or pale grey rocks (usually limestone) (except for hard-water aquaria)
- fossiliferous rocks (except for hard-water aquaria)
- rocks with metallic or rust-coloured veins or deposits
- rocks containing veins of crystals, especially coloured crystals
- brightly coloured rocks.

The above list is by no means exhaustive, but should suffice for buying rocks from aquarium stores; a basic geological guide is advisable for collecting or purchasing elsewhere. Avoid collecting rocks in areas where metal ores or minerals are mined, and where there is any likelihood of contamination, for example from pesticides or radioactivity.

All rocks should be thoroughly scrubbed in clean water before use.

Granite (top left) and gneiss (bottom left) are safe for use in both hard and soft water aquaria. Limestones (including tufa) will increase hardness and pH.

SUBSTRATE MATERIALS

Substrate materials should be suitable in chemical composition, grain size, and texture for the fish concerned.

'Hardness-free' gravel is available, but not always as inert as purported. It may be wise to ask for a small sample (a teaspoonful is enough) and ask a pharmacist (or school chemistry teacher) to test it using a strong acid. If the sample contains any material likely to affect water chemistry, it will 'fizz' in strong acid. (Note: home-testing with vinegar or lemon juice, while often advocated, is unreliable.) Coral sand and coral gravel are unsuitable substrate materials for freshwater aquaria, although a small percentage (5 to 20 per cent) of coral sand can be mixed with ordinary aquarium gravel to act as a pH buffer for fish from hard alkaline waters such as the East African Rift Valley lakes.

Sharp substrate materials are unsuitable for fish which habitually rest on the bottom or burrow in, dig, or sift it, and for bottom-dwelling catfish and loaches, whose delicate barbels may be damaged. Grain size should be appropriate to mouth size for species that need to dig, and fine material is necessary for sifting-feeders that pass substrate out through their gills. Artificially coloured gravels may be toxic; even those with a plastic coating are suspect, as

Corals should never be used in freshwater aquaria. Not only will they harden the water, but fish may injure themselves on the sharp material. Coral gravel may cause damage to mouths and gills, and coral sand particles in suspension lead to gill irritation.

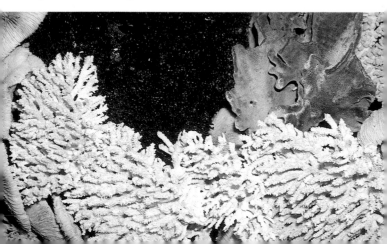

Fish whose behavioural repertoire includes digging should be allowed to do so. Depriving them of substrate to prevent this is unkind.

Some shell-dwellers use their mouths to dig in order to bury their shells: fine substrate is essential for their small mouths.

Some items of decor are essential to some fish. Lake Tanganyika shell-dwelling cichlids must be provided with shells.

plastic sooner or later degrades, and friction between the grains (digging fish, gravel cleaning) may accelerate the process. All substrate materials should be thoroughly washed to remove dust and dirt before use.

WOOD

Commonly used wood items are bogwood, driftwood, cork bark, bamboo, and coconut shells. All of these may leach tannins and other substances into the aquarium water; although this is sometimes desirable, the rate of leaching cannot be controlled and there are safer methods, for example peat filtration. Driftwood from the seashore may contain considerable SALT (3) residues.

All wooden items should be presoaked for a long period (weeks or months rather than days) to eliminate contaminants; the process can be speeded up by boiling or using repeated changes of hot water. Any soft material should be scooped out or scraped away as much as possible.

Varnishing wooden decor (with a waterproof non-toxic varnish) is commonly advocated as a quick solution to the problem of leaching. But in practice almost every piece of wood has cracks and interstices which it is impossible to seal effectively; moreover some fish (e.g. cichlids of the genus *Uaru* and some catfish) gnaw or rasp wood, and may be poisoned even by nominally safe varnish.

PLANTS

Some plants sold for aquarium use are not true aquatics (and thus likely to die and decay); some, e.g. *Dieffenbachia*, are actually poisonous. Others are reputed to affect water chemistry. Check the suitability of any plant (in a good aquarium handbook) before purchase.

It is preferable not to buy plants from aquaria containing fish, as they may harbour DISEASE (3) and/or PARASITES (3); check the leaves of any purchase for SNAILS (3) to avoid inadvertent introduction of the latter. Unfortunately any chemical genuinely effective against 'intruders' is likely to harm the plant in the process. Plastic plants (intended for aquarium use) are safe, but avoid those with unnatural colours (see below).

Clay flowerpots and drainage saucers, inverted and modified ('doorway') make excellent caves.

UNNATURAL DECOR ITEMS

A number of domestic items are commonly used in aquaria, favourites being plant pots and pipes, utilised to provide instant 'caves'. Plastic plant pots and pipes should be avoided, not being made of food-grade plastic. Clay pots and pipes should be new, to avoid any danger of chemical residues (pesticides, fertilisers); new ones may, however, affect water chemistry, increasing hardness and pH, so if this is undesirable they should be pre-soaked in regular changes of water until they cease to affect water chemistry.

Nowadays artificial rocks and woods are available; they are extremely realistic, and although expensive, are a safer choice if in doubt about the suitability of the real thing.

Also available is the most astonishing array of plastic trivia – galleons, mermaids, skulls, divers, etc., sometimes air-operated, and worst of all, spinning kaleidoscopic wheels. On a par with these are underwater spotlights and fibre-optic lights. These are at best unnatural and totally inappropriate to what is, after all the fishes' home, not a toybox; at worst, some, at least, are undoubtedly stressful to the fish and thus likely to compromise their well-being.

GLUES, PAINTS, ETC.

Any glues or paints or varnishes used in the creation of decor internal to the aquarium must, of course, be waterproof and non-toxic. Aquarium silicon sealant /adhesive is the best and safest for most purposes.

Chapter Five

FISH COMPATIBILITY

While most fish illness can be attributed to poor environmental conditions, many INJURIES (3), and a significant number of deaths, are caused by the mixing of incompatible species. Many aquarists make the mistake of assuming that environmental compatibility – sharing a habitat in nature, or requiring similar environmental conditions although not sympatric – is sufficient justification for housing fish species together. A little thought, however, will indicate that nothing could be further from the truth. A single biotope may be home to a considerable size range of fish – for example, Lake Tanganyika is home to a variety of fish which range in adult size from 3/4in. (2 cm) to 36in. (90 cm). Such size differences within a given ecosystem often correlate with predator/prey relationships.

PREDATION
Few aquarists would deliberately house fish of such diverse size together, but an astonishing number buy juveniles of large species, ignorant of their eventual size (not all shops automatically volunteer this information), and are horrified to find their community is decimated as the youngsters grow.

The problem of predation may not always be as obvious and immediate: for example, angelfish (*Pterophyllum* spp.) and tetras (small characins) are commonly housed successfully together if bought as youngsters and grown on together. But the tetras are normally shorter-lived, and, when losses through old age are replaced with new, small, specimens, the latter are promptly eaten by the angels. Equally, some piscivores are capable of consuming fish up

Small crabs and lobsters are sometimes sold for aquaria, but should not be kept with fish as their pincers can inflict serious injuries.

Oscars (Astronotus ocellatus) are all too often bought as youngsters by aquarists ignorant of their eventual size and habits. On a diet of small tankmates they rapidly grow to 30 cm (12 ins) or more!

to two-thirds of their own size, and tankmates should be chosen accordingly. Others, unable to swallow the prey whole, may take bites out of other fish and should be housed alone.

Fin-nipping can also be a problem, though not generally life-threatening. A few species of fish, for example the cichlid *Genyochromis mento* from Lake Malawi, have trophic specialisations based on scraping scales or biting pieces of fin from other fish, and can cause havoc in the confines of the aquarium. But many otherwise innocuous fish may find it impossible to resist long and/or trailing finnage such as that of angelfish, gouramis (e.g. *Colisa* or *Trichogaster* spp.), or Siamese fighting fish *(Betta splendens)*, which they may not even see as part of a larger fish, but simply as something potentially edible moving through the water. Commercially produced, long-finned varieties of popular aquarium fish are more prone to having their fins nipped than their normal-finned counterparts.

TERRITORIALITY

Behavioural incompatibility is not confined to predation. Some fish, particularly those which practise parental care of eggs and/or fry, occupy and defend (potential) breeding territories, to the detriment of tankmates. The problem can reach dire proportions if natural territory size equates with, or is larger than, aquarium size, such that other fish have no refuge space available. (See also Section I: Breeding.)

Some non-parental species occupy territory for other reasons (e.g. shelter, feeding) and exhibit behaviour which to the uninitiated may appear to be simple bullying. Dominant individuals may endeavour to lay claim to the feeding area – often only at feeding time – and drive away competitors.

In most cases of territoriality, the concomitant AGGRESSION (3) is usually more marked towards or between conspecifics, which are in direct competition for the resources in question, or towards species of similar appearance as regards colour or markings. Even juvenile fish can be extremely territorial among themselves, sometimes more so than adults.

STRESS

Even where no direct aggression and/or physical harm results from mismatching of fish, there may be dire long-term or short-term side effects, from STRESS (3). Continuous chivvying is clearly highly stressful, but there are less obvious causes of stress. A small fish will not understand that a large obligatory vegetarian is harmless, but will live its life in fear of being eaten. Boisterous, fast-moving species may cause unease, and often panic, in fish to whom rapid movement signifies approaching danger. Panic-stricken flight may in turn cause physical injury if the fish dashes itself against the aquarium glass or decor items. Timid fish may be afraid to approach the feeding area and be slowly starved out of existence. Severe short-term stress can lead to death; in the longer term stress, especially chronic stress, reduces a fish's immune capability so that it is more susceptible to disease and less able to cope with any environmental problems that may occur.

Guppies (Poecilia reticulata), top left), and rams (Microgeophagus ramirezi) are commonly kept together, although their water chemistry requirements are totally different.

EFFECTS OF INCOMPATIBILITY
Apart from the obvious physical injury caused by biting, the following are common effects of incompatibility:
- Frayed fins (and the likelihood of bacterial FIN ROT [3])
- Loose or missing scales
- Torn lips or dislocated jaws (in species that lock jaws and 'mouth-fight')
- Scrapes or cuts from collisions with hard objects (and the possibility of subsequent FUNGUS (3) attack)
- Eye damage or loss from collision
- Internal injuries from butting of the abdomen (typically SWIM-BLADDER DISEASE [2]), sometimes fatal
- RESPIRATORY STRESS (3) resulting from continuous flight

Many small fish (these are harlequin rasboras, Rasbora heteromorpha) require the security of the shoal.

- Exhaustion
- Malnutrition or starvation
- Shyness, timidity, NERVOUSNESS (2)
- Lying on the substrate or HANGING (3), head-up, in the top corners of the aquarium.
- Abnormal COLORATION [2] ('fright pattern')
- Any other abnormal BEHAVIOUR (2).

Some of these may, of course, equally be due to other environmental factors or disease.

POSITIVE COMPATIBILITY

Some fish prefer to shoal with members of their own species. Shoaling allows certain advantages over solitary swimming, such as improved predator surveillance, improved chances of locating food, and increased opportunities for mating. In the case of open-water fish such as small characins, shoaling reduces the chances of any individual being predated upon, because predators find it more difficult to track and target an individual within a large, closely moving group. Individuals of naturally shoaling species may suffer STRESS (3) if kept alone or in just two or threes, and this could affect their long-term well-being. The sociable behaviour of some other, often benthic, fish (e.g. *Corydoras* catfish) which live in small groups, is less well-understood, but apparently equally important. Again, failure to observe the social requirements of such fish may lead to stress-related disorders.

AVOIDING INCOMPATIBILITY PROBLEMS

Temperament and behaviour must be researched when planning the initial population of any aquarium, and new fish should *never* be added without first evaluating their impact on the existing community – and *vice versa*. In the event that an incompatibilty situation arises, it should, if possible, be rectified before any lasting damage occurs.

Chapter Six
PURCHASING, TRANSPORTING AND INTRODUCING STOCK

It is essential to get off to a good start by buying only healthy fish, and then transporting them safely home and introducing them to their new home with the minimum of STRESS (3). Being caught, bagged, transported (sometimes for long distances), and finally decanted into unfamiliar surroundings, is an extremely stressful experience; one which may leave the fish susceptible to DISEASE (3), or even kill it outright if not handled correctly.

VETTING THE SUPPLIER

It is advisable, before buying any fish from a particular shop, to check the premises over. If the shop is untidy or disorganised, chances are their maintenance regime is equally haphazard. Take a good look at the tanks – all of them, not just the ones containing fish that interest you. Are they clean and well cared for? A little mulm, and algae on the rear and sides, is acceptable, but if the bottom of the aquarium is littered with rubbish and the front glass dirty, shop elsewhere. Dead or dying fish are, obviously, a warning sign.

If, however, a tank with sick fish in is clearly marked "quarantine" or "not for sale", this indicates a responsible attitude. Newly arrived fish do sometimes fall ill, and not all shops have an extensive quarantine facility backstage. Those premises which possess a quarantine facility are, however, more likely to have healthy fish for sale. Even so, this is not to condemn small dealers without such facilities out of hand, as some are true enthusiasts. You can always come back next week to buy, if the fish are still healthy.

Try to establish the dealer's attitude, as the quality of his

Crowded tanks tend to contain stressed fish, and water quality may be less than optimum.

fish will often reflect this. If he is helpful, and ready to answer questions, that is a good sign. So is meticulous, up-to-date, labelling of tank contents.

Beware of shops with centralised filtration systems, which are an excellent way of filtering tanks but also of ensuring that any disease is quickly spread throughout the establishment. Some premises which rely on centralised systems utilise mechanical filtration (e.g. sand filters) and/or UV STERILISATION (3) sterilisers to help reduce the chances of spreading pathogens; however, neither of these disease control methods is foolproof. On the other hand, full marks to the shop that has a separate net for each tank, or that keeps or dips nets in a disinfectant bath between use on different tanks. These precautions will reduce the likelihood of transmitting infections between tanks.

SELECTING STOCK
(See also Section I: Signs of a Healthy Fish; Breeding)
Although it may not be possible to choose a particular individual from a large shoal (though it is quite acceptable to ask for a specific fish, especially if the price is high), do not be afraid to reject any specimen caught which does not appear to be in good condition. Ask the dealer to trap the fish between the net and the front glass, while you look closely at it, and check it over again once it is in the bag.

Some shops employ poorly trained staff with little idea of

A bag of fish, newly arrived from the wholesaler, equalising temperatures in a sale tank. Beware, this dealer does not quarantine his stock! Note too, the bag should have been undone before equalisation, there are too many fish in the bag, and the corners have not been tied off to prevent injury. A shop to avoid!

All credit to the dealer who endeavours to make his fish feel at home during their stay in his shop. The fish on the left is far less likely to be stressed than one 'stocked' in a bare tank (lower picture).

how to catch a fish. You do not want to buy a creature that has been badly stressed, and perhaps physically injured, by a lengthy pursuit. You are at liberty to protest and, if you feel all the fish in the tank are now thoroughly stressed, not to buy at all.

Ask the dealer to trap the fish against the front glass with the net, so you can inspect it before confirming purchase.

PACKING AND TRANSPORTATION

Always insist on proper packing, assuming it is not routinely offered. Small fish can become trapped, and crushed, in the corners of polythene bags, which should be cornered, or tied off, with rubber bands or tape, or knotted. Double bags should be used, as a safeguard against leaks; this is particularly important when transporting catfish and other fish which possess long sharp spines. The bags should be large enough for their occupants (in general, the width should be at least twice the length of the fish, and the length three to four times the width), and contain a large air space (60-80 per cent of the bag volume) above the water, to allow for gas exchange. Some shops are equipped with oxygen cylinders enabling them to fill the 'air space' with pure oxygen, useful for long journeys. The water should be put in the bags before any fish are caught, as otherwise it is likely to contain irritating suspended detritus stirred up from the bottom during capture.

It is acceptable to pack several small, peaceful, fish of the same species in the same bag. Larger fish, and those of dubious temperament (e.g. cichlids) should be packed individually. Insist – or you may find you have brought home one live fish and a corpse or two. Better still, take your own containers, such as tightly-lidded plastic buckets, for transporting both difficult fish and easy ones.

The bags of fish should be placed in a box, or opaque outer wrapper or bag, so that the occupants are not exposed to bright light and other stressful external stimuli. Ideally, take an insulated container or ask for a 'fish box', to prevent chilling in cold weather or overheating during a heatwave. Any spare space in the box should be packed with crumpled paper or spare, air-filled, polythene bags, to prevent the occupied ones from rolling about. Taking a spare bag is also a good idea, just in case of leakage during transit. The fish, once bagged, should be taken home and unpacked as soon as possible.

UNPACKING

It is normal to suspend bags of newly-purchased fish in the aquarium to which they are to be introduced, so that the water temperatures may equalise and TEMPERATURE SHOCK (3) is avoided. Bags should be undone before this equalisation, preferably while they are still in their outer wrapper or box rather than terrifying the fish by waving them around in mid air. Although some people float the still sealed bags, they then have to be removed from the tank – and the fish thus subjected to additional disturbance – while undoing them. The tank light should be switched off before equalisation.

There is a myth that equalisation should take about half an hour (in practice it generally takes about five minutes for temperatures to equalise), during which water from the tank should be periodically baled into the bags to "equalise water chemistry and avoid chemical shock." This will not, however, significantly lessen the impact of a major change in water chemistry, although no physiological response may be apparent for 12 to 72 hours.

What the process *is* likely to achieve is a vast increase in stress, as the fish is subjected to a series of disruptions while suspended for 30 minutes in a very confined space and exposed to external stimuli, possibly surrounded by inquisitive future tankmates from which it cannot hide. The only way to avoid chemical shock, if there is a significant difference in water chemistry between that to which the fish are accustomed and that for which they are destined, is slow adjustment over a period of days or weeks. A tank with the current correct water conditions must be provided; the adjustment process can effectively be combined with QUARANTINE (3) (*see also below; and Section I: The Correct Environment*).

RELEASING THE FISH

Once the temperatures have equalised – carefully and quietly check with a thermometer after five minutes – gently submerge the necks of the bags and allow the fish to swim out, gradually raising the bottoms of the bags so they have to leave. Always check that none are left in the now water-less bags.

The newly-introduced fish may seek cover among the decor, or rest on the bottom (SHOCK [3]). Do not interfere, and never try and coax them from hiding, as this will only cause them more stress. Simply leave the light off, and avoid too much activity near the aquarium, until the next day when, provided you have managed the transportation and introduction process correctly, the newcomers will generally be acting as if they had been there for years.

QUARANTINE

Even if you are satisfied that the shop is safe to patronise, and your new fish appear healthy, it is still a sensible precaution to quarantine them before introducing them to an established aquarium of healthy fish, just in case they are harbouring some latent disease. Bear in mind that TRANSPORTATION STRESS (3) can itself sometimes bring on a disease condition, even if the fish appeared perfectly healthy in the dealer's aquarium.

The quarantine tank need not be an elaborate affair, but it should be large enough for the fish involved, and be appropriately furnished so as to provide any basic shelter they require – i.e. a clay flowerpot for cave-dwellers or a few plastic plants (live ones may be damaged by any medication required) for those that seek cover among vegetation. It should have a basic filtration system capable of dealing with the expected loading, and the filter must be properly matured before any fish are introduced. If the tank cannot be kept up-and-running all the time, then it can be brought into use quickly by filling with matured water from the main aquarium; and by using a sponge or box filter which has been kept running in a corner of the main aquarium for just such an eventuality, and thus has the necessary bacterial population. If it proves necessary to medicate the aquarium, bear in mind that some medications are bactericidal and will eliminate filter bacteria as well as pathogens *(see also Section I: Treating Fish Diseases).*

As well as allowing an opportunity to see if the new arrivals develop any illness, a quarantine period of between two and three weeks will allow the new fish to recover from the stress of capture and transportation, without having simultaneously to cope with the often quite hectic environment of the community tank, whose occupants are likely to be interested in, and possibly a little hostile to, new arrivals. If the fish have been kept in water of different chemistry to that of their new home, then quarantine provides an ideal opportunity for gradual adjustment.

It is important to note that fish which remain healthy throughout the quarantine period are not necessarily 100 per cent disease-free. For example, some pathogens may be present in a dormant, inactivated state within the fish's tissues and can remain this way for many months or even years without causing any obvious disease. This dormancy or latency is a feature of some VIRUS (3) infections. The dormant pathogen may eventually be activated, perhaps long after quarantine, as a result of physiological changes to the host, such as chronic STRESS (3) or SENILITY (3). Some other pathogens undergo a very slow development in their host, such that the fish may remain seemingly healthy throughout the quarantine period.

Quarantine is therefore not always foolproof, but it is nevertheless an extremely important disease prevention measure and one which should be practised wherever possible.

NITRATE SHOCK
A regrettably large number of fish die through POISONING (3) by nitrate (NITRATE SHOCK [3]) a day or two after purchase, the fault usually being laid, through ignorance, at the door of the dealer, for selling fish in poor condition.

Shop display aquaria normally contain very good quality water. In addition to regular partial water changes as part of routine maintenance, they receive frequent additional small changes as the water used in bags (of fish sold) is replaced. Many home aquaria, by contrast, have very high nitrate concentrations because water changes have not been adequate to keep levels down, or water has not been changed at all. The resident fish survive because they have adjusted gradually to the slowly increasing pollution. New arrivals, by contrast, are subjected to a sudden vast increase, which proves toxic.

The same problem may, of course, occur when fish are transferred from a low-nitrate quarantine tank to a high nitrate community.

Chapter Seven

NUTRITION

Fish, in common with other vertebrates, require a variety of nutrients in order to supply their energy requirements for their daily existence and growth. The various food constituents each have their own important role in the living processes of fish: proteins, lipids, and carbohydrates are necessary for providing energy; and protein is additionally important for growth. The composition of these various food types is also important. For example, the protein must provide the fish with all the essential amino acids, and lipids must contain the right types of fatty acids. Several other nutrients are also required, though in much smaller quantities, namely various vitamins and minerals.

The relative proportions and amounts of these various nutrients which are required by a fish will depend on several factors, including the species, its stage of development, and its reproductive status, and external factors such as temperature, habitat, and season.

Fish species have evolved to fill almost every conceivable trophic niche, consuming not only obvious foods such as each other, plants (including algae), and aquatic invertebrates, but also more bizarre items such as fins and scales, fruit, detritus, and mud. They have also evolved a myriad different ways of securing their food, in their efforts to gain a competitive advantage.

DIET AND DIGESTION
More important, from the aquarist's point of view, is the fact that fish have evolved differences in their digestive systems to enable them to process different food items. Some fish are primarily algae or plant eaters (herbivores), others

ABOVE: Pike cichlids (Crenicichla sp.) are piscivores which can consume fish up to two-thirds of their own size. Petenia splendida (behind) is another piscivore with a capacious mouth.

RIGHT: A Lake Malawi rock cichlid picking at algae on a rock. Many of these fish are partially vegetarian.

Photo: Ad Konings.

primarily meat-eaters (carnivores), while many are omnivorous and will accept both types of food. Fish can be further classified according to their more specific dietary preferences; thus carnivores may be subdivided into insectivores, molluscivores, and piscivores, though in practice most fish are more catholic in their feeding habits.

Feeding the right sort of diet for the species of fish in question is paramount for the animal's well being. A herbivorous fish needs to process large quantities of low grade (= low digestibility coefficient) food, that is vegetable material, in order to obtain sufficient nourishment. Such fish have a long intestine which can accommodate the continuous slow throughput of vegetable matter required. In some species the digestive system may sustain beneficial bacteria which break down plant fibre (for example cellulose) to release simple sugars which can then be easily taken up across the fish's gut.

A piscivore, on the other hand, is physiologically adapted to process a whole fish. It has no need for a long intestine but is equipped with a stomach in which to accommodate the bulky food while it is being digested by gastric acid and various enzymes.

It should thus be obvious that nutritional problems will arise if we feed vegetable food to a piscivore, and raw fish to a herbivore. Assuming the piscivore can be induced to eat the food at all – it will not recognise it as such – then its gut will be inefficient in digesting and assimilating the food. Regardless of whether or not the fish eats the food, in the long term the result will be the same – death by slow starvation and/or nutrient imbalance (that is, it can be a quantitative and/or qualitative process).

While many piscivores are more or less obligatory, most nominal herbivores are in practice facultative feeders – they have evolved to eat vegetable matter because that is the food most often available to them, but they relish other, more nutritious foods when available. So a herbivore may well devour the raw fish offered to it, and, because of its relatively high nutritional value (as compared with the normal vegetable diet) the fish may receive far more nutrients than required. And it will probably continue feeding regardless of being sated, nutritionally speaking, as continuous intake is habitual and normally necessary for its survival.

Excess protein (and this applies to all fish) will be used as an energy source and may be catabolized in preference to carbohydrate and lipid. The disproportionately large amounts of protein in the food will be excreted in the form of AMMONIA (3) which may pollute the aquarium, whereas the products of carbohydrate breakdown are simply energy plus water and carbon dioxide. Moreover the fish may suffer from CONSTIPATION (3) through lack of the roughage which forms a major part of its natural diet.

These are, of course, the extremes of what is an exceedingly complex trophic spectrum in terms of both diet and feeding behaviour. An inappropriate diet may not be quite as serious for the less specialised feeders such as omnivores, but may, nevertheless, pose long-term nutritional problems.

DEVELOPMENT OF TROPHIC SPECIALISATIONS

It should also be noted that highly specialised feeders are normally more generalised in their trophic behaviour as fry and juveniles, for a number of reasons. Firstly, they may be unable to ingest the preferred food of adults, for example, piscivore fry are unlikely to be able to find fish smaller than themselves to eat. Secondly, its nutritive value (essentially its protein composition) may be inadequate to produce optimum growth – thus even those species which are herbivores when adult are commonly omnivorous or insectivorous during their juvenile stage. Thirdly, their small size means that they can detect and make good use of small food items such as aquatic invertebrates – such prey being often too small to be of interest or value to, or even detected by, adults. Thus many fry feed initially on micro-organisms, progressing to larger (but still small) live foods as they grow, before eventually switching to their adult diet. It is important to bear this in mind when rearing fry.

DIETARY COMPROMISES

The dietary needs of any species should always be taken into account in captivity. This, of course, can present problems in the community aquarium, which may contain a mixture of insectivorous, herbivorous, and omnivorous species – but not piscivorous!

The normal solution is to feed a compromise, omnivore diet. Although it is often suggested that additional vegetable food should be provided for herbivores, in practice the latter will usually eat their fill of omnivore food before starting on the presumably less palatable vegetable, and thus overfeed. However, while few nominal omnivores will tackle fresh vegetable matter, most will eat vegetable-based dried foods (flake, pellets – see below), so a regime based on alternation of omnivore foods (any type) and vegetarian dried foods, combined with careful monitoring for any adverse effects of the diet on the health of all the fish concerned, may achieve the desired result.

Highly specialised feeders, however, may refuse to eat items other than those which they would encounter in the wild (or local analogues – it is not necessary to import the exact dietary items from the tropics!), or may become unhealthy if fed 'artificial' alternatives. Under no circumstances should the health of the fish be compromised. If the aquarist is unable, or unwilling, to provide what is required, he should not even try to keep that species. 'Unwilling' covers any personal qualms, from distaste at feeding one live creature to another, to trying to impose a personal vegetarian ethos on one's pets.

At the same time, the practice of feeding one living fish to another can hardly be regarded as enjoyable or desirable, even though it is a natural process for both predator and prey. Most piscivores can be 'trained' to take small dead fish, like whitebait and lancefish, or pieces of larger ones such as cod and coley. They will react instinctively to anything dropped into the aquarium, and, perhaps after a few rejections, realise the substitute is just as palatable as the 'real thing'.

Although the constant sacrificing of healthy live fish should be avoided, the feeding of surplus or defective fry to piscivores and omnivores is commonplace, and probably the most practicable and humane method of disposing of them. Sick fish should, of course, never be used as food for others, because of the risk of disease transmission. (See also CANNIBALISM [3]).

Fish should never be held 'morally' responsible for eating the 'wrong' things – usually each other and the aquarium plants. The fault lies with the unthinking or ignorant aquarist who gave them the opportunity!

TYPES OF AQUARIUM FOODS

LIVE FOODS
These include, as well as live fish, items such as earthworms, and aquatic invertebrates such as *Daphnia* and various insect larvae. Some can be bought, some cultured, and some collected. Some fish, especially wild fish, may be unwilling, or even refuse, to eat anything else.
Advantages: Many live foods are the natural prey of fish, or are closely related or analogous to natural prey species.

Earthworms, whole (as here) or chopped are a favourite fish food and often the object of competition.

They generally contain significant amounts of roughage and are unlikely to cause DIGESTIVE DISORDERS (2). They are clearly psychologically beneficial – few, if any, fish will choose flake food if live food is offered simultaneously. They may help bring fish into breeding condition and trigger spawning, especially in species where the breeding season in nature is preceded by an increase in the live food supply.

Disadvantages: Live foods are often seasonal, and can be labour-intensive to harvest or culture. They may introduce disease or pests: specifically, *Tubifex* worms, which commonly live in polluted mud, may import undesirable bacteria; the same charge has been levelled at commercially produced red mosquito larvae ('bloodworm'). Pests such as dragonfly larvae and *Hydra,* which may predate on tiny fish fry, can be accidentally introduced with 'pond foods' such as *Daphnia* and *Cyclops,* though careful screening should prevent this. 'Pond foods' are sometimes cited as introducing diseases and parasites, and this is indeed possible, but seems rarely actually to produce problems. The individual aquarist must decide whether the reward outweighs the risk in each case. There is, after all, little point in avoiding any risk of introduced disease if the fish ends up unhealthy – or dead – through starvation. *(See also LIVE FOODS AS VECTORS OF DISEASE[3]).*

FRESH FOODS

A number of human foods are more or less suitable for feeding to fish. Only foods reasonably analogous to the

A selection of human foods sometimes used for fish: white fish (Coley), prawns and mussels, peas, lettuce, courgette, and cucumber are all acceptable, but liver and other foods of mammal/bird origin may lead to health problems.

natural diet should be considered. Foods of mammal or bird origin (e.g. heart), while formerly commonly used, are rich in the wrong types of fatty acids and should be avoided, otherwise the fish may become obese or develop damaging fatty deposits. (See FATTY LIVER[3]).

Advantages: Vegetable items such as lettuce, spinach, peas, cucumber, and courgette are particularly useful for herbivores, and will be eaten only by them (note: these foods have a higher cellulose content than aquatic plants, and generally require scalding before use, to break down the cellulose and render them digestible). Prawn, shrimp, and mussel are reasonably natural aquatic foods, now often used instead of mammalian protein in the production of dried foods (see below). Raw fish is the natural diet of piscivores, but some other fish apparently find it unpalatable. Hard cod roe is an excellent fry growth food, or an occasional treat for small adult fishes.

Disadvantages: Vegetables may contain undesirable chemicals unless organically grown. Seafoods may be polluted if collected from certain locations, and for this reason only those sold for human consumption should be purchased.

FROZEN FOODS
A number of 'live' and fresh foods are available in frozen form.

Advantages: Although they lack the 'wriggle factor', many fish find them highly palatable, especially the 'live' type (e.g. frozen bloodworm). Although they may not be 100 per cent safe, they are far less likely to introduce disease. They are available all the year round.

Disadvantages: Water content is often high, and as the water contains nutrients from the food, it may cause pollution. Some live foods, e.g. *Daphnia,* disintegrate when frozen, and the defrosted product is a highly nutritious soup, useless for feeding fish but very likely to pollute the aquarium. The water in frozen *Artemia* may be salty. Frozen heart is just as unsuitable as fresh. Some people find it distasteful to store pet foods in the domestic freezer; however, this should not present any hygiene problems if fish foods are stored in a separate container and the freezer is functioning properly.

BOTTLED FOODS

These are the most recent innovation in convenience fish foods: a number of popular live food species are now available in a preserved, bottled form. Although the first samples proved unpalatable because of the preservative used, subsequent, preservative-free versions are proving successful.

Advantages: As for frozen foods, but no freezer required, and no disintegration upon defrosting.

Disadvantages: None apparent to date, now that the unpalatibility problem has been addressed.

FREEZE-DRIED FOODS

A variety of live foods are available in freeze-dried form.

Advantages: A convenient method of feeding natural foods in a sterile form (and useful if no freezer facility is available).

Disadvantages: Some fish may be reluctant to eat some or all freeze-dried foods. Pre-soaking sometimes apparently increases palatability. They may be lacking in certain vitamins.

DRIED FOODS

Dried foods are probably the most popular and convenient method of feeding aquarium fish.

Although good-quality flake and pellet dried foods have for many years provided a balanced diet designed to cater

Tablet food.   *Flake food.*

for community aquaria housing a mixture of omnivores, carnivores, and herbivores, it is only comparatively recently that manufacturers of these foods have started to produce special separate 'carnivore' and 'herbivore' dried foods.

A considerable volume of nutritional research has gone into the production of many dried foods. It is important to buy only such scientifically developed formulations, produced by a reputable company, and only those designed specifically for aquarium fish, even if cheaper alternatives are available.

Advantages: Convenience of storage and use; constant availability; all essential dietary elements present; enjoyed by most general community fish species; no danger of introducing disease.

Disadvantages: As varieties tend to be concentrated and easily digestible, the majority of aquarists tend to be far too generous with them, and the fish, designed to process large quantities of lower-grade food, consume all that is offered. This can in turn lead to pollution of the aquarium with AMMONIA (3) and NITRITE (3), and although an efficient biological filter will probably cope with these most of the time, there will be an accompanying serious increase in nitrate levels.

Some fish seem prone to CONSTIPATION (3) and other DIGESTIVE DISORDERS (3) if fed only, or mainly, dried foods, and some types of fish (e.g. many killifishes and dwarf cichlids) are reluctant to eat them. Certain vitamins, notably Vitamin C, may degrade with long-term storage. Flake foods are more prone to leaching vitamins upon contact with the aquarium water than are pelleted foods.

THE IMPORTANCE OF VARIETY
Except where the fish naturally enjoys a specialised, restricted, diet, varying the diet is generally highly advantageous. An ideal diet for captive fish will include a mixture of convenience (i.e. frozen, freeze-dried, bottled, and dried), live, and fresh foods, appropriate to the species. Variety increases the likelihood that all essential dietary constituents are provided; it avoids the fish becoming bored with a single food, and at the same time ensures that they do not come to recognise only one or two items as food, problematical if those items cease to be available; it reduces the likelihood of digestive disorders.

FRESHNESS AND CORRECT STORAGE
Aquarium foods should always be discarded once their 'use-by' date has expired, so a large pack may not be the economy it seems if only a few fish are kept, or the suggested varied diet is utilised.

Dried foods should be stored in a cool, dry, dark, place in order to avoid deterioration (see AFLATOXINS[3]) and vitamin degradation. If a large quantity of dried food is purchased, it is better to decant one to two weeks' supply into a smaller container for regular use instead of opening the bulk supply daily, and a sachet of silica gel (available from photographic shops, *inter alia*) can be kept in the bulk container to absorb atmospheric moisture and thus prevent deterioration.

HOW MUCH AND HOW OFTEN?
Most aquarists overfeed their fish, partly because of the high nutritional value of the dried foods commonly used, partly because feeding the fish is an enjoyable activity, during which they are generally all in view and active. The fish themselves are very efficient feed converters and require less food per unit of body weight than do birds and mammals. Also, being cold-blooded creatures, fish do not have to metabolise food for generating body heat.

"As much as they will eat in five minutes" is an oft-quoted formula, based on avoiding polluting the tank with uneaten food rather than other considerations, but one which fails to take into account the fact that some fish are delicate pickers, while others can consume a prodigious amount in a short time.

There is no hard and fast formula to decide "how much", and, equally, "how often" depends entirely on the fish concerned. We have already seen how a piscivore may gorge itself every few days and eat nothing in between; on the other hand the majority of herbivores, insectivores, and omnivores will, in nature, feed regularly, perhaps almost continuously, on relatively low-grade foods throughout their active period each day. The aquarist must use common sense in establishing a feeding regime for the specific fish he owns. If there are constant problems with NITRO-GENOUS WASTES (3), due to overfeeding, or, less likely, fish exhibit serious EMACIATION (2), then adjustment is necessary.

However, it is important to avoid leaving large amounts of 'dead' food uneaten to pollute the tank; it is more sensible to feed 'continuous-feeding' fish a small amount several times a day than a single heavy meal; and it is important to make sure certain fish get enough – for example, those which are shy by nature or low in the tank 'pecking order', those which feed on the bottom, who may miss out on floating or slow-sinking foods, and those that feed at night, which may require special feeding.

It does no harm, and probably much good, to include a periodic fast day in the regime, say once every two weeks – but not when rearing fry, which must be given frequent feeds or they will quickly starve.

Chapter Eight

BREEDING

The purpose of breeding aquarium fish is generally for the pleasure of observing behaviour, as the hobbyist, especially in cold and temperate climates where artificial heating is necessary, is unlikely to be able to compete, price-wise, with mass-produced stock from commercial breeders. Much mass-produced stock is, however, of dubious quality, and there remains a niche for the amateur breeder producing good-quality young fish, especially young of species not yet produced commercially. He is unlikely to make his fortune so doing, but can hope perhaps to cover his outlay on equipment and running costs. If not, there is still the enjoyment, plus the fact that the captive breeding of fish may help reduce fishing pressures on wild stocks and therefore has environmental value.

PLANNING
Provided individuals of both sexes are present, and environmental conditions are appropriate, then many

Some fish lay their eggs on plants: Symphysodon aequifasciatus (discus) guarding eggs.

LEFT: Mollies (Poecilia sphenops) are livebearers.

BELOW: A mouthbrooding cichlid releasing her fry.

freshwater tropical fish will spawn (or, in the case of livebearers, produce fry) in captivity without any intervention on the part of the aquarist. However, it is likely that the majority, or all, of the eggs and fry produced in a community situation will be eaten by other fish, and, indeed, those species that do not practice parental care will commonly cannibalise their own offspring. Those species that are parental will usually defend their brood against any potential predators – in captivity their tankmates – who may be killed or injured in the process. Thus, if the aquarist wishes to produce and rear fry it will normally be necessary to undertake this as a special project, generally requiring additional aquaria for the parents, and, ultimately, the growing on of fry.

It is wise to canvass potential markets, usually other aquarists and local dealers, before breeding any species, as there are few things more disheartening than having to destroy healthy, well-grown, young fish because there is no market for them. It is, in any case, often necessary to cull broods down to saleable numbers, or, indeed, numbers that can be properly accommodated at the growing on stage, but this is far easier when they are small.

The diversity of breeding strategies among fish, and reciprocal strategies required by aquarists in order to breed them successfully, is far too great to be covered in this book. As ever, prior research is paramount. This should include not only breeding habits but also equipment, special foodstuffs, and anything else likely to be required. It is tragic to lose a hard-won brood of fry because the requisite first food is unavailable.

SELECTION OF BROODSTOCK

It is absolutely essential to breed from only the very best quality adult stock, that is, specimens which are in good health and typical of their species or form in all respects, e.g., *inter alia*, size, colour, finnage, behaviour. The use of inferior stock will produce inferior offspring; in the case of commonplace species these may prove unsaleable, and while poor-quality fry of a rare species may sell because of their rarity, it will do nobody any favours to sell them rubbish; and the aquarist's reputation as a breeder is likely to suffer, such that future, good-quality, fish prove unsaleable. The fish produced should, like their parents, be typical representatives of their species or variety, and fish that the breeder himself, using an experienced and critical eye, would be pleased to select for his aquaria.

The following should be avoided:
- Stock with visible DEFORMITIES (3), or stock from lines known to produce deformities. Do not buy where deformed siblings are also on sale (and do not buy from shops that sell deformed fish!). Most deformities are genetic and may be transmitted to the next generation.
- Abnormally-coloured fish, for the same reasons.
- Abnormally small or large individuals.
- Inbred stock, except where a degree of INBREEDING (3) has been used to produce a special strain. Random or unplanned inbreeding commonly results in deformities and other defects.
- Stock which is diseased or in any way unhealthy. Some

Genetically deformed fish should never be used for breeding. A healed split after injury (top) need be no bar to breeding, but an abnormal (for the species) two-part dorsal (left) is.

diseases can be passed by VERTICAL TRANSMISSION (3) to the offspring, and horizontally if adults and fry share a tank.

● Stock with behavioural abnormalities, which, like physical deformities, may be heritable or be indicative of a (heritable) physical defect.

● Artificially hatched/reared offspring of normally parental species, for example cichlids. For reasons as yet not properly understood, such fish are prone to egg or fry CANNIBALISM (3), a behavioural abnormality (in parental species) which will not be detected until breeding occurs. (However, some adults of some parental species commonly require a practice run or two before getting it right, and should not be discarded unless the cannibalism is clearly habitual.)

● Unidentified fish. It is acceptable to breed newly discovered species yet to receive a scientific name, but avoid stock which is unlabelled, or labelled generically. This also applies to species where special, named, strains are available – discus (*Symphysodon* spp.), angels (*Pterophyllum* spp.), and poeciliid livebearers (guppies, platies, swordtails, mollies). Generic labelling ('mixed Malawi cichlids', 'small discus', 'assorted guppies') generally denotes poor-quality stock of dubious provenance, often including HYBRIDS (3).

TRIGGERING SPAWNING

Species which breed year-round will not normally require any special treatment to bring them into spawning condition – if they do, then they are probably not being maintained properly. In addition, the following paragraphs apply largely to egg-layers; livebearing species do not generally require special treatment in order to stimulate reproduction – indeed the poeciliids may be considered the rabbits of the aquarium world. Seasonal spawners normally experience a succession of events in nature which combine to produce physical and psychological readiness to breed. In the tropics, where day and night are of similar length year round, photoperiod and light intensity are not normally involved in triggering reproduction, but variations in temperature, water chemistry, and diet and food supply are. Such species may require an enhanced dietary regimen – more food than normal, and different foods. Additional proteins may be required to permit and to assist the development of oocytes. There is no evidence that live foods are metabolically necessary, but there is no question that their use commonly helps to induce spawning.

Raising the temperature slightly is a method commonly used to trigger spawning in some groups of fish, but is best reserved for situations where properly housed and conditioned fish remain reluctant to spawn. In other cases, it may be necessary to first lower temperature and increase oxygen content (the rains, influx of melt water) before feeding live food while gradually raising the temperature over a period of weeks, to simulate natural events. However, in most cases this is quite unnecessary, and may even be counter-productive with species (e.g. parental species) where a secure, settled, environment is more important than climatic variations.

The front fish is fanning eggs.

THE BREEDING ENVIRONMENT

This will differ considerably depending on the species involved. Parental species may require a complete biotope simulation, and commonly the privacy of a tank allocated to a single pair, often well in advance of any reproductive activity so that they have time to settle and feel secure.

Non-parental species, on the other hand, can often be induced to spawn in temporary quarters to which they are introduced only when spawning is imminent; and which contain only the correct water and a suitable spawning medium if necessary, or some means of preventing the immediate cannibalism of the eggs, for example a gauze screen through which the eggs drop to safety. After spawning the parents are removed and the eggs hatched as appropriate to the species *(see below)*.

Even where a species will live and thrive in unnatural water conditions, the correct chemistry is commonly required for successful breeding; adverse conditions may affect egg/sperm viability and cause reproductive failure.

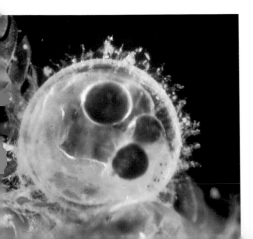

Medaka egg, 'eyed up'

POST SPAWNING REST

Spawning and parturition can be physically debilitating and sometimes stressful, and females in particular may require a period of rest and recuperation in isolation before being returned to their normal quarters. Not all species require such a rest cure, and, obviously, parental species are designed to remain with their offspring and should be allowed to do so.

HATCHING

In the case of most tropical freshwater fish, eggs normally hatch from 24 hours to five days after spawning, depending on the species and the ambient temperature. Hatching is followed by a larval stage, during which the fry slowly absorb their yolk sac and are helpless and at the end of which they become capable of independent motion ('free-swimming').

In parental species the process is best conducted under the supervision of the parent(s). Indeed, there is some evidence that fry of at least some parental species require to be 'parented' in order properly to care for their own offspring in due course, and it is thus extremely unwise to hatch the eggs of such fish artificially, even – especially – if they abandon or eat them. For example, in the angelfish, *Pterophyllum scalare*, a naturally parental species, the brood care instinct seems to have been effectively bred out of aquarium populations by failure to select parental stock,

Developing larvae. They are beginning to look like tiny fish, but still have a large amount of yolk sac to absorb.

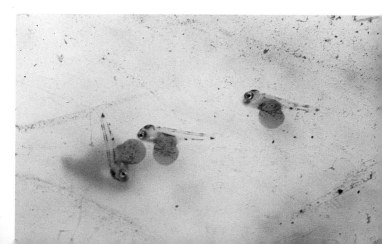

and by artificially hatching the eggs of non-parental adults.

In the case of species which do not practise parental care, hatching must be assisted by the aquarist. Water in the hatching container should be taken from the breeding aquarium so as to ensure an exact match in chemistry, or the eggs hatched in that aquarium. If the eggs are moved, they must not be exposed to air.

Hygiene in the hatching container is paramount. It is usual to treat the water with a BACTERICIDE (3) and/or FUNGICIDE (3), preferably one which degrades naturally over a short period (METHYLENE BLUE [3] is a common choice) to avoid unnecessary and possibly harmful medication of larvae and tiny fry. although in practice eggs do not normally succumb to FUNGUS (3) or BACTERIA (3) unless they are infertile or infected by adjacent infertile eggs. The whitening of initially transparent eggs is, in fact, caused by internal decomposition when unfertilised eggs fail to develop, rather than by external agency. However, such eggs may contaminate healthy ones, and should be carefully pricked out with a needle or similar, before EGG FUNGUS (3) has a chance to develop. Gentle aeration should be provided, so that the resulting current draws water over the eggs, maintaining an oxygen supply and preventing any suspended matter from settling on and contaminating them. The eggs should not, however, be placed in the stream of air bubbles, which may dislodge or otherwise damage them.

After the larvae have hatched any unhatched eggs should be removed. No food should be offered until the fry are free-swimming – prior to this they will be living on their yolk sacs, and artificial foods will simply contaminate the container.

CARE OF NEWLY-HATCHED FRY

Fry hatched in a mature aquarium, for example with their parents, will commonly find naturally occurring micro-organisms as their first food, and continue to forage from this source when nothing else is available. Fry hatched under relatively sterile conditions must be fed as soon as they become free-swimming. Common first foods are cultured micro-organisms (infusorians) for very small fry, while larger types, and those under parental care, can

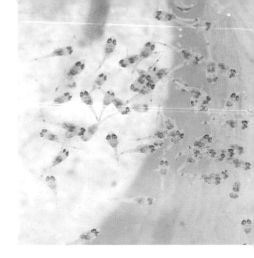

Newly free-swimming fry. It is evident that they have been fed on Artemia nauplii - their still-clear bellies are orange and Artemia eggshells can be seen floating in the bowl. These need to be removed before they decay.

usually take microworm and/or newly hatched *Artemia* (brine shrimp) nauplii. Many fry die of starvation, and probably just as many through pollution from overfeeding. Care must be taken to achieve a balance. *Artemia* nauplii are a particularly good food as their orange coloration is visible in the normally transparent bellies of the fry, providing an indication of whether or not the latter are feeding adequately. Water quality should be monitored at least daily, and small partial changes made on a daily or twice daily basis, always using water of matched chemistry and temperature. Not only are fry sensitive to tiny fluctuations in water chemistry and temperature, and to small amounts of toxicity (from both nitrogenous wastes and any other toxins present), but they also initially lack a fully developed immune system and are thus, initially, more vulnerable to infectious diseases.

A "bulb baster" (from kitchen or hardware stores) is invaluable when hatching fry. It can be used for moving eggs, larvae, or fry, for squirting Artemia nauplii into a shoal of fry, or for making small water changes on breeding containers. Because it is intended for food use it is made of non-toxic materials.

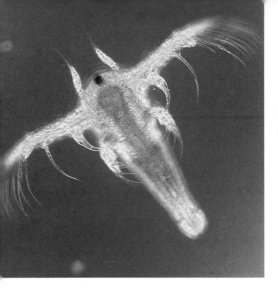

Photomicrograph of an Artemia nauplius.

Some fry may need to fill their swim bladders with atmospheric air initially, while those with accessory breathing organs will likewise need access to air above the surface. If this air is significantly cooler than the aquarium water it may cause (terminal) damage to delicate structures, so not only should an air space be left above the water's surface when breeding such species, but the tank or container should be tightly covered to retain warmth.

GROWING ON

It is essential to maintain good aquarium hygiene during the growing-on period, and to allow adequate space for the number of fry to be reared, even if this means restricting that number in accordance with the space available.

There is evidence that some fish may produce growth-retardant pheromones, either to limit size relative to population density, or, in some cases, the dominant individuals secrete such chemicals in order to limit the growth of potential rivals. The amateur will be unable to detect such substances, but regular partial water changes will help reduce their levels if they are present.

A heavy diet of growth (protein-rich) foods will produce faster growth, but possibly at the expense of water quality problems, which may retard it, and cause ill-health. A sensible balance should be achieved – fast growth is not the be-all and end-all. Specially formulated fry foods are available, and, once they are large enough, the fry can be fed many food items offered to adult fish. Numerous small feeds are preferable to occasional large ones. *(See also Section I: Nutrition.)*

Excess numbers of fry should be CULLED (3), together with any that are deformed, exhibit abnormal behaviour, or are stunted. In some species disparate growth rate is normal, commonly between the sexes, so never assume that smaller individuals are necessarily runts. Most culling should take place while the fry are still quite small and can be disposed of by feeding them to adult fish – as would happen to the bulk of any brood in nature. Any rejects too large to be disposed of in this way must be humanely despatched (see EUTHANASIA [3]).

PROBLEMS ASSOCIATED WITH REPRODUCTION
LIVEBEARER CANNIBALISM
Livebearer fry are extremely likely to be cannibalised, including by their mother, immediately after birth, or even during birth. The normal method of preventing this is to use a 'breeding trap', a container into which the gravid female is placed when parturition is imminent, and which has small apertures through which the fry can escape to safety in the tank below. This type of breeding trap is intended for use in otherwise untenanted aquaria; another type is available for community use, with a special chamber into which the fry can escape, but this is not large enough to house them for long, and they should be removed as soon as possible. Likewise females should not be kept in traps any longer than is necessary.

PRECOCIOUS BREEDING
In nature female fish – both livebearers and egglayers – probably breed as soon as they are capable of doing so. This is not necessarily desirable in the aquarium, particularly where breeding is possible at an age where siblings may still be housed together. The problem is common in poeciliid livebearers, but also in some egg-layers. Where it is likely, the sexes should be housed separately as soon as they can be differentiated. It should also be borne in mind that each episode of egg/fry production in a young female is likely to cause a check in growth.

In the wild it is highly unlikely that young males will have an opportunity to breed, because of competition from larger, stronger, older and fully grown males. In captivity infertility of first clutches from young females may be a problem where the male is also young, and not yet able to produce milt, although he may go through the motions of spawning. This can have long term ill-effects; in particular it can lead to habitual egg cannibalism in normally parental species, the habit being acquired through eating the infertile eggs when they fail to hatch. The solution is to use a mature male, or keep the sexes separate until both are fully mature.

PATERNITY IN LIVEBEARERS

Once inseminated by a male – a process that can occur very early on in young sibling fish – female livebearers commonly store sperm which is used to fertilise eggs for some months. Thus, unless a female is known to be virgin, or has been isolated until she ceases producing fry (sperm store exhausted), there is no guarantee that the selected male will be the father of any fry produced.

BREEDING-RELATED AGGRESSION.

AGGRESSION [3] (including sexually motivated harassment of females by males, and occasionally *vice versa*) is not normally a serious problem in the wild, where attacked or harassed fish have the option of leaving the scene. Within the confines of the aquarium, however, there is no escape, and there may be serious consequences – injury or death – unless the aquarist is vigilant. Males, and occasionally females, may continually pursue a potential partner which is not yet ready to spawn. Particular care must be taken where breeding stock is (temporarily) placed in small breeding aquaria, where there may be no opportunity to escape the harassment. The fish must be kept under supervision and returned to their normal quarters if it becomes apparent that one or both partners are not yet ready to spawn. Similar harassment may take place among livebearers, which, for this reason, should not be kept in too small aquaria. Over-enthusiastic males may sometimes need to be removed, especially just after a female has given birth, when she is more susceptible to mating.

Parental species, in particular cichlids, can give rise to a whole host of aggression problems, many connected with their brood care and territoriality:

- They may attack and injure/kill other fish in defence of their eggs/fry.
- With pair-bonding species, fighting may occur before the bond is established. This may be a matter of establishing individual territories, or of a potential pair testing out each other's fitness for parenthood, i.e. vigour, plus ability and willingness to defend territory and brood.
- With non-bonding species, for example many mouth-brooding cichlids, unripe females entering male territories – and tank size may give them no option – are likely to be continuously pursued (initially in courtship, ultimately in frustration), and possibly killed.
- Apparently bonded pairs may fall out for a number of reasons: loss of the brood, disturbance by the aquarist or other factors, and, where only the pair are present, the need of the male to defensively attack something, the female being the only available target.

Cichlids, the main offenders, are an extremely popular group because of their interesting behaviour, and a number of specialist books are available, providing details of the 'antisocial' behaviour to be expected in individual genera/species and methods of controlling it. Any attempt to breed cichlids should be preceded by consultation of one or more such books. *(See also Section I: Fish Compatibility.)*

OVERBREEDING

It may also be advisable or necessary to force an interval between breeding episodes, in species which spawn year-round. The normal abundance of the aquarium food supply may cause more rapid egg production and ripening, and hence more frequent spawning, than nature intended. Such species should be kept on low rations; simply isolating females to prevent spawning may sometimes lead to SPAWN BINDING (3).

Without such rest periods, the health of females may be compromised by chronic STRESS (3), not only from the repeated spawning act, but also from the sometimes almost continuous courtship of the males. Similarly, female livebearers should also be allowed to rest between broods, away from the often continuous advances of the male fish.

SPAWN BINDING
If a female is physically unable to lay her eggs for some reason, or to shed/resorb them if spawning is inappropriate (no partner; wrong environmental conditions), then she may suffer from SPAWN BINDING (3). This is a serious condition, as the eggs may ultimately degenerate and cause internal BACTERIAL INFECTION (3) of the reproductive tract, and, probably, death. Provision of a suitable breeding partner is the obvious preventative/solution in most cases. Intervention by the aquarist, by physically expelling the eggs from the female – a process commonly known as 'hand-stripping' – should be carried out only by an expert. In general, hand-stripping is inadvisable for use on very small fish (as a guide, those under five cm) as it may cause damage to the delicate internal organs, sometimes leading to death.

INFERTILITY
REPRODUCTIVE FAILURE (3) is commonly caused by infertility, which may be temporary or permanent, and due to a number of causes:
1) Genetic defect. This may be natural; or in some cases the stock may have been genetically sterilised, for commercial reasons.
2) Inappropriate water chemistry/quality or other environmental problems.
3) Side-effect of medication (possibly permanent).
4) Immature breeding stock, or stock too old.
5) Stock are all of the same sex. Even if eggs are laid, this could be due to two females 'pairing' in the absence of a male (not obvious in sexually isomorphic species).
If the problem proves long-term, and 2) and 5) have been ruled out or rectified, then replacement of stock is the only solution.

HYBRIDISATION
Crosses between species, or even genera, within a family of fish are not uncommon, particularly where they are closely related. Such crosses are largely an aquarium phenomenon, where co-housing of similar, normally allopatric, species, or other breakdown of natural barriers to cross-breeding, may result in hybrids.

The following are common causes of hybridisation:

● Absence of a conspecific breeding partner coupled with the presence of a closely related heterospecific of the opposite sex. Such mismatches should be terminated immediately, otherwise species mate-recognition criteria may be compromised and the individuals concerned subsequently fail to accept conspecific breeding partners.

● Lack of discrimination in partner choice in species of similar appearance and/or closely related, for example poeciliid livebearers, Lake Victoria cichlids. Such species should not be mixed.

● Inability of a breeding male to out-compete interested males of other, closely-related, species (common in some groups, for example Lake Malawi cichlids, where lack of natural selection has led to loss of vigour). If a wild male of the same species could reasonably be expected to hold his own against the opposition in question, then the defective male should not be used for breeding purposes.

Whatever their provenance, hybrids should be destroyed immediately, ideally at the egg stage, and steps taken to prevent any repetition. They should never be sold. It is virtually impossible to do so without dishonesty on the part of breeder or dealer or both, as there is no genuine market for casual hybrids. In addition, their release onto the market under any guise can only add to the confusion which already surrounds the identification of many aquarium fish.

Chapter Nine

TREATING FISH DISEASES

The diagnosis and treatment of diseases of pet fish is usually undertaken by the owner, sometimes following consultation with aquarium shop staff or more experienced hobbyists. Only rarely are veterinary surgeons or fish health specialists consulted. In this respect, the health management of pet fish contrasts markedly with that afforded to other pets, such as cats and dogs, where veterinary advice is usually sought. The reason for this difference relates largely to the low value of aquarium fish, particularly freshwater species, many of which sell for little more than the price of a chocolate or candy bar: only a small proportion of aquarists are prepared to pay high veterinary consultation fees for a fish which is worth only a fraction of the cost. Another influencing factor is people's perception of fish as being "cold, feeling-less creatures". Many aquarists believe that fish cannot experience pain and therefore do not require the same level of tender loving care as that given to mammals and birds. In turn the lack of demand for veterinary advice means that few vets routinely provide a service for fish, or, indeed, have the necessary knowledge and experience to do so.

This situation is far from ideal, not least because the vast majority of aquarium hobbyists have no formal training in fish disease diagnosis and treatment. As a result, it is commonplace for aquarists to select an inappropriate remedy, or worse still, to administer a series or a combination of different remedies in the hope that one will work. In other cases the sick fish may be needlessly destroyed when, in fact, a successful cure could have been effected.

Nevertheless, unless the retail price of aquarium fish rises dramatically, which is not foreseen, then disease treatment seems likely to remain largely within the hands of the aquarium owner. The aquarist should, nevertheless, seek out a local veterinarian who is prepared to provide any professional assistance that may be necessary, for example as regards EUTHANASIA (3) and the supply of medications not available 'over-the-counter' at the aquarium retailer's or local pharmacy (see below). It is prudent to arrange for this service to be available before it is actually required.

CORRECT DIAGNOSIS AND PROMPT TREATMENT

Bear in mind that many fish diseases are capable of spreading rapidly and can kill the fish within a few days. In these situations, the faster the treatment is applied, the better the prognosis for the fish. However, in no circumstances should a treatment be given without first ensuring that the disease has been correctly identified and that the treatment is appropriate for the disease in question.

It must be emphasised once again that the vast majority of aquarium fish health problems stem from poor aquarium hygiene, usually coupled with adverse water chemistry, rather than from infectious disease. With this in mind, always perform basic water tests *(see Section I: The Correct Environment)* before considering an infectious disease as the problem. Even when the fish show recognisable signs of an infectious disease, such as white SPOTS (2), it is still worth performing water tests, since adverse environmental conditions may be responsible for triggering the disease outbreak in the first place.

THE FISH MEDICINE CABINET

For most aquarists, it is not necessary to stock up with disease treatments. To do so carries the risk that the commercial stock solutions will be stored for long periods, causing some to degrade with time and lose their efficacy (not all manufacturers supply an expiry date for their products). The use of out-of-date remedies may also, under certain circumstances, contribute to the emergence of drug resistance by fish pathogens. Moreover, the availability of medications all too often leads to the temptation to use them, even where no diagnosis has been possible, in the hope of a chance cure. In practice, the opposite effect is more likely, especially if the problem is environmental.

In some situations, however, it may be prudent to stock a basic selection of disease remedies and associated equipment, just in case a fish health problem arises. This may be useful if the aquarist keeps many aquaria and frequently acquires new stock (and hence the risk of a disease outbreak is increased) or where he does not have ready access to an aquarium store or other supplier of disease remedies.

Useful items for the fish medicine chest include:

● Stock solutions of treatments for ECTOPARASITES (3), BACTERIAL INFECTIONS (3), and FUNGUS (3).

● Sodium chloride (NaCl, common salt, pure grade – but not table salt which may contain anticoagulants) or physiological salt mixes (from the aquarium store).

● Basic water test kits: AMMONIA (3), NITRITE (3), NITRATE (3), pH.

● Water conditioner (CHLORINE/CHLORAMINE (3) remover).

● Pipette (for dispensing drops of liquid remedies).

● Small measuring cylinder, e.g. 25 or 50 ml capacity, calibrated in 1 ml gradations (for measuring small volumes of liquid remedies).

● Artist's paintbrush or cotton buds (swabsticks) for topical application.

In addition, a spare 'hospital' aquarium (say, 2 to 5 gallons/9-23 litres capacity) is useful for administering short-term bath remedies and/or where only one or two fish need to be treated. It is worth keeping a note of the volume of the aquarium, so that the correct dose of remedy can be quickly calculated.

SAFETY PRECAUTIONS
HANDLING MEDICATIONS

Many fish disease remedies and water testing reagents are potentially toxic to humans, especially when in concentrated liquid form or as powders. Fortunately, most countries provide legislation on handling hazardous chemicals and this requires that warning notices and safety precautions be printed on the medication packs, where

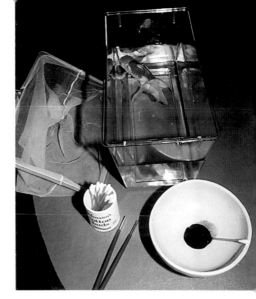

Ensure all necessary equipment is available before starting treatment. In this case, an anchor worm (Lernaea) is to be removed using forceps.

Photo: Dr David Ford.

necessary. It is wise, however, to assume that all remedies and reagents are potentially toxic, unless specifically stated otherwise by the manufacturer. As a general precaution, wear rubber gloves (e.g. washing-up gloves) when dispensing such chemicals. In the event of contact with the skin, wash off immediately; if the eyes are affected rinse away with copious cold water and seek medical assistance without delay.

Ensure that children are unable to reach the chemical disease treatments and other reagents. Do not hesitate to seek medical advice if it is known or suspected that a chemical has been accidentally swallowed.

A few chemical treatments should be handled with particular care:

● MALACHITE GREEN (3), particularly in the dry powder form which could be accidentally inhaled.

● FORMALIN (3) (sometimes used to treat parasitic infections) is a skin, eye, and respiratory irritant and should be handled in well-ventilated rooms. Stock bottles containing neat formalin (which is a 37-40 per cent solution of formaldehyde gas) should therefore be opened with special care.

● HYDROGEN PEROXIDE (3). Similar precautions as for formalin are required when handling strong solutions of this chemical. Commercial strength solutions (usually 3 per cent solution) are far less hazardous.

STAIN DAMAGE

Several of the dye-based remedies, such as ACRIFLAVIN (3), METHYLENE BLUE (3), GENTIAN VIOLET (3), and MALACHITE GREEN (3), as well as some water testing reagents, may irrevocably stain clothing, carpets, and household furnishings. It is wise to open all bottles over a sink.

STORAGE OF REMEDIES AND OTHER CHEMICALS

In general, chemical remedies and water testing reagents will have a longer shelf-life when stored under cool conditions. Certain chemicals, including several ANTIBIOTICS (3), should be stored in a refrigerator. Others, such as the powder form of the anaesthetic TRICAINE METHANESULPHONATE (3), must be stored below freezing. Refer to the product label or leaflet for any specific storage recommendations.

Certain chemicals are photo-sensitive and may degrade if exposed to sunshine or bright light, examples being certain antibiotics, for example OXYTETRACYCLINE (3) and the anaesthetic TRICAINE METHANESULPHONATE (3). Such reagents should be stored in brown-glass bottles. Check with the product instructions.

All medications should be properly labelled, and in the domestic environment it is a wise precaution to keep them under lock and key.

THE CORRECT USE OF DRUGS

It is essential, for the well-being of the fish, and sometimes of the aquarist, to follow precisely any instructions (safety, dosage, and administration) provided by the veterinarian, drug manufacturer, pharmacist, or reference material.

Treatment should be undertaken only where it has been possible to make a reliable diagnosis of the disease. Many chemical treatments are mildly toxic to fish, and although when used for the correct purpose, their benefits outweigh any disadvantages, they should never be used unnecessarily or randomly. To do so is pointless and dangerous; especially where, as is regrettasbly often the case, a number of medications are administered in succession, or even simultaneously, as is regrettably often the case, in the hope of a chance cure. A more probable result is the POISON-

ING (3) of the fish by the direct effect of the chemical (combination), or through its deleterious effects on the biological filtration.

The indiscriminate use of antibiotics and some other drugs is known to increase the likelihood of drug resistance by fish pathogens: indeed, the emergence of antibiotic resistance among certain strains of fish-pathogenic bacteria is of major concern to the ornamental fish industry.

DISPOSAL OF CHEMICALS
Any surplus, date-expired, or otherwise unwanted chemicals or drugs should be disposed of safely in consultation with a veterinarian or pharmacist. They should never be poured down a drain or included in the domestic rubbish where they may contaminate the environment or pose a risk to other people.

DISPOSAL OF DEAD FISH
Dead fish should be buried, burned, or well wrapped in polythene and disposed of in the domestic rubbish. They should not be fed to other fish, or animals, because of the risk of spreading disease or, if the dead fish has been medicated, inadvertently dosing the predator. Fish suspected of suffering from MYCOBACTERIA (3) infection (fish tuberculosis) should be handled with care because of the possibility of ZOONOSIS (3).

SOURCES OF CHEMICALS AND MEDICATIONS
The do-it-yourself approach to treating aquarium fish diseases has prompted several pet product manufacturers to develop a wide range of disease remedies which can be purchased over the counter at aquarium and pet stores, rather than having to be obtained via a vet. The majority of commonly encountered fish pathogens can be treated using these remedies. Unfortunately not all have the effect claimed, and because the chemical composition of these formulations is not always given on the bottle (whether or not such information is disclosed may depend on legislation in a particular country), the aquarist may have no way of knowing exactly what he is adding to his aquarium.

If a proprietary treatment, administered as per the instructions, proves ineffective, and the diagnosis is certain, then it may be necessary to resort to the use of specific drugs or chemicals; likewise if it is necessary or desirable to know exactly what drug or chemical is being used. In such situations it will generally be necessary to obtain the requisite medication from a vet, pharmacist, or other supplier.

In some countries, certain fish disease medications, such as ANTIBIOTICS (3), are available only on veterinary prescription, although they can be purchased freely over the counter elsewhere, for example in the USA. Because of the danger of encouraging drug resistance, it is strongly advised that such drugs be used conservatively and with informed knowledge, ideally following veterinary advice.

ACQUIRING REAGENTS

Although commercial fish breeders, large wholesale and retail outlets, and vets may wish to obtain bulk supplies of chemicals from the manufacturer, the average aquarist will normally require only a small amount. Some chemicals, e.g. METHYLENE BLUE (3), are available from aquatic retailers, otherwise the best approach is to consult a pharmacist, who will generally have (or be able to obtain) the requisite grade of chemical (for human use), and be able to provide the stock solution needed, in a suitable, properly labelled, container. It may be necessary to explain what the chemical is required for, especially in the case of highly toxic substances such as FORMALIN (3). A vet may also be able to help in this respect.

The various chemical ingredients in commercially formulated remedies are carefully chosen for their high purity. If, however, it is necessary to acquire chemicals directly from chemical suppliers (such as BDH or Sigma Chemical Co.) then it is very important to select high purity grade reagents (sometimes referred to as 'Analar' grade) rather than the cheaper 'technical grade' reagents which may contain potentially ichthyotoxic (poisonous to fish) impurities.

Some chemicals are available in pure powder or crystal form, for example METHYLENE BLUE (3) and POTASSIUM PERMANGANATE (3). These will require considerable dilution in order to achieve a working strength solution. It will usually be necessary to measure milligram quantities of these powder reagents, and this will require a highly sensitive (and expensive) chemical balance.

A background in chemistry is valuable when selecting and preparing one's own reagents. It should be mentioned that some chemicals are available from specialist chemical supply companies in a variety of salts or in hydrated form, and these may differ in efficacy or solubility. If in doubt seek professional advice.

TREATMENT

DOSING AND ADMINISTRATION ROUTES
1) VIA THE AQUARIUM WATER
Most disease remedies are added to the water (e.g. bath immersion) rather than being applied directly, externally or internally (orally or by injection), to the fish.

Nowadays a wide range of chemical remedies of this type is commercially available for treating most of the commonly encountered aquarium fish diseases, such that it is rare for the aquarist to have to prepare his own chemical treatment. A common exception is the preparation of a sodium chloride (SALT [3]) bath. It is generally far safer to use a commercially prepared treatment, where available, instead of trying to prepare one's own formulation. The use of incorrect or unpurified raw chemicals could result in fish deaths due to toxic effects of the impurities; moreover a sensitive chemical balance and other expensive laboratory equipment may be required, such that home-made remedies are not always cost-effective, even if correctly prepared.

Most commercial disease remedies are sold in liquid form which makes them easy to dispense. These commercial preparations are almost always supplied in a highly concentrated form – the stock solution – which must be diluted in order to achieve a safe, working strength (= working solution) in which the fish is then treated. The manufacturer usually provides detailed instructions regarding the amount of stock solution required for each litre or gallon of aquarium water. Commercial stock solutions are usually supplied in a dropper bottle or with either a dropper pipette or a calibrated vial, in order to allow a precise volume of liquid to be dispensed.

DURATION OF TREATMENT

This type of treatment may be either of long or short duration. Certain remedies must be applied over a prolonged period of time – usually for one or more days or, in some cases, for several weeks. Long-duration baths are necessary for combating pathogens which produce long-lived cyst or egg stages which may be impervious to chemical treatments.

Some chemical treatments are, however, effective within a short period of exposure, sometimes minutes or a few hours. Moreover, some disease remedies are significantly toxic to fish, especially when applied at the high concentrations necessary to kill some pathogens. Long-duration exposure to such chemicals may cause the fish tissue damage or even death. In these situations the fish should be exposed to the remedy for only as long as it takes to eradicate the disease: in such cases a short-duration bath is utilised, usually applied to fish in isolation, away from the main tank.

OXYGEN LEVELS

Some disease remedies, including FORMALIN (3) and PHENOXYETHANOL (3), may cause a reduction in the amount of dissolved oxygen in the water which should be compensated by increasing the level of aeration, where necessary. For the same reason aeration should also be increased where a rise in TEMPERATURE (3) forms part of the treatment, or where the fish exhibit RESPIRATORY DISTRESS (2).

REPEAT DOSING

When using reagents which have a short working life under aquatic conditions it may be necessary to redose from time to time in order to maintain an effective concentration. This may apply when performing long-duration baths and sometimes when treating the entire aquarium population *in situ*. The manufacturer will indicate if redosing is necessary and provide guidelines. Sometimes this takes the form of partial redosing, for example adding a further half dose or quarter dose every few days.

REMOVAL OF REAGENTS

In the case of persistent chemicals (that is, those which do not degrade in the aquarium within a few days) it may be necessary to undertake several partial water changes in order to dilute out the remedy from the aquarium at the end of the treatment period. A partial water change is also sometimes required between repeat treatments. Alternatively, certain chemical filter media (e.g. activated carbon) can be used to remove some medications; obviously if such media are in normal use then they will need to be removed for the duration of treatment with any relevant medication. For this reason the use of carbon and other chemical media in biological filters is inadvisable, as their removal, along with their bacterial population, is likely adversely to affect the efficiency of the system.

METHODS OF TREATMENT

Treatments added to the water may be administered by:
● bath immersion (usually performed by removing the sick fish to a small 'hospital' tank to which the treatment is added);
● adding the treatment directly to the stocked aquarium (thus the entire fish population, both sick and apparently healthy fish, are treated *in situ*).

In either case it is very important partly to dilute the stock solution in a small quantity of aquarium water before adding to the aquarium. Failure to do so may result in the fish being exposed to concentrated reagent should it, or they, happen to swim to the region of the aquarium where the stock solution is being added – exposure to undiluted disease remedies could prove fatal.

BATH IMMERSION

Sometimes it is preferable to treat one or more fish in isolation. Dosing the fish in a hospital tank should be undertaken only in situations where the pathogen is not highly infective (or has a limited host range) and is unlikely to be present as a free-living stage within the main aquarium. Certain systemic infections which are not highly contagious may be treated this way. In the case of short-duration baths, treatment of the fish in an isolation tank may obviate problems of inactivation of bio-filters by the chemical remedy. In the case of very expensive treatments,

Short-term bath in a bucket, with aeration (airstone).

A large aquarium net, with a saucer in the bottom to keep it spread and weighted, can form an impromptu nursery, prison, or hospital if no other tank is available. It cannot, of course, be used for quarantine or where medication of the water is required.

such as some ANTIBIOTICS (3), it may be necessary to transfer the sick fish to a smaller aquarium in order to minimise the amount of drug required.

The fish should be closely monitored during bath treatments, especially when using toxic chemicals. If the fish show excessive signs of STRESS (3), commonly manifesting as a loss of BALANCE (2), severe RESPIR-ATORY DISTRESS (2), or an escape response such as JUMPING (2) out of the water, then they should be removed from the bath and returned to unmedicated water – that is, returned to the main aquarium.

TREATING THE ENTIRE AQUARIUM

In the case of many infectious diseases it will be necessary to treat the stock *in situ,* rather than removing some or all of them to a treatment aquarium. This is important when combating pathogens which are able to survive off the fish and which may be present in the aquarium water or living in or on the substrate, rockwork, plants, filter, and other furnishings and equipment.

When dosing the whole aquarium, consideration must be given to the potential damaging effects of the disease remedy on the biological filter. Some disease remedies may also be harmful to aquatic plants or aquatic invertebrates (e.g. freshwater crabs and shrimps) and even some fish. The manufacturer will usually indicate if the remedy has any potential side-effects.

2) SURFACE (TOPICAL) APPLICATION

Certain DISINFECTANTS (3) can be applied topically – that is, painted onto affected areas of the body or fins. MERCUROCHROME (3) and IODINE (3) compounds, used for disinfecting WOUNDS (3) and ULCERS (3), are administered this way. Applying a topical treatment entails first removing the fish from the water and placing it on a wet cloth or towel. Small fish can be restrained within the aquarium net. Ensure that the fish is firmly but gently held so as to prevent excessive struggling or escape. Placing a strip of wet cloth over the fish's eyes may have a calming effect. The topical treatment is applied gently with a fine brush (e.g. artist's brush) or a cotton-wool swabstick. Return the fish to water as soon as possible.

3) ORAL APPLICATION

A few disease treatments are administered orally, in most cases via the food (= medicated food). In the case of medium to large fish (say, above 8 cm length) the treatment may be delivered by stomach tube. The tube itself should be narrow-bore soft flexible tubing which is fitted over a syringe needle and then attached to a syringe barrel. Insertion of the stomach tube, which must be carefully and gently navigated so as to avoid the gill arches, requires great skill and should be performed only by a vet or other suitably qualified person.

Remedies which are sometimes incorporated with the food include OXOLINIC ACID (3) (an antimicrobial) and several of the ANTIBIOTICS (3). Orally administered remedies are usually aimed at internal infections. Generally, however, oral medication is infrequently used for aquarium fish.

Medicated foods normally have to be specially prepared, sometimes by a veterinary surgeon or fish health specialist, or by the aquarist himself, using drugs obtained from the veterinarian. A few commercial medicated foods are available to aquarists in certain countries (e.g. commercial pellet or flake foods impregnated with MALACHITE GREEN (3) or ANTIBIOTICS [3]).

There are certain disadvantages to using medicated feeds. For instance, fish which are sick may lose their APPETITE (2) and therefore cannot be treated by this method. Correct dosing is also difficult, especially when treating several fish together, as some individuals inevitably take more food (and hence more medication) than others.

Calculating the dose rate is not quite as simple as that for bath treatments, since the amount of drug required will depend on the size of the fish and its daily food intake. Fortunately, dose rates have been worked out for most of the commonly applied medicated feeds used for treating aquarium fish. These are usually expressed as the amount of drug (usually in milligram or gram quantities) per weight of food (dosages are given for individual drugs in Section III). The fish is then offered one or more medicated feeds per day over a given number of days, as appropriate.

(Note: in foodfish aquaculture the dose is generally based on the weight of the fish – for example one milligram of drug per kilogram body weight. The amount of drug to be offered will depend on the expected consumption rate of food – as an average, fish are considered to eat the equivalent of 1 per cent of their body weight each day. Such calculations are difficult to apply accurately in the case of small aquarium fish weighing just a few grams).

Where it is necessary to prepare one's own medicated feed, the drug can easily be incorporated in dry pellet foods, using a size grade of pellet appropriate for the fish in question. The drug is first diluted in a small volume of water and is then soaked into the dry food. Sometimes a gelatin solution is used to assist binding of the drug to the food (this helps minimise the drug leaching into the aquarium water).

Owing to their high moisture content, 'dry foods' which have been soaked with drugs are susceptible to spoilage with moulds (see AFLATOXINS [3]): they should therefore be stored at low temperature, ideally in the freezer. For larger fish the solution of the medication can be injected into earthworms, which may prove more tempting to a sick fish than dry food.

4) INJECTION

A number of ANTIBIOTICS (3) and certain other drugs are sometimes administered by injection; however, this is feasible only in the case of fish which exceed approximately 5 cm in length.

Injecting fish is a specialised skill and should be undertaken only by a vet or other fish health specialist. Both the drug and carrier solution (e.g. saline/water) must be sterile. The drug is usually delivered intra-peritoneally (i.p.) or intra-muscularly (i.m.), the precise site being carefully determined to avoid accidental damage to the gut or vital organs. The dosage rate is usually based on the body weight of the fish.

Injecting a fish is a highly specialised skill.

REST AND RECUPERATION

Fish sometimes benefit from isolation in the hospital tank, without the need for any medication, for example in cases of STRESS (3), SHOCK (3), exhaustion, and stress-induced loss of APPETITE (3), or for a post-spawning rest.

FACTORS GOVERNING CHOICE OF TREATMENT

Often a particular treatment can be administered by only a single route, but it is not uncommon for a choice of treatments, administered via different routes, to be available. In such cases the aquarist should weigh up the advantages and disadvantages of the different modes of treatment. For example, if territorial fish such as cichlids are kept, any individual isolated for more than a day or two will lose its territory/status in the main aquarium, and is likely to be attacked and injured (or even killed) by tankmates on re-introduction. If treatment can be effected without isolation, then so much the better.

The following table summarises the major advantages and disadvantages of different methods of treatment.

TABLE 4

ADVANTAGES AND DISADVANTAGES OF DIFFERENT METHODS OF TREATMENT

(a) DOSING THE NORMAL AQUARIUM
Advantages: Minimal disturbance/STRESS (3). Eliminates off-fish pathogens. No problems re-introducing fish to main aquarium.
Disadvantages: May affect filtration. May medicate healthy fish. May kill plants. Not possible if some fish are intolerant of the medication.

(b) HOSPITAL AQUARIUM
Advantages: Peace and quiet for sick fish. Avoids the disadvantages of (a). May be easier to to provide optimal conditions for treatment.
Disadvantages: Stress of move and strange environment. Stress of eventual re-introduction to main aquarium/ tankmate AGGRESSION (3).

(c) SHORT-TERM BATH
Advantages: Avoids the disadvantages of (a). Sometimes more effective than longer-term more dilute medication. Fish can often be returned immediately to familiar environment.
Disadvantages: May cause STRESS (3)/SHOCK (3).

(d) TOPICAL TREATMENT
Advantages: Avoids the disadvantages of (a). Has the

advantages of (c). Treats only the affected area. No environmental side-effects.
Disadvantages: Handling causes stress, but less so than a strange environment.

(e) MEDICATED FEED
Advantages: Stress-free. No environmental side-effects. Optimum method for certain gut infections.
Disadvantages: Unaffected fish treated. Difficult to obtain. Sick fish lose appetite. Difficult to dose fish accurately due to variable appetites.

(f) INJECTION
Advantages: Avoids disadvantages of (a). Has advantages of (c). No environmental side-effects.
Disadvantages: Requires professional assistance. Not for small fish. Likely to cause stress.

CALCULATING DOSAGES

AQUARIUM VOLUME
The capacity of a rectangular aquarium is calculated by multiplying its internal dimensions (length x width x height) in inches or centimetres, to give its volume in cubic inches or cubic centimetres. 1 cubic foot (144 cu.ins) contains 6.23 imperial gallons, while 1,000 cubic centimetres = 1 litre.

When treating furnished aquaria – that is those containing substrate and/or decor – allowance should be made for the water displacement caused by these furnishings. A more precise value can be derived by using a bucket which is calibrated or of known volume to fill the furnished aquarium when first set up, or, in the case of large aquaria, by filling from a clean hosepipe connected to a water meter, if available. Record the volume for future reference. Such methods are also useful when dealing with non-rectangular aquaria.

WEIGHING FISH
(e.g. for oral medication or injection)
Scientific chemical balances will be required to weight very small fish (under 5-10 g). For larger fish (say, above 10 g) a good-quality top-pan letter scales, sensitive to 0.5g or 1g

accuracy, may be used. Weighing fish out of water can cause stress, and the fish will invariably struggle so that an accurate weight determination is difficult. It is preferable to weigh the fish in water, as follows: first weigh a small jar or other vessel containing a small volume of aquarium water (sufficient to comfortably house the fish for the brief weighing session); then add the fish to the container, using a net, and re-weigh. The difference corresponds to the weight of the fish.

For example:

Weight of container plus water = 267 g

Weight of container plus water plus fish = 276 g

Therefore, weight of fish = 9 g

CALCULATING DOSAGES
WORKED EXAMPLES

Example 1
We need to treat 54 litres of water with a liquid disease remedy to be administered at the rate of 1 part per thousand (1 ppt).

Procedure: we know that 1 ppt = 1 ml per litre. Thus, we need to add 54 ml of the remedy to treat the aquarium.

Example 2
We need to treat 100 litres of water with a commercial liquid remedy at the rate of two drops per gallon (imperial gallon).

Procedure: first convert the aquarium volume into imperial gallons. One litre is approximately 0.22 gallons (Table 5), thus 100 x 0.22 = 22 imperial gallons. To achieve a dose rate of 2 drops per gallon, we must therefore add 44 drops to the aquarium water (22 x 2 = 44).

Example 3
A 28 g fish needs to be injected with 15 mg of antibiotic per kilogram body weight. Procedure: The stock solution of antibiotic is 5 mg per ml in sterile saline. Amount of antibiotic required = 28 divided by 1000 x 15 = 0.42 mg. If the stock solution contains 5 mg per ml then we need to inject 0.42 divided by 5 = 0.084 ml (= 84 microlitres).

Note: if the injectable volume is too small to be accurately administered then some of the stock solution can be further diluted as required.

TABLE 5
WEIGHTS AND MEASURES

Imperial
1 imperial gallon* of water weighs 10lbs
1 lb = 16 oz
1 lb = 0.454 kilos
1 cubic foot of water = 6.23 gallons
1 imperial gallon = 4.55 litres*
1 pint = 0.568 litres
*1 US gallon = approximately 0.8 of an Imperial gallon or
3.79 litres

1 inch = 2.54 cm

Metric
1 litre of water weighs 1 kilo
1 kilo = 1,000 g
1 kilo = 2.205 lb
1000 cc (ml) = 1 litre
1 litre = 0.2198 gallons
1 litre = 1.756 pints

1 cm = 0.3937 inches

SECTION II

SIGNS OF DISEASES
AND HEALTH
PROBLEMS

HOW TO USE THIS SECTION

Diagnosis of a particular condition or disease in fish is rarely simple; only in a few rare circumstances is there a single diagnostic sign pointing to a particular ailment. Moreover, a number of signs are indicative of a multitude of possibilities, often indicating nothing more specific, individually or collectively, than that the fish is unwell or suffering some type of irritation.

In most cases it is necessary to evaluate the significance of a number of different signs, and, just as important, to take both environmental factors and circumstances into account. The aquarist must look for signs of disease in the fish; check environmental factors such as water chemistry, quality, and temperature; and consider anything unusual that may have happened in or near the aquarium, or to the affected fish, in the recent past. For example, the same signs may be indicative of completely different problems depending on whether the tank is recently set up or long-established, or whether the affected fish are recent introductions or long-term residents. No possible variable, however apparently trivial, should be discounted in the initial analysis of the situation.

Diagnosis of the probable cause of any problem is often best achieved via a process of elimination rather than by positive identification. For example, a number of different causes may lead to MUCUS HYPERPRODUCTION (2). Consider the following hypothetical scenario: the owner of an established aquarium, with no recently introduced fish, has returned from his holiday to find his fish exhibiting a thick coating of mucus and signs of IRRITATION (2).

As the aquarium and its fish are long-established, there have been no recent introductions, and the fish have not previously shown any signs of irritation, it is fairly unlikely that the problem is FLUKES (3); the pH checks out as normal and, again, there are no new fish, so ACIDOSIS (3) and ALKALOSIS (3) can be ruled out. However, the NITRATE (3) level proves to be much higher than desirable, probably because no water changes were performed while the aquarist was on holiday. So there is a possibility that the fish are suffering from one or more of the ectoparasitic PROTOZOA (3) that are sometimes present in aquaria in small numbers. Normally, the fish's immune system keeps their numbers in check so they do no significant harm to their host. However, if the fish's immunity is weakened for some reason, especially adverse environmental conditions, then the ectoparasites are able to multiply and cause SKIN SLIME DISEASE (3). Other signs such as SCRATCHING (2) and RESPIRATORY DISTRESS (2), plus the fact that all the fish are affected, tend to confirm this tentative diagnosis.

With practice the process of diagnosis by positive identification and elimination may become automatic, but inexperienced aquarists may find it helpful to make a list of any symptoms, plus other possibly relevant factors. The latter may include:

● water parameters.
● type/species, age, status (new or long-term resident) of fish affected.
● status of aquarium – how long established, recent alterations (to water, decor, equipment (including filter maintenance), diet, etc.).
● external factors (recent use of ichthyotoxic products such as insecticides in room, disturbance by visitors (boisterous children/dogs), etc.).

Against each sign of disease should be listed likely causes as indicated in this section. This may immediately permit the elimination of some possibilities: for example, although SHIMMYING (2) may be a sign of NITRITE (3) toxicity, it is normally seen only in small fish, and can be ruled out immediately if the fish is 12" long and the nitrite level is (near) zero!

The next stage is to look up each remaining possibility in SECTION III, and see if the causes and other signs given there match the signs and circumstances on the list. Again, it should be feasible to rule out certain possibilities, although even so a positive diagnosis may require post-mortem examination in some cases.

Note on the entries

Some signs of ill health in fish, e.g. CLAMPED FINS (2) and CLOUDY EYE (2), are generally known by such specific designations and are included as individual entries here. Some are obvious physical abnormalities such as GROWTHS (2), or SPOTS (2) which do not form part of normal COLORATION (2). Others relate to behavioural abnormalities such as loss of APPETITE (2) or BUOYANCY (2), or abnormal SWIMMING (2), and are referenced by the aspect affected, rather than under "loss" or "abnormal". Finally, (possible) abnormalities of anatomical features, e.g. FINS (2) or GILLS (2), are referred to the relevant feature. This system may involve some duplication, but should assist in diagnosis.

ANOREXIA
See APPETITE (2)

APATHY
See LETHARGY (2)

APPETITE, Loss of

Loss of or reduction in appetite may have several causes:

● An unwillingness to feed by one or more fish may be an early sign of a DISEASE (3), STRESS (3), or water-quality (or other environmental) problem; thus the fish should be closely inspected for any manifestations of disease and basic water testing should be undertaken (e.g. AMMONIA (3), NITRITE (3), NITRATE (3), pH (3), TEMPERATURE [3]).

● Loss of appetite in an individual fish may be the result of DIGESTIVE DISORDER (3) or chronic AGGRESSION (3) by tankmates. In the latter circumstance, separation of the affected fish from its attacker(s) is the only solution. Removal of the aggressor rather than the victim should be considered.

● Newly-introduced fish may be slow to feed initially until they have recovered from the STRESS (3) and SHOCK (3) associated with the move. They may also initially resist a change of diet.

● Wild-caught fish may initially refuse to eat unfamiliar foods such as dried or frozen formulations. A period of "weaning" may be required, during which time the fish is offered a mixture of natural (e.g. live) and artificial food items, until it learns to recognise the latter as being edible.

● Certain species of fish may persistently refuse anything but live foods. Examples include the pygmy sunfish (*Elassoma* spp.) which often accept only live aquatic invertebrates, and the pike livebearer *(Belonesox)* which preys on live fish. A year-round supply of the appropriate food items is essential when keeping these fastidious eaters, otherwise the fish may slowly starve to death.

Fortunately, most fish are able to survive a fairly long time without food, so a brief period of reduced appetite generally causes no long-term harm. An exception is fish fry which do require regular meals, otherwise they may quickly succumb, or, if they survive, be subject to STUNTING (2).

See also: EMACIATION (2), GENERAL MALAISE (2), NERVOUSNESS (2); SECTION I: The Correct Environment; Fish Compatibility; Nutrition.

BALANCE, Loss of
See BUOYANCY (2), SWIMMING (2)

BEHAVIOUR, Abnormal or Unusual
Any deviation from normal behaviour for a species, or indeed, for an established (in the aquarium) individual of a species, should be regarded as cause for concern, or at least further monitoring. To this end the aquarist should familiarise himself with the norm for his fish, by background reading coupled with careful observation.

Although changes in behaviour may simply denote life-cycle variations (e.g. the onset of reproductive activity), they are commonly a sign that something is amiss.

For some (possibly) unusual or abnormal types of behaviour, see also GENERAL MALAISE (2), IRRITATION (2), SWIMMING (2), BUOYANCY (2), NERVOUSNESS (2), COPROPHAGY (2).

Killifish are normally surface dwellers; this specimen is behaving abnormally, probably because of stress at being taken to a fish show.

BLOATING
See DISTENDED BODY (2)

BLOTCHES
See SPOTS (2)

BODY, Abnormal Shape
See DISTENDED BODY (2), DEFORMITY (2), EMACIATION (2), GROWTHS (2).

BUBBLES
● On the decor, glass, and fish: possibility of GAS BUBBLE DISEASE (3).
● In the FAECES (2) may indicate DIGESTIVE DISORDER (3).

BUGS (on fish, in the aquarium)
See PESTS (2).

BUOYANCY, Loss or Disturbance of
Loss of buoyancy or buoyancy control, evidenced by resting on the bottom of the aquarium or floating to the surface, and/or swimming at odd angles, is commonly indicative of swimbladder dysfunction. Sometimes the fish retains normal buoyancy, but cannot control the angle at which it swims. This may denote problems with the swimbladder itself or an inability to control its deflation/inflation and thus regulate buoyancy.

Buoyancy problems are a common sign of a number of diseases (especially in their terminal stages) and disorders:
● Loss of buoyancy/buoyancy control may be symptomatic of SWIM BLADDER DISEASE (3).
● Loss of buoyancy or buoyancy control may be the consequence of internal INJURY (3) resulting from AGGRESSION (3) (especially lateral ramming).
● Loss of buoyancy in a fish which shows signs of GENERAL MALAISE (3) or those of an obvious condition such as DROPSY (3) or MALAWI BLOAT (3), may be a side-effect of another illness, i.e. developing pressure on the swimbladder or disruption of the central nervous system leading to loss of buoyancy/attitude control.
● In newly-introduced fish, or following sudden changes to environmental parameters (e.g. temperature, pH), resting on the bottom may denote SHOCK (3), ACIDOSIS (3), or ALKALOSIS (3).
● Resting on the bottom may also be a sign of STRESS (3).
● Lack of buoyancy in fry may signify BELLYSLIDING (3); however, it is normal for larvae to lack buoyancy until they have used up their yolk sac.

Always remember that some fish are naturally lacking in buoyancy or habitually swim at strange angles, and that some (e.g. cichlids) commonly rest on the bottom at night.

CHOKING

The fish forcefully opens and closes its mouth, particularly after having taken a large item of food. Fish may exhibit this choking or coughing response soon after eating food items which are too large to be swallowed, or, indeed, if any other object, e.g. gravel, becomes lodged in the gullet.

● Many fish swallow their food whole rather than breaking it up in the mouth by chewing. The fish may try and ingest a food item which is too large to be swallowed whole and does not easily break down in the mouth. Fish which have taken relatively large prey such as earthworms may have problems in swallowing the food. The choking reflex is often followed by the ejection of the food via the mouth, only to be re-swallowed.

● Certain fish species which are accustomed to browsing over the substrate, such as cyprinids, may accidentally pick up a piece of gravel which may become lodged in the buccal cavity, causing a choking response. This may also occur with species which sift substrate through their gills in order to extract edible morsels, e.g. the cichlids *Geophagus* and *Lethrinops,* or any fish which uses its mouth to shift substrate to customize its environment (most cichlids).

In most cases, large food items are eventually either expelled or ingested, and the aquarist need not intervene. In the case of gravel ingestion, it may be necessary to carefully extract the stone from the mouth with the aid of fine forceps (tweezers), but only if the obstruction is easily dislodged; in difficult cases it may be necessary to take the fish to a vet.

● Transient choking action may also be observed in fish during recovery from ANAESTHESIA (3).
See also: COUGHING (2), VOMITING (2), RESPIRATORY DISTRESS (2).

CLAMPED FINS

The fins are clamped against the body and the tail is not spread properly. This is an extremely common sign that the fish is feeling unwell, and often the first warning that something is amiss.

● If all or most of the aquarium occupants exhibit continuously clamped fins then water parameters (chemistry and quality) should immediately be checked and rectified if necessary, otherwise the fish should be closely observed for the appearance of additional, more specific, signs of disease.

● Fish which are victims of AGGRESSION (3), or suffering from STRESS (3) and/or SHOCK (3), commonly exhibit clamped fins.

● The transient clamping of one or more fins usually indicates a passing irritation and is not a cause for concern. The spreading and folding of fins may also be used in display and other forms of communication.

See also: GENERAL MALAISE (2), IRRITATION (2).

CLOUDY EYE

Whitish clouding or the appearance of a whitish film over the eye of the fish.

● The majority of cases result from poor water quality (NITROGENOUS WASTES [3]), which should always be investigated first.

Cloudy eye can also denote:

● SECONDARY INFECTION (3) (FUNGAL INFECTION [3]), following mechanical damage.

● MUCUS HYPERPRODUCTION (2) as a reaction to a PROTOZOAN PARASITE (3) infestation (SKIN SLIME DISEASE [3]); poor water quality (AMMONIA (3], NITRITE [3], NITRATE [3]); inappropriate pH (ACIDOSIS [3]; ALKALOSIS [3]); POISONING [3] (including with CHLORINE (3) and/or CHLORAMINE [3]), or an inappropriate or incorrectly administered chemical medication.

● Eye Fluke (*DIPLOSTOMUM* [3]) – in this case the white clouding is in the lens rather than on the surface.

Catfish with cloudy eye, probably caused by adverse environmental conditions.

● External BACTERIAL INFECTION (3).
● VITAMIN DEFICIENCY (3), especially vitamins A, B$_2$, C.
   Associated signs may include EXOPHTHALMIA (2), and where environmental causes are involved, GENERAL MALAISE (2) and IRRITATION (2).
See also EYES (2).

CLOUDY WATER

Although not a sign of disease, cloudy water is a sign of problems that commonly affect the health of the aquarium occupants, and hence it is included here.

   The aquarium water may become cloudy for a number of reasons.

● Bacterial bloom. This is normally seen only in newly set-up aquaria, and can be expected to dissipate naturally during the maturation period *(see SECTION I: The Correct Environment)*. A bacterial bloom in an established aquarium is very unlikely, and if it does occur is indicative of such atrocious organic pollution that in all probability most, if not all, of the fish will already be dead. Survivors should be moved to alternative accommodation while the aquarium is thoroughly cleaned, preferably set up again from scratch.

● Suspended material in the water. Common causes are:

– Dirt from improperly washed decor – usually substrate, but bear in mind that it is impossible to get substrate materials totally clean. A slight cloudiness from this source is acceptable, and will settle out (into the substrate) very quickly during maturation, before fish are added.

– Accumulated (in the substrate) organic material or inert nitrogen-cycle residue, usually stirred up accidentally by the aquarist during maintenance, or deliberately by the fish when sifting/digging. If the mechanical filtration is suitable/adequate for the tank and its occupants, this should not be a major problem.

– Particles of food escaping from the gills of feeding fish. A common problem with some types of (usually large) fish and some foods. Many proprietary dried foods, mussel, and liver (which should not, but is, used as a fish food) can produce such particles, which soon settle out into the substrate or are filtered out, but may lead to raised levels of AMMONIA (3), NITRITE (3), and, in the longer term, NITRATE (3), or encourage infestations of PLANARIANS

(3). In addition some poor-quality foods may break up before ingestion by the fish, clouding the water with particles and with the same attendant pollution risk.

• Tiny particles of substrate material. Coral sand is the commonest source, and the particles can cause irritation leading to SCRATCHING (3) and possible gill damage.

• Incorrect use of chemical pH adjusters. Failure to follow the manufacturer's instructions, in particular if the chemicals are added to the aquarium neat, instead of pre-diluted, commonly leads to the formation of a whitish precipitate which covers surfaces and clouds the water. If this results in illness in the fish, survivors must be removed immediately to alternative, unpolluted, accommodation, as for POISONING (3).

• Proliferation of unicellular organisms (e.g. ALGAE (3) causing green water), usually associated with excessive lighting and high NITRATE (3) levels. More common in unshaded ponds than in aquaria. Not normally harmful *per se*, but possibly indicative of underlying equipment/ nutritional/maintenance problems.

• Staining. Wooden decor items and filtration through peat (or use of peat extract) commonly stain the water tea-coloured. This is harmless (provided no toxic effects or undesirable changes in pH occur simultaneously) and characteristic of the natural environment of some fish. The water should, however, be perfectly clear. Some medications may also stain the water. Many types of staining can be remedied by filtration over activated carbon, if desired.

See also: SCUM (2).

COLORATION, Abnormal or Changes in

Abnormal coloration may denote abnormality for the species or for the individual.

An individual may deviate from the norm for the species through genetic mutation, as in ALBINISM (3) and MELANISM (3). Such mutations occur from time to time, and some have been fixed by selective breeding following the initial accidental occurrence, in order to produce fancy varieties, e.g. black angelfish *(Pterophyllum scalare)* and albino kribensis cichlids *(Pelvicachromis pulcher).* Although such fish may be subject to particular health

Colour may vary with mood. The blue fish (left) is a dominant breeding male cichlid; the olive fish in the foreground (right) is a subordinate, slightly stressed, male of the same species. The subordinate male colour is often similar to that of the female, seen in the background (right).

problems associated with their mutation (e.g. heightened light sensitivity in albinos), provided their colour remains normal for the variety there is no cause for concern.

Changes in the coloration of a fish may give a clue to its health status or behaviour. Fish which have become noticeably darker (sometimes lighter) may be suffering from STRESS (3) or DISEASE (3), these changes in pigmentation being under the influence of hormones and the central nervous system.

In order to evaluate the significance of colour changes it is important to be aware of the normal repertoire of variations for the type of fish concerned. In many fish coloration is relatively static, such that any significant change may prove to be a cause for concern. Some fish, however, change colour as a function of their age/development, while in others colour variation may be behavioural, denoting, *inter alia*, communication, status, sexual status, and courtship display. The fish's general environment may also be influential, in that some fish tend to become darker or paler according to their surroundings.

Nevertheless any change should be regarded as suspicious if accompanied by other signs of malaise. For example, abnormally (for the fish) dark or pale coloration, coupled with NERVOUSNESS (2), loose SCALES (2), and frayed FINS (2), will probably indicate AGGRESSION (3), while heightened coloration coupled with glazed EYES (2) and erratic or uncontrolled SWIMMING (2) may be a sign of acute POISONING (3).

Coloration changes indicative of particular problems:

• Dark or discoloured patches on the body may be the result of BURNS (3) or superficial INJURY (3).

• Dark areas around the mouth in cichlids may signify the condition known as BLACK CHIN (3).

• A grey cast may be the result of MUCUS HYPER-PRODUCTION (2); a yellowish one caused by the presence of *PISCINOODINIUM* (3).

• Reddened areas of skin may be damage caused by some ECTOPARASITES (3); or skin irritation resulting from ACIDOSIS (3) or ALKALOSIS (3) or AMMONIA (3); or inflammation/haemorrhaging caused by systemic BACTERIAL (3) or VIRUS (3) infection. Can also be the result of Vitamin C deficiency.

• Extensive pale red coloration of the abdomen is associated with DROPSY (3) and certain other systemic infections (BACTERIA (3) or VIRUS (3)).

• Fading of colour, sometimes accompanied by the appearance of whitish or greyish patches under the skin, in characins and less frequently some cypriniforms, is a sign of *PLEISTOPHORA* (3) (Neon Tetra Disease).

• Abnormally pale coloration may denote, *inter alia,* MYCOBACTERIOSIS (3) (Fish TB), SHOCK (3), or OSMOTIC STRESS (3).

• Discoloration of the FINS (3) (lightened, grey-white, ragged edges, with or without reddening through inflammation; and/or red streaking of the affected fin[s]) may be indicative of bacterial FIN ROT (3).

• Overall permanent dark coloration is a common feature of BLINDNESS (3), perhaps because the fish perceives its environment to be dark and endeavours to adjust to it (camouflage).

• Abnormally dark coloration is a common sign of STRESS (3), but may be associated with DISEASE (3).

• An asymmetric dark area, commonly one side of the head, may be symptomatic of localised nerve damage inhibiting control of the melanophores. Possible causes are TUMOURS (3), BURNS (3), INJURIES (3), or localised BACTERIAL INFECTIONS (3). If the damage is permanent then permanent discoloration is likely as well.

• Heightened or otherwise abnormal coloration accompanied by loss of BALANCE (2), erratic SWIMMING (2),

RESPIRATORY DISTRESS (2), glazed EYES (2) may be indicative of POISONING (3), ACIDOSIS (3), or ALKALOSIS (3), or other conditions (e.g. GILL (2) problems) causing OXYGEN STARVATION (3) with a general deleterious effect on the central nervous system and loss of control of the chromatophores.
See also: SPOTS (2), GROWTHS (2), GILLS (2).

COPROPHAGY
See FAECES (2).

COTTON WOOL
Cotton wool-like GROWTHS (2) are normally FUNGUS (3) or, especially if around the mouth, COLUMNARIS (3).

COUGHING
Fish occasionally make coughing motions. The occasional cough is generally not a cause for concern, but regular or repeated coughing may be a sign of a health problem.
Coughing may be symptomatic of gill irritation, HYPOXIA (3), and/or other respiratory problems, caused by:
● Environmental problems such as POISONING (3) (including AMMONIA (3), NITRITE (3), NITRATE (3), CHLORINE AND CHLORAMINE [3]), excess CARBON DIOXIDE (3), CLOUDY WATER (2), incorrect pH (ACIDOSIS (3), ALKALOSIS [3])
● Pathogens affecting the gills, e.g. BRANCHIOMYCOSIS (3), GILL PARASITES (3), SKIN SLIME DISEASE (3), *ICHTHYOPHTHIRIUS* (3), *PISCINOODINIUM* (3).
● Coughing may also occur in fish recovering from ANAESTHESIA (3).
Associated signs may include: GENERAL MALAISE (2), IRRITATION (2), RESPIRATORY DISTRESS (2), CHOKING (2), VOMITING (2).

DARTING
Abnormal short rapid swimming movements, sometimes associated with POISONING (3), ACIDOSIS (3), ALKALOSIS (3), ICHTHYOPHTHIRIASIS (3), and ECTOPARASITES (3). Darting is sometimes also a sign of STRESS or OSMOTIC STRESS (3).

See also: BEHAVIOUR (2), SWIMMING (2), IRRITATION (2), NERVOUSNESS (2).

DEFORMITY

The distortion, normally genetic in origin, of any physical feature, external or internal. Common deformities involve the spine (SCOLIOSIS (3), LORDOSIS (3)), the operculum (wholly or partly missing), and fins (divided, abnormal in size/shape, or missing). SIAMESE TWINS (3) occasionally occur. A condition known as BELLYSLIDING (3) is caused by deformity of the swimbladder. Stunting, of genetic origin, may also be regarded as a deformity.

There are a number of possible causes of deformity in fish:

● Genetic: single deformities may occur even where top-grade breeding stock has been used, but are commonly the result of INBREEDING (3).

● Cultivated: a few 'man-made' varieties of fish have been intentionally produced to possess deformed body shapes or other unnatural body features. Most of the extreme examples are to be found among goldfish varieties; however, one tropical example is the 'balloon molly', which, as its name suggests, possesses an unnaturally rounded belly region which gives the fish an overall deformed body shape. A hybrid cichlid, known commonly as the 'red parrot', also possesses a deformed stumpy rounded body. The extreme distension of the body in these cultivated varieties may cause the fish swimming problems. The ethics of intentionally producing such deformed fish should be questioned.

● Environmental: exposure to adverse water conditions during early development may also be a cause of some deformities.

● Pathogenic: certain systemic BACTERIAL INFECTIONS (3), notably those caused by MYCOBACTERIA (3), can result in a deformed body. An infectious disease should always be suspected as the cause of deformities occurring in previously normal fish.

● Parasitic: *PLEISTOPHORA* (3) may cause deformity in tetras and a few other types of fish.

● Dietary: VITAMIN DEFICIENCY (3) may lead to SKELETAL DEFORMITY (3).

● TUMOURS: these, while not actually deformities, may

Balloon Molly: A cultivated variety which has been intentionally produced to have a deformed body shape.

produce the appearance of a deformity. *See also: DISTENDED BODY (2), ABNORMAL FINS (2), ABNORMAL GILLS (2), GROWTHS (2), STUNTING (2); SECTION I, BREEDING; SECTION III: DEFORMITY, SKELETAL DEFORMITIES.*

DISTENDED BODY

The fish has an abnormally swollen body or swollen belly region. There are several possible causes for this condition:

● DROPSY (3). The distension is commonly accompanied by protruding scales, giving a pine-cone-like appearance.

● Reproductive status. Female fish which are gravid (pregnant) or ripe with eggs may have distended bellies. This can be very pronounced in the case of livebearing fish (poeciliids and goodeids) which are close to term. With egglayers, the female will generally remain swollen with eggs until spawning. Prolonged carriage of eggs may lead to the condition known as EGG-BOUND (3).

● Distension resulting from a large meal. Certain carnivorous and predatory fish consume large items of food which may last them for several days. This feeding behaviour is commonly encountered with some of the predatory catfish, such as the red-tailed catfish *Phractocephalus hemioliopterus*. The fish's belly region may become grossly distended following ingestion of a large meal and this is quite normal. In the absence of further meals, the belly should gradually return to its 'normal' size within a few days.

● DEFORMITY. Certain popular species of aquarium fish

have been selectively bred in order to achieve varieties with distended or rounded bodies: these unnatural shapes are considered desirable or attractive by some aquarists. (See also DEFORMITY, above.)

● Tapeworms (CESTODES [3]). Some tapeworm species are parasitic as the adult worm which resides within the fish's gut, while others exist as the larval form within the body cavity (peritoneal cavity). Some species are quite large and several tapeworms may be present within a fish, causing gross and sometimes asymmetrical distension of the belly region.

● Organ TUMOUR (3). A large tumour mass (neoplasia) of an internal organ may cause gross body distension and give rise to dropsy-like symptoms.

● MALAWI BLOAT (3) (East African mouthbrooding cichlids only).

● OBESITY (2), normally resulting from long-term unsuitable diet. The condition normally develops slowly, and may affect other parts of the fish, notably the chest. *(See also SECTION I: Nutrition, SECTION III: OVER-FEEDING).*

● *VIBRIO* (3) (rare).

● Distension following death. This post-mortem condition arises from gas production by bacterial fermentation. The gas-inflated corpses may float to the water's surface. Distension of the corpse cannot be taken as an indication of the cause of death.

This fish has slight obesity resulting from an unsuitable diet (beef heart).

Associated signs may include: GENERAL MALAISE (2), loss of BUOYANCY (2), abnormality of the SCALES (2), EXOPHTHALMIA (2).

EGG Abnormalities and Problems
Eggs may fail to hatch because they have not been fertilised or because of attack by EGG FUNGUS (3).
See also: SECTION I: Breeding; SECTION III: REPRODUCTIVE FAILURE.

EMACIATION
Emaciation may result from a number of factors:
● Direct pathogenic effect of an infection, e.g. systemic FUNGAL (3) (rare) or (more likely) BACTERIAL INFECTION (3) (in particular with MYCOBACTERIA (3) (Fish tuberculosis)).

Emaciation in a wild-caught female guppy (Poecilia reticulata).

● Heavy infestation with WORMS (3), including ACANTHOCEPHALANS (3), may cause emaciation (due to their utilisation of host food), although the abdomen may be distended by the bulk of the worms living in the gut/body cavity. *(See DISTENDED BODY [2]).*
● *PLEISTOPHORA* (3) (in small characins and some other fish).
● HEXAMITIASIS (3) (in cichlids).
● *HETEROSPORIS* (in angelfish (*Pterophyllum* spp.)).
● Incorrect diet (NUTRITIONAL DISEASES (3), DIGESTIVE DISORDERS (3), VITAMIN DEFICIENCY (3)).
● Long-term shortfall in food intake. This may itself have numerous causes:

– Chronic STRESS (3).

– Chronic disease and concomitant malaise resulting in loss of interest in food.

– Inadequate food supply.

– Food offered unpalatable (unsuitable for the fish, stale or contaminated (AFLATOXINS (3)).

– Nocturnal species may receive insufficient food if their feeding habits are not specially accommodated.

– Bottom-dwelling fish, or 'scavengers', kept to clear up residues, may receive inadequate food if little or none is left uneaten by midwater or surface-dwelling species.

– A nervous fish may be naturally reluctant to assert itself at feeding time, and hence receive insufficient food; or AGGRESSION (3) by competitive or territorial fish may prevent other individuals from receiving their share.

– FEEDING (2) difficulties.

● Species which do not feed during brood care (e.g. mouthbrooding species) may become very emaciated.

● Spawning, especially if the eggs are large or numerous, may result in a sudden reduction in the girth of the female.

Note: Wild-caught fish offered for sale are commonly slimmer than their captive counterparts; natural food supply is sometimes less abundant than that in captivity, and the STRESS (3) of transportation, and the need to adjust to captivity and a new diet can lead to further weight loss. Such fish are not necessarily unhealthy, but should be seen to be feeding before purchase. Aquarium fish offered for sale are sometimes emaciated due to an irregular feeding regime during the various stages in the supply chain, including inadequate feeding during their stay in the retail premises.Associated signs may include: GENERAL MAL-AISE (2), Loss of APPETITE (2), NERVOUSNESS (2).

EXOPHTHALMIA or EXOPHTHALMUS

An eye condition, commonly known as "pop-eye", characterised by the swelling of one or both eyes, so that they clearly protrude from the orbit more than is normal. It is important to note that some fish (e.g. some types of fancy goldfish) are bred with protruding eyes which are 'normal' for the fish concerned; mercifully this practice, which is widely condemned as being cruel, has not yet been applied to freshwater tropical fish.

Exophthalmia accompanied by cloudiness of the eye and infection of the orbit.

CLOUDY EYE (2) commonly accompanies, and sometimes precedes, the swelling, which sometimes becomes so extreme that the eye literally 'pops out' of its socket and is lost.

Exophthalmia is a symptom of a build-up of fluid in or behind the eye, rather than being a disease in its own right, but has nevertheless also been included in SECTION III for ease of reference.

Causes of the condition include the following:

● Eye PARASITES (3), e.g. *DIPLOSTOMUM* (3).

● Systemic BACTERIAL INFECTION (3) such as FISH TB (*MYCOBACTERIUM* [3]) or bacterial DROPSY (3). In such cases exophthalmia is usually one of a number of symptoms, which may include EMACIATION (2) or DISTENDED BODY (2), ULCERS (2), and generally very poor condition.

● Systemic FUNGUS INFECTION (3) such as *ICHTHYOPHONUS* (3) (uncommon).

● Nutritional deficiencies, including VITAMIN DEFICIENCY (3).

● Metabolic disturbances, i.e. any disturbance to the biochemical functions of the fish.

● Reactions to poor water quality (NITROGENOUS WASTES (3), especially high NITRATE (3) levels).

Of these the last is by far the most common.

It should be noted that where the cause of exophthalmia is environmental or nutritional, it is common for only a single, susceptible, species – or even individual – to be affected in the first instance. Environmental/nutritional causes should thus not be ruled out simply on the basis that the problem is specific to one or a few fish, rather than general.
See also: EYES (2); SECTION III: EXOPHTHALMIA.

EYES, Abnormal

The eyes of fish may be affected by a number of infectious diseases, as well as by adverse water conditions, physical INJURY (3), AGGRESSION (3), or nutritional pathologies: The following table shows symptoms affecting the eyes, and possible causes in order of probability.

TABLE 6
EYE SYMPTOMS AND POSSIBLE CAUSES

SYMPTOM: **Cloudy/opaque appearance**
(CLOUDY EYE [2])
POSSIBLE CAUSE:
1) Water quality problem (e.g. exposure to CHLORINE (3), excessive NITROGENOUS WASTES (3).
2) BACTERIAL INFECTION (3), possibly linked with STRESS (3) and/or poor water conditions.
3) Abrasion, such as caused by poor handling (e.g. use of nets made of rough material).
4) SENILITY (3)
5) VITAMIN DEFICIENCY (3) (Vitamin A) (highlyunlikely if a balanced diet is given).
6) Eye-fluke (occasionally encountered in wild-caught or pond-reared fish) (See *DIPLOSTOMUM* [3])
7) Genetic problem (probably INBREEDING [3])

SYMPTOM: **Cottonwool-like covering to eye**
POSSIBLE CAUSE:
FUNGAL INFECTION (3), possibly linked with STRESS (3) and/or poor water conditions, or following INJURY (3)

SYMPTOM: **One or both eyes bulge outwards**
POSSIBLE CAUSE:
1) Poor water conditions (NITROGENOUS WASTES [3]) (EXOPHTHALMIA[3])

2) Incorrect water chemistry
3) Internal BACTERIAL (3), VIRAL (3), or FUNGAL (3) infection
4) SENILITY (3).
5) VITAMIN DEFICIENCY (3) (unlikely if a balanced diet is fed)

SYMPTOM: **One or both eyes missing**
POSSIBLE CAUSE:
1) AGGRESSION (3) (including predation) by tankmates
2) Other INJURY (3)
3) Severe EXOPHTHALMIA (3)

SYMPTOM: **Both eyes glazed and immobile/ apparently unseeing**
POSSIBLE CAUSE:
1) POISONING (3) (including by AMMONIA [3] or NITRITE [3])
2) Severe SHOCK (3)
3) HYPOXIA (3), possibly resulting from gill damage caused by gill diseases or GILL PARASITES.

See also: CLOUDY EYE (2) , EXOPHTHALMIA (2).

FAECES
The colour and consistency of fish faeces vary according to the species of fish, and, in particular, its diet (e.g. some commercially produced colour-enhancing foods (generally produced in flake or pellet form) may colour the faeces). Normal faeces are usually brownish or greenish and of a regular diameter typical for the fish concerned. They commonly break off soon after emerging from the vent. Intestinal PARASITES (3) and their eggs may be passed in faeces, but can be detected only by microscopic examination. Any abnormality which cannot be explained in terms of the recent diet should be regarded as possibly suspicious, particularly if persistent.
● Gas bubbles in faeces may indicate a DIGESTIVE DISORDER (2) or dietary problem.
● Irregularly formed faeces ditto.
● White, stringy, faeces are a characteristic sign of HEXAMITIASIS (3) or *CAPILLARIA* (3).

● Faeces with dark and light segments alternating may be indicative of *CAPILLARIA* (3).

● Absence of faeces for any significant period may indicate loss or absence of APPETITE (2) (eventually leading to EMACIATION (2)), or CONSTIPATION (3). A constipated fish may continue to feed, at least in mild cases.

● Worms protruding from the anus are a sign of *CAMALLANUS* (3) infestation.

Many fish will forage on the faeces of other fish or on their own faeces. COPROPHAGY (3) (literally, "eating faeces") is a route by which certain pathogens and parasites may be transmitted from one fish to another.

See also: SECTION I: Nutrition.

FEEDING difficulties

This may take a number of forms:

● Food may be ingested, but subsequently ejected or not swallowed. This may denote an obstruction (see CHOKING (2) or VOMITING (2)), or loss of genuine (rather than instinctive) interest in food due to DISEASE (3). The fish instinctively grabs a piece of food but then rejects it.

● The mouth may be fixed open, which again may denote a blockage, or a dislocated lower jaw (maxilla), requiring veterinary attention in medium to large fish, and usually EUTHANASIA (3) in very small ones.

● The mouth opening may be obstructed by GROWTHS (2).

● In pufferfish (Tetraodontidae) the problem may be overgrown TEETH (3).

See also: APPETITE (2), MOUTH (2), GAPING/GASPING (2).

FIN CONGESTION

Abnormal red streaks on one or more fins, caused by congestion of the blood vessels. A common sign of bacterial FIN ROT (3), sometimes preceding noticeable decay of the fin edges. May also be due to certain systemic VIRUS (3) and BACTERIAL INFECTIONS (3).

See also: FINS (2), HAEMORRHAGE (2).

FIN EROSION

The disintegration (necrosis) of the outer edges of the fins,

in particular the unpaired fins (dorsal, anal, caudal), rarely the pelvic (ventral). Characterised by a paling of the fin edge (not to be confused with white or light-coloured edgings normal in some fish) and often accompanied by fraying and splitting. Fin erosion may result from AGGRESSION (3) or poor water quality (the commonest causes), or be a sign of VITAMIN DEFICIENCY (3), some PARASITES (3) (FLUKES (3), SKIN SLIME DISEASE (3), *ICHTHYOPHTHIRIUS* (3), *inter alia*). It may develop into FIN ROT (3).
See also: FINS (2).

FINS, abnormal

A number of problems can affect the fins:
● Fins can be subject to genetic DEFORMITIES (2) of various kinds, deformity denoting that the fins are atypical for the species concerned. For example, they may be missing (totally or in part), divided or forked, smaller or larger than normal. Some fin deformities (e.g. multiple tails in fancy goldfish, overdeveloped finnage – 'longfin varieties' in some tropicals) are considered attractive in some quarters, and have been developed by selective breeding regardless of any swimming difficulty they may cause the fish. Fin damage may result in acquired (rather than inbred) deformity, for example splits which have failed to heal completely, and age may lead to distortion of the fin

A Geophagus with a split and frayed tail, probably caused by aggression.

rays, but these acquired deformities need not bar the fish concerned from breeding, as they are not heritable.

● Split or frayed fins, especially the posterior parts of the dorsal and anal fins, and the tail, are usually a sign that the fish has been a victim of AGGRESSION (3) (including fin-nipping).

● CLAMPED FINS (2) are a common sign that all is not well with the fish, and may both presage and accompany an outbreak of disease. They are also highly indicative of STRESS (3) and environmental problems.

● Fin damage may also occur as a result of mishandling and poor packing during transportation.

● Abnormal lightening (in colour) of the fin edges, coupled with a ragged appearance, is, together with FIN CONGES-TION (2), an early sign of bacterial FIN ROT (3). If left untreated the discoloured area will spread inward, with reddish inflammation, and the parts first affected will drop off. In severe cases the entire fin may rot away and the infection spread to the body.

● Cotton wool-like growths on the fins are FUNGUS (3).
See also: FIN TWITCHING (2), FIN EROSION (2), FIN CONGESTION (2), SPOTS (2).

FIN TWITCHING

This is generally indicative of poor water quality, ECTOPARASITES (3), or ICHTHYOPHTHIRIASIS (3). However, occasional twitching of a fin may be due simply to a transitory irritation, and no cause for concern.
See also IRRITATION (3), FINS (2).

FLASHING

A term used to describe swimming behaviour in which a fish twists on to its side and rubs its flanks against a rock or other solid object within the aquarium. This action may help relieve a skin irritation, just as when humans scratch themselves to relieve an itch. Occasional flashing should not cause alarm; however, when one or more fish are observed repeatedly to flash against objects then this may indicate:

● Most commonly, irritation proceeding from poor water quality, including suspended matter in the water. In particular, high NITRATE (3) levels and tiny particles of coral sand substrate (and some other types of CLOUDY WATER [2]) are common causes of flashing.

● Infection with skin or gill ECTOPARASITES (3) such as FLUKES (3), *TRICHODINA* (3) (and other pathogens causing SKIN SLIME DISEASE (3)), *PISCINOODINIUM* (3), or *ICHTHYOPHTHIRIUS* (3).

Flashing is commonly accompanied by other signs of IRRITATION (2), such as SCRATCHING (2), COUGHING (2), SHIMMYING (2), HEAD SHAKING (2), and YAWNING (2), as well as CLAMPED FINS (2).

FOOD REJECTION
See FEEDING (2), APPETITE (2).

GAPING and GASPING
The fish hangs, head up, tail down, with its mouth gaping at or just below the surface; or rests on the bottom, mouth agape and gills heaving; or, less frequently, swims in its normal position but with the mouth agape, with or without increased gill rate.

● Gasping at the surface is normally a sign of OXYGEN STARVATION (3), usually environmental (inadequate oxygen content in the water) rather than physiological in origin. The affected fish are seeking out the area where oxygen content is highest.

● Gasping away from the surface (typically lying on the bottom) is also indicative of ill health, and may include cases of OXYGEN STARVATION (3) where the fish has become too weak to remain at the surface.

● Gasping may also be indicative of GILL PARASITES (3) or other GILL DISEASE (3), but these should be suspected *only if* other possibilities have been eliminated.

● A wide-open mouth may sometimes indicate a blockage of the gullet (see CHOKING (2)).

● If the mouth appears immobile (does not shut), the problem may be a dislocated lower jaw. This may sometimes rectify itself; if not, then in very small fish EUTHANASIA (3) may be necessary to prevent a slow death by starvation. In larger fish it may be possible to manipulate the jaw back into place, but this should be attempted only by an experienced person. Again, euthanasia may be necessary. Note: Some fish, e.g. *Corydoras* catfish, routinely visit the surface to take a gulp of air, and some, of course, are surface-dwellers (*inter alia,* toothcarps (Cyprinodonts), and hatchet fish (e.g.*Gasteropelecus* spp.)). *See also: HANGING (2), RESPIRATORY DISTRESS (2), FEEDING (2), MOUTH (2).*

GENERAL MALAISE
The following signs (which should be looked up individually) commonly indicate, singly or collectively, that the fish is unwell, but without indicating any specific cause:
- Loss of APPETITE (2)
- Abnormal BEHAVIOUR (2)
- Abnormal COLORATION (2)
- CLAMPED FINS (2)
- LETHARGY (2)
- RESPIRATORY DISTRESS (2)
- Abnormal SWIMMING

Fish exhibiting any of these signs should be kept under close observation for additional signs of a specific problem, and levels of NITROGENOUS WASTES (3) in the aquarium should be checked.

GILL COVER
See OPERCULUM (2)

GILLS, Abnormal
Normal gills are red in colour, which can be difficult to see when the fish is in good health, as the operculum (gill cover) will open only slightly and slowly with each respiratory beat, (although normal gill rate may vary considerably from

A missing operculum (genetic deformity) provides an unusual opportunity to see the fish's healthy bright red gills.

species to species, and some variation is likely according to activity).

Irritation of the gills by chemicals or pathogens may cause a tissue response involving MUCUS HYPER-PRODUCTION (2) and/or gill cell proliferation (= gill hyperplasia). Excess gill mucus may be seen trailing from beneath the opercula. Damage to the gills resulting from gill pathogens or adverse water conditions may impair gaseous exchange across the gill membrane, causing the fish to suffer RESPIRATORY STRESS (3) and OSMOTIC STRESS (3). Affected fish may exhibit abnormal behavioural changes, such as GASPING (2) at the water surface (where oxygen levels are richer) and increased opercular beats. It should be borne in mind that respiratory problems can occur even in the absence of gill damage, for example if the dissolved OXYGEN (3) level in the water falls below a critical level.

It should be noted that temporary flaring of the gills forms part of the courtship/defensive/aggressive display of some fish. Apparent abnormality of one gill (especially in inactive fish hovering in one spot or resting on a substrate) may be due simply to environmental factors such as exposure to the current of water from the filter return, in which case the fish can be expected to 'recover' when it changes position.

The following table lists abnormalities of the gills and likely causes:

TABLE 7
GILL ABNORMALITIES

SYMPTOM: **Discoloration (too pale)**
POSSIBLE CAUSE: ANAEMIA (3)

SYMPTOM: **Discoloration (dark or grey spots)**
POSSIBLE CAUSE: Iron deposition during ACIDOSIS (3)

SYMPTOM: **Discoloration (grey-white mucus coating)**
POSSIBLE CAUSE: Reaction to irritation by GILL PARASITES (3), POISONING (3) (including AMMONIA (3), NITRITE (3), CHLORINE/CHLORAMINE (3), COPPER [3]), ACIDOSIS (3) or ALKALOSIS (3), suspended matter *(see CLOUDY WATER [2])*.

SYMPTOM: **Discoloration (mottled dark red and light)**
POSSIBLE CAUSE: BRANCHIOMYCOSIS (3)

SYMPTOM: **Discoloration (brownish)**
POSSIBLE CAUSE: NITRITE (3)

SYMPTOM: Swollen, gill cover constantly expanded
 (increased respiratory effort)
POSSIBLE CAUSES:
(a) Gill damage or irritation from PARASITES (3),
POISONING (3) (including AMMONIA (3), NITRITE
(3), CHLORINE/CHLORAMINE (3), COPPER [3]),
ACIDOSIS (3) or ALKALOSIS (3), suspended matter
(see CLOUDY WATER [2]), sifting sharp substrate
material
(b) Exertion resulting from evading AGGRESSION (3),
from reproductive activity (courtship, spawning,
 mouthbrooding), and from panic-stimulated flight (see
 also NERVOUSNESS [2])
(c) Respiratory difficulties caused by obstruction of the
gullet (see also CHOKING [2])

SYMPTOM: **Erosion (rotting away) of gill filaments**
POSSIBLE CAUSES: BRANCHIOMYCOSIS (3),
BACTERIAL INFECTION (3)

SYMPTOM: **Worm-like parasites, visible to the naked eye**
POSSIBLE CAUSE: *ERGASILUS* (3)

SYMPTOM: **Gas bubbles on gill filaments**
POSSIBLE CAUSE: GAS BUBBLE DISEASE (3)

SYMPTOM: **Operculum wholly or partly missing**
POSSIBLE CAUSES: (a)DEFORMITY (2)
 (b) INJURY (2) (rare)

See also: RESPIRATORY DISTRESS (2), IRRITATION (2).

GREEN WATER
See CLOUDY WATER (2)

The strange hump on the head of this blockhead cichlid (Steatocranus casuarius) is perfectly normal for the species.

GROWTHS

Lumps, growths, or swellings on the body surface may be due to one of several causes:

● *APIOSOMA* (3). Small whitish lumps on the skin and fins. Easily confused with *ICHTHYOPHTHIRIUS* (3) or *LYMPHOCYSTIS* (3) (but far less likely than either).

● BACTERIAL INFECTIONS (3). Raised lumps or 'lesions' may form as a result of certain bacterial infections such as FISH TUBERCULOSIS (3). The lumps may have a pale to white necrotic region (sometimes with an ulcerated pit) and a reddened haemorrhagic region.

● COLUMNARIS (3) disease may manifest as a whitish cotton wool-like growth, commonly affecting the mouth. *See also FUNGUS (3).*

● DIGESTIVE DISORDERS (3). Digestive blockage (including CONSTIPATION [3]) occasionally results in an asymmetric bulge, usually on one side of the abdomen.

● *EPISTYLIS* (3). Tiny whitish fungus-like tufts, commonly on hard tissue, e.g. fins, opercula.

● FISH POX. Greyish or whitish patches resembling MUCUS HYPERPRODUCTION (2), soft when new, but hard and waxy in time. Very uncommon in tropical fish.

● FUNGUS (3). The fungal growth is white or greyish and resembles a tuft of cotton wool, commonly at the site of an INJURY (3). *See also COLUMNARIS (3).*

● HELMINTH (3) larvae. Encysted larval helminths residing beneath the skin may appear as smallish growths on the body. The larvae, which are curled within the rounded cyst wall, may number just one or a few. They sometimes appear pale to dark grey when present beneath the skin of light-coloured fish (e.g. pink kissing gouramis *(Helostoma temminckii)*).

• ICHTHYOPHTHIRIASIS (3). The slightly raised white spots (blisters) caused by this protozoan parasite are sometimes referred to as lumps or growths, but are very small, typically less than 1 mm in diameter. The white spots may be very numerous (tens, or hundreds, or more) and occur over the body surface and fins. Normally accompanied by signs of IRRITATION (2).

• *LYMPHOCYSTIS* (3). The growths are always whitish and may appear singly and/or in grape/cauliflower-like clusters, and are especially noticeable on the fins. Each growth is roughly globular and generally much larger than the growths caused by *Ichthyophthirius* (but can range from being just visible to the naked eye up to several millimetres in diameter). Usually without signs of IRRITATION (2).

• MICROSPORIDIAL INFECTIONS (3). These PROTOZOAN (3) parasites are a less likely cause of growths in aquarium fish. The growths or 'nodules' may be of the same coloration as the surrounding skin, or may appear pale-coloured. They can vary greatly in size, and may also be present in deeper tissues.

• Normal feature. Some fish develop large lumps (humps) on the head when adult (especially in males), and this is quite normal.

• TUMOURS (3). These may appear almost anywhere on the body. Often only one tumour is present, but sometimes more. Tumours may be the same colour as the surrounding skin or sometimes black (Melanoma). They vary greatly in size (and shape), some reaching several millimetres or even centimetres across.

See also: SPOTS (2); SECTION III: CYSTS.

HAEMORRHAGE (skin, fins)

Reddening of the skin or red streaking in the fins, caused by rupturing of capillaries as a result of systemic VIRUS (3) or BACTERIAL INFECTION (3). Skin damage caused by blood-feeding ECTOPARASITES (3) can also lead to skin haemorrhaging.

See also: FIN CONGESTION (2), COLORATION (2).

HANGING (at the surface, in corners)

• Hanging head-up at the surface is commonly a sign of OXYGEN STARVATION (3) (see also GASPING [2]).

The fish pictured above are hanging head down, near the surface, to avoid attack by an aggressive fish, keeping as far from the aggressor as possible. The fish below are hanging head-up, adopting a submissive posture, to avoid antagonising the fish lurking in the lower background. Note the clamped fins.

● This behaviour, together with hanging in corners, is sometimes seen in (bottom-dwelling) fish, typically cichlids, attempting to evade AGGRESSION (3). Unable to find safety elsewhere, they attempt to elude persecution by retreating to the upper levels.

● Species which have been bred to have abnormally long finnage, especially the tail (e.g. many fancy guppy *(Poecilia reticulata)* varieties), may swim slightly head-up because of the weight of their unnaturally heavy appendages.

● Hanging head-down, in species for which this is abnormal behaviour, is indicative of various types of STRESS (3).

● Victims of AGGRESSION (3) or nervous fish sometimes adopt a slightly head-down position at the ends/rear of the tank, and may back away from any (perceived) threat, assuming a more extreme head-down position as their tail encounters the background/glass and is pushed upwards.
● Swimming head-down may also denote SWIM-BLADDER DISEASE (3).
● Occasionally a head-down position may be adopted as a reaction to problems with NITROGENOUS WASTES (3) or OXYGEN (3) depletion.
● It may also be caused by the weight of a stone or other foreign body wedged in the mouth/gullet (see CHOKING [2]).

HEAD SHAKING

The fish swims 'on the spot' and shakes its head, the movement sometimes continuing along the body in an overall sinuous movement. May be associated with SHIMMYING (2) and YAWNING (2), and is usually symptomatic of a slight aberration in water quality, commonly raised NITRATE (3) levels or suspended matter (CLOUDY WATER [2]).
See also: IRRITATION (2).

HIDING

Hiding is generally a sign of NERVOUSNESS (2) and sometimes of ill health; however, some fish are naturally secretive, for example many ambush predators and breeding cave-spawners. Nocturnal fish hide during the day. Fish which are victims of AGGRESSION (3) may hide, and some livebearer females do so when about to give birth. Newly introduced fish commonly hide until they have recovered from TRANSPORTATION STRESS (3) and familiarised themselves with their surroundings and new tankmates.

HOLES

● In the head may be the nostrils or the sensory pores. If the latter become enlarged and infected in cichlids, HEXAMITIASIS (3) should be suspected. Enlargement or erosion of the sensory pore openings, without infection, is sometimes a sign of SENILITY (3).
● In the fins are usually INJURIES (2).

● In the body may be INJURIES (2), WOUNDS (3) left by ECTOPARASITES (3), or ULCERS (3).

● The row (or rows) of small holes along each flank of the fish consist of the pore openings of the lateral line. These, like the head pores, may be affected by HEXAMITIASIS (3).

HOLLOW BELLY
See EMACIATION (2)

HYPERACTIVITY
See DARTING (2), JUMPING (2)

INJURY
Although manifestly a problem in itself, an injury may be indicative of other problems, in particular AGGRESSION (3) and STRESS (3). Fish may be injured directly by other fish; or injure themselves on decor items during flight from an aggressor, or in panic triggered by external stimulus such as human disturbance in or near the aquarium.

See also: SECTION I: Fish Compatibility; The Correct Environment; SECTION III: INJURY, WOUNDS.

IRRITATION
The following signs, individually and collectively, may indicate that the fish is experiencing irritation of the skin and/or gills, normally by adverse water conditions or, less frequently, PARASITES (3) (ECTOPARASITES (3), *ICHTHYOPHTHIRIUS (3)*):

● FIN TWITCHING (2)
● DARTING (2)
● JUMPING (2)
● SCRATCHING (2)
● FLASHING (2)
● COUGHING (2)
● YAWNING (2)
● SHIMMYING (2)
● HEAD SHAKING (2)
● CLAMPED FINS (2)
● RESPIRATORY DISTRESS (2)

JUMPING
Jumping, together with PANCAKING (2), is an escape

response. It may be provoked by:
- AGGRESSION (3) or expected aggression (including predation)
- Panic at external stimuli (e.g. sudden or unusual movement near the tank, appearance of a net in the tank)
- POISONING (3), especially as an escape reaction to chemicals (including CHLORINE (3), CHLORAMINE (3), and some medications).
- ACIDOSIS (3) or ALKALOSIS (3)
- Irritation by ECTOPARASITES (3)

See also: DARTING (2), BEHAVIOUR (2), SWIMMING (2), IRRITATION (2).

LETHARGY

A common sign of ill health. The fish is less active than normal, and may rest on the bottom or skulk in corners or under/among rocks or other decor items. A common early indication of a problem, lethargy usually increases as the illness worsens. Nocturnal species may appear lethargic by day, and diurnal ones by night, and this is quite normal. TRANSPORTATION STRESS (3) and SHOCK (3) commonly result in this behaviour, as do many environmental and pathogenic diseases.

See also: GENERAL MALAISE (2), APPETITE (2), BEHAVIOUR (2).

LUMPS

See GROWTHS (2)

MOUTH, abnormal

The lips of fish are sometimes affected by GROWTHS (2), e.g. TUMOURS (3), *LYMPHOCYSTIS* (3), and COLUMNARIS (3). They are also subject to INJURY (2) from sharp substrates in species that use their mouth to dig, or from AGGRESSION (3) in species that 'mouth-fight' (chiefly cichlids). This may result in permanent distortion even after the injury has healed.

See also: FEEDING DIFFICULTIES (2), CHOKING (2), GAPING/GASPING (2).

MUCUS HYPERPRODUCTION

Under certain circumstances fish may produce abnormal

Uaru amphiacanthoides fry feeding on mucus of the parent fish.

quantities of skin mucus in response to external stimuli. In most cases these are health problems; however, some fish, notably discus (*Symphysodon* spp.) and *Uaru* spp. produce extra mucus as a first food for their fry.

The SKIN (2) takes on a greyish or whitish COLORATION (2); however, this may not always be evident. The increase in mucus may be patchy, and sometimes affects the eyes (CLOUDY EYE (2)). There may be associated signs of skin IRRITATION (2) such as FLASHING (2) and SHIMMYING (2), and if the problem affects the gills, some RESPIRATORY DISTRESS (2) (increased respiratory rate).

● Mucus hyperproduction may be caused by any irritant, e.g. ECTOPARASITES (3) such as FLUKES (3) and PROTOZOA (3) (e.g. *PISCINOODINIUM* (3), *ICHTHYOPHTHIRIUS* (3), and those causing SKIN SLIME DISEASE (3)), or adverse water chemistry/quality (ACIDOSIS (3), ALKALOSIS (3), POISONING (3), AMMONIA (3), NITRITE (3), NITRATE (3), CHLORINE (3), CHLORAMINE (3)).

● Overdosing with chemical disease remedies can also irritate the skin, leading to mucus hyperproduction.

● Sloughing of body mucus (e.g. in *Symphysodon* (discus) and *Uaru* spp.) may be a reaction to STRESS (3) (especially TRANSPORTATION STRESS (3)), incorrect environmental conditons, or a change (often only minor) in environmental conditions. In actuality the fish apparently produces additional mucus as a reaction to the 'hostile stimulus', but the problem generally goes unnoticed until the excess mucus is lost, by which time the crisis is generally over.

NERVOUSNESS

Nervousness commonly manifests as a tendency to hide,

and/or to panic and endeavour to escape perceived threats/dangers by DARTING (2) across the aquarium, JUMPING (2), and/or PANCAKING (2). This can result in serious INJURY (3), and in turn cause stress and nervousness among tankmates. Reduced APPETITE (2) commonly results from nervousness, and may ultimately result in EMACIATION (2). Chronic nervousness can lead to immunosuppression as a result of the serious STRESS (3) involved.

● Nervousness is normally a sign of SHOCK (3) or STRESS (3), or of conditions likely to cause stress unless remedied, for example disturbing stimuli outside the tank, or inappropriate conditions, in particular lack of suitable shelter, in the tank. Unsuitable tankmates (e.g. too large, too boisterous) can also cause nervousness, even if no physical bullying takes place. Inappropriate lighting – too bright, or from below in substrate-free tanks – also commonly results in nervousness, as will the lack of a 'dawn' and 'dusk' period between the turning on/off of the room light and that of the aquarium.

● Some diseases can also involve nervous behaviour, or skittish behaviour resembling that caused by nervousness, for example parasitisation by ECTOPARASITES (3) such as *ARGULUS* (3) or LEECHES (3) or the PROTOZOANS (3) responsible for SKIN SLIME DISEASE (3).

● Newly introduced fish are commonly nervous for a variable period following their arrival, until they have settled in and accustomed themselves to their surroundings, tankmates, and owner's routine. They should be allowed to adjust in their own time; any interference, albeit well-meant (e.g. adjusting the decor) is likely to prolong the problem, although intervention is desirable in the event of serious AGGRESSION (3) from any tankmate. In such circumstances removal of the offender is preferable to removal of the victim.

● Shoaling species may be nervous if kept singly or in too small a group, thus lacking the protection of the shoal important to their psychological security.

● Some species have a reputation for particular nervousness, but chronic nervousness is generally indicative of poor husbandry and resultant STRESS (3).

A particularly striking example is the discus

(*Symphysodon* spp.), an extremely popular cichlid which has acquired a totally unjustified reputation for delicateness and nervousness. When these fish were first imported, aquarium technique was relatively primitive, and losses were high. The myth thus developed that discus require extremely hygienic conditions such as only bare tanks can provide (another myth – bare tanks are more likely to have problems with AMMONIA (3) and NITRITE (3) toxicity than those with decor), and so they were kept in bare aquaria. In nature, discus have ample cover available, and live in shady areas among roots and fallen branches. Kept in bare aquaria under glaring lighting, they not surprisingly become nervous and suffer extreme stress, and often die. In the interests of hygiene these calm-water fish are also subjected to often violent turbulence from power filters, adding to their misery. It is a minor miracle that any survive at all, let alone breed. Yet, discus kept properly, in a suitably decorated, illuminated, and filtered aquarium, are as easy to keep, as hardy, and as confident and outgoing as their close relatives the angelfish (*Pterophyllum* spp.), found in the majority of community aquaria all over the world. Discus likewise kept in such aquaria, often by aquarists ignorant of their 'delicate nature', seem to thrive equally readily.

See also: SECTION 1: The Correct Environment; Purchasing, Transporting, and Introducing Fish; Fish Compatibility.

OBESITY

True obesity is symptomatic of long-term OVERFEEDING (3) on an unsuitable diet.

See also DISTENDED BODY (2).

OPERCULUM, abnormal

- The operculum may be wholly or partially missing, normally as a result of genetic DEFORMITY (3), but occasionally due to INJURY (3).
- A distended operculum may be caused by a tumour, or by problems affecting the GILLS (2).
- The opercula are commonly distended in brooding mouthbrooders, returning to normal after fry release.
- Expanding the opercula is a form of display, usually threat, in some fish – a purely transitory phenomenon.

181

Fish with missing operculum, probably genetic in origin.

PANCAKING

An escape reflex, usually seen in flat-sided fish such as discus (*Symphysodon* spp.) and angels (*Pterophyllum* spp.), in which the fish shoots along the surface of the water on its side.

See also: DARTING (2), JUMPING (2), BEHAVIOUR (2), NERVOUSNESS (2), SWIMMING (2).

PATCHES

See SPOTS (2), GROWTHS (2), MUCUS HYPER-PRODUCTION (2), COLORATION (2).

PESTS

A variety of creatures sometimes appear in aquaria, in the water, on the decor and/or glasses, and/or on the fish. Some of these invaders may be introduced with LIVE FOODS (3), with decor, or on fish.

● Some are harmless, but may signal environmental degradation, e.g. PLANARIANS (3).

● Some, e.g. LEECHES (3), *ARGULUS* (3), *LERNAEA* (3),

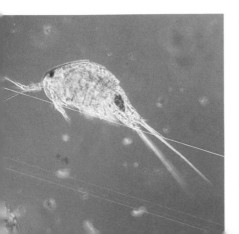

A copepod, about 1mm in length. The occurrence of large numbers of copepods in the aquarium is unusual since these crustaceans are readily eaten by most fish. Their proliferation may indicate an organic pollution problem.

ERGASILUS (3), are PARASITES (3) of fish.

● Others may or may not prove a nuisance, e.g. SNAILS (3), *HYDRA* (3), COPEPODS (3).

● *TUBIFEX (3)* worms sometimes colonise the substrate if not eaten immediately, but are generally eventually eradicated by the fish.

● Non-parasitic NEMATODES (3) – 1-3 cm long, non-segmented, red-brown worms – may also colonise the substrate and biological filter.

● Worms protruding from the anus of a fish are *CAMALLANUS* (3).

RELATIVE SIZES OF FISH PATHOGENS AND PARASITES

LARVAL TAPEWORMS	20cm+				
PISCICOLA: Fish leech.	5cm				
CAMALLANUS: Roundworm.	2cm	VISIBLE TO NAKED EYE			
SAPROLEGNIA: Fungus.	Microscopic to 1cm or more				
LERNAEA: Anchor worm.	8mm				
ARGULUS: Fish louse	6mm		HAND LENS		
DIPLOSTOMUM: Eye worm (Metacercarial stage)	1mm				
ICHTHYOPHTHIRIUS: Whitespot protozoan (trophont stage)	0.4mm			ORDINARY (LIGHT)MICROSCOPE	
GYRODACTYLUS: Skin fluke	0.1-0.2mm				
PISCINOODINIUM: Velvet protozoan	0.1mm				
TRICHODINA:	50 um– 0.1mm				
ICHTHYOPHTHIRIUS: Whitespot protozoan (free-living theront stage)	50um				ELECTRON MICROSCOPE
HEXAMITA:	10–20 um				
PLEISTOPHORA: (spore)	5um				
BACTERIA: (various species)	0.5 – 10um				
VIRUSES: (various)	0.01 – 0.5um				

Measurements: 1cm = 10mm

1mm = 1,000 microns (um)

RESPIRATORY DISTRESS

A group of signs affecting fish which are suffering from insufficient OXYGEN (3) reaching their tissues. A degree of respiratory distress is common in most cases of illness in fish.

Major signs of respiratory distress are:
● Increased rate of gill beats (increased breathing rate).
● GASPING (2) or gulping – the fish may be at the water's surface, where the oxygen level is higher, but ultimately may become too exhausted to remain there.
● Swollen GILLS (2) and expanded opercula.

Associated signs may include COUGHING (2) and/or CHOKING (2), GENERAL MALAISE (2) and/or IRRITATION (2).

Increased gill rate is almost always a sign that something is amiss, and often one of the earliest signs of a serious problem impending, although it may be simply a response to increased activity (e.g. spawning) or temporary circumstances (e.g. fright by external stimulus). Fish exhibiting this sign should be kept under careful observation until the cause manifests or the gill rate returns to normal. Levels of NITROGENOUS WASTES (3) should be checked as an additional precaution.

The various possible environmental and physiological causes of respiratory distress are discussed in SECTION III: OXYGEN STARVATION.

RESTING (on the bottom, on decor items)
See BUOYANCY (2)

SCALES, Abnormal

Scale abnormalities are generally of two kinds:
● Raised scales: the scale edges are raised from the body, giving a serrated ('pine-cone') effect to the body contour. This condition is generally associated with DROPSY (3) and is caused by an accumulation of fluid in the body pushing the scales outwards. *TETRAHYMENA* (3) may also cause 'bristly' scales.
● Missing scales: scales may be lost through INJURY (2) or a number of diseases (e.g. ULCER (3) disease, severe SKIN SLIME DISEASE (3)). A small number of fish predate on the scales of other fish (see PARASITIC FISH (3)). Loss of

scales may open the way for SECONDARY INFECTIONS (3).
See also: SKIN PROBLEMS (2), SCRATCHING (2); SECTION III: WOUNDS.

SCRATCHING

Scratching against decor items, including the substrate, is indicative of irritation of the skin and/or gills, arising from a variety of causes. It differs slightly from FLASHING (2) in that the typical sideways twist of the body that characterises the latter is absent, but by many aquarists the two terms are regarded as synonymous. Scratching on hard decor items may cause loss of scales and other INJURIES (3).

• Scratching is most commonly the result of contamination of the aquarium water with dissolved toxins (AMMONIA (3), NITRITE (3), NITRATE (3), POISONING (3)).

• It may also be due to the presence of suspended matter (CLOUDY WATER [2]).

• Less commonly it is a sign of ECTOPARASITE (3) attack (e.g. SKIN SLIME DISEASE (3), FLUKES (3), ICHTHYOPHTHIRIUS (3), PISCINOODINIUM (3), ARGULUS (3)).

See also IRRITATION (2).

SCUM

• In newly set-up aquaria, scum on the surface may be caused by bacterial activity or particles of dirt from the substrate (which can never be washed completely clean). In such cases it normally dissipates within a few days, during the maturation process of the aquarium. As no fish should be present at this juncture, it is unlikely to prove harmful.

• Scum on the surface of a mature aquarium may, if oily, reflect diet. Although unlikely to prove harmful to fish directly, it may reflect unsuitable foods, and/or inadequate or incorrectly installed filtration.

• If the room is heated by a self-contained oil or paraffin heater, then an oily scum on the water's surface may indicate contamination by fumes, with the possibility of harmful effects (POISONING [3]) on fish health. The aquarium hood should be tight-fitting to prevent direct ingress of fumes from the room, and the air-pump should be sited in an unpolluted area, or air pumped through a water-filled pre-filter to avoid pumping fumes into the aquarium. Alternatively, a different type of room heater can be used.

● A layer of scum on the surface may be indicative of (possibly) insufficient surface movement leading to OXYGEN (3) depletion, and may further inhibit the essential gas exchange that takes place at the air-water interface.

● A thick scum-like green coating, often containing gas bubbles, on the substrate and decor items is usually CYANOBACTERIA (3). ALGAE (3) may also coat decor but are less invasive and much slower-growing.

See also: CLOUDY WATER (2); SECTION I: The Correct Environment; Nutrition.

SHIMMIES, SHIMMYING

The shimmies or shimmying is a condition in which the fish flexes its body from side to side, without travelling forward through the water, i.e. swimming on the spot. HEAD SHAKING (2) is commonly associated with shimmying, and sometimes YAWNING (2). Shimmying may alternate with periods of normal swimming activity. Several causes have been implicated, including:

● A change in water chemistry.

● Poor water quality (including high NITRITE (3) levels and other forms of POISONING (3)).

● Suspended matter (CLOUDY WATER [2]) causing skin/gill irritation.

● Chilling (e.g. during transportation or resulting from heater failure).

● COLUMNARIS (3) disease (*FLEXIBACTER* (3) infection), especially in poeciliid fish.

See also: IRRITATION (2).

SHYNESS

See NERVOUSNESS (2)

SKIN PROBLEMS

Clinical signs of disease associated with the skin include MUCUS HYPERPRODUCTION (2), HAEMORRHAGE (2), ULCERS (2), abnormal SCALES (2), GROWTHS (2), SPOTS (2), changes in COLORATION (2).

• Skin conditions are commonly a reaction to environmental problems such as adverse pH (ACIDOSIS (3), ALKALOSIS [3]) or high levels of AMMONIA (3) and some other TOXINS (3). Skin reddening is common, but not invariable, with these problems.

• Skin abnormalities may also be symptomatic of SKIN DISEASES (3) caused by BACTERIA (3), VIRUSES (3), FUNGUS (3), PROTOZOANS (3) (SKIN SLIME DISEASE (3), *PISCINOODINIUM* (3), *ICHTHYOPH-THIRIUS* (3)), and other ECTOPARASITES (3) (e.g. FLUKES [3]).

• Some SKIN PARASITES (3) may be visible to the naked eye, e.g. *LERNAEA* (3), *ARGULUS* (3), and LEECHES (3).

• Red patches on the skin may be WOUNDS (3) left by large parasites, BURNS (3), or other INJURIES (3); such breaches of skin integrity may be subject to SECONDARY INFECTIONS (3) with BACTERIA (3) or FUNGUS (3), and/or develop into ULCERS (2). They may also lead to OSMOTIC STRESS (3).

• Sloughing of areas of skin is symptomatic of COLUMNARIS (3) and severe ECTOPARASITE (3) infestation, e.g. *PISCINOODINIUM* (3), *ICHTHYOPH-THIRIUS* (3), SKIN SLIME DISEASE (3).

• MUCUS HYPERPRODUCTION (2), producing a greyish coating, is symptomatic of a number of skin problems, both environmental and parasitic.

• A yellow-brown coating normally indicates *PISCINOODINIUM* (3) (Velvet disease).

• Sloughing of body mucus (e.g. in discus (*Symphysodon* spp.) and *Uaru* spp.) may be a reaction to STRESS (3) (especially TRANSPORTATION STRESS (3)), incorrect environmental conditons, or a change (often only minor) in environmental conditions. In actuality the fish apparently produces additional mucus as a reaction to the 'hostile stimulus', but the problem generally goes unnoticed until the excess mucus is lost, by which time the crisis is normally over.

SLIMY SKIN
See MUCUS HYPERPRODUCTION (2)

Patches of slimy skin are particularly evident along the dorsal ridge and upper head of this tetra. Note extreme opacity of the eye.

SPOTS

Spots and blotches of various colours may appear on the skin, fins, and gills in association with a number of diseases. It must be remembered that spots are a common feature of normal coloration, sometimes present in only one sex, or in some individuals of one or both sexes, or not developing until adulthood. The anal fin ocelli (eggspots) of many mouthbrooding cichlids are good examples of such variable spots. As ever, the aquarist should familiarise him or herself with the norm and degree of variability for each species.

Light-coloured spots:

● Pinhead-sized white spots on the head, body, and fins may be *ICHTHYOPHTHIRIUS* (3) (Whitespot) or newly-developing *LYMPHOCYSTIS* (3) cysts. The latter are typically far less numerous, often pinkish-white in colour, and reach a larger size, eventually forming cauliflower-like growths. *APIOSOMA* (3) and systemic fungus-like infections such as *DERMOCYSTIDIUM* (3) produce similar spots, but are far less common.

● Whitish spots, which on closer inspection can be seen to be tiny tufts protruding from beneath the edges of scales, may be due to systemic FUNGUS INFECTION (3), which is, however, very rare.

● Small whitish FUNGUS (3)-like tufts, especially on hard tissue (fins, opercula) may be *EPISTYLIS* (3).

● Grey spots or patches on the skin of angelfish (*Pterophyllum* spp.) may be caused by *HETEROSPORIS* (3).

● Small whitish patches in poeciliids may signify *TETRAHYMENA* (3).

• Grey-white patches under the skin, in tetras and some other fish, may be caused by *PLEISTOPHORA* (3).

• A white spot obscuring the lens of the eye may be caused by *DIPLOSTOMUM* (3) or blindness arising from INBREEDING (3). (See also CLOUDY EYE (2).)

• Greyish or whitish patches are likely to be MUCUS HYPERPRODUCTION (2) (q.v. for possible causes).

• Tiny off-white spots on the fins are commonly tiny injuries, but may sometimes look like *ICHTHYOPH-THIRIUS* (3) (Whitespot). Newly-purchased fish showing such spots should be kept under close observation, but whitespot is unlikely in established aquarium residents.

• Whitish circles may be WOUNDS (3) left by LEECHES (3).

Dark-coloured spots:

• Black spots on the body/fins are usually the encysted larval HELMINTHS (3) causing BLACK SPOT (3) disease.

• Black spots or patches round the mouths of East African cichlids are symptomatic of BLACK CHIN (3).

• Dark or discoloured patches on the body may be the result of BURNS (3) or superficial INJURY (3).

• Dark spots on the gills may be iron deposited during ACIDOSIS (3).

Red spots:

• Red spots on the skin may be WOUNDS (3) caused by ECTOPARASITES (3) such as LEECHES (3), or subcutaneous HAEMORRHAGES (2).

• Red spots or streaks on the FINS (2) (FIN CONGESTION [2]) are associated with FIN ROT (3).

Other spots:

• Tiny yellow-green spots, sometimes in huge numbers to produce a coating of the same colour, are *PISCIN-OODINIUM* (3).

• Encysted larval HELMINTHS (3) under the skin may appear as smallish spots on the body. The larvae, which are curled within the rounded cyst wall, may number just one or a few and sometimes appear pale to dark grey when present beneath the skin of light-coloured fish.

- MICROSPORIDIAL INFECTIONS (3). These PROTO-ZOAN (3) parasites are a less likely cause of spots in aquarium fish. The growths or 'nodules' may be of the same coloration as the surrounding skin, or may appear pale-coloured. They can vary greatly in size, and may also be present in deeper tissues.
- TUMOURS (3). These may appear almost anywhere on the body. Often only one tumour is present, but sometimes more. Tumours may be the same colour as the surrounding skin or sometimes black (Melanoma). They vary greatly in size (and shape), some reaching several millimetres or even centimetres across.
See also: COLORATION (2), GROWTHS (2).

STUNTING
Restricted growth may be the result of:
- Genetic deficiency, sometimes resulting from INBREED-ING (3).
- Poor diet (AFLATOXINS (3), VITAMIN DEFICIENCY (3), NUTRITIONAL DISEASES (3); *(see also SECTION 1: Nutrition).*
- Lack of APPETITE (2) caused by chronic AGG-RESSION (3), STRESS (3), DISEASE (3), or incorrect environment (NITRATE (3), NITRITE (3), AMMONIA (3), OXYGEN STARVATION (3), POISONING (3); *See SECTION 1: The Correct Environment.*
- Direct biochemical effects of adverse water conditions, as above.
- Insufficient living space. *See SECTION 1: The Correct Environment.*
- Over-frequent breeding (females). *See SECTION 1: Breeding.*
- Direct result of pathogenic DISEASE (3).
- Growth-inhibiting hormones. It has been demonstrated for a small number of species that the dominant (largest) individual in a brood produces growth-inhibiting hormones, preventing further growth by potentially competing siblings.

Stunting may be temporary or permanent, depending on the cause. Obviously genetic stunting is irremediable; however, some other types may respond to amelioration of the underlying problem. The sooner the 'treatment', the better the chance of a 'cure'. *See also: DEFORMITY (2), NERVOUSNESS (2).*

SWELLING(S)
See LUMPS (2), SPOTS (2), DISTENDED BODY (2).

SWIMMING, abnormal
As with other behavioural factors, awareness of the norm for the fish concerned is essential.

Many swimming abnormalities are a reaction to poor or inappropriate water conditions, and a check on water chemistry and quality parameters is a sensible precaution if any unusual swimming BEHAVIOUR (2) occurs, unless an alternative explanation is immediately obvious (e.g. adverse reaction to a treatment).

● Abnormal rapid DARTING (2), perhaps coupled with JUMPING (2) out of the water/and or PANCAKING (2), is an escape reaction indicative of POISONING (3), including with CHLORINE (3) or CHLORAMINE (3); it may be a sign of ACIDOSIS (3) or ALKALOSIS (3); or of adverse reaction to a chemical treatment *(see SECTION I: Treating Fish Diseases).*

● Rapid swimming with no apparent control of movement (e.g. rotating, whirling) may be indicative of POISONING (3) or OXYGEN STARVATION (3) (including that resulting from serious gill damage caused by gill diseases such as BRANCHIOMYCOSIS (3) or GILL PARASITES (3)).

● PANCAKING (2) along the surface, and/or JUMPING (2) from the water, is an escape reaction used in nature to elude predators; in captivity, usually stimulated by sudden or violent movement or vibration near the aquarium or the use of a net; or it may be a reaction to some chemical treatments, POISONING (3), acute ACIDOSIS (3) or ALKALOSIS (3).

● Diving into the substrate is also sometimes an escape reaction, but may also be a feeding mechanism or part of the spawning ritual (e.g. in some egg-laying cyprinodonts (killifish)).

● Some pathogenic diseases may lead to abnormal swimming, e.g. the muscle-wasting caused by *PLEIST-OPHORA (3)*.

● Normal speed or slower than normal swimming, coupled with loss of equilibrium (swimming nose-down, on one side, or upside-down), is indicative of SWIM BLADDER DISEASE (3).

● The weight of a large TUMOUR (3) may cause erratic, unbalanced, or laboured swimming.

● DEFORMITIES (2), including deliberately cultivated abnormally long finnage, can cause swimming difficulties.

● Swimming on the spot (see SHIMMYING (2)), HANGING (2) head-up or head-down (often in corners), resting on the bottom (unless normal for the species) (see BUOYANCY [2]) are all swimming abnormalities which should be regarded as warning signs that something may be amiss.

● Swimming up and down the aquarium glasses, as if trying to find a way out, is common in newly-introduced fish (TRANSPORTATION STRESS (3)), or, less frequently, in cases of severe STRESS (3), particularly when caused by AGGRESSION (3). It can, however, also be an attempt to solicit food!

● Fish which have accidentally picked up a piece of gravel may swim with their head pointing downwards, as a result of the weight of the stone, or with their mouth permanently open (GAPING (2)).

Associated signs may include: GENERAL MALAISE (2), IRRITATION (2), SHIMMYING (2), FLASHING (2), SCRATCHING (2), NERVOUSNESS (2), BUOYANCY (2), CHOKING (2).

SWIMBLADDER PROBLEMS
See BUOYANCY (2)

TIMIDITY
See NERVOUSNESS (2)

ULCERS
Open sores or lesions on the body, often with reddening around the perimeter, and often symptomatic of a general systemic BACTERIAL INFECTION (3). Ulcers may develop SECONDARY INFECTIONS (3), (FUNGUS [3] and/or ECTOPARASITES [3]), and may be associated with other symptoms of systemic bacterial infection, such as

Skin ulcers. Tissue necrosis has resulted in cratering of the body surface.

DISTENDED BODY (2) (i.e. DROPSY [3]) or EMACIATION (2), and/or EXOPHTHALMIA (2).

The open ulcers may severely weaken the fish, allowing the influx of water and causing significant OSMOTIC STRESS (3), as well as opening the way for Secondary infection (3).

● Ulcers are commonly a sign of chronic systemic BACTERIAL INFECTION (3), caused by, for example, *AEROMONAS* (3), *PSEUDOMONAS* (3), MYCOBACTERIA (3) and *VIBRIO* (3).

● Secondary infection of WOUNDS (3) can also lead to ulceration.

● Ulcer disease is closely linked with STRESS (3) caused by transportation, handling, and/or water quality problems. *See also SECTION III: ULCERS.*

VOMITING

The ejection of partially digested or undigested food from the mouth. This may serve as a means of eliminating toxins and other noxious substances which may have been accidentally taken in with the meal.

● Under aquarium conditions, some fish (e.g. the redtailed catfish, *Phractocephalus hemioliopterus*) are known occasionally to vomit their meal. This may be the result of an incorrect diet, or be due to environmental STRESS (3) or a sudden disturbance to the fish.

● Fish which repeatedly vomit may be suffering from a DIGESTIVE DISORDER (3) such as a BACTERIAL INFECTION (3), inflammation, or physical blockage (the latter possibly due to CONSTIPATION (3) or to having swallowed a piece of gravel/rock or item of aquarium equipment). *See also: COUGHING (2), CHOKING (2), FEEDING DIFFICULTIES (2); SECTION III: VOMITING.*

WASTING
See EMACIATION (2)

WORM-LIKE CREATURES (on fish, in the aquarium). *See PESTS (2)*

YAWNING
Fish are occasionally seen to stretch their mouths open in a manner comparable to human yawning. This behaviour is little understood, but may be a response to gill irritation, perhaps an attempt to dislodge some irritant by flushing water through the gills.

● In at least some cases this appears to be a response to poor water quality; a check on AMMONIA (3), NITRITE (3), and NITRATE (3) levels is therefore indicated. Other sources of gill irritation should also be considered:

● OXYGEN (3) depletion or excess CARBON DIOXIDE (3).

● Incorrect pH (ACIDOSIS (3), ALKALOSIS (3)).

● POISONING (3) (including CHLORINE (3) AND CHLORAMINE (3)).

● Gill PARASITES (3) such as *GYRODACTYLUS* (3), *ERGASILUS* (3).

● Other pathogenic diseases affecting the gills, e.g. BRANCHIOMYCOSIS (3), SKIN SLIME DISEASE (3).

Associated signs may include: SHIMMYING (3), HEAD SHAKING (3), GENERAL MALAISE (3), IRRITATION (3).

SECTION III

TREATMENT OF DISEASES AND HEALTH PROBLEMS A–Z

Note on medications:
The availability of many of the medications listed herein may differ from country to country. If in doubt, advice should be sought from a veterinarian or pharmacist. Unless otherwise specified, dosages for bath immersion treatments are for a one-off application, i.e. the water is treated once only. By contrast, dosages for oral medication via food are normally daily dosages, the quoted quantity to be administered each day for the prescribed period, unless otherwise stated.

P Prescription-only chemical, or available from a pharmacist. (Note: in certain countries some of these may be readily available without a prescription from a vet or pharmacist.)

A

ACANTHOCEPHALANS

ENDOPARASITIC (3) worms belonging to the phylum Acanthocephala. Also known as spiny-headed or thorny-headed worms. Several species are intestinal PARASITES (3) of fish. One species occasionally encountered is *Pomphorhynchus laevis,* which is transmitted by freshwater shrimps (*Gammarus*).

The adult worm inhabits the fish's gut, where it attaches to the gut wall with the aid of its elongate proboscis which is equipped with spines and hooks. Adult worms vary in length, according to the species, and measure typically between 1.5 and 3 cm.

Female acanthocephalan worms release their eggs into the fish's gut lumen where they are subsequently vented with the faeces. Within the aquatic environment the eggs must be eaten by a CRUSTACEAN (3) (such as *Gammarus*), whereupon they continue development within the crustacean's gut. Crustacean intermediate hosts include certain species of amphipods, isopods, COPEPODS (3), and ostracods. The fish contracts the acanthocephalan through eating an infected crustacean.

Acanthocephalans are largely associated with cyprinid fish, and are generally restricted to wild-caught and pond-farmed fish rather than those reared under aquarium conditions.

SIGNS
Acanthocephalans rarely present health problems in tropical aquarium fish. In many cases the parasite does little visible harm to its host and an infected fish may appear asymptomatic. In heavy infections, however, the fish may

exhibit EMACIATION (2) and be hollow-bellied. Often, a mild infection is discovered only by chance during post-mortem examination of the fish's intestine which may reveal one or more parasites attached to the gut wall. In some cases, the fish's gut may be slightly enlarged and contain rounded nodules, visible on the outer surface, which are formed as a host-response to the parasite. Diagnosis may be achieved by examination of the fish's faeces for the presence of eggs, though this requires specialist knowledge in order to differentiate from the eggs of other intestinal HELMINTHS (3).

PREVENTION AND TREATMENT
Control measures are entirely preventative rather than curative as there are no commercial treatments available at present. Fortunately, the parasite is unlikely to cause serious harm to its host. Acanthocephalans are unlikely to transmit under aquarium conditions because the intermediate crustacean host is not normally present, although it is possible for aquarium fish to become infected through ingesting certain LIVE FOODS (3) such as wild-caught freshwater shrimps and COPEPODS (3) collected from waters inhabited by fish. Adult worms in the intestine have a limited life and eventually die (usually within a few months), hence the infection normally clears by itself with time.

ACHYLA
A genus of parasitic fungus belonging to the Class Oomycetes. *See FUNGAL DISEASES (3).*

ACIDOSIS
A condition caused by the pH of the aquarium water falling below the optimal pH range for the fish species affected.

SIGNS
These vary depending on whether the pH drop is rapid (acute acidosis) or gradual (chronic acidosis).
● Acute acidosis: A rapid fall in pH can lead to excitable BEHAVIOUR (2), rapid DARTING (2) swimming movements, and JUMPING (2). Death may follow rapidly.
● Chronic acidosis: A slow decrease in pH over time pro-

duces less obvious behavioural signs. Fish often GASP (2) and COUGH (2) as a result of gill damage and due to a reduced capacity for blood haemoglobin to carry oxygen. Gills and skin appear turbid and milky as a result of MUCUS HYPERPRODUCTION (2). There may also be reddened skin areas as a result of the acidity irritating external body surfaces. At a pH of less than 5, dark grey marks appear on the gills as a result of iron being deposited.

CAUSES
Most fish which are accustomed to a pH of around neutral (pH 7) exhibit signs of acidosis when the pH reaches about 5.0 and below. Fish from naturally alkaline waters, e.g. Lakes Malawi and Tanganyika, may be affected as soon as the pH drops below neutral. The acid conditions directly irritate the fish's external body surfaces and cause adverse biochemical changes, in particular the fish is unable to maintain a stable acid/base balance within its blood.

Sudden drops in pH (except for those occurring where a fish is transferred from one aquarium to another without due attention to water chemistry) usually occur only in mineral-depleted water containing minimal dissolved salts and hence possessing little or no buffering capacity. The pH of such water is commonly unstable.

Slow decreases in pH are generally the result of inadequate partial water changes, such that the acidic by-products of the nitrogen cycle slowly acidify the aquarium water. Excess CARBON DIOXIDE (3) may also be a contributory factor, particularly in heavily-planted aquaria or those where CO_2 injection is used to promote plant growth.

Fish from naturally alkaline waters may suffer from chronic acidosis if maintained, through ignorance or negligence on the part of the aquarist, in a lower pH than that experienced in nature.

TREATMENT
Acidosis should be treated by correcting the pH level.

In cases of chronic acidosis, raise the pH slowly until it lies within the optimal range of the species of fish being kept. This can be achieved using bicarbonate of soda or a proprietary alkaline pH buffer. The rate of pH increase should not exceed 0.3 of a pH unit per day, so as to allow the fish to adjust its biochemical processes gradually. (Note: check that AMMONIA (3) is not present, since raising the pH will make this more toxic.)

In cases of acute acidosis the fish is unlikely to survive such a rapid drop in pH unless the problem is rectified immediately rather than gradually, and a better course of action is to return it as soon as possible to its accustomed pH range, and then adjust gradually to optimal pH for the species. It must be accepted, however, that acute acidosis is commonly fatal.

It is also important to identify the cause of the pH collapse and eliminate/remedy it. In soft water aquaria the inclusion of some calciferous material in the system (e.g. a bag of dolomite (limestone) chips suspended in the aquarium or placed in the filter) will provide a buffer against pH instability. Improved husbandry may be required to remove nitrogen cycle by-products (NITROGENOUS WASTES [3]) and excess CO_2. Monitor the fish and be prepared to identify and treat SECONDARY INFECTIONS (3) caused by immuno-suppression and opportunist pathogens infecting irritated gill and skin membranes.

See also SECTION I: The Correct Environment.

ACRIFLAVINE

Acriflavine, a mixture of 3, 6-diamino-methylacridium chloride and 3, 6-diaminoacridine, was once widely used (bath treatment) for treating infections caused by certain BACTERIA (3) and PROTOZOAN ECTOPARASITES (3), but is nowadays less popular (though it is still used as a constituent in some commercial remedies). It is harmful to aquatic plants and considered a possible cause of REPRODUCTIVE FAILURE [3] (proven in the case of guppies [*Poecilia reticulata*]). It is sometimes applied as a topical DISINFECTANT (3) on minor skin WOUNDS (3).

AEROMONAS

A genus of BACTERIA (3) commonly found in the aquatic environment. Aeromonads may be present on seemingly healthy fish; however, certain species are pathogenic, causing skin sores or ULCERS (3). BACTERICIDES (3) and ANTIBIOTICS (3) are used for eradicating aeromonad infections.

AFLATOXINS

Toxic and potentially lethal substances produced by certain types of mould (fungi) which sometimes colonise, *inter alia,* improperly stored fish foods. Although the vast majority of reported cases relate to foodfish species, aflatoxin POISONING (3) could conceivably afflict aquarium fish.

SIGNS
Diagnosis of aflatoxin poisoning is difficult as the symptoms may be vague: poor growth, ANAEMIA (3). Death may occur in extreme cases. Fish which ingest aflatoxins may develop liver TUMOURS (3); however, bear in mind that tumours are more likely to arise through disease, genetic defects or other causes. Aflatoxin poisoning should be suspected if the above symptoms coincide with the discovery of contaminated fish food.

CAUSE
Improper storage of dried foods. Foods kept under warm, damp conditions are prone to colonisation by certain aflatoxin-producing fungi, such as *Aspergillus, Fusarium,* and *Penicillium.*

PREVENTION AND TREATMENT
Prevention relies on the proper storage of dried food preparations: cool, dry conditions. Do not store opened pots of dried foods in fish houses or other warm, humid places.

AGGRESSION

Undoubtedly the commonest cause of INJURY (3) in aquarium fish, and of many deaths, either through physical damage or STRESS (3).

SIGNS
Apart from overt aggressive behaviour, look for warning signs in victims, such as split FINS (2) or dislodged SCALES (2), NERVOUSNESS (2), and loss of APPETITE (2). Aggressive behaviour may cease when the aquarist is near the aquarium (supplanted by the feeding reflex), so observation from a distance may be necessary to determine the identity of the aggressor.

Mouth-fighting can lead to injuries to the lips and even a dislocated lower jaw.

Threatening behaviour: the dominant fish (front) is threatening the other fish. Note the flared gills and throat of the aggressor.

CAUSE

Fish rarely launch unprovoked attacks on one another; what is often regarded as aggression is usually either predation or territoriality (the defence of territory, mate, and/or eggs/fry).

Predation does not always involve the death of the victim; a few predators, e.g. scale-eaters, fin-biters, consume only specific parts of the other fish. In nature the same victim is unlikely to be attacked repeatedly, but in the aquarium repeated assaults may eventually prove fatal. Fin-nipping may be regarded as a form of predation. Victims normally have long, trailing or flowing, finnage which other fish mistake for something edible.

Territoriality can be a major problem in the confines of the aquarium, where there is often insufficient space to provide the natural territorial requirement of the offending fish as well as accommodating tankmates. The 'aggressor' regards other fish as intruders or fry predators (the latter often with some justification) and constantly attacks them. Serious injury or death may result – whereas in the wild the intruder would simply swim away from the sensitive area.

A tank divider (glass or plastic) can be used to prevent aggressive contact. Note the flared gills of this firemouth cichlid (Thorichthys meeki).

Long-finned varieties, such as this White Cloud Mountain minnow, (Tanichthys albonubes) are more susceptible to fin-nipping.

A further, related, form of aggression involves a male fish attacking the female(s) provided for him (or, more rarely, *vice versa*). Such attacks may be motivated by territoriality, e.g. if pairing has yet to occur or the pair bond has been broken, so that the victim is, effectively, an intruder in the territory of the aggressor; or the 'aggression' may be simply chasing with a sexual motive. Again, injury or death may result; again, in the wild, the victim would simply retreat to safety.

PREVENTION AND TREATMENT

Problems of this kind can largely be avoided by researching the behaviour of aquarium inmates and not mixing those unsuited to one another's company. The aquarist must accept that some species eat others, some require space and privacy, and that males and females do not necessarily spend their entire lives together. Mistakes are best avoided, but if they do occur, should be rectified, by rehousing or rehoming, ideally before serious damage occurs. A tank divider can be used as a temporary measure to separate aggressor(s) and victim(s).

Sometimes removing a persistent aggressor for a few weeks may resolve the problem. The victim(s) are given an opportunity to recover, and when the aggressive fish is subsequently re-introduced, it will be a 'stranger' in the tank, and thus at a disadvantage. This 'treatment' can be particularly useful where newly-introduced fish are the objects of aggression because they are not yet accepted as members of the community.

See also SECTION I: Fish Compatibility; Breeding.

ALBINISM

Albino fish lack body pigmentation. True albinos are white to cream in coloration and possess red eyes (the eyes are actually unpigmented, the red colour being due to blood capillaries within the eye). Some fish have non-pigmented bodies but black or otherwise pigmented eyes: these are not considered to be true albinos but leucistic.

Albinism is caused by a failure in the biochemical synthesis of the pigment melanin, and this defect may have a genetic origin. Ornamental fish farmers have selectively bred several albino forms of popular aquarium species including *Corydoras* catfish, tiger barbs *(Barbus tetrazona)*, and kribensis cichlids *(Pelvicachromis pulcher)*. Albinism may also occur naturally in wild fish, although wild albinos

Albino catfish.

Albino cichlid.

are relatively rare since their light bodies make them conspicuous to predators.

It is thought that albino fish tend to be less hardy than their normally pigmented counterparts and this may be due to physiological weaknesses which coincide with the albinistic state. The non-pigmented eyes of true albinos are especially photosensitive and for this reason such fish should be kept under subdued lighting or provided with areas of shade within the aquarium.

ALGAE

These primitive plants are found in all aquaria, either attached to submerged surfaces or living freely in the water.

In general, algae are not harmful to aquarium fish. In fact, certain types of algae serve as a food source to vegetarian fish and fish fry. Clumps of algae may also harbour micro-organisms (= 'infusoria') which are themselves important first foods for many fish fry. Some algae also utilise toxic AMMONIA (3), thus removing it from the water. True algae differ from the 'blue-green algae', which are now classified as CYANOBACTERIA (3).

SIGNS

Aquaria vary in terms of the species and abundance of algae they harbour. Algae may be seen as green, red, or brown clumps or filaments which are attached to the aquarium glass, decor, and sometimes to the stems and leaves of live aquatic plants. Free-swimming algae are invisible to the unaided eye but when present in large numbers may impart a green taint to the aquarium water. In extreme cases, notably if the aquarium is exposed for long periods to very strong illumination, usually direct sunshine, the water may

Colonisation by algae makes the rockwork more natural in appearance.

Filamentous green algae, as seen under the microscope.

become extremely turbid, taking on a 'pea-green soup' appearance (GREEN WATER (2), as often occurs in the summer pond). It should be noted that some commercially produced vegetable foods may also impart a faint green or green-blue colour.

CAUSES

Rampant growths of algae may indicate undesirably high levels of certain dissolved nutrients in the aquarium water (e.g. NITRATE [3], phosphate) or incorrect lighting. Aquaria which have a high organic load, caused by an excessive stocking density, overfeeding, or infrequent water changes and cleaning, are prone to algal problems. The level of nitrate in the mains (tap) water may itself be high, depending on its geographical source and sometimes varying with the season. The type of algae which colonises the aquarium is partly influenced by the light intensity, with bright lighting favouring green algae.

PREVENTION AND TREATMENT

Good aquarium management and hygiene *(see SECTION I: The Correct Environment)* will help minimise the organic loading in the aquarium and this, in turn, will limit the amount of nutrients available for algal growth. A lush growth of aquatic plants will also help control algae by competing for nutrients. Chemical formulations which destroy algae (algicides) are commercially available from aquarium stores; however, these should be used only as a last resort (the decaying dead algae may overload the filtration system), and periodic redosing may be required. It is far preferable to address the underlying cause(s) of the problem rather than to rely on chemical control methods.

ALKALOSIS

A condition caused by an increase in the pH of the aquarium water significantly above the upper limit of the natural range of the fish species in question. Alkalosis is less common than ACIDOSIS (3), its acid water counterpart, as the dissolved minerals which give water its alkalinity also help to stabilise pH.

SIGNS
BEHAVIOUR (2) of fish suffering from alkalosis is very similar to that experienced as a result of ACIDOSIS (3). If the onset of the problem is rapid (acute alkalosis) then the fish may become excitable, swimming with DARTING (2) movements and JUMPING (2). A slow increase in pH (chronic alkalosis) is likely to be less dramatic in its effect and simply lead to a general deterioration in health. GASPING (2) and COUGHING (2) are caused by alkaline conditions damaging the gills. MUCUS HYPER-PRODUCTION (2) and reddening of gill and SKIN (2) surfaces are caused by the caustic alkaline conditions.

CAUSES
In acidophile species a pH as low as 8 may cause alkalosis, while those from neutral or slightly alkaline waters may not show signs below a pH of 10-11.

Alkalosis endangers fish by direct damage caused by caustic conditions and by disruption of biochemical processes. (Note: any AMMONIA [3] present will be significantly more toxic at these high pH levels.)

Acute alkalosis is likely only where fish are transferred from tank to tank without due attention to differences in water chemistry, or in the event of gross accidental overdose with chemical pH adjusters.

Chronic alkalosis may occur where fish are kept at a pH higher than that experienced in nature, due to ignorance or negligence on the part of the aquarist; where the pH of the water gradually increases as soluble minerals dissolve out of decor items (although pH is unlikely to reach critical levels if regular partial water changes are made); or where evaporation (which leaves dissolved salts behind) is regular and replaced with mineral-rich water, thereby slowly increasing both mineral content and pH.

TREATMENT
Correct the pH level. In cases of chronic alkalosis decrease the water pH slowly to the ideal pH range for the species of fish being kept. This can be achieved by partial water changes using replacement water with a low(er) mineral content, thereby simultaneously reducing the overall aquarium mineral content at the root of the problem. This method is preferable to using a proprietary acid pH buffer, which will not deal with the underlying cause. Reduce the pH by no more than 0.3 of a pH unit per day, allowing the fish's biochemical processes to adjust gradually.

In cases of acute alkalosis the fish is unlikely to survive a sudden change in pH unless the problem is rectified immediately rather than gradually, and a better course of action is to return it as soon as possible to its accustomed pH range (and, subsequently, ideally, to optimal for the species). It must be accepted, however, that acute alkalosis is commonly fatal.

It is important to identify and eliminate any deficiencies in husbandry which led to the high pH, otherwise a recurrence is likely.

Monitor for SECONDARY INFECTIONS (3) caused by immuno-suppression or opportunist infection of irritated areas of gill or skin tissue.

AMMONIA, AMMONIA POISONING

Ammonia is a toxic waste product of the breakdown of protein and is excreted by fish, mainly via the gills, as well as being produced during the bacterial processing of wastes that forms part of the nitrogen cycle. In closed systems such as ponds and aquaria, ammonia may build up to toxic levels unless it is removed by an effective biological filter. An increase in ammonia may arise from overcrowding, overfeeding, excessive nitrogenous decay, or as a result of inadequate or inactivated biological filtration *(see SECTION I: The Correct Environment)*.

SIGNS
Ammonia POISONING (3) in fish causes the following symptoms:
• RESPIRATORY DISTRESS (2): increased gill rate and GASPING (2) caused by pathological changes to the gill

resulting in reduced efficiency in OXYGEN (3) uptake, together with reduced oxygen-carrying capacity of the blood.

● MUCUS HYPERPRODUCTION (2) causing a white clouding of skin and gills, particularly obvious on dark skin colours and normally transparent fins and eyes.

● reddening of areas of skin caused by HAEMORRHAGE (2) from blood capillaries in the skin and internal organs.

● unusual BEHAVIOUR (2): hyperactivity and excitability, erratic SWIMMING (2) and twitching caused by ammonia damaging the brain and central nervous system.

● increased urine production in freshwater fish caused by ammonia disturbing the osmoregulatory system by increasing gill permeability.

CAUSE
Ammonia poisoning is caused by high levels of toxic free ammonia (NH_3) in the water. Ammonia dissolved in water quickly associates with the water molecule, H_2O, to form ammonium (NH_4-) and hydroxyl (OH-) ions, but as pH and temperature rise, the process is reversed with dissociation producing progressively more free ammonia (NH_3) (plus water, H_2O). Free ammonia is far more toxic than ammonium ions, so ammonia POISONING (3) is more likely in alkaline than in acid water, with the problem greater the higher the pH/temperature.

Ammonia problems are generally the result of inadequate filtration or overfeeding, or a combination of the two. Ammonia toxicity is also likely where fish have been added to a biologically immature system (NEW TANK SYNDROME [3]) or where the aerobic bacteria population of the filter has been reduced/eliminated by replacement or incorrect cleaning of the filter medium *(see SECTION I: The Correct Environment)*.

PREVENTION AND TREATMENT
Immediate remedial action is required, either by removal of the fish to an ammonia-free aquarium, or by frequent partial water changes in order to dilute the ammonia to comparatively safe levels. Low levels of ammonia toxicity can be remedied by using zeolite (a natural ion-exchange compound) as a short-term (chemical) filter medium, or by

transferring a biologically mature filter from another aquarium.

The aquarist must identify and eliminate the cause of the high ammonia level. This usually means reviewing the biological filtration system and/or feeding regime. (See SECTION I: Providing the correct environment; Nutrition.) It is also advisable to monitor for SECONDARY INFECTION (3) caused by immuno-suppression or opportunist invasion of irritated gill or skin areas.

ANAEMIA

This disease is caused by a deficiency of haemoglobin in the blood, often due to insufficient numbers of red blood cells within the circulatory system.

SIGNS

The GILLS (2) of the fish appear very pale, as opposed to their normal bright red colour. Autopsy may reveal abnormally pale internal organs.

CAUSES

Heavy infestations of blood-sucking parasites, such as LEECHES (3), may cause significant loss of blood, resulting in this condition. Heavy infections with blood-dwelling TRYPANOSOMES (3), or microbial infection of haematopoietic (blood-producing) organs, are further possible causes of anaemia. The presence of high levels of NITRITE (3) in the aquarium water reduces the fish's blood haemoglobin levels by converting this molecule into methaemoglobin; however, nitrite poisoning may cause the gills to turn a brownish colour rather than pale.

PREVENTION AND TREATMENT

Treatment must be by identifying and remedying the cause, if possible. See also the prevention sections of the entries for the possible causes listed above.

ANAESTHETICS   P

Anaesthetics are sometimes used to calm (sedate) fish in preparation for surgical procedures (such as the removal of a TUMOUR (3)), for long-distance transportation, or for humane killing (EUTHANASIA (3)).

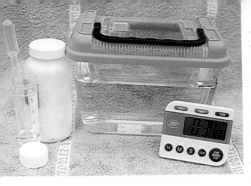

Preparing the anaesthetic tank. A timer is useful for monitoring the duration of anaesthesia. A second tank containing aerated, anaesthetic-free water is required for recovery.

TYPES OF ANAESTHETICS

Several types of anaesthetics have been used on fish, including CARBON DIOXIDE (3) gas, cooling, and chemical anaesthetics. Of these, chemical anaesthetics are the most commonly used for aquarium fish.

Three frequently applied chemical anaesthetics are BENZOCAINE (3), PHENOXYETHANOL (3), and TRICAINE METHANESULPHONATE (3). These chemicals are normally administered by immersion rather than by injection, their uptake (and excretion) being via the fish's gills. The anaesthetic dosage is calculated according to water volume rather than the fish's body weight. The optimal dosage will vary according to the species of fish as well as other biological and environmental factors such as the fish's fat content, its general health status, and the water temperature.

Of the other anaesthetic methods, carbon dioxide (CO_2) has been used in the past and is administered by bubbling the gas through water containing the fish. One disadvantage of carbon dioxide anaesthesia is the difficulty in monitoring and controlling the concentration, such that its use is now mostly restricted to food-fish aquaculture. Cooling the fish (e.g. by placing them in a small volume of water which is placed within a refrigerator) has been widely used as a method of euthanasia but is now considered inhumane and should no longer be practised.

ADMINISTRATION OF ANAESTHETICS

If incorrectly administered, anaesthetics may cause the fish STRESS (3), pain, or unnecessary death. Anaesthesia should therefore be performed only by experienced persons.

Different species vary in their susceptibility to anaesthesia. If in doubt, increase the dose slowly over time until anaesthesia is achieved. Those fish which are able to utilise atmospheric oxygen (facultative air-breathers) may take longer to become anaesthetized.

IMPORTANT: when exposed to a moderate dose of anaesthetic (e.g. the level used to achieve heavy sedation) there will be a tendency for the fish to fall into deeper stages of anaesthesia until ventilation arrest and death occurs. It is therefore very important to monitor the fish and ensure that it is returned to anaesthetic-free water as soon as possible. It thus becomes clear why anaesthesia should be performed only by experienced persons.

For the purposes of removing blood (e.g. for examination) or for taking X-RAYS (3), the fish will need to be held in anaesthetic until it turns belly-up. Mild sedation is sometimes required for calming a fish in preparation for extensive WOUND (3) treatment and similar out-of-water procedures where the fish may otherwise struggle and injure itself.

ANCHOR WORM
An ECTOPARASITIC (3) COPEPOD (3) of the genus *LERNAEA (3)*.

ANOXIA
This literally means no oxygen in the tissues (cf. HYPOXIA (3) = a diminished amount of oxygen in the tissues). See OXYGEN (3) and OXYGEN STARVATION (3) for an explanation of the various environmental and physiological causes of anoxia and hypoxia.

ANTHELMINTHICS   **P**
Chemicals which are effective in killing NEMATODES (3), HELMINTH ('worm') PARASITES (3) such as FLUKES (3), and CESTODES (3).

Anthelminthics are generally administered via medicated food, though some are effective as a bath treatment. Those which have been used for treating fish parasites include LEVAMISOLE (3), MEBENDAZOLE (3), Oxamniquine, PIPERAZINE (3), PRAZIQUANTEL (3), TRICH-LORFON (3), and NICLOSAMIDE (3). In most countries a veterinary prescription is required to obtain these drugs, as many are still important for treating human helminth diseases. Others, such as trichlorfon, are highly toxic ORGANOPHOSPHORUS COMPOUNDS (3), the supply of which is restricted in many countries. Where no dosage is given under entries for individual anthelminthics, veterinary advice should be sought regarding this subject.

ANTIBIOTICS

These bactericidal chemicals were originally derived from certain species of fungi and bacteria, but nowadays several synthetic derivatives are commercially available.

Numerous types of antibiotics have been used to treat BACTERIAL DISEASES (3) of aquarium fish. The following list is by no means exhaustive: ampicillin, Chloramphenicol, doxycycline, enrofloxacin, KANAMY-CIN (3), neomycin, and OXYTETRACYCLINE (3). Note that the quinolone compounds, such as OXOLINIC ACID (3), are not true antibiotics and are therefore not discussed here.

In certain countries (e.g. the UK) antibiotics for aquarium use are available only through veterinary prescription, but elsewhere (e.g. the USA) a range of antibiotics are freely obtainable over the counter at aquarium stores. The restrictive use of antibiotics in some countries seems warranted in view of the increasing number of bacteria strains which have developed resistance to these drugs. The indiscriminate use of antibiotics and incorrect treatment regimes have undoubtedly contributed to the alarming incidence of multiple-antibiotic resistance among fish-pathogenic bacteria. Based on current trends, antibiotic resistance seems likely to become a major health problem in the aquarium and pond fish industry.

Injection of a large fish (a koi carp) with antibiotic.

SELECTION OF ANTIBIOTICS

Ideally, the causative bacterium should be first identified and antibiotic sensitivity testing undertaken in order to ensure that an effective antibiotic is selected. However, the inevitable time delay between submitting samples for laboratory analysis and receiving the results often means that such investigations have to be omitted owing to the acute progression of many bacterial diseases which can quickly spread within the confines of an aquarium. The costs of submitting samples for bacteriology and antibiotic testing may also be inhibitory, except in the case of fish which have high economic or sentimental value. Instead, antibiotic selection is often based on a presumptive disease diagnosis, taking into account the clinical signs, species of fish, and other background history. The likelihood of antibiotic resistance will also be influential in making a selection. The majority of antibiotics used for treating fish are effective against gram-negative bacteria, since most fish-pathogenic bacteria belong to this group.

ADMINISTRATION OF ANTIBIOTICS

Antibiotics are generally more effective when administered by injection rather than by bath immersion. However, injection is not feasible with very small fish such as tetras and livebearers. Some antibiotics are effective when administered orally, via the food.

TABLE 8
EXAMPLES OF ANTIBIOTICS AND DELIVERY ROUTES

Chloramphenicol:	Injection
Kanamycin sulphate:	Bath immersion Injection Orally
Oxytetracycline hydrochloride	Bath immersion Injection Orally
Neomycin sulphate	Bath

Note: the purity (or concentration) of the antibiotic will vary according to its source and intended purpose (i.e. some are obtainable in powder form of varying degrees of purity, others in injectable liquid form). Seek advice from the manufacturer or veterinary surgeon regarding the correct dosage for the particular route of delivery.

EFFECTS ON BIOLOGICAL FILTRATION
Several antibiotics are harmful to the nitrifying bacteria found in biological filters, examples being neomycin and erythromycin. On the other hand, penicillin and tetracyclines are considered to be harmless to nitrifying bacteria when used at normal therapeutic levels.

GENERAL CONSIDERATIONS REGARDING USE OF ANTIBIOTICS
● It is wise to seek advice from a vet or fish health professional before using antibiotics, even if these drugs are available without prescription (as is the case in some countries).
● If considering treatment by bath immersion, ensure that the antibiotic selected is suitable for this delivery route: some antibiotics are not water soluble, or are poorly absorbed into the fish's tissues via the water.
● Ensure that the dose is correct for the proposed delivery route (i.e. the amount required for a bath immersion will be different to that needed for injection, or via the food).
● Fish vary between species and groups in their tolerance to certain antibiotics. Do not overdose with antibiotics and monitor all fish during the course of treatment.
● Ensure that the full course of antibiotics is given, even if the fish appears to have recovered early on in the treatment. Failure to do so could result in a resurgence of the infection, and even the development of antibiotic resistance.
● Several antibiotics will destroy nitrifying bacteria: check before adding antibiotics to biologically filtered aquaria.
● The antibiotic therapy may fail. Assuming the bacterial pathogen has been correctly identified, and the antibiotic dose was appropriate, then failure could be due to antibiotic resistance by the bacteria. In some cases, a second and different antibiotic may be prescribed.
● Antibiotics should not be used as prophylactics (i.e. they should be used only to cure a bacterial disease, and never simply to prevent one from occurring). The prophylactic use

of antibiotics, although practised by some ornamental fish farmers and traders, leads to an increase in antibiotic resistance by bacteria, and should therefore be discouraged. Fish which have been routinely exposed to antibiotics during their life may have a reduced immunity to bacterial pathogens: this may explain why some farm-reared aquarium fish quickly succumb to bacterial infections following their importation.

ANTISEPTICS **P** (some)

Antiseptics help inhibit or destroy microbial pathogens. They are sometimes applied either as a bath immersion or topically to disinfect body WOUNDS (3) caused by INJURY(3) or ECTOPARASITE (3) damage. Some antiseptics are IODINE (3)-based and these are available under various trade names; refer to the manufacturer's instructions for dosage and method of application.

MERCUROCHROME (3) is also commonly used as an antiseptic, and is sometimes applied topically (as a 0.2% to 1% aqueous solution) to body wounds.

Antiseptic solutions are also sometimes used to irrigate infected gills. Gill antiseptics (gill-wash solutions) are available commercially for this purpose and are sold primarily for use on large pond fish (e.g. koi carp) but may be used to treat large tropical aquarium fish as well.

APIOSOMA

A genus of ciliate PROTOZOA (3) which live, usually harmlessly, on the body surface of freshwater fish.

Apiosoma are stalked, cylindrical, or bell-shaped organisms which attach to the fish's skin and gills. They are considered to be commensal rather than parasitic, since they do not usually harm the fish and do not feed on its body

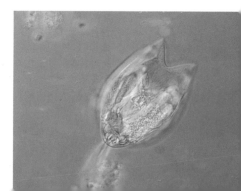

A free-living stalked protozoan, as seen under the microscope. Note the basal stalk.

tissues. These ciliates probably benefit from being attached to a moving surface (i.e. the fish), as this enables them to trap food particles and bacteria as the fish feeds and swims through the water. A related genus is *EPISTYLIS* (3), which is similar in shape and biology to *Apiosoma* but is known to be pathogenic under certain circumstances.

SIGNS
Often there are no visible signs. Sometimes these protozoa may form congregations which appear as whitish GROWTHS (2) on the skin or fins, sometimes on the edge of fin rays or, in the case of catfish, on the tips of the pectoral spines. These SPOTS (2) can be confused with those caused by *ICHTHYOPHTHIRIUS* (3) or *LYMPHO-CYSTIS* (3), both of which are more common. Diagnosis should therefore be confirmed by examining a sample of the white mass under a microscope and checking for the presence of stalked protozoa.

Apiosoma* may sometimes occur in high numbers on tissues which have been damaged by INJURY (3) or DISEASE (3). There is some evidence that large numbers of gill-dwelling *Apiosoma* may cause RESPIRATORY DISTRESS (2).

CAUSE
One common species is *A. piscicolum,* which may be found on a wide range of tropical fish species, notably those from southern Africa. It reaches about 0.1 mm in length.

PREVENTION AND TREATMENT
Good aquarium hygiene may help reduce the chances of *Apiosoma* or *Epistylis* outbreaks. In most cases, these protozoa are few in number on the fish and do no harm, such that treatment is usually unnecessary. However, if a serious outbreak is diagnosed then a SALT (3) bath treatment may be effective, administered to the whole aquarium community at the rate of 2 grams per litre, for three to seven days. (Check that the fish species to be treated are salt-tolerant; in the case of salt-intolerant fish it may be possible to effect a cure using a general anti-protozoan treatment.)

ARGULUS

This ECTOPARASITIC (3) CRUSTACEAN (3) from the family Branchiura is also known as the fish louse. *Argulus* is more commonly encountered on coldwater aquarium and pond fish than on tropical species; occasionally, however, one or a few *Argulus* parasites may be introduced via LIVE FOODS (3). About 30 species are known, although only three are common. Two species are associated with aquarium fish: *Argulus foliaceus* and *A. japonicus*.

Argulus are temporary parasites which may find their host by random encounter. They attach to the fish's skin with powerful suckers, then use needle-like mouthparts to inject an anti-coagulant before feeding on the fish's blood. The louse is not fixed to one position on its host and is able to move over the fish's body surface as well as leaving its host when engorged, becoming free-swimming for a time before locating a further host. Under tropical conditions *Argulus* can survive for several days off the fish.

Argulus mate in open water, with the female laying long strips of 100 or more eggs on solid surfaces. In the case of *A. japonicus* the eggs hatch in about two weeks at 25 degrees C; however, individual eggs within the egg mass hatch at different times. The 0.6mm juveniles are planktonic before they attack fish, and moult eight times before reaching adulthood at a size of 3-3.5mm, after around five weeks.

The severity of an *Argulus* infestation depends on the size of fish and the numbers of these parasites within the aquarium. Mild infestations are themselves rarely life-threatening; however, the puncture WOUNDS (3) made by

Argulus on tail of fish.

Adult Argulus: Male (left) and female.

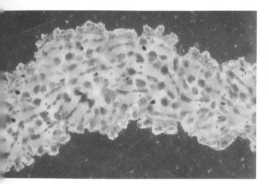

Section of egg mass of Argulus, as seen under the microscope.

the feeding *Argulus* are vulnerable to SECONDARY INFECTION (3) by FUNGAL (3) and BACTERIAL (3) pathogens. Severe infestations can result in significant blood loss, and in cases of severe epithelial disruption caused by *Argulus* wounds the fish may suffer OSMOTIC STRESS (3) and possibly death. *Argulus* have also been implicated as carriers of pathogenic bacteria.

SIGNS
Argulus feed on the fish's tissues, causing a haemorrhagic response which is visible as a small red wound. Diagnosis is based on the presence on the fish's skin of the parasite or the reddened wounds made by its feeding. One or several adult lice may be observed on the surface of infested fish. The adult parasite is visible to the naked eye as a semi-transparent flattened disc of between 5 and 12 mm in diameter. A pair of dark compound eyes are clearly visible near its anterior end.

Affected fish may be restless. The feeding *Argulus* irritate the fish's skin, sometimes causing the fish to DART (2) about and/or JUMP (2), as well as SCRATCHING (2) itself on the substrate and aquarium decor in an attempt to rid itself of the irritation. Heavy infestations may cause the fish to exhibit LETHARGY(2) and lose its APPETITE (2), and the skin may become slightly opaque due to MUCUS HYPERPRODUCTION (2).

PREVENTION AND TREATMENT
ORGANOPHOSPHORUS COMPOUNDS [3] *(see MET-RIPHONATE [3])* are effective in eradicating this parasite. Alternative treatments are a short-term bath in (a) FORMALIN (3) (standard 37-40% solution, at the rate of 0.125 ml/litre for 1 hour) or (b) POTASSIUM PERM-ANGANATE [3] (10 mg/litre for 30 minutes). It is advisable to aerate the water during the bath. Proprietary anti-crustacean parasite treatments are also available.

Small numbers of parasites may be carefully removed from large fish using forceps; the fish being restrained in an aquarium net or by partly covering its body in a wet cloth or paper towelling. The puncture wound left by the *Argulus* should be treated with a topical ANTISEPTIC (3) to minimise the chances of a secondary infection. As the aquarium is likely to be infested with free-swimming *Argulus*, this treatment will be effective only if the fish is simultaneously moved to an *Argulus*-free aquarium.

Prevent introduction of *Argulus* to the aquarium by careful examination of fish, eradicating any parasites present during the QUARANTINE (3) period, or, preferably, not purchasing infected individuals. Wild-collected live foods, such as *Daphnia* and bloodworm, should be inspected for the presence of adult *Argulus*. Plants and rocks which are freshly collected from ponds and rivers may harbour the eggs of this parasite.

ASCITES
See *DROPSY (3)*.

B

BACTERAEMIA

The presence of BACTERIA (3) in the blood. This may occur in certain systemic bacterial infections, and is potentially fatal unless quickly treated, e.g. with ANTIBIOTICS (3).

BACTERIA AND BACTERIAL INFECTIONS

A bacterium is a microscopic single-celled living organism varying in size from 0.5 to 10 microns. Only when they form large colonies are some species (e.g. *FLEXIBACTER* spp.) [3] visible to the unaided eye. Normally, however, they can be seen only under high powers of the light microscope (ca. 400 x magnification and higher). Bacteria occur singly or in groups or colonies and can be broadly classified according to their shape – spheres (coccus), rods (bacillus), and spirals (spirillium). Some contain coloured pigments.

Bacteria have a tough but permeable cell wall so that they can feed by simply absorbing their food through the wall of the cell. Some bacteria can swim through fluids by beating their tail-like flagellum; others drift through the water, while many are sedentary and live attached to surfaces, such as the substrate, rocks, and submerged vegetation. Bacteria reproduce simply, and often very rapidly, by division, such that millions can be produced in only a few hours under optimal conditions.

A few species have the capacity to survive unsuitable conditions by forming spores which are resistant to extremes of temperature, desiccation, and most chemical treatments. These spores can survive for months or even years until suitable conditions return. Numerous species of bacteria are normally present in the aquarium water and many others live harmlessly on the fish's skin or within the gut. Certain types of bacteria are actually advantageous to the aquarium, notably *Nitrobacter* and *Nitrosomonas,* which are important in biological filtration *(see SECTION I: The Correct Environment.)*

BACTERIA AS PATHOGENS

A number of bacteria species are (potentially) pathogenic to fish and cause a variety of external and internal diseases, such as ULCERS (3), DROPSY (3), FIN ROT (3) and FISH TUBERCULOSIS (3) (= fish TB). Fish pathogenic bacteria include species of *AEROMONAS* (3), *FLEXIBACTER* (3), MYCOBACTERIA (3), and *VIBRIO* (3), to name but a few. Some of these disease-causing bacteria occur freely in the aquarium or may even form part of the fish's normal gut flora, becoming pathogenic only under certain circumstances. For example, they may cause disease when the fish's immune system is compromised by adverse factors such as poor aquarium hygiene, incorrect water conditions (chemistry and/or quality), STRESS (3) (e.g. due to overcrowding or AGGRESSION (3)), or INJURY (3).

Bacteria can also be the causative agents in SECOND-ARY INFECTIONS. For example, WOUNDS (3) and other tissue damage caused by injury, or by PARASITES (3) such as *ARGULUS* (3), *HEXAMITA* (3), and *ICHTHY-OPHTHIRIUS* (3), may sometimes become infected with bacteria (and/or FUNGUS (3)).

IDENTIFICATION OF BACTERIA
Because of their small size and paucity of external features, it is not possible to identify bacteria purely by their appearance, nor is it possible visually to distinguish between pathogenic and non-pathogenic species. Bacteria can be identified only with the aid of special staining methods and biochemical tests. One major classification criterion is whether they stain positive or negative in a special dye test known as the gram stain. Most fish pathogenic bacteria are gram-negative, and hence most of the commonly applied aquarium ANTIBIOTICS (3) specifically target gram-negative bacteria.

The various microbiological and biochemical tests required are generally undertaken by a specialised fish health laboratory. Unfortunately, these tests are relatively expensive and time-consuming to perform, such that few aquarists bother to use this service. Instead, bacterial disease diagnosis is usually based on clinical symptoms alone, and although this is not fool-proof it is the most practical method routinely applied.

TREATMENT OF BACTERIAL DISEASES
In the case of aquarium fish, bacterial diseases are generally treated with BACTERICIDES (3) (including ANTI-BIOTICS [3]). Several commercial bactericidal treatments are available and these are commonly referred to as anti-bacteria or anti-internal bacteria remedies. Most of these remedies can be obtained from the aquarium store without the need for a veterinary prescription. In situations where a bacterial infection fails to respond to commercial bactericidal remedies it may be necessary to resort to antibiotics. Internal bacterial infections such as fish TB (caused by MYCOBACTERIA [3]) will usually respond only to antibiotic treatments. In the future it may be possible to use VACCINES (3) in order to protect aquarium fish against certain bacterial infections.

BACTERIAL GILL DISEASE
See MYXOBACTERIA (3).

BACTERICIDES
P (some)

Chemicals used to kill bacteria. Notable bactericides are the ANTIBIOTICS (3) as well as other chemicals such as OXOLINIC ACID (3). DISINFECTANTS (3) and ANTISEPTICS (3) are also bactericidal. (Strictly speaking, some of these anti-bacterials are in fact bacteriostatic rather than bactericidal, i.e. they act by preventing the bacteria from multiplying rather than killing them outright.)

Several commercial bactericidal treatments are available and these are commonly referred to as anti-bacteria or anti-internal bacteria remedies. Most of these remedies can be obtained from the aquarium store without the need for a veterinary prescription.

Some bactericidal chemicals, such as antibiotics and oxolinic acid, are not generally available from aquarium stores (but may be freely available in certain countries, such as the USA) and have to be obtained either with a veterinary prescription or, in some cases, directly from chemical supply companies such as BDH or Sigma, or from specialist aquaculture health product suppliers.

BELLY SLIDING
A congenital problem in fry.

This sick livebearer fry remains on the substrate and moves by a belly-sliding action.

SIGNS
Fry lack BUOYANCY (2) (in normally buoyant species), and 'hop' along on their bellies instead of swimming properly.

CAUSE
Inherited swimbladder dysfunction, usually the result of IN-BREEDING (3).

TREATMENT
None. Affected fry normally die after a few days, but should otherwise be CULLED (3).

BENZOCAINE   **P**
Chemical name: ethyl-p-aminobenzoate. A chemical ANAESTHETIC (3) used for the sedation of fish or for EUTHANASIA (3), usually supplied as a white powder. It is poorly soluble in water and must be initially dissolved in absolute alcohol or acetone. Benzocaine may be stored as a stock solution in the solvent (e.g. 10g per litre) and will retain its activity for several months provided it is stored away from light (e.g. in a dark glass bottle).

DOSAGE AND ADMINISTRATION
Benzocaine is applied as a bath immersion. The actual dosage required for anaesthesia or euthanasia will vary according to the fish species as well as environmental factors (see discussion under ANAESTHETICS [3]).

• For anaesthesia with recovery: in general, 40-100 mg per litre (e.g. 4 to 10ml per litre of stock solution (assuming stock solution strength of 10 g per litre, as above) will induce anaesthesia in fish within a few minutes, and will allow recovery if the fish is subsequently transferred to aerated, anaesthetic-free water. Higher dosages may be required to anaesthetize some species – but be careful not to overdose, as death may ensue.

● For euthanasia: use an overdose level of 200-300 mg per litre (e.g. 20-30 ml per litre of stock solution (solution strength as above)). Higher levels may be required for some species.

Safety note: always wear rubber gloves when immersing hands in anaesthetic solutions.

See also: TRICAINE METHANESULPHONATE (3), PHENOXYETHANOL (3).

BLACK CHIN

An apparently environmentally-induced skin condition in cichlids, particularly East African Rift Valley cichlids.

SIGNS

Small grey-black irregular SPOTS (2) or blotches appear on, initially, the lower jaw area, sometimes in time spreading back along the underside to the ventral insertion. In severe cases the entire lower head and chest may develop a mottled grey-black appearance.

CAUSE

The condition has not been clinically investigated, but appears to be related to increased NITRATE (3) levels. Rift Valley cichlids originate from waters which are virtually nitrate-free.

*Black Chin in
Melanochromis
auratus.*

TREATMENT
Improve water quality, in particular reducing nitrate levels to minimal. The condition usually disappears in a matter of days.

BLACK SPOT DISEASE
Caused by larval FLUKES (3) which reside in the fish's skin, musculature, or internal organs. Generally harmless, except in very heavy infestations.

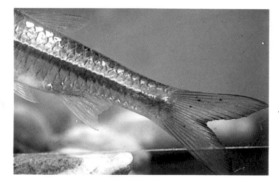

Wild-caught Rasbora showing a few black spots on the tail fin.

SIGNS
One or more small dark SPOTS (2) are present on the fish's skin and/or fins. Each spot is typically well defined, approximately circular in shape, and 1-2 mm in diameter. The spots are usually black in colour. Infested fish generally possess only one or a few spots, but in heavy infestations the fish may be covered in hundreds of black spots. Unless the infestation is extremely heavy, the fish generally exhibits no ill effects, though it may look unsightly.

CAUSES
Blackspot is caused by the larval stage of a number of digenetic fluke species (DIGENEA (3)), which invade the body tissues of fish. The fluke larva (known as a metacercaria) may become impregnated with host pigment cells (melanophores) causing the characteristic black spot appearance. The PARASITE's (3) life-cycle (see DIG-ENEA [3]) involves sequential transmission from a bird (final host), via its droppings to a freshwater snail (intermediate host), and then a fish (second intermediate host). The full life-cycle is completed when a suitable bird

host happens to eat an infected fish. The parasite is unable to multiply within the fish.

Because of its complex multi-host life cycle, blackspot disease does not occur on fish which have been reared throughout their lives indoors (e.g. in aquaria) but it is relatively common on fish which have been kept outdoors or wild caught. It is remotely possible that recently wild-caught freshwater SNAILS (3) could transmit the disease to aquarium fish.

TREATMENT
Fortunately, the disease is rarely life-threatening and should not give the aquarist cause for concern. In any case, no effective treatment is available to eliminate blackspot. The black spots sometimes fade with time. As a result of its multi-host life-cycle the parasite is not infectious under aquarium conditions and therefore infected fish do not require isolation.

BLEACH
Bleach is a solution of sodium hypochlorite, which is sold as a household DISINFECTANT (3). Despite its ease of availability and disinfecting powers, bleach is not recommended for use with aquaria as it is highly toxic to fish. Even residual amounts may cause serious damage to the fish's gills and skin. Bleach is also highly corrosive to some items of aquarium equipment, including nets.

For recommended alternatives to bleach see DISIN-FECTANTS (3).

BLINDNESS
Blindness due to the loss of one or both eyes is not uncommon among fish. This is often because the eyes have been damaged by attack by other fish or through rough handling. Environmental or genetic factors may also cause this condition, as can nutritional disorders and some parasites. Partial or complete blindness in fish is generally not as debilitating as it is for higher vertebrates.

SIGNS
One or both eyes may be absent, clouded, or have an opaque (white) pupil (CLOUDY EYE (2)). Fish which are totally

Barb with loss of one eye. The socket has healed over, and the fish is otherwise perfectly healthy.

Eye loss in a cardinal tetra, possibly as a result of attack.

Photo: Mike Sandford.

blinded may exhibit a marked increase, or sometimes a decrease, in pigmentation. Swimming behaviour and navigation ability may, however, appear normal, because fish have other sensory systems which help them detect their surroundings and avoid collisions with other fish or objects.

CAUSES

Eye loss is frequently due to AGGRESSION (3) by other fish, or perhaps from capture or handling injuries. BACTERIAL (3) or FUNGAL INFECTIONS (3) are common causes of eye opacity, and these infections are often exacerbated by poor aquarium hygiene. Fish which are suffering from STRESS (3) may have reduced immune competence and are therefore more susceptible to eye infections. Eye opacity can also result from a VITAMIN DEFICIENCY (3) (notably Vitamin A) though this is highly unlikely if a good-quality balanced diet is provided. The presence within the eye of larval DIGENEAN FLUKES (3) (e.g. *DIPLOSTOMUM* [3]) can reduce visual acuity: eye-flukes are sometimes encountered in pond-reared or wild-caught fish, but not aquarium-reared specimens. A mild and usually transient opacity to the eyes can result from CHLORINE (3) damage, due to exposure to heavily chlorinated tap water. Damage to the eye caused by EXOPHTHALMIA [3] (bubble-eye or pop-eye) and chronic GAS BUBBLE DISEASE [3] (nitrogen super-saturation) may reduce visual acuity. Finally, blindness may be inherited, commonly as a result of long-term INBREEDING (3).

TREATMENT
Fish which have lost or are otherwise blind in one or both eyes may continue to swim and feed, in which case it is not necessary to consider EUTHANASIA (3). Those species which hunt by sight (rather than by smell) will be seriously disadvantaged if blinded in both eyes and euthanasia may be necessary in order to prevent death through chronic starvation.
See also SECTION II: CLOUDY EYE.

BLOOD PARASITES
Blood-dwelling parasites rarely present a health problem in tropical aquarium fish. Affected fish may show no clinical signs of disease. Wild-caught fish may sometimes harbour TRYPANOSOMES (3). These blood-dwelling PROTO-ZOA (3) are transmitted by fish-parasitic LEECHES (3).

SIGNS
Mild trypanosome infections may be asymptomatic but fish which are heavily infected can exhibit EMACIATION (2) and LETHARGY (2): however, these are vague non-diagnostic symptoms which are far more likely to be the result of other diseases or adverse water conditions. Confirmation of trypanosome infection must therefore rely on the examination of a drop of blood under the high-power objective of a microscope. The trypanosomes are typically about 15-25 microns in body length and actively swim within the blood plasma.

PREVENTION AND TREATMENT
There are no chemical treatments available for combating blood parasites of fish. Practical control must therefore rely

on preventing the accidental introduction of leeches into the aquarium. Aquatic plants, rocks, or live foods which are collected from rivers or ponds (natural or ornamental) may harbour leeches and should therefore be closely examined for the presence of adult leeches or their egg cocoons.

BLUE-GREEN ALGAE
See CYANOBACTERIA

BRANCHIOMYCOSIS
An infection of the gills, also known as gill rot, caused by a phycomycete FUNGUS (3) called *Branchiomyces*.

Branchiomycosis: Fish infected with gill fungus.

Photo: Ian Wellby.

SIGNS
Branchiomycosis causes typical signs of RESPIRATORY DISTRESS (2): increased gill rate, GASPING (2) at the surface, HANGING (2) in fast-moving water and/or near the bubble streams from airstones. On examination the gills visibly exhibit MUCUS HYPERPRODUCTION (2) and appear mottled with dark red and pale patches. In severe cases the gill literally rots away. SECONDARY INFECTION (3) with another fungus species (SAPROLEGNIA (3)) may also be present. At high temperatures death may occur rapidly, within 2-4 days. Microscopical examination of infected tissue reveals a network of branched fungal hyphae throughout the gill. The hyphal strands are 9-30 microns in width.

CAUSE
Branchiomyces may already be present in the aquarium, or introduced by infected fish. It is spread by spherical spores,

which are produced and released by the hyphae.

Outbreaks of gill rot are most common at water temperatures above 20 degrees C (68 degrees F) and are usually linked with high levels of organic toxins (AMMONIA (3), NITRITE (3), NITRATE (3)), high stocking levels, and green water (ALGAE (3) blooms).

PREVENTION AND TREATMENT
Take steps to rectify the causative factors, i.e. by reducing stocking, improving water quality, and eliminating algal blooms, as appropriate. Use a proprietary anti-fungus bath treatment containing PHENOXYETHANOL (3) (= phenoxethol). Increase oxygen levels to reduce mortality (i.e. to alleviate RESPIRATORY STRESS [3]) during treatment. Gill regeneration after treatment takes a few weeks in young fry but months in older fish.

BUBBLE EYE
See EXOPHTHALMIA (3).

BURNS
Certain bottom-dwelling fish have very occasionally sustained skin burns as a result of resting on an aquarium heater. The habit of resting either on the aquarium heater or between the heater and aquarium glass is more common among certain catfish (notably *Plecostomus* spp. and other loricariids) as well as some loaches. Cichlids and other hole-dwellers sometimes hide beneath the heater and receive dorsal burns.

SIGNS
Burn wounds are difficult to distinguish from other injuries or skin infections. Fish which show a preference for resting on or beneath the aquarium heater should be considered at risk of burns.

CAUSE
Heat damage to the skin, and sometimes underlying tissue, as a result of the heater switching on while the fish is resting upon/under it.

PREVENTION AND TREATMENT
This problem can be prevented by purchasing a heater guard which slips over the heater tube. Positioning the heater at a steep angle, rather than horizontally, and at a reasonable distance from the substrate, should help prevent burns. Providing adequate caves for reclusive species is an additional deterrent to improvisation. Severe burns should be treated with a topical ANTISEPTIC (3). Anti-bacterial or anti-fungal remedies may be required in the event of SECONDARY INFECTION (3) of burn WOUNDS (3).

C

CAMALLANUS
A genus of NEMATODE WORMS (3) of the family Camallanidae.

SIGNS
It is very difficult to identify low-level infection with intestinal worms. Typically, the first signs of *Camallanus* infection are when one or more worms protrude from the fish's anus. *Camallanus* are red-brown in colour, and are visible to the unaided eye, reaching up to 1-2 cm in length. Severe infestations may result in spinal DEFORMITY (3), and possibly EMACIATION (3). Livebearers seem particularly susceptible to this parasite.

CAUSE
The main species of *Camallanus* found in ornamental aquarium fish is *C. cotti*, which grows to 12 mm ($^1/_2$in.) in length. The adult worms live in the fish's gut where they feed on their host's blood. The normal life-cycle of this parasite often involves a COPEPOD (3) as the intermediate host (see LIVE FOODS AS VECTORS OF DISEASE (3)), but in the aquarium they may multiply for several generations without any intermediate host; susceptible fish become infected either through the ingestion of eggs or adults in fish faeces (see COPROPHAGY [3]) or through CANNIBALISM (3) of dead fish.

TREATMENT
Treat with an ANTHELMINTHIC (3) such as FENBEN-DAZOLE (3) (available in the form of certain brands of equine worm treatment (the powder rather than the paste formulation should be used for aquarium treatment). Administer via medicated food (0.25% inclusion) or, more easily, the aquarium water can be medicated at the rate of 2mg/litre. Three treatments are required, at weekly intervals.

CANCERS
See TUMOURS

CANNIBALISM
Predation by a fish on others of its own species is relatively common.

Many species of fish will consume the eggs and fry of other fish and even of their own species, often even their own offspring. Except in the case of those species which exhibit parental care, such as the cichlids, it is preferable to separate the eggs or newly hatched/born fry from the parents in order to prevent cannibalism. Even parental species may practise cannibalism when the fry reach a size where, in nature, they would disperse, usually to clear the territory in preparation for a further brood, or because the young fish have become large enough to represent competition. Cannibalism is thus not always a simple feeding behaviour.

Cannibalism is also common during the growing on of fry, especially where there is a large size difference between individuals within a brood, as commonly happens. It may be total or partial, i.e. young fish may eat not only entire siblings, but small pieces of each other, eyes and fins being

Young cichlid with fins and belly eaten away after death.

favourite targets. This sibling cannibalism can be reduced by the frequent sorting and separation of fry according to size. It is also common for fish to feed on the corpses of both conspecific and heterospecific tankmates that have died of other causes.

Certain infectious diseases may be transmitted by cannibalistic behaviour, such as *CAMALLANUS* (3), MYCOBACTERIA (3), and *PLEISTOPHORA* (3). Given that many aquarium fish will eagerly forage on the carcases of their tankmates, it is very important to remove dead or dying fish from the aquarium as soon as possible, particularly if an infectious disease is suspected.

CAPILLARIA

A genus of NEMATODE WORMS [3] (threadworms) which are parasitic within the gut or liver of some fish species. The PARASITE's (3) life-cycle is direct, with the adult worms producing eggs which hatch into infective larvae. Those *Capillaria* species of aquarium importance parasitise the guts of discus fish (*Symphysodon* spp.), angelfish (*Pterophyllum* spp.), and other cichlids.

SIGNS
Infestations may be asymptomatic.

Heavy infestations with gut-dwelling *Capillaria* may cause EMACIATION (2) and loss of APPETITE (2). The fish's FAECES (2) may appear thin and white, or as light and dark segments. In the case of dead fish, diagnosis can be made by examining the gut for the presence of these worms, which are thread-like and usually between 0.5 and 2 cm in length (a strong magnifying lens or microscope will be required as the worms are only of hair thickness). With live fish, a faecal smear can be taken and microscopically examined for the presence of eggs. Egg morphology varies with parasite species but typically the eggs are quite distinctive, being ovoid or cylindrical in shape and with a small bulging 'plug' (operculum) at each end. (Note: parasitological examination of the faeces requires specialist training, otherwise misdiagnosis may result.)

CAUSE
Outbreaks of *Capillaria* are generally the result of a recent

introduction of infested fish. No intermediate hosts are involved (in contrast with many other nematode parasites which must pass through aquatic invertebrates in order to complete their life cycle).

PREVENTION AND TREATMENT
An ANTHELMINTHIC (3) is required, such as LEVAMISOLE (3) or PIPERAZINE (3). Isolation of the sick fish is advisable, since their faeces may contain infective eggs which can be transmitted to other fish through being eaten (see COPROPHAGY (3)).

It is often stated that discus should not be kept with angelfish in order to avoid cross-infection of the former with *Capillaria*; however, as discus are in any case just as likely to be infected as angels, this is a rather pointless precaution, outweighed by the potential benefits (discus are often nervous, and this can be reduced by allowing them to shoal with the more confident angelfish) of housing the two genera together.

CARBON DIOXIDE
A colourless, odourless gas (CO_2).

Under aquarium conditions carbon dioxide is generated as a by-product of respiration by fish. It is also produced by aquatic plants which respire during the hours of darkness, whereas they absorb this gas during the process of photosynthesis which occurs in the presence of light. For this reason, CO_2 is sometimes deliberately added to the aquarium in order to promote plant growth (a technique commonly known as "CO_2 injection", from a gas cylinder).

CO_2 dissolves in water to form carbonic acid (H_2CO_3), and may thus have an acidifying effect on the aquarium, particularly in soft water with little or no buffering capacity. Atmospheric CO_2 is partly responsible for the natural acidification of RAIN WATER (3).

PROBLEMS ASSOCIATED WITH CARBON DIOXIDE
CO_2 may be a contributory factor in cases of ACIDOSIS (3).

High levels of free CO_2 may cause RESPIRATORY STRESS (3) in aquarium fish, particularly those from moving, well-oxygenated, waters. It is most likely to be a problem during transportation and in heavily (over-) stocked freshwater aquaria where respiratory carbon dioxide levels may build up to the danger level of around 25 mg/litre.

Fish vary from species to species in their tolerance of high CO_2 levels, and some can slowly adapt to elevated levels, provided these are not excessively high. Even when significantly below 25 mg/litre, CO_2 will affect some species especially if combined with low pH or OXYGEN (3) levels. Excess carbon dioxide affects fish by inhibiting the diffusion of CO_2 from the blood via the gills and by reducing the oxygen uptake capability of the blood haemoglobin, and thus makes asphyxiation more likely even when aquarium oxygen levels are normal.

Living constantly at elevated (for the species) but sub-lethal carbon dioxide levels may also cause damage to the kidneys as a result of calcium deposition. High carbon dioxide levels may also reduce the fish's APPETITE (2), growth rate, and ability to cope with other STRESS (3).

Too low a level of carbon dioxide can also cause problems. Levels below 1 mg/litre may kill fry by causing hyperventilation, which leads to terminal blood pH problems.

REDUCTION OF CO₂ LEVELS
Heavy aeration and increased circulation/turbulence will drive off carbon dioxide into the atmosphere, reducing carbon dioxide levels effectively. Care should be taken to ensure that heavily planted aquaria are adequately aerated at night, and CO_2 injection should also be employed with suitable circumspection. It should be mentioned that carbon dioxide test kits for aquaria are available, though generally there is no need to perform such tests. *(See also SECTION I: The Correct Environment.)*

CAULIFLOWER DISEASE
See LYMPHOCYSTIS (3).

CESTODES
Cestodes (tapeworms) are ribbon-like segmented worms which vary in length from a few centimetres to up to 40 cm (16 in.), depending on the species. About 1500 species have

LEFT: Triangular head of a fish tapeworm (stained red). Photo: Ian Wellby.

BELOW: Massive infection of Ligula intestinalis. All of these larval tapeworms were removed from one fish. Photo: Ian Wellby.

been recorded from fish, all of them parasitic. Tapeworms live either within the gut or in the body cavity of the fish, where they absorb nutrients from their host. Adult worms residing in the gut lumen of the fish have an anterior sucker for gripping onto the gut wall.

Cestodes are HELMINTH (3) PARASITES (3) whose complex life-cycle involves a number of hosts. In some species the fish is an intermediate host and harbours the larval stages of the cestode; while in others the fish is the final (= definitive) host – i.e. it harbours the adult tapeworm.

An example of the cestode life-cycle is provided by *Ligula intestinalis,* in which the mature cestode lives in the gut of piscivorous birds. Eggs pass out in the droppings, falling into the water where they hatch into free-swimming larvae. These larvae are eaten by COPEPOD (3) crustaceans (e.g. *Cyclops*) in which they develop into the next larval stage. If an infected copepod is eaten by a fish, the *Ligula* larvae burrow into the gut wall where they continue to develop. The cycle is completed when the fish is consumed by the definitive bird host.

Cestodes are very rare in aquarium-reared fish, usually occurring only in wild-caught specimens and those farmed in open systems, such as ponds. Due to the complex nature of their life-cycle, cestodes cannot transmit under aquarium conditions though they may be introduced via certain LIVE FOODS (3).

SIGNS
At low levels there are no signs of infection. Heavy infection may result in significant swelling of the fish's belly (DISTENDED BODY (2)), and can cause damage to the internal organs and may impair BUOYANCY (2) and swimming. Heavily infected fish may exhibit EMAC-IATION (2). In extreme cases it is possible for the body wall to rupture.

Adult worms will be found upon dissection of the gut, and these are typically segmented, up to several centimetres in length, and pale to white in colour. In the case of larval tapeworms, these may be found upon removal of the fish's belly skin to reveal the internal organs over which the larvae may be found. Larval tapeworms are less obviously segmented but may be equally large and of a similar pale coloration to the adults.

The microscopic examination of the fish's faeces may reveal tapeworm eggs, but only in the case of those species which occur as adults in the fish's gut. Faecal examination and parasite identification is a specialised skill.

CAUSE
Any of a large number of cestode species. From the aquarist's point of view, the actual species is unimportant; however, when considering chemical treatments it is important to ascertain whether the tapeworms exist in the fish as adults or as larvae.

PREVENTION AND TREATMENT

Since copepods can act as an intermediate host, the aquarist may prefer not to use live foods from natural sources (even fish-free waters, because of the transmission by birds), as these might prove a source of infestation.

Administering ANTHELMINTHICS (3) via the food has proved effective in eradicating adult tapeworms residing within the fish's gut. (The demonstration of tapeworm eggs in the fish's faeces is conclusive evidence of adult tapeworms residing in the gut.) Anthelminthics are not recommended for use against larval tapeworms which inhabit the body cavity, as the dead, decomposing worms cannot be vented from the fish. Suitable chemicals include NICLOSAMIDE (3) (50-100 mg/kg of fish) or PRAZIQUANTEL (3) (50-100 mg/kg of fish). These anthelminthics are usually mixed with a five-day ration of food and fed over five consecutive days. This regime is then repeated after ten days to eliminate all signs of infection.

CHEMICAL SHOCK
See SHOCK (3).

CHILODONELLA

A genus of PROTOZOAN (3), CILIATE PARASITES (3), one of a number of pathogens responsible for causing SKIN SLIME DISEASE (3). Can be differentiated from the others, such as *ICHTHYOBODO* (3) (*Costia*) and *TRICHODINA* (3), only by microscopic examination.

Most species of *Chilodonella* are harmless to fish, but a few are fish pathogens and others may cause harm to fish under certain circumstances (e.g. heavily polluted water conditions). Notable among the fish pathogenic species is *Chilodonella piscicola,* which is 30-70 microns in length and, on microscopic examination (45-120 x magnification) appears heart- or bean-shaped, with rows of hair-like cilia which are used for locomotion. The fish pathogenic species of *Chilodonella* are obligate parasites and so can survive only on the host fish, where they feed mainly on dead skin cells.

In small numbers *Chilodonella* does little harm, but if fish are STRESSED (3) by other factors its numbers may increase rapidly and start attacking healthy tissue.

Chilodonella piscicola is highly adaptable to environmental conditions, including a broad temperature range, and so may occur in all freshwater fish species. It spreads entirely by direct physical contact between fish and so is more commonly found in heavily-stocked aquaria.
For signs and treatment see SKIN SLIME DISEASE (3).

CHLORAMPHENICOL $\quad$ **P**
See ANTIBIOTICS.

CHLORINE AND CHLORAMINE TOXICITY
Chlorine and Chloramine are chemicals added to domestic water supplies as disinfectants. Chlorine (Cl) is a greenish-yellow gaseous element with an irritant smell (familiar from the heavily chlorinated water of swimming pools), while chloramine (NH_4Cl) is a chlorine/AMMONIA (3) compound. Chlorine is relatively unstable in water and quickly dissipates into the atmosphere. Chloramine is much more stable and thus is being increasingly used by water authorities in summer water temperatures and long supply lines.

Chlorine and chloramine are highly toxic to fish since they both combine with water to form hypochlorous acid which is thought to destroy cell proteins and enzyme systems. The toxicity of chlorine and chloramine is increased at lower pH and higher temperatures (this is because chlorine exists in water as either a dissociated hypochlorite ion or as hypochlorous acid which is more toxic; the proportion present as the toxic hypochlorous form increases with decreasing pH and increasing temperature).

To avoid chronic effects, residual chlorine should not exceed 0.003 mg/litre, while 0.2 to 0.3 mg/litre is sufficient to kill most fish rapidly.

SIGNS
Affected fish initially exhibit an escape response, DARTING (2) around the aquarium in an attempt to find chlorine/chloramine-free water. They then begin to tremble and discolour, eventually becoming listless and weak. Chlorine/chloramine directly damages the gills so this type of POISONING (3) also causes signs of HYPOXIA (3) (e.g. RESPIRATORY DISTRESS (2)), increased gill rate,

GASPING (2) at the surface, and HANGING (2) in areas of high water flow and aeration.

PREVENTION AND TREATMENT
Prevention is paramount – tap water should always be dechlorinated, mechanically or chemically, before use. Check with the water company to see which disinfectant(s) is/are in use. Chlorine can be driven off by vigorous aeration or by running the tap water hard into a bucket; alternatively the water can simply be left to stand overnight, preferably with aeration, and the gas will dissipate into the atmosphere.

Another option is to use a proprietary dechlorinator, available from aquarium retailers. This last option is essential if the water contains chloramine, and it is important to check that the dechlorinator purchased is intended for use against chloramine as well as chlorine – not all are! *(See also SECTION I: The Correct Environment.)* These proprietary dechlorinators contain SODIUM THIOSULPHATE (3), which rapidly binds up the chlorine chemically.

Chloramine is more difficult to deal with since the sodium thiosulphate removes the chlorine but leaves the toxic AMMONIA (3) behind. Some dechlorinators (those intended for use with chloramine) also contain an ammonia-binding chemical; otherwise it is necessary to run the dechlorinated water through zeolite (an ammonia-removing ion exchange compound) to render it safe for aquarium use.

Dechlorinators should be used to treat water before it is added to the aquarium; they should be added to the aquarium itself only in emergencies.

In the event that chlorine/chloramine poisoning does occur, immediately moving the fish to another, uncontaminated aquarium, is the best course of action. Alternatively, add enough dechlorinator to treat the whole tank volume, in order quickly to neutralise the chlorine/chloramine. In either situation, an increase in aeration may assist any RESPIRATORY STRESS (3).

CHONDROCOCCUS
A synonym of *FLEXIBACTER* (3). See also COLUM-NARIS DISEASE (3).

CILIATE PARASITES

These PROTOZOA (3) belong to the phylum Ciliophora. Most species of ciliates are harmless, free-living organisms but a few are important pathogens of freshwater aquarium fish, notably *ICHTHYOPHTHIRIUS* (3) (which causes whitespot disease). Less commonly encountered is a species of *TETRAHYMENA* (3) which causes GUPPY DISEASE (3).

Fish which have died or are severely immunosuppressed may be colonised by certain species of ciliates which are normally free-living and harmless. These opportunistic parasites may be present in large numbers feeding on the skin and gills. Attack by free-living ciliates is usually associated with very poor aquarium hygiene leading to water pollution and low dissolved OXYGEN (3) levels.

See also SKIN SLIME DISEASE (3), CHILODONELLA (3), TRICHODINA (3).

CLOUDY EYE

Although sometimes considered a disease, cloudy eye is in fact a sign of a number of health problems, and is thus included in SECTION II. See also BLINDNESS (3).

COLUMNARIS DISEASE

A BACTERIAL INFECTION (3) responsible for the disease also known as Mouth Rot or Mouth Fungus.

SIGNS
Small off-white or grey lesions or marks concentrated on the head, fins, gills, and mouth cavity. These areas develop into off-white cottonwool-like GROWTHS (2), mainly around the mouth region. The more greyish colour of these tufts commonly distinguishes this condition from FUNGAL INFECTIONS (3) (*SAPROLEGNIA* (3), *ACHYLA* (3)), which are normally whiter, although the two diseases are nevertheless commonly confused. High-power microscopical investigation is required for a positive diagnosis (by the presence of rod-shaped bacteria, often seen moving in a gliding fashion, and sometimes forming aggregations; an absence of fungal hyphae excludes *Saprolegnia/Achyla* as the cause).

In the chronic slow-acting form of mouth fungus, with the

classic symptoms of external fungus-like lesions described above, death occurs only after significant skin damage. There is, however, an acute fast-acting form, which generally occurs at higher temperatures. This acute systemic infection, which incubates for less than 24 hours and kills fish in 2 or 3 days with few or no external symptoms, may well be the cause of some unexplained fish deaths.

CAUSE
FLEXIBACTER (3) *columnaris,* a rod-shaped gram-negative bacterium (sometimes incorrectly referred to in the aquarium literature as Myxobacteria), present in most aquaria in the water, on dead organic matter, or even on healthy fish skin. Mouth fungus normally occurs at temperatures above 20 degrees C (68 degrees F) when one or more of the following contributory factors is applicable:

● INJURY to the skin, e.g. through netting, handling, or AGGRESSION (3). The bacteria infect the open WOUND (3) and spread to the surrounding healthy tissue.

● VITAMIN DEFICIENCY (3), which can cause poor skin condition, which allows the infection to gain a foothold and/or spread.

● Poor water quality – high levels of AMMONIA (3), NITRITE (3), and/or NITRATE (3); incorrect pH; low OXYGEN (3) levels.

PREVENTION AND TREATMENT
Because of the difficulty in differentiating columnaris and fungal infections without microscopical investigation, the medication should be both bactericidal and fungicidal, to cover both eventualities. Bath immersion using a proprietary treatment containing PHENOXYETHANOL (3) (Phenoxethol) is normally effective. In advanced cases, especially where the disease invades internal tissues, it may be necessary to treat with ANTIBIOTICS (3).

Any underlying causes such as poor water quality should be remedied, and good husbandry will minimise the likelihood of any (further) problem. *Flexibacter columnaris* prefers hard water with a pH above 6. Fish that survive infection may develop an acquired immunity which will confer some protection against any subsequent exposure to this pathogen.

CONSTIPATION

SIGNS
Loss of APPETITE (2), absence of FAECES (2), LETHARGY (2) (including resting on the substrate); in severe cases RESPIRATORY DISTRESS (2) and DISTENDED BODY (2).

CAUSES
Normally unsuitable diet, commonly over an extended period.

PREVENTION AND TREATMENT
Discontinue feeding if the fish is still eating. Treat with an EPSOM SALTS (3) bath. Raise the TEMPERATURE (3) slightly (within the tolerance range of the species) to increase the metabolic rate. Feeding, in the first instance lightly and ideally on high-fibre foods such as *Daphnia* and mosquito larvae, may be resumed when faeces production resumes.

Rectify the diet to avoid recurrence. Supplementing the diet with high-fibre foods such as *Daphnia* may be beneficial. Death from constipation is not unknown, and avoidance (See SECTION I: Nutrition) is advisable.

COPEPODS

Copepods are small CRUSTACEANS (3). Most species are harmless, and some are popular live foods for fish. A few species, however, are parasitic on freshwater fish. Copepods may be intentionally introduced into the aquarium as a LIVE FOOD (3) or accidentally brought in via water used to transport fish or aquatic plants.

Free-living copepod, about 2 mm in length.

FREE-LIVING (HARMLESS) COPEPODS

An infestation of free-living copepods usually indicates an unhealthy build up of organic matter in the aquarium which must be rectified. Free-living copepods generally range between 0.5mm and 3mm in length, and are therefore visible to the unaided eye. They typically swim by short hops and often rest on surfaces within the aquarium. In heavy infestations they may be evident in large numbers on the aquarium glass.

Many aquarium fish will readily devour copepods; however, large species such as large cichlids will ignore such small prey. In the absence of suitable fish predators, copepods may rapidly multiply in the aquarium. Sudden infestations of copepods may indicate excessive organic matter in the aquarium, which should be addressed by cleaning the gravel and decor, and by partial water changes. It may also be necessary to review the feeding regime to prevent further outbreaks.

COPEPODS AS VECTORS OF DISEASE

Although some species, notably *Cyclops,* are of nutritional value to fish, there is a small risk that copepods harvested from the wild may harbour larval TAPEWORMS (3) which could be transmitted to aquarium fish.

PARASITIC COPEPODS

The major parasitic copepod of aquarium importance is the anchor worm, *LERNAEA* (3), which attaches to the surface of its fish host. *Lernaea* is clearly distinguishable from free-living copepods by its much larger size (reaching 20 mm in length) and by its ECTOPARASITIC (3) habit when adult.

COPPER TREATMENTS

Copper is sometimes used for treating ECTOPARASITES (3) such as the skin-dwelling PROTOZOA (3) and monogenetic FLUKES (3) (MONOGENEA [3]). It is usually applied as copper sulphate, as the hydrated form ($CuSO_4 \cdot 5H_2O$) which is available in dry form (blue crystals) or as a commercially prepared solution. Some proprietary treatments use chelated copper because this complexed copper is less toxic and more stable.

Unfortunately, copper treatments are potentially toxic to

fish (= ichthyotoxic) and hence the correct dosing is essential; overdosing may cause the fish chronic tissue damage or even death. The risks of copper ichthyotoxicity are higher under softwater conditions and the tolerance to copper varies between fish species.

The efficacy of copper treatments varies according to aquarium conditions, with a decrease in efficacy with increasing pH and in aquaria which contain calcareous materials or a high organic load. Test kits are commercially available for monitoring copper levels in the treatment aquarium.

Copper compounds must never be used in aquaria housing freshwater crabs, shrimps, or other invertebrates, since it will seriously interfere with the respiratory function of these creatures. Copper is also an effective molluscicide (snail destroyer). Several copper-based snail treatments are commercially available; however, these should be applied with caution, for the reasons given above.

DOSAGE AND ADMINISTRATION
Long-term bath for several days. A therapeutic level of between 0.15mg to 0.20 mg of free copper per litre of water is recommended. Higher doses are potentially lethal to some fish [See also POISONING (3), TOXINS (3), CHEMICAL SHOCK (3)].

COPROPHAGY
Many fish will forage on the faeces of other fish or on their own faeces. Coprophagy (literally, "eating faeces") is a route by which certain pathogens and PARASITES (3) may be transmitted from one fish to another. Certain gut-dwelling parasites are capable of being transmitted by coprophagy, including some NEMATODE WORMS (3) such as *CAMALLANUS* (3) (which is sometimes found in livebearing poeciliid fish) and *CAPILLARIA* (3) (found mostly in cichlids). CANNIBALISM (3), also prevalent among fish, is another related potential route of disease transmission.

COSTIA, COSTIASIS
Costia is a synonym of *ICHTHYOBODO* (3). For costiasis see SKIN SLIME DISEASE (3).

COTTONWOOL DISEASE

General term for a number of FUNGAL (3) and BACT-
ERIAL INFECTIONS (3) characterised by fluffy, usually
whitish, cotton-wool-like areas or tufts, commonly
SECONDARY INFECTIONS (3) at the site of an INJURY
(3) or other WOUND (3).

See also ACHYLA (3), SAPROLEGNIA (3), COLUM-
NARIS (3).

CRUSTACEAN PARASITES

Crustaceans (class Crustacea) are a diverse group of animals
which includes the crabs, shrimps, Daphnia, and
COPEPODS (3). A few species are parasitic on freshwater
fish, those of aquarium importance being the anchor worm
(LERNAEA [3]) and the fish louse (ARGULUS [3]).

CULLING

Culling is the selective elimination of defective or
superfluous individuals in a group. As applied to fish, it may
refer to the reduction in numbers of a brood of fry too
numerous to rear (or sell), or the destruction of individuals
displaying unwanted characteristics. The latter may be
physical DEFORMITY (2), STUNTING (2) (runts), or,
where the aquarist is endeavouring to develop or maintain a
special strain, deviation from the desired standard.

Culling should not be performed simply on a size basis in
species which are sexually dimorphic in size, as sex-based
differential growth may be apparent even in young fry.

Culled fry are normally destroyed by feeding them to other
fish, which is, after all, what happens to the bulk of fry
hatched in the wild.

See also EUTHANASIA (3).

CYANOBACTERIA

A major group of micro-organisms responsible for the
phenomenon known to aquarists as "blue-green algae", an
ALGAE (3)-like growth with a tendency to blanket the
entire aquarium rapidly. Its appearance is sometimes linked
to high levels of NITRATE (3) and phosphate, and
remedying these problems and their underlying causes
(OVERFEEDING (3), overcrowding, poor maintenance,
polluted tap water – see SECTION I: The Correct Environ-

ment), as well as removing as much of the nuisance as possible with a siphon or gravel cleaner, may eventually effect a cure. Although not known to be harmful to adult fish, it is possible for the blanket of blue-green algae to engulf fry, for example, when the latter are resting on the substrate or other decor at night, resulting in their suffocation. It also smothers plants.

CYCLOCHAETA
A synonym of *TRICHODINA* (3). See also SKIN SLIME DISEASE (3).

CYSTS
Cysts or 'nodules' may occur on the skin, gills, muscle, or internal organs of fish. Probably all fish species are capable of developing cysts. Some cyst-causing PARASITES (3) have a narrow host range, affecting just one or a few fish species.

SIGNS
Cysts are typically smooth and roughly spherical GROWTHS (2), and white to yellow in colour (see also SPOTS (2)). Cysts developing just under the skin may appear blotchy in colour due to the covering of epithelial pigment cells. Cysts vary considerably in size, reaching several millimetres across. Definitive diagnosis relies on microscopical detection of the causative spore pathogen stage(s) i.e spores/pathogen stage(s) within the cyst tissue, often possible only on dead fish.

CAUSES
Cysts are mostly the result of infection by various spore-forming PROTOZOA (3), FUNGI (3), and larval helminths (FLUKES (3)). The virus *LYMPHOCYSTIS* (3) also produces cyst-like growths.
Other cyst-causing pathogens include *DERMOCYSTIDIUM* (3), which is possibly related to the fungi. Internal nodule or cyst-like swellings may also be the result of infection with MYCOBACTERIA (3). [Note: some parasites, such as *ICHTHYOPHTHIRIUS* (3) (white spot), produce reproductive cysts; however, these are present in the water and not on the fish.]

PREVENTION AND TREATMENT

No chemical treatments are available for use with fish. Preventative measures are therefore paramount, involving visual screening of new fish for the presence of cysts. It is prudent to isolate any fish which develops cyst-like growths.

D

DACTYLOGYRUS

A genus of MONOGENETIC FLUKES (3) which parasitise the gills of fish. There are some 50 known species varying from 0.15 to 2 mm in length. They are exclusively fish PARASITES (3), occurring predominantly on the gills but occasionally on other parts of the body.

The life cycle of *Dactylogyrus vastator* (a species found on cyprinids) begins when female flukes release their eggs, which drop to the bottom where they hatch (after 3-4 days at 20 degrees C [68 degrees F]) into free-swimming larvae. The latter have 4-8 hours to find a host, or else they will die. When they find a host they attach to the gill area, maturing after 7-8 days and laying their own eggs in turn.

Fish may harbour a few flukes without obvious signs of disease. In heavy infections (e.g. around 20-40+ flukes on a 2cm [3/4 ins] fish), the infection is far more serious and can be fatal.

SIGNS

These are variable, depending on the extent of the parasite burden. Fish with only one or two gill flukes may show no signs, or occasional FLASHING (2) or SCRATCHING (2) prompted by momentary irritation. Fish with more severe infestations exhibit RESPIRATORY DISTRESS (2), (GASPING (2) and an abnormally fast gill rate). They may COUGH (2), apparently in an attempt to alleviate/remove the irritation. Flashing and scratching are more frequent, sometimes frenzied. Affected fish often exhibit CLAMPED FINS (2) and loss of APPETITE (2).

Acute symptoms may occur when fish are suddenly exposed to large numbers of flukes, e.g. when an infected

LIFE CYCLES OF *DACTYLOGYRUS* (GILL FLUKES) AND *GYRODACTYLUS* (SKIN FLUKES)

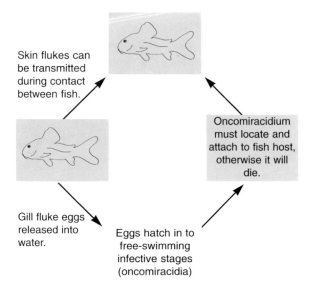

Skin flukes can be transmitted during contact between fish.

Oncomiracidium must locate and attach to fish host, otherwise it will die.

Gill fluke eggs released into water.

Eggs hatch in to free-swimming infective stages (oncomiracidia)

fish is introduced into a previously unaffected aquarium. Gill damage results in HYPOXIA (3), with associated loss of SWIMMING (2) control, glazed EYES (2), and heightened COLORATION (2), symptoms which can easily be confused with acute POISONING (3). The carrier fish remain unaffected.

On examination the gills of affected fish appear pale with grey edges and there is significant MUCUS HYPERPRODUCTION (2) around the gills. Low-power microscopic examination of the gill shows a classic club shape caused by gill membrane cell build-up. A scrape of the gills will show easily identified gill flukes under the microscope.

It should be noted that scratching is only rarely a sign of gill fluke parasitisation; in the vast majority of cases it is the result of environmental problems such as CLOUDY WATER (2) and/or NITROGENOUS WASTES (3).

CAUSE
Any species of *Dactylogyrus*; the exact identity is unimportant from a treatment point of view.

TREATMENT
Proprietary bath remedies are available for the treatment of *Dactylogyrus* and other monogenean flukes.

Dactylogyrus are generally more difficult to eradicate than skin flukes (e.g. *GYRODACTYLUS* [3]) since they are oviparous, producing eggs which are resistant to chemical treatments. It is therefore essential to follow the prescribed course of treatment in order to target the newly-hatched larvae. Alternatively a FORMALIN (3) bath can be used. In the case of persistent infections, ANTHELMINTHICS (3), such as PRAZIQUANTEL (3), can be used. Treatment with the anti-parasite drug TOLTRAZURIL (3) has given some success in eliminating monogeneans, and may offer future potential for treating aquarium fish.

In some cases, the aquarium can be rid of *Dactylogyrus* (and other monogeneans) by leaving it free of fish for 3 to 4 weeks (though some flukes produce dormant eggs which may survive this period). The infected fish must of course be treated with a suitable chemical remedy during the isolation period, otherwise they will re-introduce flukes into the aquarium upon their return.

There is some evidence that host immunity may help protect the fish against fluke infection; the provision of STRESS (3) -free conditions will therefore help ensure that the fish's immune system is not compromised.

DEFORMITY
The distortion of any physical feature, external or internal.

SIGNS
Common deformities involve the spine (SCOLIOSIS (3), LORDOSIS (3)), the operculum (wholly or partly missing), and fins (divided, abnormal in size/shape, or missing). SIAMESE TWINS (3) occasionally occur. A condition known as BELLYSLIDING (3) is caused by deformity of the swimbladder. STUNTING (2) of genetic origin may also be regarded as a deformity.

CAUSES
● Genetic: Single deformities may occur even where top-grade breeding stock has been used, but are commonly the result of INBREEDING (3).

Deformity of the spine, resulting from inbreeding.

● Cultivated: A few 'man-made' varieties of fish have been intentionally produced to possess deformed body shapes or other unnatural body features.

● Environmental: exposure to adverse water conditions during early development may also be a cause of some deformities.

● Pathogenic: certain systemic bacterial infections, notably those caused by MYCOBACTERIA (3), can result in a deformed body. An infectious disease should always be suspected as the cause of deformities occurring in previously normal fish.

PREVENTION AND TREATMENT

No treatment possible. Deformed fish should be CULLED (3) if their deformity is considered likely to cause suffering (minor deformities of the fins and/or operculum are unlikely to cause the fish problems). Fish with inherited deformities (born/hatched deformed) should never be used for breeding. Adults that regularly produce deformed fry, and the siblings of such fry, should also be regarded as unsuitable for breeding stock. Inbreeding should be avoided. Maintaining good-quality water conditions will reduce the likelihood of environmentally induced deformities. *See also SECTION I: Breeding; SECTION II: DISTENDED BODY, abnormal FINS, abnormal GILLS.*

Because deformity is commonly a sign of health problems as well as a problem in itself, it has also been included as an entry in SECTION II.

DERMOCYSTIDIUM

A spore-forming pathogen which manifests as whitish CYSTS (3) occurring on the skin and gills of fish.

Dermocystidium is a rarely encountered disease of tropical aquarium fish. The PARASITE (3) is of questionable taxonomic status but may be related to the fungi. In terms of pathological damage to the fish and control and treatment, *Dermocystidium* is quite distinct from the more commonly encountered opportunistic FUNGUS (3) species such as *SAPROLEGNIA* (3). The disease is mostly recorded from temperate and sub-tropical fish, including koi carp and goldfish.

SIGNS
Whitish GROWTHS (2) (cysts or nodules), around 1 mm in diameter, may be present on the gills and/or the skin. Possible diagnostic confusion may occur with the more commonly encountered *LYMPHOCYSTIS* (3), a VIRUS (3) disease. Microscopical examination of an excised *Dermocystidium* cyst will reveal many thick-walled spores of variable size: such spores do not occur in *Lymphocystis*.

CAUSES
Dermocystidium koi is associated with the disease in goldfish and koi carp. Certain other *Dermocystidium* species have been found infecting some tropical fish, including cichlids.

PREVENTION AND TREATMENT
There is no treatment. Infected fish should be kept in isolation in order to prevent possible transmission.

DIGENEA, DIGENETIC FLUKES
Also known as digenetic trematodes. Digenetic FLUKES (3) parasitise the skin, body tissues, internal organs, or blood of fish, the actual site(s) depending on the fluke species. The majority are parasitic on fish as the encysted larval (metacercarial) stage, examples being BLACKSPOT (3) disease and *DIPLOSTOMUM* (3) (= eye fluke). In a few species, however, it is the adult fluke which is present in the fish, one notable example being the blood flukes, *Sanguinicola* spp. (these are unlikely to be found in tropical aquarium fish).

Digenetic flukes have complex life-cycles involving both vertebrate and invertebrate hosts. Aquatic molluscs (e.g.

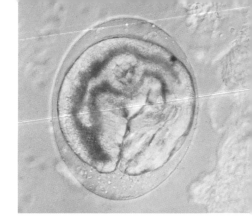

Embryonated fluke, from fish tissue.

LIFE CYCLE OF DIGENETIC FLUKES

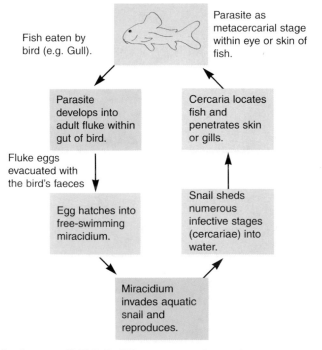

Fish eaten by bird (e.g. Gull).

Parasite as metacercarial stage within eye or skin of fish.

Parasite develops into adult fluke within gut of bird.

Cercaria locates fish and penetrates skin or gills.

Fluke eggs evacuated with the bird's faeces

Egg hatches into free-swimming miracidium.

Snail sheds numerous infective stages (cercariae) into water.

Miracidium invades aquatic snail and reproduces.

freshwater SNAILS [3]) serve as invertebrate hosts in virtually all of the fish-parasitic digenean life cycles. Due to the additional involvement of a vertebrate host (often a piscivorous bird), digenetic fluke infections are rarely encountered among aquarium-reared fish but may be found in fish which have been farmed outdoors or wild caught. For similar reasons, infected aquarium fish need not be isolated. Fortunately, metacercarial fluke infections are generally not life-threatening to the fish and are often asymptomatic.

DIGESTIVE DISORDERS

These usually result from incorrect feeding *(see SECTION 1: Nutrition)*, but may be the by-product of other ailments. They are characterised by loss of APPETITE (2), absence of or abnormal FAECES (2), DISTENDED BODY (2) or EMACIATION (2), all of which may, however, be symptoms of other disorders. Probably the commonest digestive disorder is CONSTIPATION (3).

See also OVERFEEDING (3), VITAMIN DEFICIENCY (3), NUTRITIONAL DISEASES (3).

DI-METRONIDAZOLE   P

See METRONIDAZOLE (3).

DINOFLAGELLATE PARASITES

These PROTOZOA (3) belong to the order Dinoflagellida, which contains both parasitic and non-parasitic species. The only species of importance in tropical freshwater fish belong to the genus *PISCINOODINIUM* (3), which causes the disease known under various common names: velvet, rust, or gold-dust disease.

DIPLOSTOMUM

A parasitic DIGENETIC FLUKE (3) (phylum Platy-helminthes) whose larval (= metacercarial) stage resides in the eyes of fish, causing the disease known commonly as eye fluke.

The adult PARASITE (3) lives in the gut of fish-eating birds, where it lays eggs which are shed in the birds' droppings. If the infected droppings land in water, the fluke eggs hatch into larvae (known as miracidia) which then invade the tissues of aquatic snails. Within the snail the larval flukes transform into a reproductive stage and multiply. The snail eventually sheds the flukes (known as cercariae) which swim in the water in search of a fish host. Invasion of the fish is normally via the gills, with the flukes being carried via the blood to the small capillaries within the fish's eye where they transform into metacercariae. It has been suggested that the cercariae may also be able to directly penetrate the lens from the water. Once inside the eye the flukes grow to full size within 4-5 weeks and may remain in the lens for up to 4 years. Over 500 metacercariae

Eye opacity, probably caused by the presence of eye-fluke in a pond-reared sunfish (Lepomis). Confirmation of eye-fluke is generally possible only at post-mortem.

have been found in a single fish eye. In nature, the life-cycle is completed when an infected fish is eaten by a suitable bird host. (See DIGENEA [3] life-cycle.)

Diplostomum has a wide host range, having been recorded in over 100 fish species. However, due to the complex life-cycle and need for a bird as the final host, this parasite is normally restricted to fish which have been either wild-caught or reared in outdoor ponds. It is, however, possible for the inadvertent introduction of infected SNAILS (3) to lead to an outbreak in the aquarium. If eye flukes are introduced into the aquarium in this way, cercarial larval invasion of the fish may occur in such large numbers that gill trauma may result from the penetration wounds, sometimes leading to host death.

SIGNS

The parasite invades the lens, vitreous humour, and retina, causing impaired vision and occasionally severe eye damage. Small white cataracts may occur. One or both eyes may appear cloudy. Chronic infection can result in severe lens damage and detachment of the retina, leading to blindness. EXOPHTHALMIA (2) is sometimes associated with this disease.

The fluke metacercariae may sometimes be seen, under low-power magnification, within the eyes of a restrained or sedated live fish, but confirmation is generally feasible only at autopsy, the eye being dissected so as to reveal the metacercariae within.

The aquarist should bear in mind that CLOUDY EYE (2) is more likely to be the result of microbial infections or environmental problems than infection with eye-fluke *(See SECTION II: CLOUDY EYE for other causes of this condition.)*

Aquatic snails serve as the intermediate host for eye flukes.

CAUSE

Infection caused by the metacercarial stage of the digenean fluke *Diplostomum*. Several *Diplostomum* species are known to infect the eyes of fish, a common species being *D. spathaceum*.

PREVENTION AND TREATMENT

Fish which have cloudy eyes or cataracts should not be purchased.

Fish can become infected only in outdoor bodies of water which harbour aquatic snails and which are visited by piscivorous birds. The only conceivable means by which aquarium-reared fish could contract eye fluke is by exposure to infected snails, and this is highly unlikely unless snails are inadvertently introduced from ponds or streams, e.g. on plants or with LIVE FOODS (3).

In most cases, the infected fish remain otherwise healthy and do not need to be kept in isolation. EUTHANASIA (3) is necessary only if the fish's vision is severely impaired such that it is unable to locate food and is suffering as a consequence (however, bear in mind that many fish are able to locate food without relying on vision, exceptions being certain predatory species).

Evidence suggests that certain ANTHELMINTHICS (3), such as PRAZIQUANTEL (3), may destroy the larval flukes. In general, however, chemical treatments are not warranted, and in any case, by the time the symptoms have been detected, any ocular damage to the fish will probably have already occurred.

DISEASE

This can be defined as a state of ill-health. Diseases may be classified as either infectious or non-infectious.

INFECTIOUS DISEASES

These are caused by a pathogen and are transmitted from one fish to another, either directly or indirectly, depending on the pathogen species involved. In the case of indirect transmission, this may involve non-fish hosts such as aquatic SNAILS (3), crustaceans (e.g. COPEPODS (3)), and in some cases, piscivorous birds or even mammals. Examples of infectious diseases are those caused by VIRUSES (3), BACTERIA (3), FUNGI (3), PROTOZOA (3), and HELMINTH (3) PARASITES (3).

Under aquarium conditions, however, certain pathogen-borne diseases are, in practical terms, non-infectious. Notable among these are those diseases caused by DIGENETIC FLUKES (3) in which the parasites must pass through one or more non-fish hosts (such as a bird) before being infective to other fish: clearly, this sequence of transmission is unlikely to occur in the home aquarium!

NON-INFECTIOUS DISEASES

These are not caused by pathogens. Non-infectious diseases include TUMOURS (3), genetic defects (e.g. some cases of DEFORMITY (3)), and physiological or organ disorders. As far as aquarium fish are concerned, most non-infectious diseases are environmentally induced, notably caused by poor aquarium hygiene and/or adverse water conditions.

Environmental health problems and infectious diseases can be easily confused: both may result in large numbers of fish becoming ill within a relatively short period of time. In general, when several previously healthy fish are observed simultaneously and suddenly (i.e. within a few hours) to become ill, this is almost invariably the result of a water quality problem and not an infectious disease.

DISINFECTANTS

Disinfectants are occasionally used on aquarium equipment, but generally only following a serious disease outbreak, particularly involving highly pathogenic microbes (e.g. BACTERIA [3] or VIRUSES [3]) which may persist on aquarium equipment and auxiliary items such as siphons and buckets.

Aquarium disinfectants include the chlorine-based and IODINE (3)-based chemicals, such as BLEACH (3) and

IODOPHORS (3), respectively. These are used to destroy a wide range of pathogens. Both these groups of chemicals are inactivated by organic matter and for this reason any dirty equipment should be washed prior to exposure to the disinfectant.

These types of disinfectants must never come into direct contact with fish or other aquatic animals: it is therefore imperative that the equipment is thoroughly rinsed prior to re-use. For the same reason, great care must be taken when disinfecting porous materials, such as some aquarium substrates or filter media, due to the difficulties in removing all traces of the chemical. Bleach is particularly toxic to fish and is corrosive to metals and nylon nets. Needless to say, bleach will kill plants.

Iodophors are preferred and are less toxic to handle. Commercial iodophor solutions may be purchased from some aquatic stores or a veterinarian. The stock solution requires dilution and is normally applied as a bath or as a surface wipe (refer to the manufacturer's instructions for dilution and exposure times).

See also POISONING (3).

DROPSY (Ascites)

A common cause of DISTENDED BODY (2). Strictly speaking, dropsy is a symptom rather than a disease in its own right, but is commonly regarded as the latter in the aquarium hobby, and hence is included here.

SIGNS

Significant SWELLING (2) of the abdominal area of the fish; the swollen body may cause the SCALES (2) to stick

Cichlid with abdominal swelling due to dropsy.

Dropsy in Labeo bicolor. Note the abdomen is swollen and the abdominal scales are projecting outwards.

Photo: Mike Sandford.

outwards, giving a serrated appearance to the body outline (sometimes known as the pinecone effect): this is often more noticeable when the fish is viewed from above. Dissection reveals a build-up of fluid or jelly-like material in the abdominal cavity and swelling of organs, which causes the abdominal distension. Other associated symptoms include LETHARGY (2) (often showing a poor escape reflex), RESPIRATORY DISTRESS (2), skin turning a pale red colour, and, in chronic cases, EXO-PHTHALMIA (2) and boils or ULCERS (2).

CAUSES
The cause may be infection with a VIRUS (3), BACTERIUM (3) [*AEROMONA* (3), MYCOBACTERIA (3), *NOCARDIA* (3)], or PARASITE (3) (e.g. *HEXAMITA* (3)). Adverse water conditions (e.g. poor aquarium hygiene; accumulation of NITROGENOUS WASTES [3]) may predispose fish to this condition. Most of the bacteria which cause dropsy symptoms occur widely in the aquatic environment both in the water and organic detritus (mulm) in the aquarium, and in the flora of the fish's gut.

Osmoregulatory problems may also cause this condition.

Disease outbreaks usually occur as a result of a combination of circumstances – in particular the presence of a particularly virulent and infectious strain of bacteria combined with adverse environmental conditions and general poor aquarium hygiene. Other predisposing factors may includ: immune suppression (e.g. caused by chronic STRESS (3)), poor nutrition, genetic weakness due to INBREEDING (3), SENILITY(3). The primary infection route is via the gut, as a result of the fish foraging on pathogen-contaminated faeces and other detritus, or through CANNIBALISM (3) of an infected fish (corpse).

As in most bacterial infections there can be three forms of the disease:

● Acute: rapid onset of disease resulting in death before significant symptoms are exhibited, although some body distension is usually noticeable.

● Chronic: slow, systemic development of disease with a wide range of disease symptoms, typically progressing from body distension to ulceration and exophthalmia.

● Latent: very low levels of infection. Infected fish often show very little sign of disease but may act as carriers.

PREVENTION AND TREATMENT

Preventative methods are paramount since a cure is often difficult or impossible. Ensure optimum environmental conditions and good aquarium hygiene *(see SECTION I: The Correct Environment; Nutrition)*. Avoid STRESS (3).

Affected fish should be isolated and maintained under optimal conditions. A proprietary anti-internal bacteria treatment, applied as a long-duration bath, may be effective in some cases. If the fish does not respond, then effective treatment may sometimes be achieved using medicated foods, for example, OXYTETRACYCLINE (3) or CHLORAMPHENICOL (3), in either case at the rate of 55 mg/kg of fish daily for ten days; or sulphamerazine at 265 mg/kg for three days.

E

ECTOPARASITES

PARASITES (3) which live on the exterior surfaces of the fish, i.e. on the skin, fins, gills, and/or eyes. Examples include: some PROTOZOANS (3), e.g. those causing SKIN SLIME DISEASE (3); skin and gill FLUKES (3); CRUSTACEANS (3) such as *ARGULUS* (3) and *LERNAEA* (3); and parasitic annelid worms such as the fish LEECH (3) (*PISCICOLA* (3)).

Some ectoparasites are large and visible to the naked eye, e.g. leeches, *Lernaea,* and *Argulus,* while others are microscopic and noticeable only by the clinical or behavioural symptoms they cause, such as MUCUS HYPERPRODUCTION (2) and irritation evidenced by SCRATCHING (2) and FLASHING (2), and, in the case of gill parasites, RESPIRATORY DISTRESS (2). However, these symptoms are far more commonly the result of poor environmental conditions, which should be eliminated as potential causes before parasites are suspected.

Specific signs and treatments are detailed under the entries for individual types of ectoparasite.

EGG BOUND, EGG BINDING

Also known as spawn binding. When a female fish is ripe with eggs but is unable to spawn for some reason, then her ova may eventually become necrotic and this can ultimately lead to the fish's death. This egg-bound condition is more likely to arise in those species which rarely spawn under aquarium conditions, or in situations where ripe females do not have access to adult male fish. Khuli loaches (*Acanthophthalmus/Pangio* spp.) are examples of well-known aquarium fish which rarely spawn in captivity, and which may die as a result of becoming egg-bound. Adjusting the aquarium conditions to trigger spawning, or the introduction of male fish, will lessen the chances of this condition occurring.

EGG FUNGUS

Fish eggs are susceptible to attack by aquatic fungi. The fungus invariably attacks infertile eggs but may spread to adjacent fertile ones.

The eggs of virtually all fish species are potentially at risk

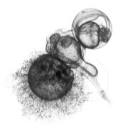

Fungused cyprinid egg (bottom) smothered by fungal hyphae. Remarkably, the middle egg has escaped fungal attack and has just hatched, and the top egg is developing normally.

of FUNGUS INFECTION (3). The degree of susceptibility varies between fish species, with some producing tough eggs which are relatively resilient to fungal attack.

SIGNS
Eggs which are attacked by fungus are typically surrounded by white fungal hyphae, giving them a fluffy or spiky-looking contour: these white hyphal filaments may be clearly seen with the aid of a high magnification hand lens. Where eggs are laid closely together in clutches, as in the case of substrate-spawning cichlids, the fungus may easily spread from dead to viable eggs and can eventually destroy the entire clutch.

It is a common misapprehension that white or opaque eggs are fungused even if no hyphae are apparent. In practice some eggs are opaque and whitish when laid, and nevertheless perfectly viable; clear eggs which are infertile commonly turn white within 24 hours of spawning but fungal hyphae do not normally appear until some time thereafter.

CAUSE
Several species of fungus may attack fish eggs, including those of the genera *SAPROLEGNIA* (3) and *ACHYLA* (3).

CONTROL AND TREATMENT
In those groups of fish which exhibit parental care, notably the cichlids, the parent fish often pick off dead eggs before they fungus, thereby preventing any chance of infection of the remaining clutch. In other cases, the aquarist may intervene by physically removing any fungused eggs using a pipette, needle, or fine tweezers/forceps.

Where eggs are incubated independently of the adult fish, they can be maintained in a long-term bath of METHYLENE BLUE (3) (2 mg per litre) which will minimise the chances of fungal attack. In those fish species which have a moderate to long incubation time (4+ days) it will be necessary to redose with methylene blue every second or third day. **WARNING:** methylene blue is potentially harmful to biological filtration.
See also SECTION I: Breeding.

ENDOPARASITES

PARASITES (3) which live within the body of the fish. By contrast, those which live on the surface of the fish's body, fins, or gills are known as ECTOPARASITES (3). Examples of endoparasites are TAPEWORMS (3), DIGENETIC FLUKES (3), and some PROTOZOAN (3) parasites, e.g. *HEXAMITA* (3). The protozoan *ICHTHY-OPHTHIRIUS* (3), which causes whitespot disease, is, strictly speaking, an endoparasite since it resides under the fish's skin; however, it is widely referred to in the aquarium literature as an ectoparasite.

In terms of treatment, endoparasites are generally more difficult to eradicate than are ectoparasites, because of their enclosure (and hence protection) within the fish's body, such that they are not directly exposed to chemical treatments administered by bath immersion.

EPSOM SALTS

Hydrated magnesium sulphate ($MgSO_4.7H_2O$). Used to increase mineral content *(See SECTION I, The Correct Environment)* and sometimes effective against CONSTIPATION in fish.

DOSAGE AND ADMINISTRATION
As a laxative: 1 level teaspoon per 4 gallons (2.5 g per 18 litres), dissolved in a small volume of aquarium water and added to the aquarium. Raising the TEMPERATURE (3) slightly (within the physiological tolerance limits of the fish) may assist by increasing the fish's metabolic rate.

EPISTYLIS

A genus of ciliate PROTOZOANS (3). Although regarded as commensals rather than true PARASITES (3), these sessile, stalked protozoans sometimes use fish as a surface upon which to attach. *Epistylis* may sometimes colonise host tissues already infected with bacteria, upon which these ciliates feed. Infrequently encountered on aquarium fish.

SIGNS
Epistylis tend to colonise the fish's harder tissue surfaces, such as the tips of fin rays and opercula. The small colonies may appear like tiny tufts of FUNGUS (3). The host fish

will generally show signs of a BACTERIAL INFECTION (3), since *Epistylis* is often found in association with an infected WOUND (2).

Microscopic examination of a colony reveals several cylindrical or bell-shaped protozoans each supported by a long stalk which is used for attachment. The stalk may reach 1.2 mm in length, depending on the species, and may be branched supporting several protozoan 'bodies' (known as zooids).

There is evidence that the stalk of *Epistylis* may penetrate the fish's skin, thereby aggravating the damage already caused by the bacterial infection. However, it is generally believed that the clinical features mostly relate to the underlying bacterial infection rather than the concomitant *Epistylis*.

CAUSES
High organic pollution and an existing bacterial infection are major contributing factors in *Epistylis* colonisation of fish.

Several species are known, including *E. colisarum* which has been recorded from gouramis. Differentiation between *Epistylis* species is not necessary as far as control and treatment is concerned.

PREVENTION AND TREATMENT
An improvement in aquarium hygiene and prevention /treatment of bacterial infections will greatly reduce the chances of *Epistylis* attachment and damage. A SALT (3) bath can be used to eradicate this protozoan. Any concomitant bacterial infection will also require treatment with proprietary anti-bacterial remedies or ANTIBIOTICS (3).

ERGASILUS
A genus of COPEPOD (3) (CRUSTACEAN [3]) PARA-SITES (3) of the gills of fish, sometimes known as gill maggots.

Only the female is parasitic: after fertilization she attaches to the fish's gill using her antennae which either pierce or clamp onto the filament. The male and larval stages are free-swimming. The parasite's body is 0.5-3 mm long, and her egg pouches measure an additional 1-3 mm in length – it is the latter that are the visible 'maggots'. Nauplii hatch out of the egg pouches after 10-12 days at 16 degrees C (61 degrees F) or as little as 3 days at 32C (89.5F), and the female then extrudes the next batch of eggs. The nauplii mature in 8-10 weeks and mate, after which the females seek out a host. A female can produce over 40,000 parasites in a single year.

Although relatively common on wild and pond-reared fish, gill maggots are rarely encountered under aquarium conditions.

SIGNS
Affected fish exhibit RESPIRATORY DISTRESS (2): high gill rate, gasping, and COUGHING (2). Naked-eye examination of the gills will reveal MUCUS HYPER-PRODUCTION (2) and clearly visible maggot-like egg pouches.

CAUSE
Approximately 65 species of ergasilid parasites are recorded from freshwater fish. From the aquarist's point of view exact identification is unnecessary.

Ergasilus are usually introduced via infected fish or as free-swimming larvae in fish-bag water, though this is unlikely if the fish have been aquarium reared. It is possible that wild collected LIVE FOODS (3) could harbour the larval stages within the water.

PREVENTION AND TREATMENT
Prevention of an outbreak is best achieved by QUAR-ANTINE (3). Treatment is via proprietary anti-crustacean medication, METRIPHONATE (3), or a short-term (30 minute) POTASSIUM PERMANGANATE (3) bath.

EUTHANASIA
It may sometimes be necessary to kill fish which are suffering as a result of an incurable disease or from a serious injury.

The decision whether to put a fish out of its misery or keep it alive in the hope that it may recover is often a difficult one to make. In some cases it may be worth seeking expert opinion, by taking the fish to a reputable aquarium store or veterinary surgeon – however the additional STRESS (3) involved in disturbing and transporting the fish may itself be unkind, or even the 'final straw' as regards possible survival.

ACCEPTABLE METHODS OF EUTHANASIA
When considering euthanasia, bear in mind that fish are capable of experiencing pain and stress and must therefore be killed humanely. Acceptable killing methods include concussion, decapitation, and ANAESTHETIC (3) overdose. Concussion and decapitation may seem barbaric, but if conducted properly, are fast and humane killing techniques. If the aquarist feels unable to perform euthanasia then the fish can be taken to a vet or professional aquarist who is skilled in such techniques.
● Concussion: The body of the fish is wrapped in a cloth, with the head exposed. The fish's head is then hit forcefully against a hard surface, such as the edge of a table. Alternatively, a hard object can be hand-held and brought down forcefully on the fish's head. (In the case of large fish, it is possible to purchase a special club known as a "priest" from fishing tackle (bait) shops, which is sold for the humane despatch of trout, bass, etc.) In either method, the brain should be destroyed by penetration with a scalpel or sharp scissors, otherwise the fish may subsequently recover.
● Decapitation: In the case of small fish the head can be quickly removed with the aid of a sharp scalpel, knife, or scissors. The brain should then be destroyed, as for concussion. The need to destroy the brains of decapitated fish may seem unnecessary; however, it is known that fish's brains are highly tolerant of HYPOXIA (3), such that the animal may remain 'conscious' for some time after its head has been severed from the body.
● Anaesthetic overdose: This method is ideal for killing any size of aquarium fish. It is also ideal for simultaneously killing large numbers of fish (e.g. when CULLING [3]). Immersion anaesthetics, such as TRICAINE METHANE-SULPHONATE (3) and BENZOCAINE (3), are ideal for euthanasia. The effective killing dose will depend to some extent on the species of fish and other conditions. For example, a prolonged exposure to 300 mg per litre of

Tricaine methanesulphonate is sufficient to cause death in most tropical aquarium fish. It is advisable to leave the fish in the anaesthetic solution for a long period of time (e.g. for a couple of hours or more) to ensure that recovery does not occur following removal from the anaesthetic solution. If in any doubt, physical destruction of the brain can be performed, as outlined for concussion, above.

UNACCEPTABLE METHODS OF EUTHANASIA
It is considered cruel to kill fish by the following methods:
● flushing them alive down the lavatory
● removing them from the water until death occurs
● plunging them into boiling water
● plunging them into iced water
● slowly chilling them (with or without water) (note: this method is still commonly advocated in the aquarium literature, but is now considered to cause the fish unnecessary pain)
● breaking their neck, without subsequent destruction of the brain.

SAFE DISPOSAL OF CARCASSES
The aquarist should take responsibility for the safe and hygienic disposal of fish carcasses. The dead fish should first be wrapped in newspaper or absorbent tissue and then placed in a leak-proof plastic bag for domestic disposal. Alternatively, it can be burned, or buried in the garden. Never feed diseased dead (or live) fish to other fish as certain pathogens can be transmitted by this route. Similarly, do not flush dead fish down the lavatory as this could conceivably result in the infection of native fish with exotic pathogens.

EXOPHTHALMIA, EXOPHTHALMUS
An eye condition, commonly known as "pop-eye", characterised by the swelling of one or both eyes, so that they clearly protrude more than is normal.

SIGNS
One or both eyes swell and protrude from the orbit. CLOUDY EYE (2) commonly accompanies, and sometimes precedes, the swelling, which sometimes

*"Pop-eye" in a
cyprinid.*

becomes so extreme that the eye literally 'pops out' of its
socket and is lost.

CAUSE
Exophthalmia is a symptom of a build-up of fluid in or
behind the eye, rather than being a disease in its own right.
It has nevertheless been included here, as well as in
SECTION II, for ease of reference, as many aquarists regard
it as a discrete illness.
  Causes of the condition include the following:
● Reactions to poor water quality (NITROGENOUS
WASTES (3), especially high NITRATE (3) levels).
● Eye PARASITES (3), e.g. *DIPLOSTOMUM* (3).
● Systemic BACTERIAL INFECTION (3) such as Fish TB
(*MYCOBACTERIUM*) (3) or bacterial DROPSY (3).
VIRAL (3) infections may also be the cause. In these cases
exophthalmus is usually accompanied by other symptoms,
which may include EMACIATION (2) or DISTENDED
BODY (2), ULCERS (2), and generally very poor
condition. Often poor aquarium hygiene is the underlying
cause of such infections.
● Systemic FUNGUS INFECTION (3). *ICHTHYO-
PHONUS* (3), or *Ichthyophonus*-like fungus, has, on
occasion, been known to infect freshwater fish.
● Nutritional deficiencies (see VITAMIN DEFICIENCY
[3]).
● Metabolic disturbances, i.e. any dysfunction of the
biochemical processes of the fish.
Of these the first – poor water quality – is by far the most
commonplace underlying factor.

TREATMENT
Prompt action is necessary at the first sign of exophthalmus,
before permanent damage to the eye(s) occurs. Often
improvement of water quality, by partial water changes,

may effect a cure, although the swelling may take several days or even a week to subside. Any accompanying external eye cloudiness normally abates more quickly. If adverse water chemistry is found to be the underlying cause, this must likewise be remedied in order to effect a long-term cure. If an infectious disease has been diagnosed, then treatment should be as for the relevant infective agent. If environmental and pathogenic problems have been ruled out, then improving the diet may be tried *(See SECTION I: Nutrition; VITAMIN DEFICIENCY [3].)*

EUTHANASIA (3) should be considered in cases where exophthalmus is accompanied by dropsy or other debilitating symptoms and fails to respond to treatment.

EYE FLUKE or EYE WORM
See *DIPLOSTOMUM* (3).

F

FATTY LIVER
A pathological condition of the liver caused by incorrect dietary fats. Foods which contain significant amounts of animal fat or other highly saturated fats are responsible for this condition. Saturated fats are not easily digested by the fish and are instead deposited in the liver. An excessive accumulation of fat within the liver may be fatal but is not usually detected until at autopsy. Feeding a well-balanced diet will prevent this condition.
See also NUTRITIONAL DISEASES (3), OVER-FEEDING (3); SECTION I: Nutrition.

FENBENDAZOLE   P
An ANTHELMINTHIC (3) commonly used to treat equine worm infestations, but also of aquarium use, e.g. for NEMATODES (3) such as *CAMALLANUS* (3). If a proprietary horse-wormer is employed for aquarium treatment, the powder/granular form (not paste) should be purchased.

DOSAGE AND ADMINISTRATION
Treatment is via long-term bath at the rate of 2-3 mg per litre, with repeat doses added at days 7 and 14 (i.e. a three-week course of treatment).

FIN-NIPPING
See AGGRESSION (3).

FIN ROT
Fin rot is the progressive erosion and disintegration of the fins.

SIGNS
An outbreak starts with the appearance of a grey-white line along the outer margin of the affected fin(s), followed by 'fraying' of the soft tissue (fin membrane) at the fin edge(s) and eventually of the fin ray(s) as well. The area of rot on the margin of the fin is typically reddened and inflamed. Congestion of the blood vessels (FIN CONGESTION (2)), resulting in red streaks on the fin, is often a warning sign that a fin rot outbreak is about to occur. In some cases the fin rot attacks the cartilage at the base of the fin and the whole fin drops off.

Fin rot symptoms are sometimes seen in association with with rough and ragged skin, usually when the latter is one of the symptoms of COLUMNARIS (3) disease (mouth fungus). SECONDARY INFECTION (3) with FUNGUS (3) is very common in cases of fin rot, leading to the appearance of COTTON-WOOL-like GROWTHS (2) on the rotting fin. Untreated fin rot may advance towards the body, and in the case of tail rot may progress to the body tissue. In such cases death usually follows rapidly.

Tail of a cichlid with fin-rot (lower right border). Note also the patch of fungus infection on the upper part of the fin.

CAUSE
BACTERIA (3), normally in association with environmental factors. A number of species of bacteria have been associated with fin rot: *AEROMONAS* (3) species *(A.liquefaciens, A.formicans)*, *PSEUDOMONAS* (3) species, *FLEXIBACTER* (3) (columnaris). All these bacteria may form part of the natural aquatic fauna and hence are commonly present within the aquarium.

There are a number of likely causes of a fin rot outbreak:
● External bacterial infection caused by reduction of the fish's natural immunity, due to poor environmental conditions or STRESS (3).
● Bacterial invasion of fin tissue following mechanical damage, i.e. INJURY (3), typically during netting, as a result of AGGRESSION (3) (including fin-nipping) or, in the case of bottom-dwelling species, abrasion by sharp substrates.
● Serious systemic bacterial infection, in which case there are normally other symptoms such as ULCERS (3) and DISTENDED BODY (2) (e.g. in cases of DROPSY [3]).

PREVENTION AND TREATMENT
The progressive nature and obvious signs of the disease mean that several days normally (but not invariably) elapse before serious fin damage occurs, so the vigilant aquarist has plenty of time to identify and treat the problem before it becomes life-threatening or likely to result in permanent fin loss.

Treatment may be achieved by bath immersion using a SALT (3) solution (provided the affected fish is/are salt-tolerant) or a PHENOXYETHANOL (3) (Phenoxethol)-based proprietary medication which will help combat both the bacterial infection and any secondary fungal attack. If only one or two fish are affected, topical application of GENTIAN VIOLET (3) is highly effective, and has also effected a cure in cases where other treatments have proved ineffective.

To accelerate recovery and fin regeneration, optimum environmental conditions and a balanced diet should be provided. If environmental problems are the root cause of the problem, these should, of course, be ameliorated: levels of NITROGENOUS WASTES (3) should be minimised, overcrowding avoided, and steps taken to prevent further aggression if that is the underlying cause.

It is impracticable totally to avoid the circumstances that may lead to fin rot; however, good husbandry, careful selection of compatible fish, and careful handling will help to minimise the likelihood of its occurrence.

FISH LEECH
See LEECHES (3), PISCICOLA (3).

FISH LICE, FISH LOUSE
See ARGULUS (3).

FISH POX
A VIRUS (3) disease, not usually life-threatening, common among cold-water fish (e.g. carp [*Cyprinus carpio*], and hence also known as carp pox) but rare in tropical aquaria. There have been no recorded cases of the disease spreading throughout an aquarium, and it should be regarded as unsightly, rather than dangerous.

SIGNS
Irregular (in shape, size, and distribution) but usually discrete, gelatinous, milky GROWTHS (2), white, grey or pink in colour, reaching between 1 and 2 mm in thickness. These growths may appear anywhere on the fins, head, and/or body, and may initially be soft but harden to a waxy consistency. In severe cases much of the surface of the fish may be covered in pox growths but this extreme form is rarely encountered in aquaria.

Fish pox growths cannot be removed, unlike mucus (but note: because removal of mucus may be harmful to the fish, this test should be made only for confirmation if fish pox is already seriously suspected), and MUCUS HYPER-PRODUCTION (2) is more uniform (flatter and a thinner layer).

CAUSE
Fish pox is caused by a herpes virus, sometimes referred to as *Herpesvirus cyprini*. The individual virus is approximately 110-150 millionths of a millimetre in diameter. Little is known about this virus, but the incubation

period appears to be about 6 months and occurrence of a pox outbreak seems to be linked with other factors, such as genetic weakness, poor nutrition and poor water quality (and in the case of coldwater fish, with changes in water temperature).

PREVENTION AND TREATMENT
There is no known treatment for fish pox. The immune response of affected fish often eventually eliminates the disease, although not necessarily on a permanent basis (the virus may remain dormant within its host). Good husbandry may considerably improve the likelihood of a self-cure. A vaccine has been produced but its efficacy has been questioned. In severe cases, if the fish is incapacitated, EUTHANASIA (3) may be necessary. The disease is infectious, but only slightly so. Obviously affected specimens should nevertheless not be purchased.

FISH TANK GRANULOMA (FISHKEEPER'S GRANULOMA)

A relatively uncommon bacterial disease of humans which can be contracted from aquarium fish. The disease in fish, which is sometimes known as FISH TUBERCULOSIS (= fish TB) (3), is caused by various species of MYCO-BACTERIA (3), including *Mycobacterium marinum*. The disease may be transmitted to humans as a result of handling infected fish or by immersing the hands in an infected aquarium. The mycobacteria can invade broken skin.

The condition in humans is normally confined to the fingers and hand. The human form is not life-threatening and is treatable with a course of antibiotics, though it may be more serious in individuals who are severely immunosuppressed. This disease must not be confused with

Mycobacterial infection of the hand following contact with infected fish or their aquarium water.

human tuberculosis (caused by another mycobacterium, *M. tuberculosis*) which is not contracted from fish. Fish tank granuloma is one of a very few zoonotic diseases *(see ZOONOSIS [3])* which can be passed from aquarium fish to humans.

The risks of contracting this disease are remote and can be further reduced by taking simple precautions, notably do not immerse hands in the aquarium if the skin is broken – wear rubber gloves.

Always seek medical advice if you suspect you have a mycobacterial infection, and mention that you keep fish. The disease is so rare that many doctors are unaware of its existence; any fishkeeper who develops a mystery (to the doctor) skin infection, or one that refuses to clear up, particularly on the hands, should inform the doctor of the possibility of the disease and, if necessary, request a specialist opinion (e.g. referral to a dermatologist).

FISH TUBERCULOSIS, FISH TB

A systemic bacterial disease caused by various species of MYCOBACTERIA (3). Mycobacterial diseases are fairly commonly encountered among tropical aquarium fish.

SIGNS

The infection may progress slowly. Emerging clinical signs may include one or more of the following: LETHARGY (2), loss of APPETITE (2), EMACIATION (2) (hollow belly), EXOPHTHALMIA (2) (pop-eye), and pale COLORATION (2). These symptoms may be accompanied by persistent skin ULCERS (2) which can vary in severity, and sometimes by the onset of skeletal DEFORMITIES (2).

Autopsy may reveal large numbers of white or pale

Mycobacterial lesions on a gourami. Photo: D. Bucke.

coloured nodules (each around 2-3 mm in diameter) within the internal organs. Similar internal nodules may also be found in *ICHTHYOPHONUS* (3) infections (although the latter is very rare in freshwater fish) (see FUNGAL DISEASES (3)). Confirmation of mycobacteriosis requires special staining of the bacteria (known commonly as the acid-fast stain).

CAUSES
Mycobacterium marinum and *M. fortuitum* are known to cause fish TB. Poor aquarium hygiene may predispose fish to these infections.

PREVENTION AND TREATMENT
The careful selection of new stock, and the maintenance of good aquarium hygiene, will go a long way towards preventing outbreaks of mycobacteria. It is advisable to isolate any fish showing signs of mycobacteriosis. The mycobacteria may be transmitted through CANNIBALISM (3) of infected fish tissues and possibly also by COPROPHAGY (3). Open ulcers provide another route by which the mycobacteria can enter the water from the bodies of live fish. There is also evidence for VERTICAL TRANSMISSION (3) in the case of some fish groups (e.g. poeciliids)

Mycobacterial infections are difficult to treat, although ANTIBIOTICS (3) may sometimes be effective. EUTH-ANASIA (3) should be considered in the case of badly infected fish.

Note: there is a small risk of humans contracting myco-bacterial infections from diseased fish or their water – see FISH TANK GRANULOMA (3).

FLAGELLATES
A group of PROTOZOANS (3) which includes both free-living and parasitic species. Fish-parasitic flagellates include *HEXAMITA* (3) and the blood-dwelling TRYPANOSOMES (3); however, the latter are of little aquarium importance.

FLATWORMS
Worm-like creatures belonging to the phylum Platy-

helminthes. As both common and scientific names suggest, these creatures have characteristically flattened bodies, with some species being extremely elongate and segmented. Includes several groups of aquarium importance: Tapeworms (CESTODES), FLUKES (3) (DIGENEANS [3] and MONOGENEANS [3]), and the free-living PLAN-ARIANS (3).

FLEXIBACTER
A genus of BACTERIA (3) which can cause tissue necrosis of the skin, fins, gills, and mouth of fish. *Flexibacter* is associated with clinical diseases such as COLUMNARIS (3), also known as Cotton Wool Disease or Mouth Fungus. The most common freshwater species is *Flexibacter columnaris,* which has a broad host range but is considered to be more pathogenic under warm water conditions. Possible predisposing factors include poor water conditions, for example. a high level of organic pollution (high NITRATE [3]) and STRESS (3).

FLUBENDAZOLE   **P**
This ANTHELMINTHIC (3) is a chemical analogue of MEBENDAZOLE (3).

FLUKES
A generic term for a number of HELMINTH PARASITES (3) of fish, in particular *DACTYLOGYRUS* (3) (gill flukes), *GYRODACTYLUS* (3) (skin flukes), and *DIPLOSTOMUM* (3) (eye flukes). Flukes may be MONOGENETIC (3), i.e. the parasite requires only a single host during its entire life cycle, or DIGENETIC (3), where two or more different host species are required.

FORMALDEHYDE
A pungent gas, also known as methanal, which dissolves readily in water to produce FORMALIN (3). Treatments which, in fact, utilise formalin occasionally erroneously refer to formaldehyde.

FORMALIN
A 37-40% aqueous solution ("commercial strength formalin") of FORMALDEHYDE (3) (methanal) gas, with

antiseptic, germicidal, and preservative properties.

Formalin was formerly commonly used as a treatment for ectoparasites, in particular FLUKES (3) and SKIN SLIME DISEASE (3), against which it has proven effective. Unfortunately it is also highly toxic to fish, such that the safety margin is very low, sometimes resulting in fish deaths due to the formalin itself rather than the disease against which it is directed. Although still widely used in foodfish aquaculture and sometimes for certain pond fish, formalin is now rarely used for aquarium fish.

Nowadays it is more commonly used as a preservative for specimens to be retained for identification or post-mortem (the latter ideally performed on fresh material, however). The fish to be preserved should be humanely despatched (EUTHANASIA [3]) if not already dead, and placed in a 10% solution of formalin in a tightly-lidded container.

ADMINISTRATION
Long-term (several days) or short-term (10-30 minutes) bath. Formalin may affect biological filtration and is best administered, if at all, in an isolation aquarium. This has the added advantage that if the fish show(s) any signs of distress they/it can be returned to the normal, untreated, environment.

DOSAGE
Different authorities have traditionally quoted rather variable dosages, perhaps because different fish species, and, indeed, different individuals, may vary in their tolerance to formalin. The effects – beneficial or adverse – of the dosages given below cannot therefore be guaranteed. Short-term high-strength baths, in particular, should be administered only with considerable care. The fish should be observed during treatment – continuous observation is vital during short-term baths – and the treatment suspended if any distress, particularly severe RESPIRATORY DISTRESS (2) or a JUMPING (2) escape response, occurs.
● Long-term bath (for small ECTOPARASITES (3), e.g. those causing SKIN SLIME DISEASE (3)): 0.15-0.25 ml of commercial strength (37-40%) formalin per 10 litres (approximately 1-2 drops per gallon), mixed with some aquarium water and added to the treatment tank. After 2-3

days return the fish to the normal environment, or perform a 30% water change if treating the main aquarium.

● Short-term bath (for larger ECTOPARASITES, e.g. FLUKES): 2 ml of commercial strength formalin per 10 litres (approximately 17 drops/gallon). The bath should be prepared in advance of the fish being added, to ensure the chemical is properly dispersed. Treatment should last no longer than 30 minutes – less if the fish becomes distressed. Provide aeration during bath treatment.

WARNING Formalin is extremely dangerous if splashed on skin or in eyes, and must be rinsed off immediately with plenty of water, and medical attention sought. It also produces toxic fumes – stock bottles should not be opened in a confined area. It should not be exposed to light, but kept in a dark bottle, as otherwise paraformaldehyde may form as a whitish deposit. Paraformaldehyde is highly toxic to fish, even in extremely low concentrations. It is also potentially explosive and must therefore be disposed of carefully; seek expert help if necessary.

FUNGICIDE

A number of proprietary aquarium fungicides are available from aquarium retailers, normally involving treatment by long-term bath. Some of these are also suitable for the prevention of EGG FUNGUS (3), and those containing PHENOXYETHANOL (3) (Phenoxethol) are also effective against external BACTERIAL INFECTIONS (3). In addition METHYLENE BLUE (3) is commonly used as an aquarium fungicide, and SALT (3) is sometimes effective (but should be used only for those fish species which are salt-tolerant).

Topical application of GENTIAN VIOLET (3) has the advantage of treating only the affected localised area in cases where just one fish has a slight infection.

There is a regrettable tendency for some aquarists to regard treatment of the aquarium with fungicide as a routine curative – or even a prophylactic! – instead of dealing with the underlying cause(s). Prolonged or continuous exposure to some fungicides may have harmful effects, and unnecessary or avoidable use of them is inadvisable.

See also AGGRESSION (3), INJURY (3); Section I: The Correct Environment.

FUNGUS and FUNGAL INFECTIONS

The fungal diseases of aquarium fish are most commonly attributed to fungi of the genera *SAPROLEGNIA* (3) and *ACHYLA*. (3). (In fact, many fungal infections attributed to *Saprolegnia* are actually caused by other types of fungi, and sometimes several fungal species may simultaneously colonise a lesion.)

Most fish-pathogenic fungi generally invade only those tissues which have already been damaged through INJURY(3) or DISEASE (3). Fungi may also attack fish eggs (see EGG FUNGUS (3)). In addition to injuries, poor aquarium hygiene, adverse water chemistry, chills, and other stressors are predisposing factors in fungus outbreaks. Fish which are very old (see SENILITY[3]) are more prone to fungus attack. Fortunately, several effective treatments, known collectively as aquarium FUNGICIDES (3), are available for treating fungus infections in fish.

Only rarely do fungal infections invade deep within the tissues. One infrequently encountered systemic 'fungus' is *ICHTHYOPHONUS* (3) (which is extremely rare in freshwater fish), whose status as a true fungus has been questioned. *Ichthyophonus* invades the major organs and causes tissue nodules which are similar to those found in FISH TUBERCULOSIS (3). Confirmation is based on the microscopical examination of diseased tissue for the presence of fungal spores.

There are no commercial treatments for systemic fungal infections of fish, although bath immersion using MALACHITE GREEN (3) has been suggested as a possible treatment.

The disease known as COLUMNARIS (3) (or mouth fungus) can easily be confused with some external fungi, but is, in fact, bacterial in origin.

FURANACE   **P**

Also known as Nifurpirinol. This antimicrobial chemical is used primarily for treating internal BACTERIAL INFECTIONS (3) (e.g. systemic bacteria).

DOSAGE AND ADMINISTRATION
Generally applied as a bath, or orally, via medicated food.
● Short bath: 1-10 mg/litre for 5-10 minutes.
● Long term bath: 0.01-0.1 mg/litre, for several days.
● Orally: 2-4 mg per kg of fish, daily for 5 days. Medicated
food should be fed exclusively during the treatment period.

G

GAS BUBBLE DISEASE
This environmental problem, caused by gas saturation of the
aquarium water, is analogous to the 'bends' in human
divers. Fish which are exposed to supersaturated water will
breath in excess concentrations of gas which may
subsequently come out of solution in the blood, forming
dangerous emboli in the tissues (a gas embolism is the
obstruction of the blood vessels by gas bubbles). Although
a major problem on some ornamental fish farms, such as
those which extract water from boreholes, it is rarely a
problem in aquaria. Nitrogen is the gas most commonly
linked to this disease.

SIGNS
In acute cases, the affected fish may have BUBBLES (2)
around their head region, each bubble being up to several
millimetres in diameter. The fish may exhibit LETHARGY
(2) without showing any other disease symptoms.
Microscopical examination of the gills may reveal small
bubbles within the gill lamellae. The aquarium itself may

The finger test: Appearance of numerous bubbles on the immersed fingers is an indication of gas supersaturation of the water. Note bubble formation on the aquarium glass – another indication.

also have gas bubbles on the glass and on other submerged surfaces.

Measuring the nitrogen gas concentration requires highly specialised and expensive equipment – unavailable to the aquarist. On the other hand, the 'finger test' provides a rough indication of possible gas supersaturation of the water: immerse a dry finger in the aquarium water and hold it there for about a minute. If numerous bubbles form over the finger surface, then the water may be supersaturated.

CAUSES
Gas bubble disease is caused by gas supersaturation of the water, mainly nitrogen gas which is toxic to fish above 104% saturation or thereabouts. This condition may arise when cool and gas-rich water is quickly warmed. As the water temperature rises, its gas-carrying capacity is reduced, causing gas (and hence nitrogen) supersaturation. The leakage of high pressure pump tubing or connectors, causing a venturi effect, is another potential cause of gas supersaturation on fish farms, but is extremely unlikely to occur under aquarium conditions. Gas supersaturation may also occur where newly set up aquaria have been filled with cold tap water and quickly warmed to operating temperature (but, of course, no fish should be present at this stage!), or where aquaria have been refilled with freshly drawn cold (or quickly heated) tap water during a large partial change (again very bad practice).

PREVENTION AND TREATMENT
Gas supersaturation can be avoided by ensuring that fish are not exposed to cold water which has been recently and rapidly warmed. Instead, the water should be left for some time, and ideally aerated, in order to allow the gases to equilibrate.

If gas supersaturation of a stocked aquarium is suspected, immediately agitate or aerate the water in order to drive off the excess gas.

Although large water changes, using freshly drawn water, are sometimes necessary as emergency measures, e.g. in cases of POISONING (3), the water should be vigorously aerated before use to drive off the excess nitrogen.

GENTIAN VIOLET
P

A combination of three dyes – methyl rosaniline, methyl violet, and crystal violet – with antiseptic, bactericidal, and fungicidal properties.

DOSAGE AND ADMINISTRATION
A 1% solution can be used for topical treatment of FIN ROT (3) and FUNGUS (3). The dye should not be allowed to contact the fish's eyes and/or gills.

This compound will stain human skin and clothing bright purple!

GILL FLUKES
See DACTYLOGYRUS (3).

GILL MAGGOTS
See ERGASILUS (3).

GILL ROT
See BRANCHIOMYCOSIS (3).

GILL WORMS
See DACTYLOGYRUS (3).

GOLD SPOT or GOLD DUST DISEASE
See PISCINOODINIUM (3).

GREEN WATER
See SECTION II: CLOUDY WATER; ALGAE (3).

GUPPY DISEASE
Common name given to the disease caused by infestation with *TETRAHYMENA (3) corlissi*, a ciliated PARASITE (3).

GYRODACTYLUS
Gyrodactylus is a genus of MONOGENETIC FLUKES (3), commonly known as skin flukes, of which numerous species have been recorded from fish. Virtually all groups of freshwater fish are known to be susceptible to these PARASITES (3); however, individual fluke species each tend to have a limited host range, though this may be less

restrictive under aquarium conditions. *Gyrodactylus* species are mostly associated with the skin but may also be found on the gills and fins.

These ECTOPARASITES (3) typically reach 0.4 mm in length (a few exceed 1 mm). In general, they are slightly elongate (basically sausage-shaped) and are characterised by their suckers and hooks with which they attach to the skin and gills of fish, where they feed on epithelial mucus and cells.

Gyrodactylus are obligate parasites, which generally do not survive off the host fish. They are all hermaphrodites and give birth to live young. The flukes are able to migrate over the body surface of the fish and are transmitted from fish to fish by direct contact. In the case of *G. turnbulli* (which affects guppies), and possibly other species, those parasites which accidentally get dislodged into the water have a limited chance of successfully reattaching to a fish. Infestation of the gills may well occur as a result of dislocated flukes being taken in with respiratory water passing across the gills.

SIGNS

Mild infections may not give rise to obvious disease symptoms, except FLASHING (2) and SCRATCHING (2) behaviour by the fish in an attempt to relieve the irritation caused by the feeding flukes.

Under optimal (for the flukes) conditions, the flukes are capable of reproducing at a fast rate, resulting in heavy infections and hence more serious clinical symptoms, within a short time period (e.g. days rather than weeks). The fish's skin may become cloudy, with MUCUS HYPERPRODUCTION (2), in response to the tissue damage and irritation cause by the flukes. In severe cases reddened areas, abscesses, and FIN EROSION (2) may occur. The infected fish may also exhibit general LETHARGY (2) and have CLAMPED FINS (2). Parasites on the gills may cause thickening of the gill filaments, leading to RESPIRATORY DISTRESS (2) and its associated behaviour, including GASPING (2) at the surface. Heavy infections, especially on small fish, can be fatal. Skin damage caused by the flukes can lead to SECONDARY INFECTION (3).

Confirmation of diagnosis can be made by taking a skin scrape and examining the material using a low-power microscope (40-120 x magnification) for the presence of flukes.

CAUSE
One (or more) of several species of *Gyrodactylus*. From the aquarist's point of view, the exact species involved is irrelevant.

PREVENTION AND TREATMENT
Poor aquarium hygiene, e.g. heavy organic pollution, is a predisposing factor in outbreaks of skin flukes. STRESS (3) may also render the fish more susceptible, by reducing their immune capability (there is some evidence for acquired immunity to these flukes). Given the mode of transmission, directly from fish to fish, serious outbreaks of *Gyrodactylus* are more likely under conditions of overcrowding.

Treatment is normally via bath immersion (i.e. treatment of the whole aquarium community) using a proprietary skin and gill fluke medication.

Gyrodactylus, being livebearers, are generally more easy to eradicate than *DACTYLOGYRUS (3)* (gill flukes) since the latter produce eggs which are resistant to chemical action. Nevertheless, it may sometimes be necessary to resort to other treatments in difficult cases of skin fluke. A short-term bath in FORMALIN (3) may prove effective, as can baths in SALT (3) or ANTHELMINTHICS (3) (such as MEBENDAZOLE (3)). In the case of *G. turnbulli*, raising the water temperature to 30 degrees C (86 degrees F) for 12-24 hours may kill the flukes. The host guppies should survive this heat treatment, provided they are not already experiencing obvious RESPIRATORY DISTRESS (2) and the temperature is increased slowly.

H

HELMINTH DISEASES

Diseases caused by parasitic 'worms' belonging to the Phylum Platyhelminthes. These comprise diseases caused by FLUKES (3) (MONOGENETIC (3) and DIGENETIC (3) species), and tapeworms (CESTODES (3)). Some helminth diseases are highly pathogenic, such as those caused by Monogenetic Flukes, whereas others tend to be fairly benign. Many helminth parasites have complicated life-cycles which may include one or more non-fish hosts.

Chemical treatments which specifically destroy helminths are known as ANTHELMINTHICS (3).

HEAD AND LATERAL LINE EROSION
See HEXAMITIASIS (3).

HETEROSPORIS

A genus of MICROSPORIDIAN PROTOZOA (3), generally similar in biology to the closely-related *PLEISTOPHORA* (3).

SIGNS
These include EMACIATION (2) and the presence of greyish patches or SPOTS (2) on the skin.

CAUSE
The major species of aquarium interest is *H. finki* which infects the muscles of angelfish (*Pterophyllum* spp.). The disease has caused high mortalities, particularly in young fish; adult angelfish appear more resistant. Infection may occur through CANNIBALISM (3) of dead infected angelfish.

PREVENTION AND TREATMENT
No treatment is available. Fish suspected of this disease should be isolated to prevent transmission to other fish. Badly affected fish should be considered for EUTHANASIA (3).

Hexamitiasis: Eroded sensory pores on the head of Microgeophagus altispinous.

The small orange hole in the snout of this cichlid is not hexamitiasis but the nostril. (Note the slight eye cloudiness in this specimen, almost certainly environmental.)

HEXAMITA, HEXAMITIASIS

A parasitic disease primarily of cichlid fish (family Cichlidae), although similar conditions have been reported in other families. Some authorities consider that most, if not all, aquarium cichlids are infected. The PARASITES (3) are readily transmitted from cichlid to cichlid.

SIGNS
White stringy FAECES (2), sometimes, but by no means always, accompanied by enlargement of the sensory pores of the head (and/or occasionally the lateral line), which usually also become filled with whitish pus. Dark COLORATION (2) and loss of APPETITE (2) are common in advanced cases. Both EMACIATION (2) and DISTENDED BODY (2) have been reported in association with the parasite.

CAUSE
Flagellates of the genus *Hexamita* (sometimes cited as being synonymous with *Octomitus* or *Spironucleus*). These weakly pathogenic parasites are commonly found in small numbers in the intestines of cichlids, where they do no apparent harm under normal circumstances. If, however, the fish is weakened (e.g. by other disease, environmental problems, or other STRESS (3) – or even SENILITY [3])

the parasites multiply and migrate through the fish's system. If (and only if) they reach the sensory pores do the characteristic pus-filled holes develop. Death occurs if a vital organ is invaded and fatally damaged. Many mystery deaths of cichlids may be due to *Hexamita* infestations where the sensory pores have remained unaffected.

Even if hexamitiasis does not itself prove fatal, its debilitating effect can render the fish susceptible to life-threatening infection by *AEROMONAS* (3) and some other BACTERIA (3) as well as other parasites such as *ICHTHYOBODO* (3).

PREVENTION AND TREATMENT
METRONIDAZOLE (3) and di-metronidazole may be effective, but parasite resistance to these drugs has been reported. There is no evidence that non-prescription proprietary aquarium remedies are of significant, if any, efficacy.

It is normal to treat only individuals showing signs of the disease. Although prophylaxis is possible, this is not recommended in view of the danger of resistance of the parasite to the only effective drugs known. Prevention of serious infestation by avoidance of stress is preferable. Re-infestation is virtually inevitable if untreated cichlids are subsequently introduced to a previously medicated aquarium.

HOLE-IN-HEAD DISEASE
See HEXAMITIASIS.

HOSPITAL TANK
An aquarium (usually small) used for the treatment of sick fish, in particular where isolation is required to avoid STRESS (3), infection of other fish, or environmental damage from medication, or because only one or two fish require treatment. *See also SECTION I: Treatment of Fish Diseases.*

HYBRIDIZATION
The breeding together of organisms of different species. Hybridization is not uncommon among fish, and has been used by professional breeders to produce new 'fancy'

strains (e.g. poeciliids). From the viewpoint of the amateur aquarist, however, it is undesirable. Hybrid offspring are often infertile, and no reputable dealer will buy or sell them. They may also add to the confusion surrounding the identification of many species, and the release of hybrids into the hobby carries a risk of contaminating pure stocks through subsequent (unintentional) hybrid x pure matings.

CAUSES
1) Absence of a suitable conspecific partner coupled with the presence of a heterospecific of the opposite sex, normally of a similar, usually congeneric species (common in some groups of cichlids). Repeated cross-matings may result in subsequent failure to recognise a conspecific as a suitable mate.
2) Lack of discrimination regarding partner choice in similar, usually closely related, species (e.g. poeciliids, Lake Victoria cichlids).
3) Inability of the breeding male to drive away interested males of other, closely related, species (common in Lake Malawi cichlids, where lack of natural selection in tank-bred stock has led to loss of territorial vigour).

PREVENTION
Where any of the above is known to be a problem, then, respectively:
1) Avoid keeping unmated females with males of similar species.
2) Avoid mixing species prone to indiscriminate cross-mating.
3) The inadequate male should under no circumstances be allowed to pass on his defective genes, but should be replaced with a more vigorous individual.
    Any hybrids that do nonetheless occur should be CULLED (3) immediately.

HYDRA

These small freshwater relatives of the sea anemones (phylum Coelenterata) occasionally establish in aquaria. They are completely harmless to most adult fish but may capture very small fish and fry.
    Hydra range in size from being just visible to the naked

eye up to about 2 cm in length. They may be found attached to the glass and other internal surfaces of the aquarium and may on occasion reach pest proportions. *Hydra* can be recognised by their general body shape, comprising a stalk, which is used for attachment, and tentacles which are used for capturing prey. These creatures have elastic bodies and are able to contract, giving the appearance of tiny, jelly-like blobs. They may range in colour from cream to grey or light brown.

Large numbers of *Hydra* within the aquarium can appear unsightly. However, it is generally only in rearing and breeding aquaria that *Hydra* are capable of causing damage, by capturing and ingesting fry with the aid of their tentacles. The *Hydra's* tentacles are equipped with stinging cells which quickly overpower the prey.

Complete eradication of *Hydra* may prove difficult without stripping down and scrubbing the aquarium surfaces and washing the gravel, decor, and submerged equipment in hot SALT (3) solution (above 105 degrees F; 2-5% salt).

Controlling *Hydra* in stocked aquaria may be achieved by adding salt to give a 0.5% solution, and maintaining this saline condition for about one week. Ensure that all the species of fish are able to tolerate a prolonged saline bath; most adult fish can, but most fry may not tolerate this change in water chemistry. Undertake several partial water changes after the treatment, to eliminate the salt from the aquarium.

Alternatively, keep their numbers in check by routinely wiping down areas of the aquarium glass where *Hydra* congregate, after which the detached individuals are promptly siphoned out of the tank. Decor items to which *Hydra* are attached may be routinely removed and scrubbed under a tap.

Certain types of fish, notably gouramis, are known to feed on *Hydra*, thereby helping to control the *Hydra* population.

HYDROGEN PEROXIDE (H$_2$O$_2$) **P**

A clear liquid (viscous in concentrated form) which has strong oxidising properties. Hydrogen peroxide decomposes into two harmless products: water and oxygen, and hence it is often used medically as a disinfectant since it leaves no harmful traces. It is sometimes used as an aquarium ANTISEPTIC (3).

Hydrogen peroxide may also sometimes be used as an oxygen donor, to quickly rectify hypoxic conditions within the aquarium (see OXYGEN (3)).

The strength of the aqueous solution is given either as the percentage H_2O_2 in water, or as the number of volumes of oxygen which 100 ml of the solution will produce on decomposition. Pharmacy strength solutions are 6% (= 20 volumes) UK or 3% (= 10 volumes) USA.

DOSAGE AND ADMINISTRATION

● As an anti-protozoal:
Short-term bath: 10 ml of 3% solution to 1 litre of water (40 ml per gallon). Immerse fish for 5-10 minutes maximum, or for less time if the fish appear overly stressed. Tolerance to this treatment varies from species to species.

● To remedy hypoxic conditions:
1-2 ml of 3% solution per 10 litres of aquarium water (5-10 ml per 10 gallons). It is *essential* not to overdose, otherwise the fish will be further stressed and possibly seriously harmed. It is also important partly to dilute the hydrogen peroxide stock solution beforehand, i.e. mix the required amount of 3% stock solution with about ten times its volume of water (taken from the aquarium), then add to the tank and ensure a fast dispersion (e.g. pour in front of the outflow of a power filter). Maintain aeration.

Note: this is a short-term remedy for absolute emergencies only; it is necessary to identify and rectify the cause of hypoxia in order to prevent a recurrence, and in the majority of cases remedying the cause(s) of the problem will render chemical treatment with H_2O_2 quite unnecessary.

HYPOXIA
A condition where insufficient OXYGEN (3) reaches the fish's tissues, causing RESPIRATORY STRESS (3), and often death.
See also OXYGEN STARVATION (3).

I

ICH
Commonly used abbreviation of *ICHTHYOPHTHIRIUS (3).*

ICHTHYOBODO
A flagellate PROTOZOAN PARASITE (3) of fish, one of the causative agents of SKIN SLIME DISEASE (3), formerly known as *Costia necatrix*, but now reclassified as *I. necator.* Another species, *I. pyriformis*, was once thought to exist but is now considered to be a variant of *I. necator*. *Ichthyobodo* is visible under medium power (100 x magnification) light microscopy as a reniform (kidney-bean-shaped) protozoan with two hair-like flagella.

This protozoan has a parasitic stage on the fish and a free-living stage in the water. The free-living stage (which reaches almost 20 microns in length) has two flagella of uneven length which are used for swimming. The free-living stage locates a fish host and attaches to the secondary gill lamellae and/or the dorsal fin. Both stages are able to reproduce by division.

Ichthyobodo feeds on the skin of fish, but causes significant damage only when present in large numbers. It is commonly present in small numbers in aquaria and can infect a wide range of fish. There is evidence for differences between fish species in susceptibility, although immune status may also be influential in terms of infection levels. Thus, STRESS (3) may predispose fish to outbreaks.

Ichthyobodo prefers a temperature of less than 25 degrees C (77 degrees F) and dies at temperatures about 30 C (86 F), but has the ability to encyst when conditions (including temperature) are unfavourable. The cysts, which may remain viable in the water for extended periods of time, are a possible source of reinfection. *For Signs and Treatment see SKIN SLIME DISEASE (3).*

ICHTHYOPHONUS
A systemic FUNGAL INFECTION, chiefly of marine fish, but seen very occasionally in freshwater fish fed on marine trash fish, e.g. in aquaculture.

ICHTHYOPHTHIRIASIS, *ICHTHYOPHTHIRIUS*

Also known commonly as ich or whitespot disease. An extremely common parasitic disease of aquarium fish which is highly infectious and potentially lethal, and manifests as tiny white spots over the fish's body and fins. The disease appears capable of infecting all species of freshwater fish. The wide host range of this PARASITE (3), its direct life-cycle, and speed of multiplication under tropical aquarium conditions, are contributing factors to its significance as a major disease problem in aquarium fish.

LIFE CYCLE OF ICHTHYOPHTHIRIUS

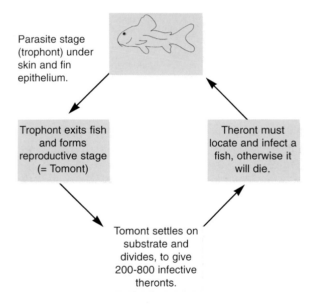

Parasite stage (trophont) under skin and fin epithelium.

Trophont exits fish and forms reproductive stage (= Tomont)

Theront must locate and infect a fish, otherwise it will die.

Tomont settles on substrate and divides, to give 200-800 infective theronts.

SIGNS

The parasite has a multi-stage life-cycle, involving infective and free-living forms (see diagram). Clinical symptoms are caused by the infective trophont stage which resides within the epidermis of the skin, gills and buccal cavity of its host. Although commonly referred to as an ECTOPARASITE (2), the trophont resides within the skin, adjacent to the basal lamina, but does not invade the underlying tissues or internal organs.

The characteristic white spots are particularly obvious on the fins of these catfish.

Cichlid with whitespot. Numerous spots are present on the posterior body of this specimen, including the dorsal and caudal fins.

Infected fish develop characteristic raised white 'SPOTS' (2) on the fins and body, and within the gills and mouth. Each 'spot' is an individual parasite which is enveloped by semi-transparent host tissue. The spots are invisible to the unaided eye at first, but increase in size as the parasite feeds and grows, eventually reaching between 0.3 to 1 mm in diameter, but rarely larger. Occasionally, in heavy infections, several parasites may cluster within a single site. The white spots are more obvious on dark-bodied fish, and may also be readily seen on the clear fins, especially when these are viewed against a dark background.

Fish which sustain light infections exhibit few symptoms other than the occasional SCRATCHING (2) of their flanks on solid objects in the aquarium, in response to the skin irritation.

Heavy infections can be lethal as a result of severe respiratory or osmotic disturbances, or through secondary invasion by bacterial pathogens. Small fish and fish fry may die within a few days of an initial heavy infection. Heavily infected fish exhibit a variety of abnormal BEHAVIOUR (2) and physiological changes. They may appear restless and swim in sudden DARTING (2) movements and have fin tremors, presumably due to irritation. In severe infections the fish exhibit LETHARGY (2) and HANGING (2) near the surface. The skin may turn pale and begin to slough away in patches, and the fins become torn and ragged. The gills also become pale. Damage to the skin and gills causes dysfunction of these organs, resulting in both OSMOTIC STRESS (3) and RESPIRATORY DISTRESS (2). Difficulties in breathing are manifested by an increased rate in opercular movements and by the fish HANGING (2) near the water surface where oxygen levels are higher. By this stage, treatment is unlikely to be effective and the fish will probably die.

CAUSE

There appears to be only one species of whitespot parasite, *Ichthyophthirius multifiliis;* however, several strains have been identified. The parasite has a wide temperature tolerance range and can be passed from coldwater fish to tropical species, and vice versa. Whitespot may be introduced into the aquarium via infected fish, or via water which harbours the free-living stages. Aquatic plants and aquatic live food organisms (e.g. *Daphnia, Tubifex* worms) are further potential sources of infection if these have recently been collected from whitespot-infected waters. Contrary to popular belief, drinking-quality tap water is not a source of whitespot infection (largely because the infective theronts can survive for only a few hours before locating a fish host, and thus would die during the water treatment process; chlorination may also harm this stage).

PREVENTION AND TREATMENT

Outbreaks of whitespot in the main aquarium can normally be avoided simply by QUARANTINING (3) new acquisitions, which are the most common vectors of the disease. Regrettably, many aquarists neglect this simple precaution.

Fortunately, whitespot disease is generally easy to cure provided treatment is administered at an early stage. Several effective anti-whitespot remedies are commercially available, and many of these are based on dye compounds (e.g. METHYLENE BLUE (3), MALACHITE GREEN [3]) and/or FORMALIN (3). However, these remedies will not destroy the infective stage present within the fish's skin. For this reason, one or more repeat treatments are normally required in order to completely eradicate whitespot from the aquarium. The development of acquired immunity in recently infected fish will also help reduce parasite numbers in the aquarium following an outbreak.

Certain types of fish, including scaleless species, are highly intolerant of some commercial whitespot remedies: the manufacturer's instructions should provide details of any fish species which must be moved prior to administering the treatment.

A long-term SALT (3) bath (2g per litre for 7 days) should eradicate *Ichthyophthirius*; however, this treatment must be administered only to fish which are tolerant of salt conditions.

The aquarium itself can be cleared of whitespot simply by removing all of the fish. In the absence of any fish, the free-living stages of the parasite will die through lack of hosts. Under tropical conditions (above 21 degrees C; 70 degrees F) the aquarium will generally be whitespot-free after 4 days, though it is best left for 7 days to be on the safe side. Similarly, aquatic plants, decor, substrate, internal filters, etc. which have been kept under fish-free tropical conditions for 7 days can be safely moved to another aquarium without the risk of transmitting whitespot.

ULTRA-VIOLET IRRADIATION (3) will help reduce the population of whitespot parasites during an outbreak, but should not be totally relied upon to eradicate the disease.

Those fish which survive an outbreak of whitespot will develop partial immunity to any subsequent exposure to this parasite. Immune protection may last for weeks or months, but can be diminished as a result of STRESS (3) or disease. The fact that some fish suffer from heavy infections following an outbreak of whitespot while others appear uninfected is largely explained by differences between individual fish in their levels of acquired immune protection to this parasite. There are probably also species differences in susceptibility to this disease. For example, the clown loach (*Botia macracantha*) is widely reported to be highly susceptible to whitespot.

The adverse effects of stress on the fish's immune system

may explain why an outbreak of whitespot often follows a deterioration in water quality or other stress-inducing conditions.

INBREEDING

The non-selective mating, often for successive generations, of closely-related individuals. Repeated in-breeding can lead to genetic disorders such as DEFORMITY (3), congenital BLINDNESS (3), melanoma (see TUMOURS (3)), REPRODUCTIVE FAILURE (3) (infertility), and BELLYSLIDING (3) fry, as well as general degradation of stock vigour.

INJURY

Injuries may occur both externally and internally, and range from trivial to life-threatening.

SIGNS
External injuries are normally obvious. Abnormal BEHAVIOUR (2) following a known possible cause of injury (see below) may indicate internal injury, e.g. loss of BUOYANCY (2) control following AGGRESSION (3) by another fish is indicative of injury to the swimbladder. However, diagnosis of the nature of most internal injuries is impossible.

CAUSES
AGGRESSION (3) by other fish is the commonest cause of injury, as the result of direct contact and for collision with hard objects during flight. Collision damage may also occur as a result of panic flight, e.g. following some sudden and unusual movement near the aquarium. Coarse substrates may cause abrasions to mouths and/or gills in species that dig and/or sift the substrate; likewise, bottom-dwellers may suffer abrasions to their undersides and/or barbels. More bizarre injuries include heater BURNS (3), crushing (by collapsing decor), and mixed injuries caused by getting trapped in equipment or decor, e.g. filter inlets, crevices in rockwork, holes in bogwood. Jumping out of the tank can cause serious external and internal injury. Clumsy netting and poor packing *(see SECTION I: Purchasing, Transporting, and Introducing Stock)* can also result in injury.

Bruising and missing scales as a result of aggression.

PREVENTION AND TREATMENT

Many injuries can be prevented by sensible choice of tankmates, decor, equipment, etc. If injury does, nevertheless, occur, the cause should, if possible, be rectified to avoid recurrence. However, it is practically impossible to avoid injuries entirely, as there is always a danger of aggression between individuals where two or more fish are kept together, and it would be impossible to breed many species without a degree of chasing and consequent minor damage. The aquarist must use his discretion to decide what degree of injury is acceptable given the species and circumstances.

Most minor injuries will clear up untreated, and provided the injured fish is behaving and feeding normally, it is best left alone rather than risking additional STRESS (3) from treatment.

Injuries which discommode the fish, or, while apparently superficial, are extensive, normally require hospitalisation *(See SECTION I: Treating Fish Diseases)*, largely in order to provide a STRESS- (3) free environment in the first instance, and to avoid the unnecessary medication of healthy fish.

A 0.1-0.2% SALT solution may help prevent SECONDARY INFECTION (3) (by BACTERIA (3) or FUNGUS [3]) of external injuries (salt-tolerant fish species only), such infections generally being more dangerous than the actual injuries. A mild salt bath will also help reduce OSMOTIC STRESS (3) in those fish which have extensive surface WOUNDS (3) and help avert FIN ROT (3) where fin damage has occurred. Raising the TEMPERATURE (3) slightly will increase the metabolic rate and thus possibly accelerate the healing process, provided the increase is within the fish's tolerance range. Aeration may need to be increased in order to ensure adequate OXYGEN (3) at higher than normal temperatures. Severe injuries commonly require EUTHANASIA (3), either immediately if there is obviously no hope of survival, or when it becomes apparent that recovery is unlikely.

INSECTICIDES　　　　　　　　P

Certain ORGANOPHOSPHORUS (3) insecticide compounds, notably TRICHLORFON (3), have been used to eradicate a number of fish ECTOPARASITES (3) e.g. infestations of gill and skin FLUKES (3), *ARGULUS* (3) (fish louse), and *LERNAEA* (3) (anchor worm). Owing to their potential neuro-toxicity to man, his pets, and the environment, the use of organophosphorus compounds for treating fish parasites is now restricted in many countries. Depending on local government restrictions, several commercial formulations of organophosphates may be available under various brand names, e.g. from horticultural and/or agricultural outlets. These formulations vary considerably between brands in the strength of the active ingredient and hence the manufacturer's instructions for dilution must be followed. Ideally, aquarium usage of these chemicals should be undertaken only under veterinary supervision.

IODINE

A non-metallic element (I), one of the halogens, with powerful DISINFECTANT (3) properties.

Iodine is also required in trace amounts in the fish's diet. Insuffient dietary iodine may give rise to thyroid TUMOURS (3); however, this is extremely unlikely in aquarium fish. Correct feeding (as outlined in SECTION I: Nutrition) should obviate any likelihood of iodine deficiency, and it is neither necessary nor desirable to take other preventative measures.

In the event that goitre is suspected (i.e. in cases of opercular swelling or growths associated with the gills, in either case which cannot be attributed to other, more probable, causes), then special iodine-medicated foods, suitable for fish, are available from the veterinarian.

IODOPHORS

IODINE (3)-based DISINFECTANTS (3).

J
NO ENTRIES

K

KANAMYCIN

This ANTIBIOTIC is sometimes used for treating certain BACTERIAL INFECTIONS (3) in fish, particularly MYCOBACTERIA (3). Administered as kanamycin sulphate.

DOSAGE AND ADMINISTRATION

Prolonged bath: usually between 10 and 100 mg/l for 5-10 days. It will be necessary to redose the water every 1-3 days, with a total of 50% of the aquarium water changed (using pre-aged water) in between. Note: the actual dose and duration may depend on the species of fish to be treated and the severity and nature of the disease: always follow professional instructions.

Kanamycin may also be administered orally with the food. Delivery by injection (intraperitoneal) has been reported as causing ichthyotoxicity in some fish species.

L

LEECHES

Leeches are elongate annelid worms which may reach several centimetres in length. They are characterised by their anterior (oral) and posterior suckers and by their

Severe leech infestations are rarely encountered under aquarium conditions. Note the red bite wounds.

Photo: Ian Wellby.

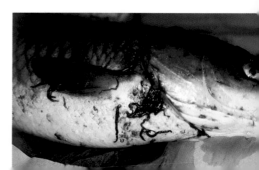

typical looping movements. Several species are encountered in freshwaters.

Leech infestations are rarely encountered in tropical aquaria but are more common in fish ponds and in the wild. Leeches may be accidentally introduced into aquaria via plants or stones which have been collected from outdoor waters, as these may harbour the eggs. There is also a small risk that LIVE FOODS (3) which have been collected from the wild may harbour leeches.

Only a few species of aquatic leech are PARASITES (3) of fish, e.g. *PISCICOLA* (3) *geometrica*, whereas others are parasitic on aquatic invertebrates or non-piscine aquatic vertebrates. Thus, not all leeches found in aquaria are dangerous to fish.

Leeches spend only a proportion of their time attached to the host. Tell-tale signs of a fish leech problem are the reddened circular bite WOUNDS (3) left on the fish's skin. If a leech problem is suspected, take a look at the underneath of aquarium stones for any signs of their eggs.

Leeches are known to transmit certain species of fish parasitic PROTOZOA (3) which live in the blood. It is speculated that leeches are also capable of transmitting pathogenic BACTERIA (3) and VIRUSES (3) to fish; however, there are only a few documented cases of this having occurred and most studies relate to food fish.

For *SIGNS* and *TREATMENT* see *PISCICOLA* (3).

LERNAEA

A large CRUSTACEAN PARASITE (3) commonly known as anchor worm, more frequently encountered in pond fish than in aquarium fish. The life-cycle is direct, with no intermediate hosts. Male and female anchor worms pair up on the surface of the fish but only the female is parasitic, the male dying after mating. The female *Lernaea* anchors to its host with the aid of a special organ, the holdfast, which is inserted into the fish's skin and may penetrate the underlying muscles. The parasite is believed to feed on host blood and cellular debris.

The female develops two distinctive egg sacs which give the parasite an overall 'Y' or 'T' shaped appearance. The eggs are released into the water where they hatch and metamorphose through several free-swimming and parasitic larval stages. The parasitic larvae (copepodid stages) generally settle on the fish's gills. The spent female may subsequently produce further pairs of egg-sacs.

SIGNS
The adult anchor worm is a large ECTOPARASITE (3) which can be clearly seen on the surface of its fish host. Fish which sustain just one or a few anchor worms may be relatively free of symptoms, apart from occasional SCRATCHING (2) or FLASHING (2) in an attempt to rid themselves of the irritation caused by the parasites. In contrast, small fish and fry can be severely weakened by this large parasite, and may die. The deep puncture WOUNDS (3) made by the parasitic female worms are vulnerable to SECONDARY INFECTION (3) with FUNGUS (3) or BACTERIA (3). Large numbers of parasitic larvae may cause gill damage, leading to RESPIRATORY DISTRESS (3) and sometimes death. Diagnosis is confirmed by the visual detection of one or more parasites on the fish's body. The gill-dwelling larval stages are too small to be detected with the naked eye and require microscopical examination of gill scrapes or gill snips.

CAUSE
Several species of *Lernaea* have been described, of which *L. cyprinacea* is the most commonly encountered in aquarium fish. This species is adapted to tropical conditions and can parasitise a broad range of fish species.

PREVENTION AND TREATMENT
Infested fish should be isolated in order to prevent any mature female worms from releasing eggs into the main aquarium. Control measures include the physical removal of adult *Lernaea* with the aid of forceps, assuming the parasitised fish is large enough to withstand such a procedure. The exposed wound should be treated with a topical ANTISEPTIC (3) such as MERCUROCHROME (3).

Chemical bath treatments can be used to eradicate the larval stages. TRICHLORFON (3), an ORGANO-PHOSPHATE COMPOUND (3), is effective at 0.2-0.3

mg/litre. Owing to the gradual degradation of this chemical in the water, this treatment will need to be repeated every seven days for four to six weeks.

Tadpoles are capable of harbouring *Lernaea cyprinacea* and hence feeding fish with live tadpoles is a possible means of introducing this parasite into the aquarium (the use of tadpoles as a live food should, in any case, be discouraged due to the decline of frog populations in Europe and other parts of the world). It is possible that the water accompanying wild-caught LIVE FOODS (3) (e.g. *Daphnia*, bloodworm) could also harbour infective stages.

LEVAMISOLE   P

This ANTHELMINTHIC (3) is used for treating NEMATODE WORM (3) infections. The drug is available as levamisole hydrochloride which is soluble in water. It appears to have only a limited, if any, effect in destroying the egg (ova) stages of nematodes.

DOSAGE AND ADMINISTRATION

Levamisole is usually delivered orally, either as a medicated food, or, in the case of large fish, by tube. It is well absorbed though the fish's body tissues.

Dosage as medicated food: 5-10 mg levamisole hydrochloride per kilogram weight of fish, daily for seven days.

LIVE FOODS AS VECTORS OF DISEASE

Popular live food organisms include *TUBIFEX* (3) worms, aquatic crustaceans, and aquatic insect larvae. These foods are readily taken by most aquarium fish and form part of a fish's balanced diet. Although of nutritional value, it must be borne in mind that some live food organisms are intermediate hosts of fish PARASITES (3), and/or may harbour fish-pathogenic BACTERIA (3) and VIRUSES (3). This is particularly the case if the live foods have been collected from ponds or rivers in which fish are present.

The feeding of wild-collected live foods to aquarium fish therefore poses a small risk but, nevertheless, one of which the aquarist should be aware. Furthermore, the water in which these organisms are collected may itself harbour fish pathogens (such as viruses, bacteria, and parasitic PROTOZOA (3)), large parasites such as the fish louse

Copepods can harbour larval stages of fish parasites.

(*ARGULUS* [3]) and *LERNAEA* (3), and/or predators such as dragonfly larvae and *HYDRA* (3).

Live food organisms which have been cultured separately from fish are unlikely to harbour diseases. Some commercially available live foods (e.g. *Daphnia*) are cultured this way and are safer to feed (however, it may be difficult for the aquarist to distinguish between genuine cultures and 'bogus' ones which have been collected from fish-inhabited waters).

Food organisms which have been frozen-irradiated (examples being frozen *Daphnia*, *Tubifex*, river shrimp, bloodworm, and many others) are generally considered to be disease-free. Live foods collected from marine environments are generally much safer to feed to freshwater fish because many marine fish pathogens and parasites are unable to survive in fresh water. Brine shrimp (*Artemia* spp.) are very safe to feed, and are available as dried cysts ('eggs') which can be easily hatched into nauplii following incubation in saline. Their marine (or salt lake) habitat and their ability to survive desiccation make *Artemia* an unlikely source of freshwater fish pathogens.

Non-aquatic live foods such as earthworms, whiteworms (*Enchytraeus* spp.), crickets, woodlice, etc. are unlikely to introduce pathogens; however, it is important to avoid terrestrial live foods which may have been exposed to pesticides (in which case they will normally be dead!).

The list below shows common live food organisms together with the types of fish pathogens or parasites they may harbour.

TUBIFEX (3) worms: Pathogenic BACTERIA (3) /VIRUSES (3)

COPEPODS (3): Tapeworms (CESTODES [3]);
                    NEMATODE WORMS [3] (*Anguillicola*)

Gammarus ('river shrimp'):   ACANTHOCEPHALAN (3)
worms

Some aquatic insect larvae (e.g. bloodworm):
Pathogenic BACTERIA (3)/VIRUSES (3)

The common procedure of dosing live foods with chemicals such as POTASSIUM PERMANGANATE (3) may help kill any fish pathogens within the water containing the live food; however, this is not a reliable method for killing pathogens residing within the tissues or gut of the live food organisms themselves. Live *Tubifex* worms probably pose the greatest disease risk to fish, such that it is wise not to feed them under any circumstances.
See also SECTION I: Nutrition.

LORDOSIS
A DEFORMITY(3) in which the backbone is 'kinked' in the vertical plane, giving the fish an S-shaped appearance when viewed from the side.

LYMPHOCYSTIS, LYMPHOCYSTIS DISEASE
A chronic viral disease of fish, often also known as Cauliflower Disease. Although capable of infecting a large number of species, the virus is restricted to highly evolved groups of fish such as the cichlids, and conversely does not infect cyprinids (barbs, rasboras, danios, and the like) or catfish.

The common name arises from the whitish CYSTS (2) associated with the disease. These cysts, which sometimes occur singly or in small clusters on the body surfaces, may in extreme cases coalesce to form larger structures similar in form and colour to a miniature cauliflower (their shape has also been likened to that of a raspberry or a bunch of grapes).

The *Lymphocystis* virus invades the fish's cells where it causes them greatly to enlarge, eventually reaching somewhere between 50 and 100,000 times their normal size. As infection proceeds, adjacent host cells also become invaded by the virus, eventually giving rise to clusters of giant cells, each harbouring thousands of viruses, which together

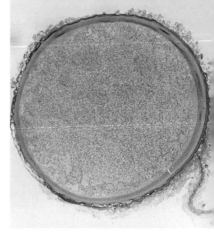

RIGHT: Electron micrograph of enlarged fish cell packed with Lymphocystis. Photo: Roy Moate.

BELOW: Lymphocystis on an artificially coloured glassfish.

manifest as the white growths (cysts). Over a period of weeks or even months, these growths may eventually reach 0.5 cm or more in size. The disease is disfiguring but rarely life-threatening, and often the fish self-cures. Large growths on the lips may, however, cause death indirectly by preventing the fish from feeding.

SIGNS

The disease typically manifests as small white, grey-white, or pinkish GROWTHS (2), occurring most commonly on the fins (especially at the fin base) but they may also appear on other parts of the fish's body. In its early stages the small developing cysts can easily be confused with ICHTHYOPHTHIRIASIS (3) (whitespot); however, the cysts caused by *Lymphocystis* grow larger and are typically far less numerous. Furthermore, Lymphocystis Disease is far less contagious than whitespot and fish sustaining this virus infection are unlikely to exhibit the RESPIRATORY DISTRESS (2) or FLASHING (2) behaviour commonly associated with advanced ichthyophthiriasis. Lymphocystis Disease may, however, sometimes cause loss of APPETITE (2), resulting in a degree of EMACIATION (2).

CAUSE
Lymphocystis Disease is caused by an iridovirus (a group of DNA viruses). Each virus particle is icosahedral in shape and approximately 180-200 microns in size. Individual viruses are far too small to be resolved by light microscopy, but may be observed using a high-power electron microscope (EM) under which their icosahedral shape typically appears hexagonal in the 2-dimensional EM picture. There is some suggestion that Lymphocystis Disease may be due to a range of closely related viruses, each possibly with a limited host range – if true, this could partly explain the observed low infectivity of the disease.

The mode of transmission is not precisely known, but is thought to involve disruption of the cysts (possibly by abrasion damage), resulting in the release of the intracellular viruses. The liberated viruses are infective in the aquarium water for a number of days and may gain entry into a fish via damaged skin. An oral route has also been suggested, and could arise through picking at the cysts on an infected fish or by ingesting free cysts or viruses in the water.

It is thought that STRESS (3) and adverse environmental conditions may aggravate an outbreak of Lymphocystis Disease (which may be lying dormant in the fish). For example, this disease appears more prevalent among artificially coloured fish, particularly the glassfish (family Chandidae); it is not clear whether this is a consequence of the stress caused by injection (typically, a large-gauge (relative to fish size) needle is used) or whether the virus can be transmitted via the syringe needle used to deliver the dye.

PREVENTION AND TREATMENT
There is no known treatment for Lymphocystis Disease; however, the disease is usually self-limiting and is rarely fatal, such that it does not normally pose a serious threat to aquarium fish. Affected fish should, however, be isolated to prevent possible spread of the disease; in time the cysts

generally break down and disappear, and it appears that affected fish commonly develop resistance to *Lymphocystis* and are not reinfected by the viruses thus released. They should, however, be quarantined for 2 months (see below) after the disease has apparently disappeared. Scarring is possible, especially in the case of large cysts.

Surgical removal of the growths is possible, but generally unnecessary and hence not recommended because of the STRESS (3) involved. The exception is in cases where the fish is seriously discommoded by a particular growth (e.g. affecting fin movement), or where the size or number of cysts on the lips is preventing it from feeding. Remedial surgery may be impracticable on small fish, and EUTHANASIA (3) may be the kindest solution in the case of extensive and/or disabling infections.

The only method of reducing the risk of introducing *Lymphocystis* into the aquarium is by extensive QUARANTINE (3), around two months being sufficent to allow visual detection of any early developing cysts. However, it is thought that the virus can remain dormant for long periods of time within a fish, without outward signs of infection, and thus it is impossible to be absolutely sure that a fish is *Lymphocystis*-free.

Quarantine against this disease is, however, unnecessary for types of fish not affected (e.g. cyprinids), and the disease is so uncommon that the majority of aquarists ignore the minimal risk of its introduction. Any fish known to have been in contact with an infected fish should be quarantined for two months, although, as mentioned above, this will not guarantee they are free of the virus. It is inadvisable ever to buy a fish with *Lymphocystis*; however, because of the generally harmless nature of this disease, it is acceptable to buy an unusual or otherwise unobtainable fish affected by the virus, provided it is isolated until free of outward signs of disease.

M

MAGNESIUM SULPHATE
See EPSOM SALTS (3).

MALACHITE GREEN
A triphenylmethane dye of the rosaniline group, formerly a popular aquarium medication used in the treatment of a wide range of pathogens and PARASITES (3), in particular PROTOZOANS (3) such as *ICHTHYOBODO* (3) and *ICHTHYOPHTHIRIUS* (3). Its popularity has diminished through concerns that it may be harmful to human health, particularly in the crystal/powder form which might be accidentally inhaled. It still, nevertheless, forms a constituent of a number of proprietary remedies, in particular when mixed with FORMALIN (3) as a general treatment for pond fish.

   Malachite green may harm biological filtration and plants, and is not well tolerated by some fish. It will also stain hands, clothing, and equipment. The dry form should be handled only by qualified persons; aquarists should obtain a ready-mixed 1% stock solution of the zinc-free grade of the chemical.

DOSAGE AND ADMINISTRATION
● 0.1-0.2 ml of 1% stock solution per 10 litres, as a long-term bath. The dosage can be repeated once or twice, at 4-5 day intervals, each repeat treatment to be preceded by a 25% partial water change
● 1-2 ml of 1% stock solution per 10 litres as a short-term (30-60 minutes) bath, repeated on alternate days for a maximum of 4-5 treatments.
The drug is easily deactivated by organic material, and ideally treatment should take place in the isolation (hospital) aquarium.

MALAWI BLOAT
A condition affecting mouthbrooding cichlids from the lakes of the East African Rift Valley, first reported from Malawian species.

SIGNS
LETHARGY (2), RESPIRATORY DISTRESS (2) (increased respiratory rate, GASPING (2) at the water's surface), loss of APPETITE (2), accompanied or followed, usually within 24 hours, by severe SWELLING (2) of the abdomen and loss of BUOYANCY (2) (resting on the bottom). Death normally follows within 72 hours.

CAUSES
Bloat has formerly been associated with BACTERIAL INFECTION (3) and an inappropriate or unvaried diet. Investigations by aquarists indicate that most cases are the result of dietary and/or environmental causes:
● A monotonous and/or unsuitable diet: dried foods and beef heart have been implicated.
● Poor water quality, in particular high levels of NITRATE (3).
● The long-term addition of SALT (3) (sodium chloride, NaCl) to the aquarium water (in the mistaken belief that this will increase water hardness).

Several simultaneous cases may be indicative of a bacterial infection, otherwise environmental triggers should be suspected, in particular where a succession of cases occurs at intervals of 2-6+ weeks.

PREVENTION AND TREATMENT
Broad-spectrum ANTIBIOTICS may help bacterial bloat. There is no known treatment for environmental bloat. Prevention is the best strategy. Recovery of affected individuals is rare, and EUTHANASIA (3) should be considered, although death from this disease is usually rapid.

MEBENDAZOLE $\qquad$ P
This ANTHELMINTHIC (3) is used to treat intestinal tapeworms (CESTODES (3)) and MONOGENETIC FLUKES (3). Chemically, mebendazole is a synthetic benzimidazole and is slightly soluble in water. Trade names include Vermox.

DOSAGE AND ADMINISTRATION
Against monogeneans:

- short-term bath: 100 mg/litre for 10 minutes.
- long-term bath: 1 mg/litre for 24 hours.

Against intestinal tapeworms:
Orally, via medicated food. Mix with food at the rate of 25-50 mg per kg of fish. Feed the medicated food once per week, for three weeks.

MELANISM

Overproduction of the dark pigment melanin, producing permanent abnormally dark coloration (relative to species norm).

Melanistic 'sports' of some aquarium fish, e.g. some poeciliids, angelfish (*Pterophyllum scalare*), have been fixed as fancy varieties by selective breeding. Accidental melanism is sometimes the result of INBREEDING (3), and the genetic stabilisation of melanic forms requires further, albeit planned, mating of closely related individuals. Hence melanistic forms are sometimes less vigorous than their normal coloured ancestors, and may be prone to genetically induced blindness and tumours.

Partial melanism in a colour variety of the angelfish, Pterophyllum scalare.

MERCUROCHROME **P**

An ANTISEPTIC (3) used for topical treatment of WOUNDS (3) and FUNGUS (3).

DOSAGE AND ADMINISTRATION
A 2% stock solution should be applied to the affected area, and the treatment repeated on alternate days if necessary,

until the condition is healed. **CAUTION**: avoid contact of mercurochrome with the gills.

METAL POISONING
Water may be contaminated by a number of metals, at source (metallic salts in natural water courses), in transit (from pipework), or in the aquarium (from unsuitable equipment). Iron, lead, and copper are the commonest causes of metal toxicity. The degree of toxicity may vary with water chemistry which influences the particular metal salts produced – metallic contamination of soft water is particularly dangerous. Susceptibility to metal toxicity varies from species to species. Test kits are available for monitoring copper levels.
See also POISONING (3); SECTION I: The Correct Environment.

METRIPHONATE/METRIPHORATE   P
See TRICHLORFON (3)

METHYLENE BLUE
A bactericidal and fungicidal thiazine dye with a number of aquarium applications, less popular nowadays because of its deleterious effects on biological filtration and its ability to stain skin, clothing, and aquarium decor and equipment (including silicon sealant). It may also be harmful to plant life. It nevertheless remains a safe and effective treatment for *ICHTHYOPHTHIRIUS* (3) and FUNGUS (3), and is the treatment of choice for the prevention of EGG FUNGUS (3). It is readily available as a 1% or 2% stock solution from aquatic retailers.

DOSAGE AND ADMINISTRATION
● For BACTERIAL (3), FUNGAL (3), and PROTOZOAN (3) INFECTIONS (3):
2 ml of 1% stock solution per 10 litres of aquarium water, as a long-term bath, preferably in an isolation aquarium because of the adverse effects on biological filtration and decor. The dye degrades after a few days, particularly in the presence of organics, and the dose should be repeated if necessary.
● As a prophylactic against egg fungus:

Nominal dosage is 2mg/litre. However, a more usual approach is to add the dye to the hatching container a drop at a time, allowing each drop to disperse throughout the water, until the latter is a slight to medium blue but the eggs remain visible for observation. The single dose is then allowed to degrade naturally, so that by the time larvae become free-swimming and feed, first food micro-organisms are not adversely affected by the chemical. In addition, small (5%) daily partial water changes, using carefully matched water (chemistry, temperature), should be made post-hatching, to help remove the dye and to compensate for the lack of biological processing of waste products in the hatching container.

Note: In species which have a moderate to long incubation time (4+ days) it may be necessary to redose with methylene blue every second or third day.

METRONIDAZOLE **P**
and DI-METRONIDAZOLE
Metronidazole and di-metronidazole are antimicrobial drugs developed for human treatment, effective against anaerobic bacteria and protozoa. In the aquarium, used to treat HEXAMITIASIS (3).

DOSAGE AND ADMINISTRATION
If only (or largely) cichlids are kept then treatment will usually take place in their normal accommodation; otherwise a hospital tank should be used to reduce costs and avoid unnecessary medication of unaffected fish. *All* cichlids from the affected aquarium should be treated. These drugs do not appear to have any deleterious effect on biological filtration.

Metronidazole:
50 mg per gallon (4.5 litres) of aquarium water. The drug is normally supplied in tablet form (usually 200 mg/tablet); the tablets should be crushed and mixed with a small amount of water which is then added to the aquarium. The treatment should be repeated on alternate days for a total of 3 treatments. A 25% water change between treatments is optional. If the fish are feeding, then metronidazole-medicated food can be given. The recommended dosage is

1% (by weight), but few aquarists are likely to have the necessary equipment to measure the tiny quantities this entails (see SECTION I: Treating fish diseases). In practice, pellets/flake can be soaked in metronidazole solution, or a little powder can be mixed with, for example, chopped shrimp or earthworms, to which it will adhere.

di-metronidazole:
25 mg per gallon (5 mg/litre), administered as above, but with three treatments at three-day intervals. Serious or persistent cases can be given a 48-hour bath, in a hospital tank, in an 0.004% solution (180 mg/gallon, 40 mg/litre).

MICROSPORIDIANS
PROTOZOAN (3) parasites which are occasionally encountered in aquarium fish, the most common being *PLEISTOPHORA* (3) sp., which causes 'neon tetra disease'. Microsporidians are very small (less than 50 microns) intracellular parasites, characterised by the production of spores. Some species cause GROWTHS (2), which may occur just beneath the skin or within the deeper tissues.

MONOGENEA, MONOGENETIC FLUKES
A group of parasitic platyhelminthic FLUKES (3), which have a monogenetic life cycle, i.e. they require only one host in order to produce the next generation (cf. DIGENEA (3) or digenetic flukes, which require two or more hosts to complete their life-cycle).

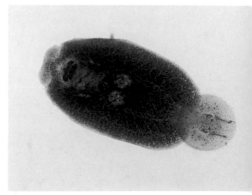

Monogenean fluke, about 2mm in length (stained red to show internal features).

MOUTH FUNGUS, MOUTH ROT
See COLUMNARIS (3).

MS222
See TRICAINE METHANESULPHONATE (3).

P

MYCOBACTERIA, MYCOBACTERIOSIS
Several species of mycobacteria are known; however, only two species infect aquarium fish, namely *Mycobacterium marinum* and *M. fortuitum*, which cause a chronic, and often lethal, systemic disease known as FISH TUBERCULOSIS (3). Mycobacterial infections are difficult to treat, but some success may be achieved using ANTIBIOTICS (3).

MYXOBACTERIA
See COLUMNARIS (3), FLEXIBACTER (3).

N

NEMATODE WORMS
A large group of threadlike organisms, also known as threadworms or roundworms, comprising both free-living and parasitic species. There are over 5,000 species of parasitic nematodes, and 650 have been identified as adults in fish. They have a cylindral non-segmented body, approximately 1mm in length, and are usually white or colourless but may take on the colour of the blood and gut content on which they feed. The nematode life cycle varies from a simple one-stage host relationship to a complex multi-host system. The larval stages of nematodes may live free or be encysted on internal organs. The adults live off the gut contents or gut lining of the fish. Severe infestation

Harmless, free-living nematode, about 2mm in length, collected from the aquarium filter.

by larval stages of nematodes can damage individual organs, while large numbers of adults in the gut generally weaken the host.

SIGNS
At low levels of infestation there will be no obvious clinical signs. Severe infestations may cause abdominal SWELLING (2) and general LETHARGY (2). In some cases spinal DEFORMITY (2) (curvature) may occur if the fish is severely affected by nematodes.

CAUSE
A number of species, notably *CAMALLANUS* (3).

PREVENTION AND TREATMENT:
Avoid feeding wild-caught LIVE FOOD (3) species, as several serve as intermediate hosts of nematodes. Treatment of adult nematodes is with ANTHELMINTHICS (3).

NEOMYCIN SULPHATE   P
See ANTIBIOTICS (3).

NEON TETRA DISEASE
A PROTOZOAN (3) disease which primarily infects the musculature of certain tetras and a small number of other freshwater aquarium fish species *(See PLEISTOPHORA [3]).*

NEW TANK SYNDROME
The term applied to the mass POISONING (3) by AMMONIA (3) and/or NITRITE (3) which commonly takes place when fish are added to newly set up aquaria before the nitrogen cycle has become established in the tank and its filter system. A similar syndrome may occur as the result of inappropriate filter maintenance (e.g. total replacement of filter medium, incorrect cleaning of medium), or of the use of chemical disease remedies which destroy nitrifying bacteria.

SIGNS
As for ammonia and nitrite poisoning, in recently set up aquaria (usually the first 21 days) which have not been

matured before fish are added. All, or most of, the aquarium population are affected, with numerous deaths. SECONDARY INFECTIONS (3) with BACTERIA (3), FUNGUS (3), and PROTOZOA (3) may occur in surviving fish as a result of the attendant STRESS (3) compromising their immune systems.

PREVENTION AND TREATMENT
Prevention is paramount – the aquarium should always be properly matured, and the initial peaking of ammonia and nitrite monitored, with no fish being added until levels of these toxins have returned to zero. Sensible stocking and feeding for a short period thereafter will prevent any residual problems as the filtration gradually adjusts to the increased loading.

New Tank Syndrome is easily avoided and there is no excuse for the problem occurring.
See also SECTION I: The Correct Environment.

NICLOSAMIDE **P**
This ANTHELMINTHIC has been used to treat intestinal tapeworms (CESTODES [3]) and ACANTHO-CEPHALANS (3). It appears to have little or no effect in destroying the egg stage of tapeworms. Proprietary names include Yomesan and Nicloside.

DOSAGE AND ADMINISTRATION
Administered orally, in food:
● 50 to 100 mg per kg weight of fish per day. The medicated food is fed exclusively for seven days. A repeat course may be required.
● (This second method obviates the need to calculate fish weight and feeding rate): 1% admixture with food (e.g. 10 mg niclosamide mixed with every gram of food), the medicated food being fed exclusively for one week. A repeat course may be required.

NIFURPIRINOL **P**
See FURANACE (3).

NITRATE
Nitrate ($-NO_3$) is the final product of the nitrogen cycle,

which converts AMMONIA (3) to NITRITE (3) and finally nitrate. Nitrate is toxic to fish at a generally much higher level than nitrite or ammonia. Resistant species such as guppies *(Poecilia reticulata)* and goldfish *(Carassius auratus)* may survive levels up to 1,000 mg/litre (which is not, however, to say that they should be expected to do so routinely, or even exceptionally). Nitrate is considered a significant cause of STRESS (3) at far lower levels, and is particularly toxic to fish fry and sensitive species (e.g. those from nitrate-poor waters such as the East African rift lakes, much of the Amazon basin, and rain forest areas in general). It is generally agreed that 50 mg/litre is the maximum level to which even tolerant fish should be exposed in captivity, with less than 25 mg/litre preferable, and even lower necessary for some species.

Test kits are available for monitoring nitrate levels. These sometimes have a limited 'shelf life' and may lull the aquarist into a false sense of security by giving a zero reading. However, a zero reading is highly unlikely, and probably totally impossible, in a system containing any form of life, and should be regarded as suspect. Rampant ALGAE (3) growth is normally a sign of high nitrate levels.

PROBLEMS CAUSED BY NITRATE
Even in the short term, exposure to undesirably high levels of nitrate may cause STRESS (3) and compromise the immune system, leaving the fish more prone to attack by pathogens. In the longer term the continuing, and often increasing, stress will gradually weaken the fish, causing general slight, or even severe, ill-health, even without pathogenic attack, symptomised by LETHARGY (2), RESPIRATORY DISTRESS (2), YAWNING (2), loss of APPETITE (2), EMACIATION (2), REPRODUCTIVE FAILURE (3), etc. High nitrate levels have been identified as a contributory factor in MALAWI BLOAT (3) and HEXAMITIASIS (3).

It is also vital to avoid NITRATE SHOCK (3) when introducing new fish to the aquarium.

NITRATE REMOVAL
Nitrate removal from freshwater aquaria can be achieved in a number of ways:

- Dilution by partial water changes. This is effective, provided the fresh-water source does not itself have a significant level of nitrate. Unfortunately, many water sources have been contaminated by nitrogen-rich fertilisers and/or inadequate purification during recycling, making them unsuitable for use with fish without pre-treatment to remove nitrate.
- Nitrate-removing ion exchange resins. These can be used to remove nitrate from source water for water changes, while some can be used in the aquarium filter. These resins exchange a chloride ion for the nitrate.
- Reverse Osmosis. This process produces almost 100% pure H_2O, removing any mineral salts as well as organics such as nitrates.
- De-nitrification. This is a process carried out by facultative anaerobic bacteria in oxygen-depleted conditions. The bacteria obtain their oxygen from nitrate ($-NO_3$) breaking it down to nitrite (NO_2) and then nitrous oxide (NO). In practice it is very difficult successfully to create the right conditions for reliable de-nitrification in the freshwater aquarium.
- Plants, including ALGAE (3), utilise nitrates. Unless the aquarium is densely planted and has a very low stocking rate, however, it is unlikely that the aquarium plants will be able to utilise all the nitrate produced.
- Some aquarium plant fertilisers, of the type added to the water rather than inserted in the substrate close to the plant, may cause a sudden dramatic increase in nitrate levels. Avoiding such products will help maintain low nitrate levels.

See also SECTION I: The Correct Environment.

NITRATE SHOCK

SHOCK (3) caused by sudden exposure to high levels of NITRATE (3). A common problem when newly purchased fish are introduced to improperly maintained aquaria where nitrate levels have gradually risen, usually over a long period of time, as a result of inadequate partial water changes.

SIGNS
Typically the fish become ill, commonly with signs of

POISONING (3), 24-72 hours after introduction. They are often found dead, with no previous sign of illness, at 'lights on' of the second or third day in their new home.

PREVENTION AND TREATMENT
A large water change or removal to a nitrate-low aquarium may help, but normally irreversible damage will have occurred and death be inevitable by the time any signs of illness manifest. Prevention is therefore paramount. New fish should never be introduced to aquaria with high nitrate levels, and such levels should in any case be avoided, as they are detrimental to the long-term well-being of the established occupants.
See also SECTION I: Providing the correct environment; Purchasing, transporting, and introducing stock.

NITRITE and NITRITE TOXICITY
POISONING (3) by nitrite (NO_2), a toxic product of the nitrogen cycle.
(See SECTION I: The Correct Environment).

SIGNS
The most common signs of nitrite poisoning are the same as for OXYGEN STARVATION (3), i.e. RESPIRATORY DISTRESS (2) (GASPING (2) at the surface, hanging in areas of water or air movement, increased gill rate and general LETHARGY (2). Examination of the gills will also reveal a pale tan to brown coloration, instead of the healthy, bright red colour normally observed. The fish may also FLASH (2) and SHIMMY (2).

Gasping at the water surface and shimmying behaviour in this molly could be the result of nitrite poisoning.

CAUSE

Nitrite is formed by the breakdown of AMMONIA (3) by *Nitrosomonas* bacteria during the nitrogen cycle; it dissociates in water to form nitrous acid, which is highly toxic to fish. The amount of nitrous acid resulting from a given level of nitrite depends on pH and temperature: the lower the pH and temperature, the more toxic nitrous acid will be present. Absorbed nitrous acid causes haemoglobin (the molecule within red blood cells which transports oxygen) to be oxidised into methaemoglobin which is inefficient at carrying oxygen.

High levels of nitrite may occur where biological filtration has not been properly matured (NEW TANK SYNDROME (3)), where its bacterial population has been compromised (e.g. by medication(s) or incorrect cleaning of filter media), or where it has been severely overloaded (e.g. by overfeeding). Regular raised nitrite levels are indicative of inadequate filtration and/or overfeeding. Any measurable nitrite level should alert the fishkeeper to the existence of a potentially long-term problem.

The levels of nitrite that any fish species can tolerate are variable, depending on the species' natural capacity to convert methaemoglobin back to haemoglobin. Some species, such as discus (*Symphysodon* spp.) can be adversely affected by as little as 0.5 mg/litre, whilst guppies *(Poecilia reticulata)* can survive levels of up to 100 mg/litre. Fry are particularly sensitive.

PREVENTION AND TREATMENT

Prevention and avoidance are preferable to rectification. As a general management principle, ensure nitrite levels are kept close to zero. Sufficient effective nitrifying filtration will eliminate nitrite as it is oxidised into NITRATE (3) by *Nitrobacter* bacteria.

If high levels of nitrite occur, adding 1 gram per litre of SALT (3) (sodium chloride) to the water significantly reduces nitrite toxicity, but may in itself prove harmful to many species. It is thought that the chloride ions reduce the amount of nitrite absorbed into the fish's bloodstream.

A safer procedure (especially for salt-intolerant species) is to change 25-30% of the aquarium water twice daily, with an 8-12 hour interval, until a safe nitrite level is reached. In some cases it may be necessary to undertake even larger water changes in order to speed the reduction of nitrite within the aquarium. Using a mature filter from another aquarium will normally reduce nitrite levels to near-zero within 24-48 hours. The optimum solution, however, is temporary removal of the fish to a nitrite-free aquarium until their own quarters can be rendered safe.

Clearly, the underlying cause of the problem must be identified and eliminated.

NITROGENOUS WASTES

A collective term for AMMONIA (3), NITRITE (3), and NITRATE (3), sometimes also known as Nitrogen Cycle by-products. *See also SECTION I: The Correct Environment.*

NOCARDIA

A genus of BACTERIA, some species of which affect freshwater fish. *Nocardia* infection is very similar to that caused by MYCOBACTERIA (3) and the transmission, control and treatment information is essentially the same. Special staining and high-power microscopy (x 1000) is required to differentiate between *Nocardia* and mycobacteria, one distinguishing feature being the presence of branched forms in *Nocardia*, but not in mycobacteria. (In fact, *Nocardia* is considered by some to be an intermediate between a bacterium and a fungus.) However, as far as the aquarist is concerned, such differential diagnosis is not generally required. ANTIBIOTICS (3) offer the best chances of a cure.

NUTRITIONAL DISEASES

Nutritional diseases mostly result from a long-term incorrect diet, and are therefore thus normally long-term, i.e. they may take weeks or months to manifest, by which time permanent damage may have occurred. A few, such as CONSTIPATION (2), may be either short or long term in origin and effect.

The signs of nutritional diseases are variable, depending on the exact nature of the underlying problem.

Nutritional problems are unlikely to occur if a varied diet of good-quality foods (which have been properly stored), appropriate to the recipients, is used. *See also AFLA-TOXINS (3), DIGESTIVE DISORDERS (3), MALAWI BLOAT (3), FATTY LIVER (3), VITAMIN DEFICIENCY (3); SECTION I: Nutrition; SECTION II: APPETITE, EMACIATION, DISTENDED BODY, FAECES, OBESITY*

O

OBESITY

An unsuitable diet can lead to obesity in fish. Obesity may cause swimming difficulties, and be associated with DIGESTIVE DISORDERS (3), FATTY LIVER (3), and REPRODUCTIVE FAILURE (3).

SIGNS
A slow and gradual increase in girth, particularly affecting the abdomen; in some fish the condition may affect the area anterior to the pelvic (ventral) insertion. Many aquarists fail to notice that their fish are becoming obese because of the gradual nature of the condition. Many fish exhibited at shows are obese, owing to overfeeding on unsuitable foods in order to achieve maximum size (and hence maximum points for size). Such treatment is deleterious to the fish's health and might thus be regarded as cruel.

PREVENTION AND TREATMENT
Prevention is the best course. Reference to photos of wild specimens, or to specimens for sale in shops, will provide a reasonable yardstick for assessing whether longer-term aquarium residents are obese. Correct diet should prevent the problem occurring. If a fish has become obese then the diet should be remedied.

It would be to the considerable benefit of many fish if show rules were amended to allow, or even require, down-pointing of obese fish, as this would act as a deterrent to unthinking owners.
See also OVERFEEDING (3); SECTION I: Nutrition.

OCTOMITUS
See HEXAMITA (3).

OODINIUM

An outdated name for the dinoflagellate parasite which causes velvet disease in freshwater fish. See *PISCINOODINIUM* (**3**).

ORGANOPHOSPHOROUS COMPOUNDS [P]
(ORGANOPHOSPHATES)

These chemicals are well known for their insecticidal activity but have also been used to treat a range of ECTOPARASITES (3) of fish: crustaceans (COPEPODS (3)), FLUKES (3) (MONOGENEA), and LEECHES (3). Unfortunately, organophosphates are neurotoxic to humans and other animals and are known to cause widespread environmental damage. These concerns have led to their being restricted or prohibited in certain countries. Where legally available, they should be handled with extreme care (wear rubber gloves) and be disposed of safely (follow the manufacturer's instructions regarding handling and disposal, or seek other expert advice).

Numerous organophosphate compounds exist; however, TRICHLORFON (3) (also known as metriphonate) is the one most commonly used for treating fish ectoparasites. Some fish parasites are known to have developed resistance to organophosphates, thereby reducing the chemical's efficacy. Certain groups of fish (e.g. characins – tetras), as well as fish fry, are sensitive to organophosphate treatments.

OSMOTIC SHOCK
See SHOCK (3), OSMOTIC STRESS (3).

OSMOTIC STRESS

Disruption of a fish's osmoregulatory system due to extensive skin permeability (e.g. arising from injury or disease) or as a result of incorrect water chemistry.

SIGNS

In the case of skin damage resulting in permeability, clinical signs of the underlying cause are usually apparent, such as INJURY (3) or severe ULCERS (2), especially when these affect a significant proportion of the body surface. In all cases there may be classic signs of STRESS (3): abnormally pale or dark COLORATION (2),

CLAMPED FINS (2), abnormal BEHAVIOUR (2) (LETHARGY (2), or, conversely, DARTING (2) escape behaviour), RESPIRATORY DISTRESS (2) (increased gill rate), and, in extreme cases, loss of balance.

CAUSE

Fish must maintain a constant salt/water balance within their bodies so as to provide optimal conditions for various physiological and biochemical processes. The salt content of freshwater fish is higher than that of the surrounding water, and this difference must be maintained by an energy-requiring process known as osmoregulation *(see SECTION I: Biology and Anatomy)*. Certain adverse environmental or disease conditions may place an extra burden on the fish's osmoregulatory system until a point is reached when the fish is physiologically unable to cope, resulting in osmotic stress and possible death.

● Skin injury or skin disease. Where the skin's natural impermeability is compromised, such as through extensive damage to the tegumentary layers, then osmotic forces will cause water to enter via the WOUND (3) and body salts to be lost from it. This poses extra work for the fish's osmoregulatory system, and in severe cases the fish may be physiologically unable to compensate, resulting in death through osmoregulatory failure.

● Incorrect water chemistry. This can arise when fish are exposed to water which is either unnaturally mineral-rich or unnaturally mineral-depleted for the species in question. Usually, osmotic stress will be greatest when fish from mineral-rich natural waters are exposed to extremely mineral-depleted water conditions (in which the osmotic difference between fish and its environment is greater). Unlike those fish which are physiologically adapted to live in waters which are mineral-poor (e.g. many South American species), the hard-water species may have less efficient osmoregulatory systems and are therefore unable to cope with the added osmotic stress. However, osmotic stress can also occur when fish from mineral-poor waters are placed in very hard water.

● Sudden changes in concentrations of dissolved salts, e.g. if a fish is moved from mineral-depleted to mineral-rich water (or vice versa) without gradual acclimatisation, are likely to cause acute osmotic stress or osmotic SHOCK (3), commonly leading to death within 24-72 hours.

• Exposure of fish to high concentration SALT (3) (NaC1) baths (e.g. for eradicating parasites) may also cause extreme osmotic shock, so fish should be removed to fresh water as soon as they show any signs of imbalance or extreme STRESS (3).

• AMMONIA (3) will also adversely affect the fish's osmoregulation.

It should also be noted that osmotic stress is only one of a number of complex biochemical problems that may occur when fish are subjected to a sudden change in water chemistry or to long-term maintenance in unsuitable conditions, and that such incorrect treatment always involves a risk to the health of the fish.

PREVENTION AND TREATMENT
Adjust the water's dissolved salts or hardness to an appropriate level.

In situations where the fish is believed to be experiencing osmotic stress resulting from extensive skin damage caused by injury or infection, add 1 to 3g/litre of a proprietary balanced physiological salt to the water. Use the 1g/litre dosage for soft water species. This will reduce the osmotic pressure (the difference between the internal and external salt content) and help alleviate the physical problems. It should be borne in mind, however, that there is a risk of this treatment causing more harm than good in the case of species accustomed to mineral-depleted, acidic water, because of the effects of a change in water chemistry on other biochemical processes. Where osmotic stress is due to incorrect water chemistry, the underlying cause should be remedied gradually to avoid CHEMICAL SHOCK (3).
See also SECTION I: The Correct Environment.

OVERFEEDING
Overfeeding is a common error made by most novice, and even some experienced, aquarists. Depending on the nature of the food offered, overfeeding can have several harmful effects to the fish and/or their environment.

• Overfeeding a balanced diet. Provided a suitable diet is

given, overfeeding is unlikely. However, the excess food will be excreted by the fish, mostly as AMMONIA (3), and may result in an overload of the biological filtration system. Even if there is no problem with ammonia or NITRITE (3) poisoning, there will be an unnecessary increase in NITRATE (3).

● Overfeeding the wrong types of food. Although the overall quantity of food may not be excessive for the fish in question, if the diet contains significant amounts of unsuitable foodstuffs (notably animal fats) then this may lead to OBESITY (3), CONSTIPATION (3) and other DIGESTIVE DISORDERS (3), and FATTY LIVER (3) degeneration.

● Uneaten food left to decompose may also seriously overload the biological filtration system, and can result in CLOUDY WATER (3) (bacterial bloom) which can deplete the oxygen level of the water.

See also SECTION I: Nutrition.

OXOLINIC ACID **P**

A synthetic ANTIBACTERIAL (3) compound (a type of quinolone) used in the treatment of systemic BACTERIAL INFECTIONS (3) (e.g. *VIBRIO [3]*).

DOSAGE AND ADMINISTRATION

Orally, via medicated food: 10 mg of oxolinic acid per kg of fish, daily for 10 days.

Long-term bath: 0.5-2.0 mg/litre for 1-2 days. The efficacy of the treatment may decline relative to increasing alkalinity, i.e. the higher the aquarium pH the less effective the medication.

OXYGEN AND OXYGEN STARVATION

Oxygen is vital for respiration in all fish; however, the aquatic environment is relatively poor in this gas. For example, a tropical freshwater aquarium (at 26 degrees C – 79 degrees F) will contain a maximum of circa 8 mg/litre of dissolved oxygen, as compared to 200 mg/litre of oxygen in the air. Thus tropical fish need to be highly efficient in extracting the meagre amounts of oxygen present in their surroundings.

Fish vary from species to species in their physiological requirements for oxygen. In general, those species which occur naturally in ponds and still waters are capable of withstanding much lower oxygen levels than those which inhabit fast running streams and rivers.

The minimum oxygen requirement for some species of tropical fish may be critically close to the oxygen saturation level of the water. As a consequence, any significant fall in the level of dissolved oxygen in the aquarium can cause some fish to experience RESPIRATORY STRESS (3) and, in severe situations, death.

SIGNS

Fish which are experiencing acute environmental or physiological oxygen starvation (hypoxia) may exhibit the following symptoms of RESPIRATORY DISTRESS (2):

● Increased gill beats (increased breathing rate).

● GASPING (2) or gulping at the water surface (not to be confused with surface feeding behaviour).

● HANGING (2) in areas of water with higher oxygen content, e.g. filter outlets at/near the surface.

If the problem is not/cannot be remedied then inadequate oxygen supply to the brain may lead to loss of motor control, glazed EYES (2) and unusual (heightened) COLORATION (2) due to impaired control of the chromatophores, signs more often associated with acute POISONING (3).

Those fish which have died through an acute lack of oxygen often exhibit flared gill opercula and gaping mouths. Large fish, and those which have a high physiological requirement for oxygen, are often the first to die should the dissolved oxygen in the water fall to a critical level. Chronic hypoxia, in which the oxygen level may be sub-optimal for the species in question but not lethal, may be far less obvious and can manifest as poor growth (STUNTING [2]) and reduced APPETITE (2), as well as GENERAL MALAISE (2) and increased susceptibility to disease.

Dissolved oxygen levels can be measured using an electronic oxygen meter or colorimetric test kit. Some oxygen testing apparatus needs to be calibrated before use (check with manufacturer's instructions). Oxygen measurements must be taken either on the aquarium water *in situ* (as is possible with electronic meters) or from a freshly drawn sample. A stored sample of water will give a misleading value.

CAUSES

Oxygen starvation in fish may arise either because there is very little oxygen in the water (= environmental hypoxia) or because the fish's ability to take up oxygen is impaired (= physiological hypoxia). In addition, fish which are subjected to unusually high levels of activity (e.g. constant AGGRESSION (3) by tank-mates, etc.) may experience hypoxia due to their increased metabolic demand, even though aquarium oxygen levels are adequate for normal levels of activity.

Causes of environmental hypoxia include:
● High stocking density of fish. In situations where a high density of fish is supported by artificial aeration then there is an increased risk of oxygen starvation occurring in the event of the aeration equipment failing.
● Excessive organic pollution (this may cause a bloom of aerobic bacteria which consume oxygen from the water) resulting from, *inter alia*, OVERFEEDING (3) and/or poor aquarium hygiene.
● Combination of the above two factors. For example, death by hypoxia is not uncommon in fish which are transported at high packing density over long distances (e.g. by air). The death of one or more fish during transit will cause organic pollution and possibly a bacterial bloom which can lead to a rapid decline in dissolved oxygen levels. Partly for this reason, anti-bacteria chemicals are often added to the transportation water.
● Increased water temperature (perhaps due to a failed thermostat causing the aquarium heater to be permanently switched on).
● Certain disease remedies may lower the dissolved oxygen level in the water (e.g. FORMALDEHYDE (3), PHENOXYETHANOL (3)).

Causes of physiological hypoxia include:
● Gill damage as a result of gill PARASITES (3) (e.g.

FLUKES [3]) or BACTERIAL (3) or FUNGAL (3) infections. Various PROTOZOAL (3) pathogens, such as *ICHTHYOPHTHIRIUS* (3), *PISCINOODINIUM* (3), and rarely *APIOSOMA* (3), may also seriously damage the fish's gills.

● Gill damage due to POISONING (3), e.g. CHLORINE (3) or AMMONIA (3) toxicity.

● Gill damage caused by ACIDOSIS (3) or ALKALOSIS (3).

● NITRITE (3) damage to the fish's red blood cells (which carry oxygen around the body). Nitrite also inhibits haemoglobin function.

● Gill damage caused by mechanical damage, e.g. sharp substrate materials in aquaria housing bottom-sifters.

PREVENTION AND TREATMENT
Environmental factors
Prevention is paramount since acute cases of hypoxia often result in death. A low to moderate stocking density, good aquarium hygiene, and proper maintenance of aeration and filtration equipment will greatly help prevent low dissolved oxygen levels from occurring. Where necessary, vigorous agitation or aeration of the water will help bring oxygen levels back towards saturation point.

Aquatic plants are sometimes sold as 'oxygenators' (particularly in the pond trade); however, they should never be used as a means of improving oxygen levels in an otherwise poorly oxygenated aquarium. Although aquatic plants (and algae) release oxygen during photosynthesis, at night they actually consume oxygen from the water. As a result, the oxygen level in a static, densely planted aquarium (or pond) may fluctuate over each 24 hour period, being high during the day and low at night. In practice, the common use of aquarium aerators and filter powerheads tends to suppress this fluctuation effect.

In emergencies HYDROGEN PEROXIDE (3) can be used to raise aquarium oxygen levels rapidly.

Physiological factors
Ammonia or nitrite damage to the gills and respiratory system can largely be avoided by the proper use of biological filtration equipment and by preventing situations

which could lead to NEW TANK SYNDROME (3). Chlorine damage to the fish's gills can be prevented by dechlorinating all tap water prior to aquarium use.

Increasing the aeration may help fish which are suffering from physiological hypoxia. However, in severe cases, the gills or respiratory system may be so damaged that no amount of dissolved oxygen will help. Mechanical damage to the gills should be avoided by choice of a substrate material suitable for the fish maintained.

OXYTETRACYCLINE

Oxytetracycline hydrochloride is an ANTIBIOTIC (3) sometimes used in the treatment of systemic BACTERIAL INFECTIONS (3) in fish. It has the advantage of versatility as regards administration.

DOSAGE AND ADMINISTRATION
Injection: 10-20 mg oxytetracycline per kg of fish (repeat if necessary).
Orally: in food, at a rate of 60-75 mg per kg of fish per day, administered for 7-14 days.
Bath immersion: long-term bath (5 days), at 20-100 mg/litre. Repeat if necessary.

OZONE

Ozone (O_3) is an unstable allotropic form of OXYGEN (3) produced by the action of ultraviolet radiation or electrical discharge on the free oxygen molecule O_2. Because of its chemical instability it is a powerful oxidising agent, the extra oxygen atom readily associating with both organic or inorganic substances. This oxidising capability makes ozone a powerful DISINFECTANT (3), which is commonly used to destroy pathogens in marine aquaria. Ozone can also be used to eliminate organic discoloration of the water.

It is of questionable value, and rarely used, for the freshwater aquarium, where quarantine and good husbandry are normally sufficient to maintain good fish health. Although eliminating free-swimming pathogens may seem advantageous, ozone is not a cure/prevent-all, and the possible dangers inherent in its use outweigh the advantages.

DOSAGE AND ADMINISTRATION

The effective dosage for killing BACTERIA (3) and VIRUSES (3) lies in the range 1-8 mg ozone per litre per minute, with a contact time of between 2 and 6 minutes.

Ozone must never be used directly on the aquarium, as it will oxidise not only any undesirable pathogens, but also the fish! It is instead used to sterilise water circulated though a separate ozonising vessel or chamber; the water should then be heavily aerated or passed through activated carbon to remove all traces of ozone before being returned to the aquarium. Because it can be applied only to the water, ozone is effective only against free-living pathogens, not those residing on or in the fish or the aquarium decor.

OZONE TOXICITY

Even at relatively low concentrations, ozone can be toxic to fish. The residual ozone concentration should be kept below 0.002 mg per litre, otherwise it may significantly STRESS (3) and perhaps kill the fish. If ozone is used as a disinfectant in a freshwater aquarium, treat as suspicious any signs of distress or IRRITATION (2) in the fish, particularly RESPIRATORY DISTRESS (2) or other signs of gill problems. Any sign of ozone odour, which is detectable by the human nose at the level of 0.02-0.05 mg/litre, indicates that the ozone is at a level which is toxic to fish.

Ozone is also dangerous to humans, causing various ailments such as nausea, headaches, and depression.

P

PARASITES and PARASITIC DISEASES

Parasites are organisms which live, for at least part of their life cycle, on the body surface or within the tissues/organs of, or in association with, another lifeform, termed the host. The parasite/host relationship is strictly one-sided, with the parasite deriving benefit (usually food) from the host without the latter receiving any reciprocal advantage. Commonly most species of parasite cannot complete their

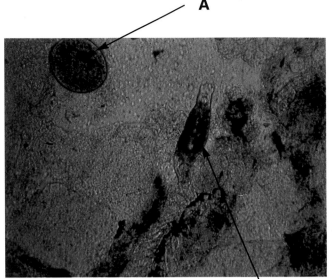

Skin smear revealing Ichthyophthirius (A) and a monogenean fluke (B). Photo: David Ford.

life-cycle without a suitable host being present (obligate parasites) while a few are capable of a free-living or commensal (e.g. as part of the fish's normal gut flora) existence but may become parasitic under certain conditions (facultative parasites or opportunistic parasites). The host, meanwhile, does not require the parasite for its survival, and is sometimes severely disadvantaged by its presence.

Parasites are commonly divided into two groups, ECTOPARASITES (3), which live on the outside of their host, and ENDOPARASITES (3) which live inside it.

PARASITIC DISEASES IN FISH
Aquarium fish are susceptible to a range of diseases caused by parasitic species of PROTOZOA (3), FLUKES (3),

Ectoparasitic isopod crustacean, isolated from a fish imported from South America.

Photo: Mike Sandford.

tapeworms (CESTODES (3)), NEMATODE WORMS (3), CRUSTACEANS (3), and LEECHES (3). (The other disease-causing organisms, notably VIRUSES (3), BACTERIA (3), and FUNGI (3), are usually referred to as pathogens or microbial pathogens).

Ectoparasites may be found on the surface of the fish's skin, fins, or gills, the actual site(s) depending on the parasite species. Examples include the skin and gill flukes, anchor worm (*LERNAEA* [3]) and the fish louse (*ARGULUS* [3]).

Endoparasites may occur beneath the fish's skin or within the muscles, blood, or internal organs; again the actual site(s) of invasion depend largely on the parasite species. Examples include tapeworms (CESTODES (3)), TRYPANOSOMES (3), eye-fluke (*DIPLOSTOMUM* (3)), the whitespot protozoan *ICHTHYOPHTHIRIUS* (3), and many others. Certain fish parasites, notably the DIG-ENEAN (3) flukes and tapeworms, typically have complex life-cycles involving two or three different types of host. Non-fish hosts include piscivorous birds (such as gulls) and aquatic invertebrates (such as SNAILS (3) or COPEPODS (3)). These multi-host parasites are generally unable to multiply under aquarium conditions but may be introduced via an intermediate host (e.g. a snail, LIVE FOOD [3]).

Many of the smaller parasites, such as the PROTOZOA (3) and monogenetic flukes (MONOGENEA (3)), can be identified only with the aid of a microscope, occasionally augmented with special staining procedures. Parasite diagnosis is an acquired skill which is best left to a qualified parasitologist or veterinary surgeon who is familiar with fish parasites.

SPECIAL IMPACT OF PARASITES ON CAPTIVE FISH

It is common for wild fish to sustain a few parasites, which do little harm as it is not normally in a parasite's best interests to kill its host. In captivity, however, under certain circumstances parasites may proliferate until their numbers are such that the host is seriously harmed. A fish whose immune system is compromised (e.g. by STRESS [3] or incorrect environmental conditions), will be more vulnerable to serious attack by, for example, protozoans, which may commonly be present in aquarium fish but in only relatively harmless numbers under normal circumstances. Fish which are suffering from SENILITY (3) or weakened by another disease may be more vulnerable than a young healthy specimen.

In the wild, parasites rarely pose serious disease problems to fish. This is because the infection levels on wild fish tend to be very low, and this stems largely from the low density of fish within the water such that parasites have difficulty in locating and engaging their host. Thus, even for those parasites which undergo extensive multiplication, only a few ever find a host and survive. Furthermore, the fish's IMMUNITY (3) is known to limit the parasite burden in the case of some parasite species (e.g. *ICHTHYOPHTHIRIUS* [3], *PISCINOODINIUM* [3]). As a result, apparently healthy wild fish may actually be harbouring low numbers of parasites and often several parasite species may be found concurrently on a single fish.

Under aquarium conditions, however, where fish are relatively crowded within a confined space, parasites are more easily able to locate a fish, resulting in much higher, and hence much more serious, infections. Furthermore, fish which are subjected to chronic STRESS (3) caused, for example, by adverse aquarium conditions, are more prone to serious parasite outbreaks due to the inhibitory effects of stress on the fish's immune system.

It is doubtful whether all parasites can be totally excluded from the aquarium, but serious infections can generally be avoided by good husbandry and meticulous QUARANTINE (3).

PARASITIC FISH

A few species of fish are themselves parasitic on other fish.

The only parasitic behaviour of aquarium importance is that occasionally displayed by certain loricariid catfish such as *Plecostomus* spp., and the Chinese algae eater or sucking loach, *Gyrinocheilus aymonieri*. Although these fish are normally quite harmless, very occasionally a 'rogue' individual will develop a taste for the skin mucus of its tank-mates, often large cichlids. The 'parasite' will use its mouthparts to attach to the flank of its host and feed on the skin. Remarkably, the host fish sometimes appears unperturbed by such activity (which may, however, induce

Ventral view of a plecostomus, showing sucking mouth.

panic in nervous species/individuals); however, the consequences can be dangerous, for the 'parasite' is likely to inflict skin abrasions which may become infected. The only remedy is to isolate the offender.

A few other species of fish, including some cichlids, feed primarily (possibly exclusively) upon the fins or scales of other fish. This remarkable behaviour is considered by some authorities to be a form of parasitism. At present the only species regularly seen in captivity is a cichlid, *Genyochromis mento* from Lake Malawi, whose coloration and form mimic those of favoured victim species, such that it is sometimes accidentally imported by mistake. The presence of such a fish is quickly apparent!

pH
pH is the measure of the acidity or alkalinity of a liquid. Incorrect pH may be responsible for a number of problems in fish, including ACIDOSIS (3), ALKALOSIS (3), and pH SHOCK (3).
See also SECTION I: Providing the correct environment; Purchasing, transporting, and introducing stock.

pH SHOCK
See SHOCK (3).

PHENOXYETHANOL (PHENOXETHOL)
P (for anaesthetic use)
Phenoxyethanol is an ANAESTHETIC (3) which also has

BACTERICIDE (3) properties, and hence is sometimes used by veterinary surgeons when undertaking surgical procedures on fish. It is also a constituent of some proprietary aquarium remedies, and also available under the name Phenoxethol.

DOSAGE AND ADMINISTRATION
Phenoxyethanol is applied as a bath immersion. The anaesthetic dose varies according to the fish species and other factors (see discussion under ANAESTHETICS (3)). For aquarium remedies containing phenoxyethanol, dosage should be as per the manufacturer's instructions.

PIPERAZINE **P**

This ANTHELMINTHIC is sometimes used for the treatment of intestinal NEMATODES (3) such as *CAMALLANUS* (3). It is purchased as piperazine citrate.

DOSAGE AND ADMINISTRATION
Administration is orally, as a medicated food.
Piperazine citrate: mixed with moistened flakes or pellets (50 mg drug per 10 g food). The medicated food is fed exclusively for a period of 7 to 10 days. A repeat course, after a further 10-14 days, may be required.

PISCICOLA

One of several genera of leeches which are PARASITES (3) of fish, feeding on their host's blood. Leeches belong to the phylum Annelida (annelid worms) and occur as both free-living and parasitic species. Leeches are sometimes found in ornamental fish ponds but are rarely encountered in tropical aquaria. Occasionally, however, adult leeches or their eggs (cocoons) are sometimes accidentally introduced into the

Adult leech, about 3cm in length.

Photo: Ian Wellby.

Brown-black leech eggs (cocoons) on the underside of an aquarium rock. These cocoons are about 4mm in size

tropical aquarium via aquatic plants, stones, or live foods which have been collected from ornamental fish ponds or natural bodies of water. Although rarely causing serious diseases themselves, leeches are capable of transmitting TRYPANOSOMES (3) to fish.

Leeches leave their host from time to time, e.g. to lay their eggs, and can survive independently for 3 months. When seeking a host the leech lies in ambush, either on the bottom or on a convenient plant; when a fish passes it quickly attaches and moves across the host, locating an appropriate place to feed. It then pierces the skin and extracts blood.

SIGNS
Adult leeches are obvious by their large size (1-5 cm / $^1/_2$ - 2ins) and their worm-like appearance. Leeches have a extensible, segmented body which terminates at each end in a disc-shaped sucker, the anterior (oral) sucker usually being noticeably smaller than the posterior one. Leeches may seen attached to the body surfaces of a fish or more often are observed off the fish. They swim by undulating movements and crawl over surfaces by a stretching-looping action. Leeches should not be confused with harmless PLANARIAN (3) worms which are considerably smaller and flattened, and move over the aquarium glass and other surfaces by a gliding rather than a looping action.

The bite WOUNDS (3) caused by leeches may appear as one or more red or whitish circles on the body surface of the fish. The wounds are susceptible to SECONDARY INFECTIONS (3). Given that some leeches hide away after feeding, the wounds may be the only visible indication of a leech infestation. However, similar tissue damage may also be caused by other more commonly encountered diseases, such as ULCERS (3). Other clinical signs of leech attack are more vague and include ANAEMIA (3) and LETHARGY (2) due to blood loss; conversely the victim may be skittish and unsettled. Rarely do leeches cause the fish serious harm.

Inspection of the lower- and under-sides of large pebbles and stones within the aquarium, and of the bases of aquatic plants, may reveal leech cocoons. The firmly attached cocoons are typically brown to black in colour and oval in shape. They may be present in clusters.

It should be kept in mind that not all aquatic leeches are parasitic on fish. Hence the presence of adult leeches (or their cocoons) living freely within the aquarium may not necessarily indicate a problem. Unfortunately, the fish-parasitic leeches are extremely similar in appearance to the harmless species.

CAUSES
Several genera of leeches are known to infest fish; however much of the aquarium literature relates to *Piscicola*, one common Eurasian species being *P.geometra* which reaches a maximum size of about 5 cm (2 ins). In North America, *P.milneri* is common, but may in fact be a variant of *P. geometra*. Being primarily cold-water leeches, *P. geometra.* and *P. milneri* are two species which could be introduced into aquaria from natural water bodies or ornamental ponds.

PREVENTION AND TREATMENT
Leeches may not be easy to eradicate from the aquarium, so prevention is by far the best policy. In particular, wild-caught LIVE FOODS (3) (e.g. *Daphnia*, bloodworm) should be carefully examined for the presence of adult leeches. Closely inspect potential fish purchases for these and other large parasites, to avoid any risk from that source. Pond plants should never be introduced into the aquarium as they may transmit leeches and other pond parasites, as may stones, wood, and gravel collected from natural bodies of water inhabited by fish.

Individual leeches may be physically removed from the substrate using an aquarium net or siphon tube. SALT (3) (sodium chloride) is often effective in encouraging a feeding leech to detach from its host. Leeches may be eradicated from aquaria using ORGANOPHOSPHORUS COMPOUNDS (3) such as TRICHLORFON (3); however these chemicals are very toxic to animals and must be handled with extreme care (see note below). Due to the chemical resistance of the cocoon stage, it will usually be necessary to redose the aquarium after 2-3 weeks. Depending on temperature the eggs take 13-80 days to hatch from the cocoon, and the young leeches are mature after 19-24 days.

Note: In view of their extreme toxicity, organophosphorus treatments should be used in aquaria only if it is proven that fish-parasitic leeches are present: either by direct observation of attached leech(es), or by the appearance of bite wounds on fish in combination with the presence of unattached leeches or their cocoons.

PISCINOODINIUM

Dinoflagellate PROTOZOA (3) which cause the potentially lethal disease known as "velvet" or "freshwater velvet". Other common names are "gold dust disease" or "rust disease". *Piscinoodinium* is an ECTOPARASITE (3) which attacks a wide range of fish but is more commonly encountered on barbs and other cyprinids, gouramis, and killifish. Note: the generic name *Oodinium* is no longer valid, despite still being commonly cited in the aquarium literature.

The life-cycle of *Piscinoodinum* bears many similarities to that of *ICHTHYOPHTHIRIUS* (3). The parasitic stage, known as a trophont, is typically pear-shaped, and between 30 and 100 microns in length. It attaches to the fish's skin, fins, or gills, and anchors itself by means of its branched rhizoids (= rhizocysts) which embed into the tissues. The trophont remains on the fish for 3-6 days at tropical aquarium temperatures, where it feeds and grows (parasite nutrition is via photosynthesis and probably also by uptake of host material). At lower temperatures the life-cycle takes longer, for example up to 11 days at 15-17 degrees C (59-63 degrees F).

The parasitic phase ends when the trophont detaches from its host and forms a free-living reproductive CYST (3) (= tomont). Within the protective cyst, a series of cell divisions yield up to 256 infective forms known as dinospores (=

LIFE CYCLE OF *PISCINOODINIUM*

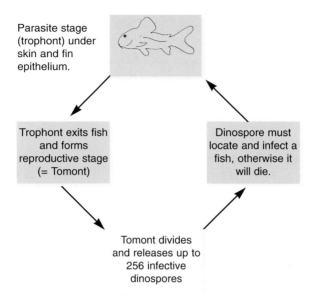

Parasite stage (trophont) under skin and fin epithelium.

Trophont exits fish and forms reproductive stage (= Tomont)

Dinospore must locate and infect a fish, otherwise it will die.

Tomont divides and releases up to 256 infective dinospores

gymnospores) which exit the ruptured cyst and become free-swimming. The dinospores are invisible to the unaided eye, usually no more than 20 microns in length and 15 microns in width. They are short-lived and must locate and infect a fish within 24-48 hours or so (at 25 degrees C (77 degrees F)), otherwise they die.

SIGNS
Piscinoodinium is capable of rapidly multiplying under aquarium conditions, resulting in the fish being exposed to waves of attack by the infective dinospores. Individual fish may sustain many tens, hundreds or even thousands of parasites. The parasitic trophonts may form clusters within areas of damaged skin. Under bright light the trophonts appear as tiny yellow-green SPOTS (2) over the fish (the colour is due to the presence of chloroplasts, used for photosynthesis). Under subdued or indirect light the trophonts appear greyish. Trophonts may reach almost 0.1 mm in length and are therefore much smaller than whitespot parasites (*ICHTHYOPHTHIRIUS* [3]).

Infected fish may exhibit a variety of symptoms,

depending on the severity of the disease, including
FLASHING (2), CLAMPED FINS (2) or FIN
TWITCHING (2), MUCUS HYPERPRODUCTION (2),
and RESPIRATORY DISTRESS (2) (increased gill rate). In
heavy infections the fish sometimes appear as if peppered
with a fine yellow-golden dust (hence the common name
gold-dust disease). Severe cases may result in areas of the
fish's skin sloughing off, possibly causing OSMOTIC
STRESS (3). Badly affected fish lose their APPETITE (2)
and exhibit general LETHARGY (2). In the absence of
treatment, heavy infections often result in death. The
disease appears to be more pathogenic to fry and juvenile
fish.

CAUSES
Two species of *Piscinoodinium* (phylum Sarcomastigo-
phora) have been recorded from freshwater aquarium fish:
P. pillulare and *P. limneticum.*

PREVENTION AND TREATMENT
Studies on the closely related *Amyloodinium* (which causes
a similar disease in marine fish) indicate that fish which
survive a dinoflagellate infection may develop a degree of
immunity to the parasite. Some fish in the aquarium may
therefore be already immune to velvet (sometimes due to an
infection prior to purchase), whereas others may be
completely susceptible. This difference in immune status
between individual fish may partly explain why some fish
suffer heavy infections during a velvet outbreak whereas
others in the same aquarium appear to sustain few or no
parasites. There are also species differences in
susceptibility. Three to four weeks QUARANTINE (3) of
newly acquired fish will enable the aquarist to screen out
most, if not all, cases of velvet.

Adverse aquarium conditions are believed to be
predisposing factors in serious outbreaks of velvet.
Maintaining the fish under optimal, STRESS (3)-free
conditions will help ensure that they are better able to
develop partial immunity to velvet and thus improve their
chances of survival.

Chemical control can be achieved using a proprietary anti-
velvet remedy available from aquarium retailers. QUININE

(3) and COPPER (3) treatments may also be effective (however, copper is not well tolerated by some species of fish, so use with caution and according to the manufacturer's instructions). Only the free-living dinospores are thought to be susceptible to chemical treatments.

The addition of SALT (3) to the water is also effective, provided the fish species to be treated are physiologically able to withstand a long term exposure to salt.

The intensity of infection within an aquarium can be reduced by keeping the aquarium dark. Dark conditions help prevent photosynthesis by the parasitic trophonts and also prevent dinospore development. This control strategy, which is useful in cases of high infection, should not be used alone but as an adjunct to chemical treatment.

An infected aquarium can usually be cleared of *Piscinoodinium* by leaving it free of all fish for a minimum of 14 days (ideally, 21 days). This fish-free period allows time for any cysts within the system to release their short-lived infective dinospores. It will, of course, be necessary to treat the removed fish before returning them to the aquarium.

Increased TEMPERATURE [3] (to 28 degrees C [82.5 degrees F]) can be used to accelerate the life-cycle of the parasite, ensuring all encysted stages hatch and are impacted by the treatment, and thus effecting a speedier cure. However, this strategy should be undertaken only with care, if at all, because of the danger of causing the fish additional RESPIRATORY STRESS (3).

PLANARIANS

These harmless, free-living flatworms are often mistaken for fish parasites such as LEECHES (3).

Planarians are elongate worms, typically measuring between 2 mm and 10 mm in length, and are usually creamy-white, grey, or brown in colour. Characteristic features are their V-shaped heads and their slow, gliding movement over aquarium surfaces. They may be accidentally introduced into the aquarium via aquatic plants or live foods.

Planarians are often first noticed on the viewing glass of the aquarium. They may sometimes reach epidemic numbers and this often reflects an accumulation of organic waste matter in the aquarium, sometimes symptomatic of OVERFEEDING (3) (uneaten food). Sensible feeding and good aquarium hygiene, including the regular siphoning of debris from the surface of the gravel, will help keep their numbers in check. Certain types of fish, such as gouramis (Anabantidae), may also help control planarians by preying on them.

PLEISTOPHORA

A genus of PROTOZOAN PARASITES (3) which infect the muscle tissues of fish. Of aquarium importance is *Pleistophora hyphessobryconis* which causes neon tetra disease. This disease was originally described from two Amazonian tetras, the neon *(Paracheirodon innesi)* and the glowlight *(Hemigrammus erythrozonus)* but has subsequently been recorded from a small number of other tetra species as well as a few cyprinids (including zebra danios *[Brachydanio rerio]*, certain barbs, and goldfish *[Carassius auratus]*).

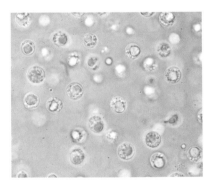

Microsporidian spores, as seen under the high-power microscope.

SIGNS
Low level infections can be asymptomatic. In moderate to heavy infections the fish's colours fade, and grey or white PATCHES (2) may appear under the skin. Destruction of muscle tissues by the parasites causes the fish's body to appear contorted and the fish may swim abnormally. The disease can spread to the organs. Those fish suffering from advanced disease may exhibit EMACIATION (2), and death often ensues.

CAUSES
The disease is caused by a spore-forming parasite, *Pleistophora hyphessobryconis* (Phylum Microspora). Fish acquire the disease through the accidental ingestion of spores, for example from foraging on a dead infected fish (see CANNIBALISM (3)). Once inside a fish's gut the parasite invades the body tissues where it multiplies and spreads, eventually forming masses of spores within the host's musculature. Each spore is oval in shape, measuring approximately 6 x 4 microns. There is a host tissue reaction which may be effective in destroying the spores.

PREVENTION AND TREATMENT
There are no effective treatments commercially available at present; however, experimental studies using TOLTRA-ZURIL (3) have shown promise. Preventative measures are therefore paramount and include isolation of affected fish and prompt removal of fish carcases from the aquarium. The infective spores may remain viable in an aquarium for many months, making it difficult to completely eradicate this disease. Given the limited host range of *Pleistophora* the likelihood of renewed outbreaks can be reduced by restocking the aquarium with fish species which are not considered susceptible to this disease. In some cases the fish's immune system may combat the parasite and hence effect a self-cure.

Note: related MICROSPORIDIAN (3) parasites of the genus *HETEROSPORIS* (3) cause muscle damage and mortalities in juvenile angelfish (*Pterophyllum* spp.) and loricariid catfish *(Ancistrus cirrhosis)*.

POISONING
Poisoning is a common cause of illness and death in aquarium fish. Poisons may be ingested, or absorbed via the gills. Poisoning is often acute, with numerous rapid deaths, and can be traced to a recent 'event' in or near the aquarium. However, a poison may sometimes be present in relatively harmless concentrations, and then, because fish tend to accumulate certain chemicals within their tissues (often reaching hundreds or thousands of times concentration), chronic poisoning may result. In such cases the problem may be difficult to diagnose, and the cause even more difficult to identify.

SIGNS

The signs of poisoning are non-specific, and other causes such as OXYGEN STARVATION (3) and infectious diseases may need to be considered.

Mild or chronic poisoning normally manifests as general slight debility, perhaps with an increased susceptibility to other diseases, e.g. SKIN SLIME DISEASE (3). The eyes may appear glazed and staring; the fish may swim on the spot and/or SHIMMY (2). Respiratory rate is usually increased. Loss of APPETITE (2) is common. Generally, some species/individuals are affected more than others. Death may eventually result unless the source of toxicity is identified and eliminated, but fish die singly rather than *en masse*.

Severe (acute) poisoning is additionally characterised by signs of serious malaise: RESPIRATORY DISTRESS (2) (GASPING [2] at the surface or 'panting' while lying on the substrate); loss of motor control; sometimes heightened COLORATION (2) due to chromatophore activation. Many or all fish die quickly and in rapid succession.

CAUSES

Toxins can be divided into the natural and the unnatural. The former are by-products of the life process and the nitrogen cycle – CARBON DIOXIDE (3), AMMONIA (3), NITRITE (3), NITRATE (3) – whose presence is inevitable but which should not normally be present in dangerous concentrations if the aquarium is properly maintained.

Unnatural toxins are legion; the following list of poisons (actually known to have been responsible for fish deaths) is by no means exhaustive – many other substances will be toxic if added to the aquarium:

Medications (overdoses and mixtures); horticultural pesticides and fertilisers (contaminated stones, flowerpots from the garden); paint or chemical fumes; domestic insecticides (e.g. fly spray, moth killer); aerosol polishes; varnish (applied to bogwood and ingested by wood-gnawing species, e.g. *Uaru* cichlids, some catfish); COPPER (3) (from modern domestic pipework and hot water cylinders); lead (from old domestic pipework); toxic minerals (e.g. arsenic) in rocks; many plastics; toxic live plants (occasionally sold for aquarium use, e.g.

Dieffenbachia); chemicals used by water companies in tap water (not just regular bactericides such as CHLORINE (3) or CHLORAMINE (3), but insecticides used to kill unwelcome invertebrates in mains pipework); metals (e.g. aluminium from saucepans used to boil peat); soaps and detergents (used to wash equipment/hands, and inadequately rinsed).

In addition, poorly stored fish foods can, in rare cases, cause poisoning due to AFLATOXINS (3).

PREVENTION AND TREATMENT
Poisoning should be avoided by exercising extreme care regarding items used in the aquarium, or chemicals and other potential toxins used in it, in its vicinity, or on its equipment. *(See also SECTION I: The Correct Environment.)*

In cases of severe toxicity move the affected fish to an uncontaminated aquarium, or if none is available, remove the source of contamination (if possible) and perform successive large water changes. This may result in an effective total change of water, not normally recommended but in some circumstances the only hope of saving any fish. It must be understood, however, that the likelihood of any fish surviving severe chemical toxicity is extremely small.

The same principles apply to mild toxicity, except that it is not necessary to remove the fish, and, once the source of contamination has been removed, a number of partial (e.g. 25-35 per cent) water changes over the next few days may eliminate the problem provided toxins have not accumulated in the fish's body tissues. The aquarist must balance the likely ill effects of the level of toxicity and of the treatment: too drastic a treatment might be more harmful than the basic problem.

In the case of natural poisons, simply increasing water circulation (aeration) should eliminate any excess of CO_2; water changes should be used to reduce levels of nitrogen cycle by-products, and in the longer term improving biological filtration and modifying the regular maintenance/feeding regime may be desirable.

Severe poisoning may have permanent or long-term effects on any survivors, and EUTHANASIA (3) may be necessary if obvious suffering is involved.

POLLUTION

Contamination of the aquarium water by organic or inorganic toxins. See also POISONING (3), RAINWATER (3), NITROGENOUS WASTES (3).

POP-EYE

See EXOPHTHALMIA (3).

POTASSIUM PERMANGANATE

This powerful oxidizing agent has been used to treat ECTOPARASITES (3) and BACTERIAL INFECTIONS (3) of the skin in pond fish; however, it is not generally recommended for aquarium fish as many species are sensitive to this chemical. The toxicity of potassium permanganate increases in alkaline pH conditions. Potassium permanganate is available in solid form (crystals) or as a stock solution.

DOSAGE AND ADMINISTRATION
Exceptionally, potassium permanganate has been applied as a short bath (5 to 10 mg/litre, for 30 minutes) to treat heavy infestations of fish louse (*ARGULUS* (3)).

Potassium permanganate can be used to sterilise aquarium plants. The plants are immersed in a very dilute solution (rose wine coloured) for 5-10 minutes.

PRAZIQUANTEL   **P**

An ANTHELMINTHIC (3) sometimes used to combat tapeworms (CESTODES (3), in the gut) and MONOGENETIC FLUKES (3).

DOSAGE AND ADMINISTRATION
Monogenea: Short-duration bath: 2 mg per litre, for 2-3 hours. A repeat bath, after 1 week, may be required.
Gut tapeworms: Orally, via medicated food: 50 mg per kg of fish body weight per day. Feed the medicated food exclusively for 1-2 days.

PROTOZOAN PARASITES

Some of the more commonly encountered infectious diseases of aquarium fish are caused by protozoan parasites, notable examples being ICHTHYOPHTHIRIASIS (3) and velvet disease (*PISCINOODINIUM* (3)). Other protozoan parasites of aquarium fish include: *CHILODONELLA* (3), *HEXAMITA* (3), *ICHTHYOBODO* (3), *PLEISTOPHORA* (3), *TETRAHYMENA* (3), *TRICHODINA* (3), and TRYPANOSOMES (3).

Protozoa are single-celled organisms, the majority of species being microscopic; however, a few, such as *Ichthyophthirius* and *Piscinoodinium,* are just visible to the unaided eye. Some species are ECTOPARASITES (3) on fish while others invade the fish's skin, internal organs, or even the blood. Many of the ectoparasitic and skin-dwelling protozoa can be combated using proprietary aquarium remedies, whereas those which invade the deeper tissues and organs of the fish tend to be more difficult to eradicate.

PSEUDOMONAS

A genus of gram-negative rod-shaped BACTERIA (3). Some *Pseudomonas* species cause BACTERIAL INFECTIONS (3) in fish, resulting in symptoms such as ULCERS (2) and/or FIN EROSION (2). Such infections may be fatal. Proprietary anti-bacterial remedies are sometimes effective, otherwise a course of ANTIBIOTICS (3) will be necessary.

Q

QUARANTINE

The segregation of one or more individual fish, or an aquarium, to minimise the risk of spreading disease.

Newly purchased fish should be quarantined for 2 to 4 weeks and observed for signs of any disease, in order to avoid introducing pathogens into an established aquarium containing healthy fish. The quarantine period also permits the new fish to recover from TRANSPORTATION STRESS (3) and provides an opportunity for any adjustments to water chemistry required.

Any aquarium affected by (suspected) infectious disease should also be quarantined. Fish, decor, equipment, hands, and accidental water splashes, can also transmit diseases

and hence the quarantine/hospital aquarium should, ideally, be physically distanced from the main aquaria.
See also SECTION I: Purchasing, Transporting, and Introducing Fish.

QUININES P

These anti-PROTOZOAN (3) compounds are well known for their value in treating human malaria and have sometimes been used to eradicate certain protozoan infections of aquarium fish.

Quinines have been used to treat whitespot (ICHTHY-OPHTHIRIASIS [3]) but have now been largely superseded by proprietary anti-whitespot remedies. Some success has been reported using quinine to combat marine velvet (*Amyloodinium*), the drug apparently killing the free-living dinospores. Its use for treating freshwater velvet (*PISCINOODINIUM*) therefore seems worth investigating.

DOSAGE AND ADMINISTRATION
For treating (marine) velvet disease: Chloroquine diphosphate:
● prolonged bath (hospital tank): 10 mg per litre, for 3 days. A repeat dose may be necessary.
● entire aquarium: dose as above. The quinine will decompose with time; however, it is best to undertake a series of partial water changes after a few days, to dilute out the drug. Filtering over activated carbon will also remove quinine from the water.

Note: Certain fish may be highly intolerant of quinine, as are many aquatic invertebrates. Monitor the fish during treatment for signs of quinine toxicity.

R

RAIN WATER *(AS A POLLUTANT)*

Rain water is frequently used as a natural water source for aquaria, particularly for fish which prefer soft, neutral to acid water conditions. Unfortunately, rain water must nowadays be considered potentially unsafe as a result of increasing atmospheric pollution, particularly in urban areas. In contrast to pure water which has a neutral pH (pH

7.0), rain water is naturally acid, averaging around pH 5.6, and this acidity is caused by its contact in the atmosphere with CARBON DIOXIDE (3) and natural sulphur compounds. Sulphur dioxide and other chemical emissions from power stations and other human industries has resulted in certain parts of the world (including Europe and North America) receiving precipitation which is extremely acid, as low as pH 4.0 – the so-called "acid rain" phenomenon. The pH of rain water should therefore be checked before adding to aquaria. Contamination of rain water with toxic metals or pollutants may occur during contact with roofs and gutters and during storage in metal and some plastic water butts.

The addition of highly acid rain water to the aquarium may cause a sudden pH drop, particularly in soft water conditions. Such sudden downward pH shifts will STRESS (3) the fish, and in extreme cases cause ACIDOSIS (3) and/or pH SHOCK (3) in susceptible species.

Reverse osmosis (RO) units provide alternatives to rain water for creating soft, acid water conditions in aquaria in regions where the mains water is mineral-rich.

See also POISONING (3).

REPRODUCTIVE FAILURE

Reproductive failure in fish is a problem commonly experienced by aquarists. It may range from failure of the fish to show any interest whatsoever in breeding, through various other manifestations to the death of fry at the newly free-swimming stage. The following are some of the commoner problems, with some possible causes:

1) Failure to spawn:
• Only one sex present.
• Environmental factors (e.g. water chemistry, quality; temperature) incorrect, causing STRESS (3).
• Necessary environmental trigger (e.g. enriched diet, change in temperature) lacking.
• AGGRESSION (3) causing STRESS (3).
• Oocytes failing to develop in ovary – probably due to environmental or dietary problems.
• Fish too old or otherwise functionally sterile.
• Fish too young.

A hybrid cichlid (Pseudotropheus socolofi x Melanochromis auratus).

● Female not ripe (i.e. eggs not yet developed sufficiently to be laid).

● In territorial species, fish unable to secure a suitable territory.

● Inappropriate decor, e.g. suitable spawning medium/ substrate absent.

● Inappropriate lighting – usually insufficient light, causing underdevelopment of gonads due to lack of stimulation of the pituitary gland *(see SECTION I: Biology and Anatomy).*

2) Eggs fail to hatch

● Functional sterility of one or both fish.

● Inappropriate (for the species) water chemistry or poor water quality affecting viability of eggs and/or sperm.

● Only one sex present. In some cichlid species two females may 'pair off' and spawn. This happens only where no male is present. Oscars *(Astronotus ocellatus),* blue acaras *(Aequidens pulcher),* and angels *(Pterophyllum scalare)* are notorious for this behaviour.

● The male is too young (or old) to produce (viable) sperm, even though he appears to fertilise the eggs. Common in young tankbred fish. In nature females would seek out older, stronger males, but in captivity do not always have this option.

● The male is not interested. This may be due to ill-health, STRESS (3), youth or old age, functional sterility. In some cases (e.g. West African cichlids of the genus *Pelvicachromis)* competition from conspecific males is sometimes necessary to stimulate male interest in the female.

● The male was driven away by a male of another, usually closely related, species, who took over his role. Such cross-matings may also result in HYBRIDIZATION (3).

3) Failure to spawn or eggs fail to hatch
● Hybrid fish (the progeny of a cross between species) may be functionally sterile or all one sex. (see also HYBRIDIZATION (3)). Breeding from hybrids is in any case undesirable.
● DISEASE (3) (e.g. TUMOURS (3), fat deposition resulting from incorrect diet) can have an adverse effect on the gonads, causing sterility.
● Certain chemical remedies, notably MALACHITE GREEN (3), are thought possibly to cause sterility in fish.
● Genetic manipulation of fish, such as hormone-induced sex reversal, is now being commercially practised on a limited number of ornamental fish species. This procedure may be undertaken in order to achieve all male fish (in those species where the males are more popular and/or command higher prices, such as guppies), or, in the case of some commercial fish breeders, to prevent competition from amateurs. Obviously, if only single sex fish are available to the aquarist then there will be no opportunities to breed from them (and hence no competition for commercial breeders), an undesirable situation from the point of view of the serious amateur aquarist.

4) The eggs fungus (EGG FUNGUS [3])
● Eggs infertile.
● Poor water quality or sudden environmental (temperature, chemistry) change harmed the eggs. Exposing eggs to unnaturally hard water (for the species in question) may cause them to fail to develop.

5) The parents ate the eggs or fry
● Cannibalism is common in non-parental species, and to be expected unless suitable precautions are taken by the aquarist.
In parental species:
● The parents realised the eggs were not viable, and recycled the protein with a view to a further spawning soon afterwards.
● The parents were subject to undue STRESS (3), and ate their eggs/fry in order to try again when conditions were more suitable.
● The brood (initially or after early losses) was too small to

be worth the 'investment' of time and effort required for rearing, in terms of the likelihood of any fry surviving to ensure genetic perpetuation.

(With reference to the above two entries, the 'economics' of brood care in cichlids has been the subject of some research: the more time the parents have 'invested' in their brood, the less likely they are to give up trying to rear them.)

● Behavioural defect. This problem is common in some species, most notably angelfish *(Pterophyllum scalare),* and appears to be linked to artificial hatching. It remains unclear whether the problem is genetic (natural selection would weed out egg/fry-cannibals among parental species) or because parental behaviour needs to be learned. The fact that F_1 offspring of wild cichlids, artificially hatched, exhibit a high rate of egg-cannibalism, points to the latter cause.

● The parents ate the fry after several days/weeks, then spawned again. In nature the fry would have dispersed before this stage was reached; in the aquarium they were unable to do so, and the parents had to eat them to create a safe environment, free of possible enemies, for the next brood.

6) Tankmates ate the eggs/fry

● This is only to be expected, although parental species may succeed in rearing part of their brood. A common problem is nocturnal predators (e.g. catfish, including 'plecostomus' types) eating the brood of largely diurnal parental fish (e.g. cichlids) during the hours of darkness. This is often wrongly interpreted as parental egg cannibalism.

7) The fry failed to become free-swimming

● Environmental problems, especially poor water quality, or sudden changes in temperature or chemistry.

● Genetic problems (e.g. BELLYSLIDING (2)), possibly due to INBREEDING (3).

8) The fry became free-swimming but died

● As for (7).

● The fry starved because the wrong type of, or insufficient, food was provided.

● CARBON DIOXIDE (3) levels were too low.

9) Some or all of the fry were deformed
● As for (7).

10) Livebearer-specific problems
● A few of the long-finned varieties of livebearer (e.g. long-finned swordtails) have an extremely elongate gonopodium (the intromittent organ) such that they are unable to copulate. Although perfectly capable of producing viable sperm, the males are functionally sterile and can only be bred by extracting their sperm via a pipette and then artificially inseminating the female.
See also SECTION I: Breeding.

RESPIRATORY DISTRESS
A condition affecting fish which are suffering from a lack of OXYGEN (3) to their tissues.
Major signs of respiratory distress are:
● Increased rate of gill beats (increased breathing rate).
● GASPING (2) or gulping (the fish may be HANGING (2) at the water's surface (where the oxygen level is higher) but ultimately may become too exhausted to remain there).
   The various possible environmental and physiological causes of respiratory distress are discussed under OXYGEN STARVATION (3).

ROUNDWORMS
See NEMATODE WORMS (3).

RUST DISEASE
See PISCOODINIUM (3).

S

SALT
Common salt (Sodium chloride, NaCl).
   Salt has long been used as an aquarium ANTISEPTIC (3) and FUNGICIDE (3). Although strong solutions were formerly used to treat actual outbreaks of FUNGAL INFECTION (3), nowadays it is more usual to use a proprietary aquarium fungicide for that purpose. Nevertheless a mild (0.1-0.2%) salt solution, preferably

administered in a hospital tank, remains a useful prophylactic against fungal and BACTERIAL INFECTION (3) following INJURY (3).

Salt was formerly commonly used routinely as a 'tonic', regardless of its appropriateness or otherwise to the water chemistry requirements of the fish concerned; its ability to inhibit bacterial and fungal infections may have encouraged this usage before it was generally understood that good aquarium hygiene, including efficient biological filtration, is a more appropriate method of preventing minor ailments.

Salt has also commonly been used to "increase hardness and pH" (which it doesn't!) for Rift Valley cichlids; this usage has been identified as a major cause of MALAWI BLOAT (3).

It is important not to use domestic table salt, which usually contains additives which may prove toxic. Block cooking salt, or crystallised sea salt, are normally safe, but the product of choice is 'aquarium salt'. Some freshwater tropical fish are highly intolerant of salt, as are many aquarium plants. Because most freshwater aquarium remedies are intended for use on brackish water fish as well, they can generally be used in conjunction with salt, unless otherwise stated in the manufacturer's instructions.

DOSAGE AND ADMINISTRATION
● As a prophylactic: 1-2 level teaspoons of salt per gallon (1-2 g/litre) of aquarium water, producing a 0.1-0.2% solution. The salt should be pre-dissolved in a suitable small amount of aquarium water, which is then added to the aquarium.
● As a treatment for fungal/bacterial infection: A solution of up to 1% (10g/litre) can be used provided the fish shows no signs of distress. This concentration should be achieved gradually over a period of 24-48 hours, to avoid OSMOTIC STRESS (3) or SHOCK (3). An initial solution of 0.1-0.2% (as above) should be increased in 0.1% increments at intervals of 4-6 hours. If the fish appears distressed by an increase in the concentration, reduce it immediately by a partial water change.
● As a means of reducing NITRITE (3) toxicity: up to 1g per litre, added to the affected aquarium.
● As a means of detaching feeding leeches (e.g.

PISCICOLA (3)): A short-duration bath in 2.5% salt solution will often cause a feeding leech to detach from the fish, but will not kill the leech.
● As a treatment for *PISCINOODINIUM* (3) (velvet disease): A long-duration bath in salt (1 level teaspoonful per 5 gallons; 10 g per 45 litres).

SAPROLEGNIA
A genus of fungus belonging to the Class Oomycetes. In the aquarium hobby, *Saprolegnia* is frequently used as a general name to describe any type of cotton-wool-like fungal growth on the body surface of fish. In fact, several genera of Oomycetes fungi are known to cause FUNGAL INFECTIONS (3) on fish.

LEFT: Saprolegnia on the tail.

BELOW: Secondary infection of an ulcer with Saprolegnia. Photo: David Bucke.

SCOLIOSIS
See SKELETAL DEFORMITIES (3)

SECONDARY INFECTIONS
Secondary infections are caused by opportunistic pathogens which invade tissues already damaged by a previous or existing infection (a so-called primary infection). Commonly encountered secondary infections include those caused by FUNGUS (3) (e.g. *SAPROLEGNIA* [3]). and

Severe skin damage by ectoparasites has resulted in secondary bacterial infection, causing skin haemorrhaging.

various pathogenic BACTERIA (3).

The tissue damage inflicted by ECTOPARASITES (3) and skin-dwelling parasites (e.g. MONOGENETIC FLUKES (3), *ARGULUS* (3), LEECHES (3), *ICHTHYOPHTHIRIUS* [3]). may lead to secondary infections.

Prophylactic treatment with anti-fungal and anti-bacterial remedies is recommended where secondary infections are likely.

SENILITY

Evidence of senility is encountered more commonly among aquarium fish (and ornamental pond fish) than in those living in the wild. This difference relates to the high risk of predation among wild fish, especially among those weakened by any factor including DISEASE (3) or INJURY (3) and/or age, resulting in very few individuals reaching an old age.

Physiologically, senility may involve the deterioration of vital organs causing their eventual failure, leading to the death of the fish. Senile fish may have a lowered immunity to disease and are therefore more prone to FUNGAL DISEASES (3) and certain other infections. Some species of cichlids may show an increased susceptibility to HEXAMITIASIS (3).

The lifespan of fish varies, often roughly in line with size, small fish being generally shorter-lived. Small fish with an adult size of 1-2 ins (2.5 - 5cm) may have a natural lifespan of only one year (and a single breeding season) in the wild, and maybe twice that in captivity. Some large (12 ins+ [30cm+]). cichlids and the giant gourami *(Osphronemus goramy)* have been recorded as living for upwards of 10 years in captivity.

Senility in Corydoras catfish

Young adult – no signs of senility.

Senile specimen (12 years old), with eroded caudal fin. The fish exhibits lethargy and poor swimming ability.

SIGNS
Clinical signs sometimes associated with senility include abnormal SWIMMING (2) behaviour (such as swimming head downwards), paling of body COLORATION (2), EXOPHTHALMIA (2), and CLOUDY EYES (2) due to cataracts. Osteoarthritis may develop and this can affect the fish's swimming ability. The fins may take on a 'gnarled' appearance with twisted rays. There may be an increased likelihood of TUMOURS (3). The fish may exhibit EMACIATION (2), either through loss of APPETITE (2) or through increasing inability to compete successfully at feeding time.

PREVENTION AND TREATMENT
Obviously ageing itself cannot be treated. However, steps can be taken to alleviate some of the associated problems. Elderly fish may require housing by themselves or with less competitive tankmates than previously, in order to avoid bullying or slow starvation through inability to secure enough food.

An elderly fish which becomes severely incapacitated in any way by its years, so as to cause obvious or likely suffering, should be regarded as a candidate for EUTHANASIA (3).

It is unwise to purchase obviously elderly fish, and it should be borne in mind that in small species this may equate with full-grown individuals.

SHOCK
A physiological response to sudden trauma of various kinds, commonly too abrupt an alteration in one or more environmental factors.

SIGNS
The nature of the clinical signs may be influenced by the cause and severity of the shock, and include: loss of colour, abnormal respiratory rate (increased or decreased), RESTING (2) on the bottom, occasionally moving to another location in jerky bursts. In more severe cases, the fish may lie on its side or even belly-up.

CAUSES
Shock is typically observed in fish newly introduced to an aquarium, but may also occur following a partial water change if insufficient attention was paid to matching the temperature and chemistry of the new water to that of the aquarium. In all types of shock, susceptibility varies from species to species and even from individual to individual.

Male Apistogramma macmasteri resting on the substrate, in shock, after having been moved to a new tank.

The same fish showing normal coloration and deportment.

Temperature shock is caused by a sudden change of temperature, with a decrease more likely to promote severe shock. Fish usually react immediately to such changes.

Osmotic or chemical shock is caused by a sudden change in water chemistry (e.g. a significant change in hardness/pH/salinity), and signs are typically delayed, manifesting only after 24-72 hours, in line with the gradual and continuous exchange of body fluids with the surrounding medium. Commonly fatal.

Toxic shock is caused by sudden exposure to high concentrations of toxins, including AMMONIA (3), NITRITE (3), and NITRATE (3). Nitrate shock may, like osmotic shock, take some time to manifest, and, like it, is often fatal.

Transportation STRESS (3) and other major disturbances to the fish may also produce shock-like signs.

PREVENTION AND TREATMENT
Prevention is paramount, as serious shock can be fatal. Immediate reversal should be effected in cases where the onset of shock is rapid – e.g. temperature, acute POISONING (3). This may entail the removal of newly-introduced fish to a more congenial environment, as adjusting the aquarium conditions rapidly is likely to in turn send resident fish into shock. Where shock follows a water change, however, the aquarium conditions should be corrected.

In the case of delayed (osmotic, nitrate) shock, any attempt to remedy the problem after it has become apparent is unlikely to be beneficial and may even cause further trauma.

In all cases of shock it is essential to minimise STRESS (3).
See also TRANSPORTATION STRESS (3); SECTION I: Purchasing, Transporting, and Introducing Stock.

SIAMESE TWINS
This is fairly common among certain livebearing fish such as guppies *(Poecilia reticulata)*. Often one of the twins is severely underdeveloped and hangs from the belly region of its sibling. In some cases the joined fry may survive to adulthood; however, their quality of life is very poor and for this reason they should be humanely destroyed at birth (see

EUTHANASIA (3)). Siamese twins have also occasionally been recorded in egglaying fish.
See also DEFORMITIES (3).

SKELETAL DEFORMITIES

Distortion of the vertebral column is often the most obvious skeletal deformity, as this can affect the fish's general body shape.

Rainbowfish with pronounced curvature of the spine.

SIGNS
The fish's backbone may appear bent, laterally (in the horizontal plane) (= scoliosis) and/or vertically (= lordosis). Swimming ability may be affected, depending on the severity of the deformity.

CAUSES
Skeletal deformity may arise from collision INJURY (3), infectious disease, nutritional deficiencies, or be the result of a genetic or developmental abnormality.
● Injury: In the case of highly active species, the fish may have collided at speed with the aquarium glass/decor, or perhaps with the aquarium cover as a result of jumping out of the water.
● Infectious diseases: Certain systemic infections, notably MYCOBACTERIOSIS (3), can cause damage to skeletal tissues, resulting in distorted vertebrae.
● Nutritional deficiencies: Deficiency in dietary phosphorus, calcium, or vitamin C may lead to skeletal deformities in fish. *See also NUTRITIONAL DISEASES (3), VITAMIN DEFICIENCY (3).*
● Genetic and developmental disorders: Skeletal deform-

ities may be the result of genetic abnormalities, perhaps due to INBREEDING (3), or they may have occurred during the early development of the fish.

● Deformed varieties: Some commercially produced varieties of 'ornamental' fish – such as the "blood red parrot" (a hybrid, not to be confused with the true parrot cichlid [*Hoplarchus psittacus*]). – possess a deformed body contour which appears as if the fish has a broken spine.

PREVENTION AND TREATMENT
The careful selection of good breeding stock and the provision of suitable water conditions during rearing should help prevent genetic and developmental skeletal deformities from occurring. Good water conditions and aquarium hygiene will also reduce the likelihood of mycobacterial infections.

Dietary-linked deformities are unlikely to occur if a well balanced and varied diet is given. Skeletal damage through collision injury is less easy to prevent, other than by providing stress-free conditions which will reduce the likelihood of the fish taking fright and darting through the water.

Once developed, skeletal deformities cannot be rectified. EUTHANASIA (3) may be necessary, and CULLING (3) of deformed fry regarded as essential.

Deformed fish should not be purchased. Given the probable suffering experienced by "cultivated deformities" such as "blood red parrots", "balloon mollies", and many "fancy" goldfish, the responsible aquarist will avoid such fish as well.

SKIN DISEASES

These are the most commonly reported diseases of fish since they usually give rise to obvious clinical symptoms such as ULCERS (2), GROWTHS (2), HAEMORRHAGES (2), sloughed skin, etc. Skin diseases may be due to environmental problems (e.g. adverse pH (ACIDOSIS [3], ALKALOSIS [3]), high levels of AMMONIA [3]), infectious diseases (e.g. BACTERIAL (3) or VIRUS INFECTIONS [3], ECTOPARASITES [3]). or non-infectious diseases (e.g. TUMOURS [3]).

Abdominal haemorrhaging on a killifish.

White patches on a female guppy. Microscopical examination is necessary to determine whether these are caused by bacteria or ectoparasites.

SKIN PARASITES

The skin of fish is the site of attack by several parasites. These include PROTOZOA (3) (e.g. *ICHTHY-OPHTHIRIUS* [3], *PISCINOODINIUM* [3], *TRICHODINA* [3]), MONOGENETIC FLUKES (3) (e.g. *GYRO-DACTYLUS*[3]), crustacea (e.g. *ARGULUS* [3], *LERNAEA* [3]), and LEECHES (3) (e.g. *PISCICOLA*[3]).

SKIN SLIME DISEASE

A general term for infection with a variety of PROTOZOAN PARASITES (3) such as *ICHTHYOBODO* (3) (Costia), *CHILODONELLA* (3), and *TRICHODINA* (3) *(Cyclochaeta)*, all of which cause MUCUS HYPER-PRODUCTION (2). Heavy infection with any of these parasites leads to skin damage, which may either allow SECONDARY INFECTION (3) (BACTERIAL (3) or FUNGAL [3]). to take hold, or lead directly to death. The disease is sometimes known as Costiasis, from *Costia*, now regarded as a synonym of *Ichthyobodo*.

SIGNS
The skin takes on a blue/white cloudiness, caused by a thick build-up of mucus (MUCUS HYPERPRODUCTION (2)),

Skin slime disease on a gourami. Note the white patches of mucus hyper-production around the upper head and back towards the dorsal fin. Parasitological exami-nation of a skin scrape may reveal the cause.

often between the head and the dorsal insertion, sometimes covering much of the head and body. The skin may appear roughened, and in severe cases scales may become detached and skin peel away in strips; there may also be FIN EROSION (2). The fish may FLASH (2) and SCRATCH (2) irritated areas against solid objects. If the gills are affected, there will be RESPIRATORY DISTRESS (2), the fish GASPING (2) for oxygen at the surface and COUGHING (2). Loss of APPETITE (2) and LETHARGY (2) (listless swimming) are also commonly associated with this disease.

CAUSE
Any one or a combination of the parasites listed above. It is not uncommon for small numbers of the causative parasites to be present on fish. If a fish harbouring low numbers of parasites is subsequently weakened or subject to STRESS (3) (for example as a result of poor nutrition, adverse water quality (NITROGENOUS WASTES (3)), or overcrowding) then the parasites may multiply and become a problem. The host's tissue response to the parasites (or even to other factors) may result in skin hyperplasia (= over-production of skin cells) and/or mucus hyperproduction, and this in turn may provide more food for the parasites, encouraging their proliferation, and leading to a vicious circle.

PREVENTION AND TREATMENT
Normally the entire aquarium is treated, because of the likelihood that all fish present will be affected to some degree. Treatment is normally with a proprietary remedy, following the manufacturer's instructions. The temperature should be raised to 28 degrees C (83F) during the treatment period. In the event that the proprietary medication proves ineffective, treatment with FORMALIN (3) or METRIPHONATE (3) is suggested.

In cases where *TRICHODINA* (3) has been microscopically diagnosed, removal (and bath treatment) of all the fish from the aquarium for 4 days should render it free of this parasite, due to the parasite's limited life away from its host. It is essential to identify and remedy the underlying cause(s) of the outbreak, otherwise recurrence is likely.

SNAILS

Although often perceived as useful 'scavengers', aquatic snails are generally undesirable in the aquarium since they frequently proliferate to epidemic numbers. Large quantities of decomposing snail faeces may cause water pollution problems, and the snails themselves are capable of transmitting certain parasitic diseases, such as *DIPLO-STOMUM* (3) (this disease risk relates only to recently wild-caught snails and not those which have been propagated in aquaria).

The snail population can be kept in check by routinely removing individuals, for example by scooping them up with a net, or siphoning them from the gravel and internal surfaces. This task is generally best undertaken in the evening, after the aquarium lights have been switched off for some time, since most snails are more active at night and will be easier to locate.

Chemicals which destroy snails (molluscicides) are commercially available and typically include COPPER (3) as the active ingredient. Unfortunately, copper is toxic to fish and hence molluscicidal treatments should be used with caution and never in overdose. Where practicable, remove the fish from the aquarium before applying molluscicides and undertake several water changes before returning the fish. Never add copper-based formulations to aquaria containing copper-sensitive fish, or invertebrates such as crabs and shrimps, as copper is highly toxic to these

A proliferation of snails in the aquarium may reflect poor environmental conditions.

creatures. Where the snail density is very high, the snail corpses should be removed following an application of molluscicide, otherwise their decomposing bodies may pollute the water. For this reason, care should be taken when using molluscicides to eradicate snails which burrow (e.g. *Melania tuberculata* – the Malayan pond snail) since their corpses may be difficult to retrieve without considerable disturbance to the substrate.

SODIUM THIOSULPHATE

This chemical is effective in neutralising toxic CHLORINE (3) in water supplies. It is usually purchased in the form of a proprietary aquarium water conditioner or dechlorinating solution. Dose rates are given by the manufacturer.

Sodium thiosulphate will also neutralise CHLORAMINE (3) but this reaction liberates toxic AMMONIA (3) which must itself be removed from the water. For this reason it is advisable to use a proprietary dechlorinator also intended for chloramine, as this will contain an ammonia remover as well.

SPAWN BINDING

See EGG BOUND (3).

SPINY HEADED WORMS

See ACANTHOCEPHALANS (3).

SPIRONUCLEUS

See HEXAMITA (3).

STERILITY (REPRODUCTIVE STERILITY)

The inability of fish to produce viable offspring.
See REPRODUCTIVE FAILURE (3); SECTION I: Breeding.

STRESS

Within the confines of an aquarium, stress situations can easily develop. Fish which are subjected to chronic stress, such as prolonged exposure to unsatisfactory environmental conditions or to constant bullying by tank-mates, are likely to suffer a gradual decline in their health, leading to death.

Stress can lower a fish's immunity and hence render it more prone to infectious diseases.

SIGNS
Stress may cause loss of APPETITE (2), or abnormal BEHAVIOUR (2) such as HIDING (2) away (including HANGING (2) in corners), erratic or panicky SWIMMING (2) (e.g. PANCAKING (2), JUMPING (2)), and general NERVOUSNESS (2). Fish which are stressed may show abnormal COLORATION (2) (commonly much darker than normal), due to the influence of stress-mediated hormones on the skin pigment cells. RESPIRATORY DISTRESS (2) (increased gill rate) is also a common symptom.

CAUSES
Aquarium stressors may be environmental (e.g. adverse water conditions, extremes of temperature, inadequate provision of shelter) or behavioural (such as AGGRESSION (3) by other fish). Several chemical disease remedies, although often of net benefit to the fish, are themselves stressors. Extraneous sources of stress, for example when a young child (or adult!) repeatedly taps on the aquarium glass, can be equally damaging to the fish. Transportation, or even movement from one aquarium to another within the domestic facility, can be extremely stressful.

PREVENTION AND TREATMENT
Providing a stress-free environment, and identifying and eliminating any cause of stress that may subsequently occur, is essential for the well-being of aquarium fish, and just as important as maintaining good water quality. This can be achieved only by meticulous attention to proper husbandry and choice of fish (as set out in SECTION I), and by continuing observation and remaining on the alert for any signs of a stress situation developing. **A stress-free aquarium is a sign of a good aquarist!**
See also TRANSPORTATION STRESS (3), SHOCK (3).

SULPHAMERAZINE   P

A sulphonamide drug which has bacteriostatic action. Once used to treat certain BACTERIAL INFECTIONS (3) such as *AEROMONAS* (3), it has largely been replaced by ANTIBIOTICS (3) and other BACTERICIDES (3).

SWIMBLADDER DISEASES

The swimbladder is a gas-filled buoyancy organ which is present in many, but not all, fish, providing them with buoyancy and avoiding the need to swim constantly to remain afloat in the water column.

Head-down posture in a "blood red parrot", caused by swim bladder disfunction.

Swimbladder problems are commonly encountered in some kinds of tropical aquarium fish (e.g. cichlids) as a result of internal INJURY (3) caused by AGGRESSION (3), as well as in certain stumpy-bodied varieties of fancy goldfish (their unnatural body shape causing swim-bladder derangement).

Some fish species, however, notably those that live in rapids (rheophilic species), commonly have a reduced or completely atrophied swimbladder, as buoyancy is a disadvantage in their specialised environment. It is perfectly normal for such fish to rest on the bottom or on decor/equipment items, and their absence of buoyancy does not denote ill-health.

SIGNS
Abnormal SWIMMING (2) behaviour, with loss of neutral BUOYANCY (2): the affected fish may have problems in keeping its position in the water column. The swimbladder may be damaged so that it is unable to deflate or inflate, causing the fish to either float to the surface or sink to the substrate, respectively. In some cases the fish may swim nose/tail down or swim/float/lie on its side or even upside-down.

CAUSES

Systemic BACTERIAL INFECTION (3) is a major causative factor. Certain species of PROTOZOA (3) (coccidia) and NEMATODE WORMS (3) (roundworms) may cause swimbladder problems in coldwater fish, but are rarely of aquarium importance in this respect. In territorial or quarrelsome fish, notably cichlids, damage is by far the most common cause of swimbladder dysfunction, usually as a result of (repeated) lateral ramming by an aggressor. Swimbladder problems may also result from pressure on the swimbladder caused by, for example, TUMOURS (3), CONSTIPATION (3), or DROPSY (3).

Loss or absence of buoyancy is a common symptom in the later stages of many other diseases, and (temporarily) in cases of SHOCK (3).

PREVENTION AND TREATMENT

Careful choice of fish and aggression management will help minimise problems caused by damage, but occasional swimbladder injuries are virtually inevitable if aggressive and/or territorial fish are kept together. Good aquarium hygiene will greatly reduce the chances of a systemic bacterial infection from occurring. Where a bacterial infection is suspected, treatment with ANTIBIOTICS (3) may sometimes remedy the swimbladder problem.

Transfer of the affected fish to an aquarium which is about 5 degrees C (9 degrees F) warmer (assuming this increased TEMPERATURE (3) is within the species' tolerance range) has sometimes proved effective, including in cases of damage. Maintaining the fish in shallow water is also considered helpful.

Where the fish is severely stressed by buoyancy problems and no improvement is apparent after 3 days of treatment, then EUTHANASIA (3) is probably the most humane solution.

Swimbladder problems are usually not infectious/contagious.

T

TAIL ROT
See FIN ROT (3)

TAPEWORMS
See CESTODES (3)

TAPWATER TOXICITY
POISONING (3) caused by any contaminant, including: agricultural chemicals (e.g. NITRATES (3), phosphates); minerals occurring naturally in the source water; metallic contamination from pipework (lead, COPPER (3)), and chemicals added by the water company (CHLORINE (3), CHLORAMINE [3]). to eliminate BACTERIA (3) and other undesirable lifeforms. May also include the effects of water chemistry unsuitable for the fish – *see SHOCK (3), ACIDOSIS (3), ALKALOSIS (3).*
See also SECTION I: The Correct Environment.

TEETH – OVERGROWN
Overgrown teeth are a problem usually restricted to pufferfish (Tetraodontidae) of which there are several freshwater species.

SIGNS
Difficulty or inability as regards taking in food; mouth open unnaturally wide, especially if associated with visible lip damage.

CAUSE
Inappropriate diet. The puffer's teeth are fused to form a beak capable of cracking open the molluscs that form its natural diet, and, just like a budgerigar's beak, they must be subjected to constant wear otherwise they can overgrow and seriously damage the mouth.

PREVENTION AND TREATMENT
Feeding pufferfish with plenty of hard foods, particularly aquatic snails which form their natural diet, will help keep

their teeth in check. If the teeth nevertheless become overgrown, veterinary assistance will be necessary.

TEMPERATURE – AS A TREATMENT

A small increase in temperature (3-5 degrees C/5.5-9 degrees F) (providing this is within the fish's tolerance range) will increase the fish's metabolic rate and immune function and hence may prove beneficial to the healing process. The life-cycles of some parasites (e.g. *ICHTHYOPHTHIRIUS* [3]). are also accelerated by temperature increases, and this can be used to effect a cure more speedily than at normal tank temperature.

Raised temperature increases OXYGEN (3) requirement and also reduces the oxygen-carrying capacity of the water, so additional or enhanced aeration may be necessary. Increased temperature should, ideally, be avoided where gill damage or inflammation is involved (e.g. in cases of gill PARASITES [3] e.g. FLUKES [3] BRANCHIMYCOSIS [3]), in order to avoid further trauma.

TEMPERATURE SHOCK
See SHOCK (3).

TETRACYCLINE   **P**
See ANTIBIOTICS (3).

TETRAHYMENA

A genus of ciliate PROTOZOA (3). Most *Tetrahymena* species are harmless to fish; however, a few are known occasionally to cause disease. *Tetrahymena corlissi* is sometimes encountered in tropical aquaria and causes "guppy disease". Although principally associated with guppies, *T. corlissi* may also attack other livebearing species and occasionally other groups of tropical fish.

SIGNS
T. corlissi may be present in large numbers over the skin, forming small white patches. In guppies, the parasites sometimes congregate around the eye. The fish's SCALES (2) may become 'bristled' and protrude. The muscles and internal organs are occasionally invaded. Infections may be rapidly fatal.

Definitive diagnosis of *Tetrahymena* requires microscopical examination of skin smears or infected tissues in order to differentiate from other genera of parasitic protozoa.

PREVENTION AND TREATMENT
Livebearing fish should be inspected for any clinical signs of *Tetrahymena* before being purchased. Mild skin infections may respond to proprietary anti-protozoa remedies. Treatment is unlikely to be successful in the case of heavy infections and where muscle or organ invasion has occurred, and EUTHANASIA (3) should be considered.

TOLTRAZURIL P

A triazinone drug with anti-PROTOZOAL (3) activity. Originally used for treating protozoal infections in chickens, toltrazuril shows promise in treating certain protozoal infections of fish. For example, it has been effective as a bath treatment in combating the parasitic trophont stage of *ICHTHYOPHTHIRIUS* (3) but not the infective theronts. Further studies on this drug, and optimisation of dosage, may pave the way for its wider application in the treatment of protozoal infections of fish.

TOXIC SHOCK
See SHOCK (3)

TOXIN
A poisonous substance. In the aquarium sense, any substance poisonous to fish (= ichthyotoxic). See POISONING (3).

TRANSPORTATION STRESS
STRESS (3) arising from transportation, including netting, packing, unpacking, and introduction to strange accommodation/tankmates.

SIGNS
The newly-released fish exhibits NERVOUSNESS (2) and may hide; alternatively it may rest on the bottom as if suffering from SHOCK (3), or swim frantically up, down, and along the aquarium glass as if trying to escape. Death

Bags of live tropical fish – ready for export.

sometimes occurs from associated physical trauma, in extreme cases actually during transit.

CAUSE
The transportation process is inevitably stressful. Some species are highly susceptible, while others seem little affected. The distance and duration of transportation is also significant. Wild fish from remote jungle streams may have been housed in small containers for days or weeks before reaching a shipping station; commercial shipping, of wild and tank-bred fish, by air freight commonly involves high packing density in small bags with no inspection for up to 36 hours – so any fish that die will pollute the water for the remainder of the journey. And while certain anaesthetics now used to keep the fish inactive (and thus permit greater packing density) also prevent aggression and act as tranquillisers, they may also have harmful (sometimes delayed) side-effects.

PREVENTION AND TREATMENT
Minimisation of STRESS (3) during and after transportation is all-important *(see SECTION I: Purchasing, Transporting, and Introducing Stock)*. Newly-introduced fish should be left in peace and quiet, with the tank light off, until they are seen to be behaving normally. Under no circumstances should they be chased from cover, prodded, or otherwise stressed further. This will achieve nothing, except, perhaps, the demise of a fish that might otherwise have recovered.

From a stress point of view, a locally-bred fish is a better proposition than one mass-produced and shipped thousands of miles, and subsequently passing through the tanks of importer, wholesaler, and retailer before reaching its eventual home.

TREMATODES
SEE FLUKES (3).

TRICAINE METHANESULPHONATE ■P

Alternative chemical name: 3-aminobenzoic acid ethyl ester. Also known under the brand name MS222.

A widely used fish ANAESTHETIC (3), sold as a white powder. Tricaine methanesulphonate has the advantage over BENZOCAINE (3) of being readily soluble in water, but is more expensive.

DOSAGE AND ADMINISTRATION

The anaesthetic is applied as a bath immersion. The actual dose required for anaesthesia or EUTHANASIA (3) will vary according to the fish species as well as environmental factors (see discussion under ANAESTHETICS [3]).

Tricaine tends to reduce the pH of water, particularly soft, unbuffered water, such that it may STRESS (3) the fish; sodium bicarbonate ($NaHCO_3$) should be added to prevent this, dosage as given below.

● For anaesthesia: In general, a dose level of between 40-100 mg per litre will induce anaesthesia in fish, and will allow recovery if the fish is subsequently transferred to aerated, anaesthetic-free water. Add twice the amount of sodium bicarbonate (i.e. to give a final bicarbonate concentration of 80-200 mg per litre) before adding the fish.

● For euthanasia: Use an overdose level of 300 mg per litre. Mix with twice the quantity of sodium bicarbonate (i.e. to give a final bicarbonate concentration of 600 mg per litre) before adding the fish. Safety note: wear rubber gloves when immersing hands in anaesthetic solutions.

TRICHLORFON ■P

Also known as metriphonate.

An ORGANOPHOSPHORUS (3) compound, used in horticulture/agriculture as an INSECTICIDE (3), and sometimes employed to eradicate a number of fish ECTOPARASITES (3) including gill and skin FLUKES (3), *ARGULUS* (3), and *LERNAEA* (3). Owing to their potential neuro-toxicity to man, his pets, and the environment, the use of organophosphorus compounds for treating fish parasites is now restricted in many countries.

Trichlorfon may be available from horticultural and agricultural outlets, but should nevertheless be used only under veterinary supervision. The various proprietary solutions differ greatly in the percentage content of trichlorfon, and will therefore need to be diluted accordingly to give the appropriate bath strength.

DOSAGE AND ADMINISTRATION
Normally applied as a long-term (7 days approx.) bath. A working concentration of 0.25 mg per litre is recommended. The organophosphate may be added directly to the aquarium and is thought not to harm biological filtration.

The activity of trichlorfon decreases with increasing temperature and increasing alkalinity (i.e. pH values above 7.0), such that redosing may be necessary in order to maintain an effective concentration – see supplier's instructions for redosing regimes. In the absence of any such information, the following may be used as a rough guide to redosing:

Long-duration bath (hospital tank or main aquarium): For the average freshwater aquarium (25 degrees C (77 degrees F), pH 6.5-7.5) a full dose (0.25 mg/litre; 1 mg per gallon) should be given on day 1, followed by a half-dose on day 3 or 4; this will compensate for degradation. Maintain fish in the bath for 7 days. Note: the bath temperature should not exceed 27 degrees C (80 degrees F), otherwise chemical effectiveness may be reduced. The aquarium water should be well aerated during treatment.

Certain sensitive fish, notably characins, should be closely monitored during treatment and removed if they exhibit signs of RESPIRATORY DISTRESS (2) or other abnormal BEHAVIOUR (2). In the case of very acidic water conditions it is prudent to undertake several partial water changes after the course of treatment in order to dilute any residual activity of the compound.

TRICHODINA
CILIATE PARASITES (3), typically betwen 50 and 100 microns in diameter, and one of the causative agents of SKIN SLIME DISEASE (3). Most of the fish parasitic trichodinids belong to this genus.

Trichodina are mainly ECTOPARASITES (3), occurring

on the surface of the fish's skin and/or gills where they attach loosely, feeding on cell debris and tissues. Most *Trichodina* species have a broad host range though some are relatively host specific, infecting just one or a few fish species. The parasites spend most of the time on their host but are capable of surviving away from the fish for up to 2 days. Transmission may occur during contact between fish, or when a dislodged free-swimming parasite encounters another fish. The parasite's sharp denticles cause their host skin damage.

Several species of trichodinids (*Trichodina* and related genera) are parasitic on fish, though precise identification is unnecessary as far as treatment is concerned.

Diagnosis is confirmed by microscopical examination (x 100 magnification) of a skin or gill scrape. *Trichodina* are characteristically highly motile, often skimming across the field of view. *Trichodina* possesses a disc-shaped body which contains an inner circle of thick denticles and an outer fringe of beating cilia.

STRESS (3), especially when caused by adverse water conditions, is a significant predisposing factor for outbreaks of *Trichodina*.

For *SIGNS* and *TREATMENT* see SKIN SLIME DISEASE (3).

TRYPANOSOMES
Flagellate PROTOZOA (3) which infect the blood of fish, and are transmitted by LEECHES (3). They are rarely of aquarium importance. *See also BLOOD PARASITES (3).*

Catfish with severe emaciation, possibly caused by trypanosome infection.

Photo: Mike Sandford.

Tubifex.

TUBIFEX WORMS

These small mud-dwelling annelid worms are red-brown in colour. Although popular as a live food for aquarium fish, *Tubifex* are known to be capable of transmitting certain microbial and parasite diseases to fish. For this reason, many aquarists will not risk feeding live *Tubifex*.
See also LIVE FOODS AS VECTORS OF DISEASE (3).

TUMOURS

Abnormal growths may occasionally develop on fish. Some types of tumour may be harmless (benign), but others can be malignant (cancerous) and spread (metastasize) throughout the body. Large tumours, whether benign or malignant, may cause serious problems as a result of their mass affecting vital organs or impeding swimming ability. Tumours on the lips, particularly the lower lip, may impede feeding. All bony (teleost) fish are potentially at risk of developing tumours, although the incidence of certain types of tumour appears to be higher among particular fish groups.
Note: the aquarium literature sometimes (incorrectly) refers to any type of swelling or growth as a tumour.

SIGNS

Tumours vary considerably in size, colour, and form according to the type of tumour cell and its position on the fish. There is possible diagnostic confusion with other GROWTHS (2), caused by microsporidial CYSTS (3), viral *LYMPHOCYSTIS* (3), and possibly with those caused by larval HELMINTHS (3) and certain other infections. If all

Tumour near base of caudal fin.

Skin tumour. Photo: Stan McMahon.

Tumour on underside of caudal penduncle. Photo: David Ford.

other types of GROWTHS (2) and SWELLINGS (2) can be eliminated from the diagnosis, then the problem may well be a TUMOUR (3).

TYPES OF TUMOURS

● Skin tumours: generally benign papillomas which do not metastasize, but which can nevertheless grow very large. Malignant skin tumours are less common.

● Connective tissue tumours (fibromas; though possibly in fact, nerve tumours) have been associated with certain fish species, such as goldfish.

● Thyroid tumours: it is difficult to distinguish true thyroid tumours (thyroid neoplasias) from goitres (thyroid hyperplasia due to IODINE (3) deficiency). Thyroid tumours may be found on the gill arches, sometimes causing the operculum visibly to distend.

● Melanomas: these are the most common forms of pigment cell tumours and manifest as dark, slightly raised growths. Often malignant. The incidence of melanomas appears to vary between species, and is relatively common in certain hybrids such as swordtail-platy crosses (due to certain genes being absent). Characins (e.g. tetras) also tend to be more susceptible to melanomas. Melanomas have also been associated with MELANISM (3) and INBREEDING (3).

● Tumours associated with internal organs: these are less likely to be diagnosed, except upon autopsy, though the sheer mass of certain organ tumours may result in outward signs such as DEFORMITY (2) or DISTENDED BODY (2) (especially if the condition is laterally asymmetric).

CAUSES
Identifying the underlying cause of tumours is virtually impossible. Extreme levels of pollution, or the presence of certain toxins, have been implicated in causing some types of tumour. VIRUS (3) infections are also a likely cause of certain tumours. Liver tumours are sometimes the result of ingesting poorly stored foods which have become contaminated with AFLATOXINS (3).

A fish's susceptibility to tumours may be influenced by the species, and by its sex, age and genetic composition. Fish which are severely stressed may have impaired immune function and this in turn could increase the risk of tumour formation.

PREVENTION AND TREATMENT
Very little can be done to reduce the occurrence of tumours other than provide optimal aquarium conditions (including diet), and avoiding inbreeding. Treatment is not usually possible. Surgical removal of tumours may be feasible in a few cases, e.g. unsightly skin tumours, or where the tumour is encroaching on the gills, mouth, or vent. If the tumour is thought to be causing STRESS (3) or other suffering then EUTHANASIA (3) is the only humane option.

Opercular swellings or growths associated with the gills should first be treated with a course of IODINE (3), in case these are the result of a goitre rather than a tumour. Iodine-medicated foods suitable for fish are available from vets.

U

ULCERS and ULCER DISEASE

Ulcers are generally a sign of various systemic BACTERIAL INFECTIONS (3) rather than a specific disease in their own right.

SIGNS

Open sores or lesions on the body, often with reddening around the perimeter, usually caused by bacterial infections. Ulcers may develop SECONDARY INFECTIONS (3) of FUNGUS (3), and may be associated with other symptoms of systemic bacterial disease, such as DISTENDED BODY (2) (DROPSY [3]), EXOPHTHALMIA (2), and EMACIATION (2).

Skin ulcer on a cichlid.

Severe ulceration may cause osmotic stress.

Photo: Beatta McDougall.

CAUSE

Skin necrosis, usually as a result of a chronic systemic infection caused by certain bacterial pathogens, notably

AEROMONAS (3), *PSEUDOMONAS* (3), MYCO-
BACTERIA (3), and *VIBRIO* (3). The open, necrotic
WOUNDS (3) severely weaken the fish. In severe cases
where there is extensive disruption to the fish's skin barrier,
this may cause significant osmoregulatory problems
(OSMOTIC STRESS [3]). and render the fish suceptible to
SECONDARY INFECTIONS (3).

STRESS (3), for example caused by rough handling,
TRANSPORTATION (3), or adverse environmental
conditions, is considered to be a significant predisposing
factor in outbreaks of ulcers. Chronically stressed fish
which happen to sustain skin damage through INJURY (3)
or ECTOPARASITES (3) may be especially prone to
ulcerative infections, due to the suppressive effects of stress
on their immune defences.

PREVENTION AND TREATMENT
Wherever possible, avoid the causative circumstances or
take steps to minimise associated stress and likelihood of
injury. If ulcers do occur, eliminate stress, improve water
quality if necessary. A prolonged SALT (3) bath (3-5 g/litre
for several days) will alleviate osmoregulatory stress in the
case of severe ulceration, and help reduce the chances of
secondary infection by fungi. Note: some fish, e.g. catfish,
are salt intolerant.

Minor, superficial ulcers may respond to a proprietary
bath treatment (e.g. an anti-ulcer or anti-systemic bacteria
remedy). More serious cases will usually require a course of
ANTIBIOTICS (3) (e.g. OXYTETRACYCLINE (3)
hydrochloride) which may be administered in the food, as a
long-term bath, or, in the case of larger fish, injected.

UV IRRADIATION
Ultra-violet irradiation (UV) has the ability to eliminate a
number of harmful or potentially harmful organisms such as
some BACTERIA (3), some free-swimming PARASITES
(3), and unicellular ALGAE (3). It must be stressed that UV
does not eradicate all types within any of these groups, and
will not necessarily *prevent* disease transmission within an
aquarium but merely *reduce* it. It should therefore never be
regarded as a foolproof means of preventing or eliminating
infectious diseases. UV sterilisation is used chiefly for

marine fish, and this is largely a reflection of their higher monetary value. UV irradiation may be of value in controlling disease outbreaks in aquaria which are constantly receiving new stock, and especially for reducing disease transmission between multi-tank systems which are linked to a central filtration unit (e.g. in wholesaler's/ retailer's premises). For the average aquarist, however, its use is considered to be largely unnecessary, and UV should never, in any case, be used as an excuse to avoid QUARANTINE (3) procedures or to be lax in maintaining aquarium hygiene and optimal water conditions. Furthermore, UV may be ineffective in destroying large parasites and cyst – or spore-forming pathogens.

The value of using UV to maintain near-sterile aquarium conditions has been questioned. It has been suggested that the relative paucity of bacteria in UV-treated aquarium water may lower the fish's natural defences due to a lack of immunological stimulation from exposure to these micro-organisms. This could present a problem if the fish is subsequently moved to an aquarium not treated with UV, since the fish would then be exposed to a range of bacteria to which it may not have acquired immunity.

UV is administered by means of a device called a UV steriliser, and it is essential to use only a model intended for aquarium use. It is also important to follow the manufacturer's instructions, and especially *never* to look directly at the UV light, as this may cause eye damage.

V

VACCINES P

The vaccination of fish against certain infectious diseases is routinely undertaken in the case of foodfish species; however, vaccination has rarely been applied to aquarium fish. At present, only a handful of commercial fish vaccines exist, and none are specifically directed against aquarium fish diseases. In the future, however, a vaccine may become available for protecting aquarium fish against whitespot (ICHTHYOPHTHIRIASIS [3]). and possibly even velvet (*PISCINOODINIUM* (3)).

Vaccine delivery by injection is not possible with small tropical fish, such as this gourami.

On-going research into non-invasive vaccine delivery routes (e.g. administered by bath or with the food) will enable tropical aquarium fish, many of which are too small to be injected, to benefit from vaccination.

VELVET DISEASE
See *PISCINOODINIUM* (3)

VERTICAL DISEASE TRANSMISSION
The transmission of an infectious disease from one generation to the next, i.e. from parents to progeny.

A number of VIRUS (3) and BACTERIAL (3) diseases of fish are known to be transmitted vertically. These include the MYCOBACTERIA (3) which cause FISH TUBER-CULOSIS (3). These pathogens may be transmitted on or within the parent fish's sperm or eggs, such that the offspring are infected before they are born or hatch. Adult stock which is known to have a history of mycobacterial or virus infection should not be used for breeding purposes.

In general, the careful selection of healthy broodstock will considerably reduce the risk of spreading vertically transmitted diseases.

VIBRIO, VIBRIOSIS
Vibrio is a genus of BACTERIA (3), several species of which may cause disease in fish; however, these bacteria are found predominantly in brackish or marine waters. One exception is a strain (known as "Type C") of *V. anguillarum* which has been recorded as a pathogen in freshwater fish. Its preferred optimum temperature of 26 degrees C (79 degrees F) and wide pH tolerance (between 6 and 9.6) mean that it is capable of thriving in tropical aquaria.

SIGNS

Vibriosis occurs in two forms, both potentially life-threatening:

● The acute form, which may kill before any significant symptoms occur, though there is sometimes skin HAEMORRHAGING (2), sometimes with sub-dermal ulcers, and necrosis or enlargement of some internal organs. DISTENDED BODY (2) (DROPSY [3]) may also occur.

● The chronic form is associated with lesions of the musculature and intestinal inflammation, these being evident upon post-mortem. Outward signs may include EXOPHTHALMUS (2), ULCERS (2), or sores.

It is not possible to diagnose and differentiate vibriosis from other systemic bacterial infections except by specialised microbiological analysis of cultured material taken from the infection site. It must be borne in mind, however, that vibriosis is uncommon in freshwater fish and hence other bacteria are more likely to be the cause of disease.

Fish may become infected with *Vibrio* either via the oral route (e.g. as a result of CANNIBALISM [3] or COPROPHAGY [3]). or by entry of the bacteria through damaged skin. Poor water quality (e.g. high organic pollution), a high AMMONIA (3) level, and other STRESS (3)-inducing conditions may increase the likelihood of an outbreak.

PREVENTION AND TREATMENT

Successful treatment of *Vibrio anguillarum* is usually achieved only with ANTIBIOTICS (3) (e.g. CHLORAM-PHENICOL [3] or furazolidone) and certain antimicrobials (e.g. OXOLINIC ACID [3]). Chloramphenicol should be administered in food at the rate of 50mg per kg of fish on day one, and subsequently 30mg per kg of fish per day for the following five days. Alternatively, furazolidone can be administered in food at the rate of 100mg per kg of fish daily for a period of six days.

VIRAEMIA

The presence of VIRUSES in the blood. Often a feature of systemic viral infections.

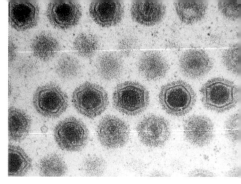

VIRUSES and VIRUS DISEASES

Viruses are extremely small (10-500 millionths of a mm in length) and can be seen only through a high-power electron microscope. They are simple organisms which invade host cells (= intracellular). They invariably damage the cells they invade, and proliferate into adjacent cells, eventually causing disease in their host. Viruses 'take over' the host cell's genetic material and 'instruct' the cell to produce copies of the virus: this is the means by which viruses multiply. In some viral diseases the infected host cells greatly enlarge and are packed with numerous viruses, as occurs in FISH POX (3) and *LYMPHOCYSTIS* (3).

Viral diseases often have prolonged incubation periods and the virus itself can become dormant or remain at a sub-acute level. Some individual fish may harbour viruses without showing any signs of ill-health: these fish are known as carriers and pose an undetectable reservoir of infection, and are thus a health risk to their tank-mates. Unfortunately, the symptomless carrier state can persist for some time, such that carriers may not necessarily be detected during routine QUARANTINE (3) procedures. Viruses are extremely resilient and can live off the fish for long periods, sometimes for many years, and can survive extremes of temperature and even desiccation.

The most commonly reported viral infections of aquarium fish are those which cause visible signs such as the white growths observed in *Lymphocystis* disease. However, many other fish viruses exist, causing symptoms such as HAEMORRHAGING (2), EXOPHTHALMIA (2), DISTENDED BODY (2) (DROPSY [3]), and other systemic problems.

Most viral diseases are difficult to diagnose, largely due to the complex laboratory procedures (and expense) involved in detecting, isolating, and characterising the causative virus.

PREVENTION AND TREATMENT OF VIRUS DISEASES
The 'free' viruses (i.e. those existing off the fish) may be killed using certain DISINFECTANTS (3). However, most disinfectants are toxic to fish and can be used only on aquarium equipment and external surfaces (followed by thorough rinsing in water). Once the virus is in the fish cell, then treatment is not possible, since the host cell would also be killed by any effective treatment currently available. Antibiotics and antimicrobials are of no use.

Fortunately, however, most of the common virus infections of aquarium fish are infrequently lethal, and in many cases the disease is self-limiting, as a result of acquired immunity by the host. The best course of action is to isolate (QUARANTINE [3]). the affected individual and all the other fish which have come into contact with it, and supply the best possible conditions in the hope that the fish's immune system will eventually overcome the infection.

VITAMIN DEFICIENCY
Fish, in common with other animals, have a dietary requirement for certain vitamins. Vitamin deficiency can lead to developmental abnormalities, reduced growth, physiological changes, and an increased susceptibility to infections.

Most reputable brands of dried aquarium fish foods (e.g. flakes, pellets) contain all the necessary vitamins for the fish's well-being, but varying the diet is nevertheless a sensible precaution to minimise the likelihood of deficiency or other nutritional problems.

Vitamin C is the vitamin most likely to be deficient in dry foods which have been stored for some time, since it degrades during storage. The development by fish food manufacturers of more stable forms of vitamins (including vitamin C) has somewhat reduced this problem.

SIGNS
Important note: most of the clinical symptoms listed below will more likely be caused by environmental problems or infectious diseases. A vitamin deficiency should be considered only in situations where the fish have been fed with an inferior or monotonous diet, or if a dry

Cloudy eye may reflect a vitamin deficiency but is more commonly the result of adverse water conditions.

food has degraded due to incorrect storage. Problems caused by a vitamin C deficiency are the most likely to occur, due to this vitamin's inherent instability and water-soluble properties.

VITAMIN DEFICIENCIES AND THE CLINICAL SIGNS THEY CAUSE

Vitamin A
- Eye disorders: EXOPHTHALMIA and/or CLOUDY EYE
- Fin or skin HAEMORRHAGE

Vitamin C
- FIN EROSION
- Fin or skin HAEMORRHAGE
- Skeletal DEFORMITY

Vitamin E
- EXOPHTHALMIA

CAUSE
Some very cheap brands of fish food may be deficient in certain vitamins. Water-soluble vitamins (vitamin B complex; vitamin C) are prone to leaching from the food upon contact with the aquarium water: the degree of leaching varies between the various brand products. Vitamin C may degrade during storage of dry foods (e.g. flake and pellet foods). Fish which have starved for a long period of time may be susceptible to certain vitamin deficiencies, especially water-soluble vitamins which are not stored in the fish's tissues.

PREVENTION AND TREATMENT
Avoid very cheap brands of aquarium fish foods as some may not provide a balanced diet. The use of a reputable brand of aquarium fish food (e.g. flake or pellet), supplemented with fresh or frozen foods, will largely

prevent vitamin deficiency problems. Dried foods should be stored in a cool, dry place, otherwise vitamin degradation may occur. Similarly, purchase only small quantities of dried foods at a time, such that they can be used up within two to three months.

A short course of vitamin supplements, administered orally or by injection, may be beneficial in suspected cases of vitamin deficiency.

VOMITING

The ejection of partially digested or undigested food from the mouth serves as a means of eliminating toxins and other noxious substances which may have been accidentally taken in with the meal.

SIGNS

Small amounts of fish vomit may go unnoticed and may, in any case, be consumed by other fish within the aquarium. In the case of very large fish a vomited meal can rapidly foul the water, causing cloudiness and possible overloading of the biological filter.

CAUSES

Vomiting serves a useful purpose for those species which include rotting carcasses (including dead fish and other animals) among their diet, such as some of the large catfish. Such fish may occasionally need to expel ingested flesh which is contaminated with, for example, bacterial toxins.

Under aquarium conditions, some fish (e.g. the red-tailed catfish, *Phractocephalus hemioliopterus*) are known occasionally to vomit their meal. This may be the result of an incorrect diet, or be due to environmental STRESS (3) or to a sudden disturbance to the fish.

Gut infections may also provoke vomiting.

TREATMENT

A single incident of vomiting should not cause alarm; however, it is very important to remove large quantities of vomited food from the aquarium in order to prevent a serious water quality problem. Fish which repeatedly vomit may be suffering from a gut problem such as an infection, inflammation, or physical blockage (the latter possibly due

*Red-tailed catfish
may sometimes
vomit their meal.*

to having swallowed a piece of rock or item of aquarium equipment). In the case of a bacterial infection it will usually be necessary to treat the fish with a course of ANTIBIOTICS (3).

A suspected blockage of the gut is difficult to investigate in all but very large fish, but may show up on X-RAY (3).

W

WASTING DISEASE
See MYCOBACTERIOSIS (3)

WHITESPOT
An extremely common and highly infectious disease which affects all species of freshwater aquarium fish. *(See ICHTHYOPHTHIRIASIS [3]).*

WORMS
This is a collective common term used to describe several groups of fish PARASITES (3), notably tapeworms (CESTODES (3)), ACANTHOCEPHALANS (3), and parasitic NEMATODES (3). The term 'worm' can be very misleading, as in the case of 'anchor worm' which is, in fact, a parasitic crustacean (*LERNAEA* [3]). and not a true worm.

Non-parasitic worms of aquarium interest include earthworms, PLANARIANS (3) and *TUBIFEX* (3).

WOUNDS
The skin serves as a protective barrier to invasion by microbial pathogens and helps maintain the fish's internal

physiological salt balance. Wound damage to the skin may render the fish vulnerable to infection and can cause OSMOTIC STRESS (3).

SIGNS
The extent and location of the wound will obviously vary according to cause. Minor wounds may entail loss of a few scales or a ripped or otherwise damaged fin. Of a more serious nature are wounds which puncture the skin epithelium. The wounded tissues may be prone to SECONDARY INFECTION (3) .

CAUSES
Wounds can be sustained mechanically within the aquarium, for example by accidental abrasion against a sharp rock. The use of dead coral as decoration in freshwater aquaria has been linked to skin wounding in fish, since certain corals are extremely sharp. Capture and rough handling may also result in skin abrasion or wounds.

AGGRESSION (3) is another cause of wounds; the eyes, fins, and flanks are usually the favoured targets for attack. Several species of freshwater crabs and lobsters are also capable of inflicting wounds on fish.

Wounds may also be caused by pathogens and parasites . Infestations with blood or tissue-feeding ECTOPARA-SITES (3), such as LEECHES (3) and *ARGULUS* (3), can also result in small puncture wounds on the fish's body.

TREATMENT
Deep wounds are vulnerable to infection and should be treated with an ANTISEPTIC (3), applied topically. Large wounds can be sealed with pharmacy-grade petroleum jelly (e.g. Vaseline) or similar non-toxic skin dressing cream (consult the veterinarian regarding the suitability or otherwise (potential ichthyotoxicity) of any such cream). The cream will serve as an artificial barrier to infection while the wound heals, and in the case of large wounds, may help reduce osmotic stress.

X

X-RAYS

This investigative procedure is rarely applied to tropical aquarium fish, except in the case of highly-prized stock, and even then it is usually undertaken only on medium to large specimens. X-rays may be useful in confirming cases of suspected skeletal damage or a gut blockage. Live fish requiring X-ray should be immobilised using ANAES-THETICS (3) and laid on a wet cloth during exposure. Fish tissues require only a relatively brief exposure to X-rays, and achieving a good contrast may require a few attempts using different exposure times.

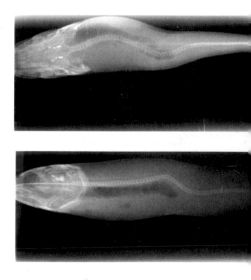

X-rays of the dorsal (upper picture) and side aspects of a bowfin (Amia calva) reveal severe spinal deformity.

Z

ZOONOSIS

Zoonoses are diseases of animals which can be transmitted to humans. In terms of human health risks, fish are among the safest of creatures to keep as domestic pets and this is one reason why aquaria are tolerated within many hospital wards.

There are a few cases of humans having contracted bacterial diseases from fish or aquarium water, including *VIBRIO* (3) spp. and *Salmonella java.* The most commonly reported zoonosis is fish MYCOBACTERIOSIS (3) (fish TB) which is caused by *Mycobacterium marinum* and related species. The human form of the disease is sometimes known as fishkeeper's granuloma, and manifests as a persistent rash to the skin, mostly the fingers and hands. The human disease is not life-threatening and is treatable with a course of antibiotics. Fish showing signs of TB should be handled with caution.

More recently, a *Streptococcus* bacterium *(S. iniae)* of farmed *Tilapia* has been shown to cause blood infections in humans. Although not yet associated with aquarium fish, it would seem prudent to consider this disease as a potential zoonosis risk to aquarists.

There are two basic human hygiene rules which should be followed by all aquarists when working with aquaria:
1. Never immerse open wounds in the aquarium water: wear protective gloves (the arm-length veterinary type are ideal – sometimes available from agricultural merchants, otherwise ask the vet).
2. When siphoning the water from an aquarium, never prime the siphon tube with the mouth. Swallowing aquarium water is unhygienic! Use a commercial siphon primer available from the aquatic store.

Persons who are severely immunosuppressed are at greater risk of contracting zoonotic infections from their fish. Those aquarists in high risk categories should take extra care when working with aquaria.